BASIC
English
Grammar

FOURTH EDITION

with Essential Online Resources

Betty S. Azar
Stacy A. Hagen

**Basic English Grammar, Fourth Edition
with Essential Online Resources**

Azar Associates: Shelley Hartle, Editor, and Sue Van Etten, Manager

Pearson Education, 221 River Street, Hoboken, NJ 07030

Staff credits: The people who made up the *Basic English Grammar, Fourth Edition* team, representing editorial, production, design, and manufacturing, are, Dave Dickey, Nancy Flaggman, Amy McCormick, Robert Ruvo, and Marian Wassner.

Text composition: S4Carlisle Publishing Services

Illustrations: Don Martinetti—pages 5, 6, 8, 9, 17, 18, 19, 21, 22, 26, 29, 31, 33, 34, 36, 40, 41, 45, 46, 47, 48, 50, 51, 52, 53, 54, 59, 61, 63, 64, 69, 71, 74, 77, 78, 79, 81, 85, 89, 90, 91, 99, 101, 103, 106, 112, 114, 117, 125, 126, 129, 130, 133, 135, 139, 142, 143, 144, 146, 147, 153, 154, 155, 156, 162, 164, 171, 172, 173, 180, 184, 187, 188, 191, 192, 193, 197, 200, 202, 203, 204, 206, 207, 208, 210, 211, 212, 213, 214, 216, 217, 219, 220, 221, 222, 223, 228, 229, 230, 234, 237, 256, 258, 260, 262, 266, 267, 278, 279, 281, 283, 286, 287, 288, 290, 292, 293, 305, 312, 320, 322, 323, 327, 329, 330, 331, 332, 340, 348, 361, 363, 365, 366, 368, 370, 376, 377, 378, 379, 380, 383, 386, 393, 398, 401, 402, 407, 411, 416, 417, 418, 419, 420, 421, 428, 431, 432, 434, 441, 447, 453, 454, 455, 456, 457, 458, 470, 471, 475, 479, 488

Chris Pavely—pages 1, 3, 13, 14, 15, 16, 21, 32, 35, 38, 39, 43, 44, 49, 52, 62, 67, 68, 75, 79, 81, 88, 92, 95, 96, 98, 102, 103, 104, 105, 107, 108, 109, 120, 124, 148, 149, 151, 158, 161, 169, 173, 174, 175, 178, 181, 185, 189, 216, 236, 241, 247, 250, 252, 255, 259, 270, 272, 274, 275, 280, 290, 291, 292, 295, 300, 304, 307, 310, 313, 315, 325, 334, 335, 336, 337, 343, 345, 352, 353, 354, 359, 362, 363, 375, 377, 391, 396, 397, 399, 400, 413, 427, 430, 431, 440, 445, 449, 466, 469, 501 (in *Let's Talk: Answers,* Chapter 4, Exercise 18, p. 106)

Photo Credits: Page 296 dieKleinert/Alamy; p. 297 Aaron Alex/Alamy; p. 367 Alexander Kaludov/Fotolia; p. 382 Christos Georghiou/Fotolia.

Library of Congress Cataloging-in-Publication Data

Azar, Betty Schrampfer, 1941-
  Basic English grammar / Betty S. Azar, Stacy A. Hagen.—Fourth Edition, with answer key
    pages cm
  Includes index.
  ISBN 978-0-13-294224-9 (with Answer Key)—ISBN 978-0-13-294230-0 (without Answer Key)
  1. English language--Textbooks for foreign speakers. 2. English language—Grammar—Problems, exercises, etc. I. Hagen, Stacy A., 1956- II. Title.

PE1128.A96 2014
428.2'4—dc23

2013042099

Printed in the United States of America

ISBN 10: 0-13-465658-X
ISBN 13: 978-0-13-465658-8

2 17

ISBN 10: 0-13-466116-8 (International Edition)
ISBN 13: 978-0-13-466116-2 (International Edition)

1 16

To Shelley Hartle

For her watchful eye, her vast expertise,
her indefatigable good cheer

Contents

Preface to the Fourth Edition

Basic English Grammar is a developmental skills text for beginning English language learners. It uses a grammar-based approach integrated with communicative methodologies to promote the development of all language skills in a variety of ways. Starting from a foundation of understanding form and meaning, students engage in meaningful communication about real actions, real things, and their own lives in the classroom context. Grammar tasks are designed to encourage both fluency and accuracy.

The eclectic approach and abundant variety of exercise material remain the same as in the earlier editions, but this fourth edition incorporates new ways and means. In particular:

- **CORPUS-INFORMED CONTENT**

  Based on corpus research, grammar content has been added, deleted, or modified to reflect discourse patterns. New information highlighting differences between spoken and written English has been added to the charts, and students practice more frequently used structures. We have been careful to keep the information manageable for beginning students.

- **PRESENTATION OF KEY GRAMMAR**

  Chapter 15 (in earlier editions of *BEG*) has been moved to Chapter 6 of this edition in order to teach possessive forms earlier and present all pronouns together.

- **WARM-UP EXERCISES FOR THE GRAMMAR CHARTS**

  Newly created for the fourth edition, these innovative exercises precede the grammar charts and introduce the point(s) to be taught. They have been carefully crafted to help students *discover* the target grammar as they progress through each warm-up exercise. The warm-up exercises can help the teacher assess how much explanation and practice students will need.

- **MICRO-PRACTICE**

  At the beginning level, a single grammar structure (e.g. basic pronouns and possessives) sometimes needs to be presented in several steps. Additional exercises have been created to give students more incremental practice.

- **LISTENING PRACTICE**

  Recent research highlights the importance of helping students at all levels understand authentic spoken English. New as well as revised exercises introduce students to relaxed, reduced speech. The student text audio is available on Essential Online Resources, and a full audio script can be found in the back of the book.

- **READINGS**

  This fourth edition now has a wide selection of readings for students to read and respond to. The content is carefully controlled so that the vocabulary is accessible to beginning students and the grammar structures appropriate to the chapter(s) studied.

- **WRITING TASKS**

  New writing tasks help students naturally produce the target grammar structures in extended discourse. These end-of-chapter activities include writing models for students to follow. Editing checklists draw students' attention to the grammar focus and help them develop proofreading skills.

Components of Basic English Grammar, Fourth Edition:

- **Student Book with Essential Online Resources** includes the access code for the audio, video, self-assessments, and teacher resources with the Student Book answer key.
- **Student Book with MyEnglishLab** that includes the access code to MyEnglishLab, an easy-to-use online learning management system that delivers rich online practice to engage and motivate students.
- A comprehensive *Workbook,* consisting of self-study exercises for independent work.
- An all-new *Teacher's Guide,* with step-by-step teaching suggestions for each chart, notes to the teacher on key grammar structures, vocabulary lists, and expansion activities.
- An expanded *Test Bank,* with additional quizzes, chapter tests, mid-terms, and final exams.
- *ExamView* software that allows teachers to customize their own tests using quizzes and tests from the *Test Bank*.
- *AzarGrammar.com,* a website that provides a variety of supplementary classroom materials, *PowerPoint* presentations for all chapters, and a place where teachers can support each other by sharing their knowledge and experience.

The Student Book answer key is available in the Teacher Resource Folder on Essential Online Resources. Teachers can choose to make the answer key available to their students. Homework can be corrected as a class or, if appropriate, students can correct it at home with the answer key and bring questions to class. In some cases, the teacher may want to collect the assignments written on a separate piece of paper, correct them, and then highlight common problems in class.

MyEnglishLab

MyEnglishLab provides a range of interactive activities that help motivate and engage students. MyEnglishLab for *Basic English Grammar,* Fourth Edition includes:

- Rich online practice for all skill areas: grammar, reading, writing, speaking, and listening
- Instant feedback on incorrect answers
- Remediation activities
- Grammar Coach videos
- Robust assessments that include diagnostic tests, chapter review tests, mid- and end-of-term review tests, and final exams
- Gradebook and diagnostic tools that allow teachers to monitor student progress and analyze data to determine steps for remediation and support
- Student Book answer key in the Teacher Resource Folder

The Azar-Hagen Grammar Series consists of

- *Understanding and Using English Grammar* (blue cover), for upper-level students.
- *Fundamentals of English Grammar* (black cover), for mid-level students.
- *Basic English Grammar* (red cover), for lower or beginning levels.

Tips for Using the New Features in this Text

WARM-UPS

The *Warm-Up* exercises are a brief pre-teaching tool for the charts. They highlight the key point(s) that will be introduced in the chart directly following the *Warm-Up* exercise. Before beginning the task, teachers will want to familiarize themselves with the material in the chart. Then, with the teacher's guidance, students can discover many or all of the new patterns while completing the *Warm-Up* activity. After students finish the exercise, teachers may find that no further explanation is necessary, and the charts can then serve as a useful reference.

LISTENING

The *Listening* exercises have been designed to help students understand American English as it is actually spoken. As such, they include reductions and other phenomena that are part of the natural, relaxed speech of everyday English. Because the pace of speech in the audio may be faster than what students are used to, they may need to hear sentences two or three times as they complete a task.

The *Listening* exercises do not encourage immediate pronunciation (unless they are linked to a specific pronunciation task). Receptive skills precede productive ones, and it is essential that students gain receptive familiarity with the speech patterns before they begin using them in their own speech.

Students are encouraged to listen to conversations the first time without looking at their text. Teachers can explain any vocabulary that has not already been clarified. During the second listening, students complete the assigned task. Teachers will want to pause the audio appropriately. Depending on the level of the class, pauses may be needed after every sentence, or even within a sentence.

It is inevitable that sound representations in the text will at times differ from the instructor's speech, whether due to register or regional variation. A general guideline is that if the instructor expects students will *hear* a variation, or if students themselves raise questions, alternate representations can be presented.

A *Listening Script* is included in the back of the book.

READING

The *Readings* give students an opportunity to work with the grammar structures in extended contexts. Vocabulary that may be new to students is presented on yellow notes for teachers to introduce. One approach to the reading is to have students read the passage independently the first time through. Then they work in small groups or as a class to clarify vocabulary questions that didn't come up in the notes. A second reading may be necessary. Varied reading tasks allow students to check their comprehension, use the target structures, and expand upon the topic in speaking or writing.

WRITING

As students gain confidence in using the target structures, they are encouraged to express their ideas in longer writing tasks. Model paragraphs accompany assignments, and question-prompts help students develop their ideas.

Editing checklists provide guidance for self- or peer-editing. One suggested technique is to pair students, have them exchange papers, and then have the *partner* read the paragraph aloud. The writer can *hear* if the content is what he or she intended. This also keeps the writer from automatically self-correcting while reading aloud. The partner can then offer comments and complete the checklist.

For classes that have not had much experience with writing, the teacher may want students to complete the task in small groups. The group composes a paragraph together, which the teacher then collects and marks by calling attention to beginning-level errors, but not correcting them. The teacher makes a copy for each group member, and each student makes the corrections *individually*.

LET'S TALK

Each *Let's Talk* activity is set up as one of the following: **Pairwork, Small Group, Class Activity, Interview,** or **Game**. Language learning is a social activity, and these tasks encourage students to speak with others about their ideas, their everyday lives, and the world around them. Students speak more easily and freely when they can connect language to their own knowledge and experiences.

CHECK YOUR KNOWLEDGE

Toward the end of the chapter, students can practice sentence-level editing skills by correcting errors common to this level. They can work on the sentences for homework or in small groups in class.

This task can easily be set up as a game. The teacher calls out an item number at random. Students work in teams to correct the sentence, and the first team to correctly edit it wins a point.

Please see the **Teacher's Guide** for detailed information about teaching from this book, including expansion activities and step-by-step instructions.

Acknowledgments

Our revision began with extensive reviews from many talented professionals. We are grateful for the expertise of the following teachers: Susan Boland, Tidewater Community College; Lee Chen, Palomar College; Gene Hahn, University of Wisconsin, Stevens Point; Kathleen Keeble, Illinois Institute of Art, Chicago; Steven Lasswell, Santa Barbara City College; Michael Pitts, Los Angeles Southwest College; Carla Reible, Riverside City College; Alison Rice, Hunter College; Maria S. Roche, Housatonic Community College; Nelky Rodriguez, Riverside Community College; John Stasinopoulos, College of DuPage; Hallie Wallack, International Language Institute; Robert L. Woods, Central Washington University.

We were assisted throughout the process by a skilled and dedicated editorial staff. We would like to thank Shelley Hartle, managing editor, for her passion for the series and gifted editing and layout skills; Amy McCormick, editorial director, for guiding the project with exceptional judgment, attentiveness, and foresight; Marian Wassner, senior development editor (and grammar master), for her superb editing and thoughtful responses; Robert Ruvo, production manager, for his deft project management, keen eye for design, and unfailing good humor; Janice Baillie, copy-editor, for her stellar editing and remarkable ability to track all manner of detail; Sue Van Etten, business and website manager, for her expert and dedicated counsel.

We'd also like to express our appreciation to the writers of the supplementary texts: Kelly Roberts Weibel, *Test Bank* and Martha Hall, *Teacher's Guide*. Their creative and fresh ideas greatly enrich the series.

Finally, our thanks to our committed leadership team at Pearson Education who oversaw the entire revision: Pietro Alongi, Rhea Banker, and Paula Van Ells.

We are grateful for the artistic talents of Don Martinetti and Chris Pavely — their colorful work brightens every chapter.

Our families, as always, support and encourage our work. They truly inspire us every day.

Betty S. Azar
Stacy A. Hagen

Chapter 1
Using Be

❑ **Exercise 1. Let's talk: class activity.** (Chart 1-1)
Introduce yourself to six classmates. Use this model.

Hi, I am _____.
           (name)

I am from _____.
              (country or city)

I speak _____.
            (language)

Write down information about six classmates you talk to.

FIRST NAME	COUNTRY OR CITY	LANGUAGE

❑ **Exercise 2. Warm-up.** (Chart 1-1)
Read the sentences and circle *yes* or *no*.

1. He is happy.   yes   no

2. She is sad.   yes   no

3. I am happy.   yes   no

1-1 Singular Pronouns + Be

PRONOUN + BE				Singular means "one."
(a)	**I**	**am**	late.	
(b)	**You**	**are**	late.	**I, you, she, he,** and **it** in (a)—(e) refer to one person.
(c)	**She**	**is**	late.	
(d)	**He**	**is**	late.	**am, are, is** = forms of **be**
(e)	**It**	**is**	late.	

(f) **Maria** is late. ↓ **She** is late.	Pronouns refer to nouns. In (f): **She** (feminine) = Maria
(g) **Tom** is late. ↓ **He** is late.	In (g): **He** (masculine) = Tom
(h) **Bus 10** is late. ↓ **It** is late.	In (h): **It** = Bus 10

❏ **Exercise 3. Looking at grammar.** (Chart 1-1)

Write the correct pronoun: *he, she,* or *it.* Some items have two answers.

1. Mary _____she_____

2. David _____

3. Mr. Smith _____

4. Canada _____

5. Dr. Jones _____

6. Ms. Wilson _____

7. Professor Lee _____

8. English _____

9. Robert _____

10. Miss Allen _____

❏ **Exercise 4. Looking at grammar.** (Chart 1-1)

Complete the sentences with *am, is,* or *are.*

1. He _____is_____ here.

2. You _____ late.

3. It _____ ready.

4. She _____ early.

5. I _____ hot.

6. He _____ cold.

❏ **Exercise 5. Let's talk.** (Chart 1-1)

Part I. Check (✓) all the words that are true for you right now.

I am . . .

1. ____ happy.
2. ____ hot.
3. ____ nice.
4. ____ hungry.
5. ____ tired.

6. ____ sad.
7. ____ cold.
8. ____ nervous.
9. ____ sick.
10. ____ funny.

She is nervous.

He is hungry.

She is tired.

Part II. Share some sentences with a partner: "I am ____."

Part III. Tell the class a few things about your partner: "He is ____." OR "She is ____."

❏ **Exercise 6. Warm-up.** (Chart 1-2)

Circle the correct answer. One sentence has two answers.

How many people?

1. We are ready.	one	two, three, or more
2. You are ready.	one	two, three, or more
3. They are ready.	one	two, three, or more

1-2 Plural Pronouns + *Be*

PRONOUN + *BE*	
(a) **We** **are** here.	Plural means "two, three, or more."
(b) **You** **are** here.	**We**, **you**, and **they** in (a)—(c) refer to two, three, or more persons.
(c) **They** **are** here.	
(d) Sam and I ↓ **We** are here.	In (d): **We** = Sam and I
(e) Sam and you ↓ **You** are here.	In (e): **You** = Sam and you NOTE: **You** can be singular or plural.
(f) Sam and Lisa ↓ **They** are here.	In (f): **They** = Sam and Lisa

❏ **Exercise 7. Looking at grammar.** (Chart 1-2)
Choose the correct pronoun.

1. Lee and Bill	(they)	we
2. Alice and I	they	we
3. Mr. and Mrs. Martin and I	they	we
4. you and Dr. Taher	they	you
5. Tony and she	they	we
6. Tony and you	they	you

❏ **Exercise 8. Looking at grammar.** (Charts 1-1 and 1-2)
Complete the sentences with *am*, *is*, or *are*.

1. We ___*are*___ ready.

2. I _____ late.

3. He _____ happy.

4. They _____ sick.

5. She _____ homesick.

6. Abdul and Taka _____ homesick.

7. You (one person) _____ funny.

8. You (two persons) _____ early.

9. You and I _____ ready.

10. It _____ hot.

11. Sara and I _____ late.

12. You and Emily _____ tired.

Exercise 9. Looking at grammar. (Charts 1-1 and 1-2)
Make complete sentences.

1. He \ here _____ *He is here.* _____

2. They \ absent _____

3. She \ sick _____

4. I \ homesick _____

5. You and I \ homesick _____

6. We \ late _____

7. Jack \ hungry _____

8. You (one person) \ early _____

9. You (two persons) \ early _____

10. Mr. and Mrs. Nelson \ late _____

11. Amy and I \ late _____

□ **Exercise 10. Warm-up.** (Chart 1-3)
Read the sentences and circle *yes* or *no*.

1. Canada is a country.   yes   no

2. Toronto is a city.   yes   no

3. Vancouver is an island.   yes   no

1-3 Singular Nouns + *Be*

NOUN + *IS* + NOUN
(a) **Canada** **is** **a country.**
 	
INCORRECT: *Canada is country.*
	In (a): **Canada** = a singular noun
	        is = a singular verb
	    country = a singular noun
	
	A frequently comes in front of singular nouns.
	In (a): **a** comes in front of the singular noun **country**.
	A is called an "article."

(b) Bali is **an** island.
 	
INCORRECT: *Bali is island.*

an island
	A and **an** have the same meaning. They are both articles.
	A is used in front of words that begin with consonants:
	b, c, d, f, g, etc.
	      Examples: *a bed, a cat, a dog, a friend, a girl*
	
	An is used in front of words that begin with the vowels
	a, e, i, and *o.**
	      Examples: *an animal, an ear, an island, an office*
	
	an ear

* ***An*** is sometimes used in front of words that begin with *u.* See Chart 7-2, p. 196.

Vowels = a, e, i, o, u

Consonants = b, c, d, f, g, h, j, k, l, m, n, p, q, r, s, t, v, w, x, y, z

❏ **Exercise 11. Looking at grammar.** (Chart 1-3)
    Write ***a*** or ***an***.

    1. ___*a*___ town

    2. _____ city

    3. _____ island

    4. _____ place

    5. _____ street

    6. _____ avenue

    7. _____ ocean

    8. _____ continent

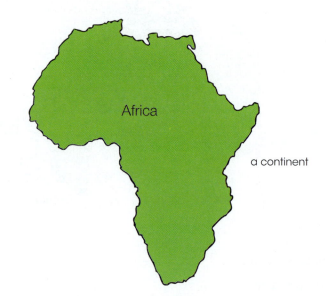

a continent

❑   **Exercise 12. Vocabulary and grammar.** (Chart 1-3)
Part I. Put the words from the box in the correct column. Some words go in two places.

✓ Arabic	Cuba	Hawaii	Mexico	Russia	Spanish
✓ Beijing	France	Japanese	Moscow	Russian	Taiwan
Chinese	French	Lima	Paris	Saudi Arabia	Tokyo

COUNTRY	LANGUAGE	CITY	ISLAND
	Arabic	*Beijing*	

Part II. Work in small groups. Check your answers. Finish the chart with your own choices. Your teacher will help you. Take turns making sentences. Share some of your sentences with the class.

Example: France, Japanese
STUDENT A: France is a country.
STUDENT B: Japanese is a language.

❑   **Exercise 13. Warm-up.** (Chart 1-4)
Complete the sentences with *a book* or *books*. What do you notice about the verbs in red?

1. A dictionary is _____.

2. Textbooks are _____.

3. Dictionaries and textbooks are _____.

1-4 Plural Nouns + *Be*

NOUN + *ARE* + NOUN (a) **Cats are animals**.	**Cats** = a plural noun **are** = a plural verb **animals** = a plural noun
(b) SINGULAR: a cat, an animal PLURAL: cat**s**, animal**s**	Plural nouns end in **-s**. **A** and **an** are used only with singular nouns.
(c) SINGULAR: a cit**y**, a countr**y** PLURAL: cit**ies**, countr**ies**	Some singular nouns that end in **-y** have a special plural form: They omit the **-y** and add **-ies**.*
NOUN and NOUN + *ARE* + NOUN (d) **Canada and China are countries.** (e) **Dogs and cats are animals.**	Two nouns connected by **and** are followed by **are**. In (d): **Canada** is a singular noun. **China** is a singular noun. They are connected by **and**. Together they are plural, i.e., "more than one."

*See Chart 3-5, p. 69, for more information about adding **-s/-es** to words that end in **-y**.

❑ **Exercise 14. Looking at grammar.** (Charts 1-3 and 1-4)
Look at each noun. Is it singular or plural? Choose the correct answer.

1. animals	one	two or more
2. a dog	one	two or more
3. a city	one	two or more
4. cities	one	two or more
5. an island	one	two or more
6. languages	one	two or more
7. a country	one	two or more

❑ **Exercise 15. Looking at grammar.** (Charts 1-3 and 1-4)
Write the plural form.

1. a book   _____*books*_____   4. an eraser   _____

2. a textbook   _____   5. a pen   _____

3. a pencil   _____   6. a dictionary _____

a pencil   an eraser

❏ **Exercise 16. Looking at grammar.** (Charts 1-3 and 1-4)

Complete the sentences. Use **a** or **an** and the words from the box.

animal	country	language
city	island	sport

1. A bird is _____*an animal*_____ .   Birds and cats are _____*animals*_____ .

2. Tennis is _____ .   Tennis and soccer are _____ .

3. Chicago is _____ .   Chicago and Berlin are _____ .

4. Spanish is _____ .   Spanish and Italian are _____ .

5. Mexico is _____ .   Mexico and Brazil are _____ .

6. A cow is _____ .   Cows and horses are _____ .

7. Hawaii is _____ .   Hawaii and Taiwan are _____ .

❏ **Exercise 17. Looking at grammar.** (Charts 1-3 and 1-4)

Change the singular sentences to plural sentences.

SINGULAR   PLURAL

1. A chicken is an animal.   →   _____*Chickens are animals.*_____

a chicken

a pea

2. A pea is a vegetable.   →   _____

3. A dictionary is a book.   →   _____

4. An airplane is a machine. →   _____

5. June is a month.
   July is a month.   →   _____

6. Winter is a season.
   Summer is a season.   →   _____

7. Egypt is a country.
   Indonesia is a country.   →   _____

❑ **Exercise 18. Game.** (Charts 1-3 and 1-4)

Work in teams. Your teacher will say the beginning of a sentence. As a team, finish the sentence and write it down. The team with the most correct sentences wins the game. Close your book for this activity.

Example:
TEACHER: Spanish . . .
TEAM A: Spanish is a language.

1. A dog . . .
2. Arabic . . .
3. London . . .
4. Summer . . .
5. September and October . . .

6. Mexico and Canada . . .
7. An airplane . . .
8. Winter and summer . . .
9. Peas . . .
10. A car . . .

❑ **Exercise 19. Let's talk: pairwork.** (Charts 1-3 and 1-4)

Your partner will ask you to name something. Answer in a complete sentence. You can look at your book before you speak. When you speak, look at your partner.

Example:

PARTNER A	PARTNER B
1. a country	1. two countries

PARTNER A: Name a country.
PARTNER B: Brazil is a country.
PARTNER A: Good. Brazil is a country.
           Your turn now.

PARTNER B: Name two countries.
PARTNER A: Italy and China are countries.
PARTNER B: Right. Italy and China are countries.
           Your turn now.

Remember: You can look at your book before you speak. When you speak, look at your partner.

PARTNER A	PARTNER B
1. a language	1. two cities
2. two languages	2. an island
3. a machine	3. two countries in Asia
4. an animal	4. a vegetable
5. two seasons	5. a street in this city

Exercise 20. Warm-up: listening. (Chart 1-5)

🎧 Listen to the conversation. Notice the words in red. Do you know the long form for them?

A: Hi. My name is Mrs. Smith. I'm the substitute teacher.

B: Hi. I'm Franco.

C: Hi. I'm Lisa. We're in your class.

A: It's nice to meet you.

B: We're glad to meet you too.

1-5	**Contractions with _Be_**					

	PRONOUN	+	_BE_	→	CONTRACTION	
AM	_I_	+	_am_	→	**I'm**	(a) **I'm** a student.
IS	_she_	+	_is_	→	**she's**	(b) **She's** a student.
	_he_	+	_is_	→	**he's**	(c) **He's** a student.
	_it_	+	_is_	→	**it's**	(d) **It's** a city.
ARE	_you_	+	_are_	→	**you're**	(e) **You're** a student.
	_we_	+	_are_	→	**we're**	(f) **We're** students.
	they	+	_are_	→	**they're**	(g) **They're** students.

When people speak, they often push two words together.
A contraction = two words that are pushed together

Contractions of a _subject pronoun_ + **be** are used in both speaking and writing.

PUNCTUATION: The mark in the middle of a contraction is called an "apostrophe" (').*

*NOTE: Write an apostrophe above the line. Do not write an apostrophe on the line.

    CORRECT: _____I'm a student_____.

    INCORRECT: _____I,m a student_____.

❏ **Exercise 21. Looking at grammar.** (Chart 1-5)

Write the contractions.

1. I am   _____I'm_____   5. it is   _____

2. she is   _____   6. they are   _____

3. you are   _____   7. he is   _____

4. we are   _____

❏ **Exercise 22. Looking at grammar.** (Chart 1-5)

Write the long form for each contraction.

1. They're sick.   _____They are_____ sick.

2. He's absent.   _____ absent.

3. It's hot.   _____ hot.

4. I'm late.   _____ late.

5. She's hungry.   _____ hungry.

6. We're students.   _____ students.

7. You're here.   _____ here.

❏ **Exercise 23. Looking at grammar.** (Chart 1-5)
Complete the sentences with pronouns. Use contractions.

1. *Sara* is a student. _____*She's*_____ in my class.

2. *James* is a student. _____ in my class.

3. *I* am at school. _____ in the cafeteria.

4. *Yuri and Anna* are absent. _____ at home.

5. *Anna* is from Russia. _____ nice.

6. *Ali and I* are in the same class. _____ friends.

7. *Yuri, Ali, and Anna* are friends. _____ funny.

❏ **Exercise 24. Listening.** (Chart 1-5)
Part I. Listen to the conversation. Write the contractions.

A: Hello. ___*I'm*___ Mrs. Brown. _____ the substitute teacher.
        1   2

B: Hi. _____ Paulo, and this is Marie. _____ in your class.
       3   4

A: _____ nice to meet you.
    5

B: _____ happy to meet you too.
    6

A: _____ time for class. Please take a seat.
    7

Part II. Listen to the conversation again and check your answers.

❏ **Exercise 25. Warm-up: pairwork.** (Chart 1-6)
Work with a partner. Complete the sentences with all the words from the box that are true.
Share a few of your answers with the class.

a baby	a husband	a teacher
a bird	a student	a wife

1. I'm not _____.

2. You're not _____.

1-6 Negative with *Be*

	CONTRACTIONS	**Not** makes a sentence negative.
(a) I **am not** a teacher.	I**'m not**	CONTRACTIONS
(b) You **are not** a teacher.	you**'re not** / you **aren't**	**Be** and **not** can be contracted.
(c) She **is not** a teacher.	she**'s not** / she **isn't**	Note that "I am" has only one
(d) He **is not** a teacher.	he**'s not** / he **isn't**	contraction with **be**, as in (a), but
(e) It **is not** a city.	it**'s not** / it **isn't**	there are two contractions with **be**
(f) We **are not** teachers.	we**'re not** / we **aren't**	for (b)—(h).
(g) You **are not** teachers.	you**'re not** / you **aren't**	
(h) They **are not** teachers.	they**'re not** / they **aren't**	

❏ **Exercise 26. Looking at grammar.** (Chart 1-6)
Complete the sentences with the negative form of *be*.

an astronaut

FULL FORM	CONTRACTION
1. I ___*am not*___ an astronaut.	I ___*'m not*___ an astronaut.
2. He _____ an astronaut.	He _____ an astronaut. OR
	He _____ an astronaut.
3. They _____ astronauts.	They _____ astronauts. OR
	They _____ astronauts.
4. You _____ an astronaut.	You _____ an astronaut. OR
	You _____ an astronaut.
5. She _____ an astronaut.	She _____ an astronaut. OR
	She _____ an astronaut.
6. We _____ astronauts.	We _____ astronauts. OR
	We _____ astronauts.

❑ **Exercise 27. Looking at grammar.** (Charts 1-5 and 1-6)
Make sentences with *is*, *isn't*, *are*, and *aren't*.

Examples: Africa \ city . . . It \ continent

   Africa isn't a city. It's a continent.

   Baghdad and Chicago \ city . . . They \ continent

   Baghdad and Chicago are cities. They aren't continents.

1. Canada \ country . . . It \ city

   _____

2. Argentina \ city . . . It \ country

   _____

3. Beijing and London \ city . . . They \ country

   _____

4. Asia \ country . . . It \ continent

   _____

5. Asia and South America \ continent . . . They \ country

   _____

❑ **Exercise 28. Vocabulary and listening.** (Charts 1-3 and 1-6)
Part I. Write *a* or *an*.

1. __*a*__ mother   8. _____ son

2. _____ mom   9. _____ aunt

3. _____ father   10. _____ uncle

4. _____ dad   11. _____ parent

5. _____ sister   12. _____ adult

6. _____ brother   13. _____ child

7. _____ daughter

Peterson Family Tree

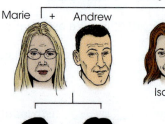

Marie + Andrew

Isabelle + David

Billy   Janey

Part II. Listen to the sentences. Choose the correct answer. *Note:* in spoken English, the "t" in negative contractions may be hard to hear.

1. is isn't	3. is isn't	5. are aren't	7. are aren't
2. is isn't	4. is isn't	6. are aren't	8. are aren't

Paul Cox   Gloria Perez   Nurse Lars Jensen

Rick Hayes   Jennifer Evans

Dr. Sana Gupta   Omar Khan   Joe Davis

Part I. Write the name of the person next to the job.

1. plumber _____*Paul*_____   5. police officer _____

2. bus driver _____   6. doctor _____

3. nurse _____   7. auto mechanic _____

4. gardener _____   8. construction worker _____

Part II. Complete the sentences. Items may vary in items 3–7.

1. Jennifer _____*isn't*_____ a gardener. She _*'s a police officer*_____ .

2. Lars _____*is*_____ a nurse. He _____ a doctor.

3. Omar _____ an auto mechanic. He isn't _____.

4. Paul _____ a construction worker. He _____.

5. Sana _____. _____.

6. Gloria _____. _____.

7. I'm not a _____. I'm _____.

❑ **Exercise 30. Warm-up.** (Chart 1-7)

Complete each sentence with a word from the box.

short	tall	young	old

1. Bill is _____.

2. He is also _____.

3. Sam is _____ and _____.

Bill   Sam

1-7 *Be* + Adjective

NOUN	+	*BE*	+	ADJECTIVE		round
(a) A ball		is		**round**.		intelligent
(b) Balls		are		**round**.		hungry ⎤ = adjectives
(c) Mary		is		**intelligent**.		young
(d) Mary and Tom		are		**intelligent**.		happy

Adjectives often follow a form of **be** (am, is, are).

PRONOUN	+	*BE*	+	ADJECTIVE
(e) I		am		**hungry**.
(f) She		is		**young**.
(g) They		are		**happy**.

In (a)—(g), the adjectives give information about a noun or pronoun that comes at the beginning of a sentence.*

*The noun or pronoun that comes at the beginning of a sentence is called a "subject." See Chart 6-1, p. 159.

❑ **Exercise 31. Grammar and vocabulary.** (Charts 1-5 and 1-7)

Find the adjective in the first sentence. Then complete the second sentence with **be** + *an adjective* with an opposite meaning. Use an adjective from the box. Write the contracted form of **be**.

beautiful	expensive	noisy	short
clean	fast	old	tall
easy	✓happy	poor	

1. I'm not sad. I *'m happy* _____.

2. Mr. Thomas isn't rich. He _____.

3. My hair isn't long. It _____.

4. My clothes aren't dirty. They _____.

5. Flowers aren't ugly. They _____.

6. Cars aren't cheap. They _____ .

7. Airplanes aren't slow. They _____ .

8. Grammar isn't difficult. It _____ .

9. My sister isn't short. She _____ .

10. My grandparents aren't young. They _____ .

11. The classroom isn't quiet. It _____ .

❑ **Exercise 32. Grammar and vocabulary.** (Charts 1-3, 1-4, and 1-7)
Complete each sentence with *is* or *are* and an adjective from the box.

cold	flat	important	small/little	sweet
dangerous	funny	large/big	sour	wet
dry	✓ hot	round	square	

1. Fire _____*is hot*_____ .

2. Ice and snow _____ .

3. A box _____ .

4. Balls and oranges _____ .

5. Sugar _____ .

6. An elephant _____ , but
   a mouse _____ .

an
elephant

7. A rain forest _____ , but
   a desert _____ .

8. A joke _____ .

9. Good health _____ .

a mouse

10. Guns aren't safe. They _____ .

11. A coin _____ small, round, and _____ .

12. A lemon _____ .

a lemon   sugar   water

lemonade

❏ **Exercise 33. Let's talk: game.** (Chart 1-7)

Work in teams. Your teacher will ask you to name things. Your team will make a list. Share your list with the class. The group with the longest list gets a point. The group with the most points at the end of the game is the winner. Close your book for this activity.

Example: round
      TEACHER: Name round things.
TEAM A'S LIST: a ball, an orange, a clock
TEAM B'S LIST: a baseball, a basketball, a soccer ball
TEAM C'S LIST: a ball, a head, an orange, a coin, a ring, a planet
                Group C wins a point.

1. hot	4. free	7. beautiful
2. difficult	5. little	8. expensive
3. sweet	6. important	9. cheap

❏ **Exercise 34. Let's talk: pairwork.** (Charts 1-5 → 1-7)

Work with a partner. Take turns making two sentences for each picture. Use the given adjectives. You can look at your book before you speak. When you speak, look at your partner.

Example: The girl . . . happy/sad
PARTNER A: The girl isn't happy. She's sad.
           Your turn now.

Example: The flower . . . beautiful/ugly
PARTNER B: The flower is beautiful. It isn't ugly.
           Your turn now.

PARTNER A	PARTNER B
1. The table . . . clean/dirty.	1. The man . . . friendly/unfriendly.
2. The boy . . . sick/well.	2. The coffee . . . cold/hot.

18 CHAPTER 1

$x^2 + 5 + 4 = (x + 4)(x + 1)$ 3. The algebra problem . . . easy/difficult.	 3. The woman . . . tall/short.
 4. The cars . . . old/new.	 4. Katie . . . old/young.

❑ **Exercise 35. Grammar and vocabulary.** (Charts 1-5 → 1-7)
Complete the sentences with *is* or *are* and the correct pronoun. Use contractions. Some sentences are negative.

1. A pea _____*is*_____ green. _____*It isn't*_____ red.

2. Carrots _____*aren't*_____ blue. _____*They're*_____ orange.

3. An onion _____ orange. _____
   brown, white, or green.

4. A strawberry _____ black. _____ red.

5. Bananas _____ yellow. _____ white.

6. A banana _____ yellow. _____ white.

7. An orange _____ orange. _____
   brown.

8. Apples _____ red or green. _____
   purple.

9. A tomato _____ blue. _____
   red or green.

❑ **Exercise 36. Let's talk: game.** (Charts 1-5 → 1-7)
Part I. Check (✓) all the words you know. Your teacher will explain the words you don't know.

1. _____ hungry		11. _____ angry
2. _____ thirsty		12. _____ nervous
3. _____ sleepy		13. _____ friendly
4. _____ tired		14. _____ lazy
5. _____ old		15. _____ hardworking
6. _____ young		16. _____ famous
7. _____ happy		17. _____ sick
8. _____ homesick		18. _____ healthy
9. _____ married		19. _____ unfriendly
10. _____ single		20. _____ shy

Part II. Sit in a circle. Student A makes a sentence using "I" and the first word. Student B repeats the information about Student A and makes a new sentence using the second word. Continue around the circle until everyone in class has spoken. The teacher is the last person to speak and must repeat the information about everyone in the class.

Example:
STUDENT A: I'm not hungry.
STUDENT B: He's not hungry. I'm thirsty.
STUDENT C: He's not hungry. She's thirsty. I'm sleepy.

❑ **Exercise 37. Let's talk: pairwork.** (Charts 1-5 → 1-7)
Work with a partner. Check (✓) each adjective that describes this city/town (the city or town where you are studying now). When you finish, compare your work with a partner. Do you and your partner have the same answers? Tell the class about some of your differences.

1. _____ big		11. _____ noisy
2. _____ small		12. _____ quiet
3. _____ clean		13. _____ crowded
4. _____ dirty		14. _____ not crowded
5. _____ friendly		15. _____ hot
6. _____ unfriendly		16. _____ cold
7. _____ safe		17. _____ warm
8. _____ dangerous		18. _____ cool
9. _____ beautiful		19. _____ expensive
10. _____ ugly		20. _____ inexpensive/cheap

❑ **Exercise 38. Warm-up.** (Chart 1-8)
Read the sentences and choose *yes* or *no*.

1. The cat is next to the mousetrap.   yes   no

2. The mouse is under the chair.   yes   no

3. The mouse is behind the cat.   yes   no

1-8 *Be* + a Place

(a) Maria is **here**.		In (a): *here* = a place.
(b) Bob is **at the library**.		In (b): *at the library* = a place. **Be** is often followed by *a place*.

(c) Maria is {	**here**. **there**. **downstairs**. **upstairs**. **inside**. **outside**. **downtown**.	A place may be one word, as in the examples in (c).

(d) Bob is {	PREPOSITION +	NOUN	A place may be a prepositional phrase (*preposition + noun*), as in (d).
	at	**the library**.	
	on	**the bus**.	
	in	**his room**.	
	at	**work**.	
	next to	**Maria**.	

ON

IN

NEXT TO

ABOVE

UNDER

BEHIND

SOME COMMON PREPOSITIONS

above	behind	from	next to	under
at	between	in	on	

❑ **Exercise 39. Looking at grammar.** (Chart 1-8)
Complete each sentence with a preposition from the box.

above	between	next to	under
behind	✓ in	on	

1. The cat is _____*in*_____ the desk.

2. The cat is _____ the desk.

3. The cat is _____ the desk.

4. The cat is _____ the desk.

5. The cat is _____ the desk.

6. The cat is _____ the desk.

7. The cat is _____ the desks.

❏ **Exercise 40. Let's talk: pairwork.** (Chart 1-8)

Work with a partner. Follow your partner's instructions.

Example:
PARTNER A: Put your hand under your chair.
PARTNER B: (*Partner B performs the action.*)

PARTNER A	PARTNER B
Put your pen . . .	*Put a piece of paper . . .*
1. on your book.	1. behind your back.
2. in your hand.	2. between two fingers.
3. next to your thumb.	3. next to your thumb.
4. under your desk.	4. in the air.

❏ **Exercise 41. Listening.** (Charts 1-1 → 1-8)

Listen to the sentences. Write the words you hear. Some answers have contractions.

The First Day of Class

Paulo___*is a student*___ from Brazil. Marie _____ student

                    1   2

from France. _____ the classroom. Today _____ exciting day.

                        3   4

_____ the first day of school, but they _____ nervous.

     5   6

_____ to be here. Mrs. Brown _____ the teacher. She

        7   8

_____ in the classroom right now. _____ late today.

     9   10

❏ **Exercise 42. Reading and writing.** (Charts 1-1 → 1-8)

Read the paragraph. Then complete the sentences with true answers. Several answers are possible for each item.

A Substitute Teacher

    Today is Monday. It is the first day of English class. Mr. Anderson is an English teacher, but he isn't in class today. He is at home in bed. Mrs. Anderson is in the classroom today. Mrs. and Mr. Anderson are husband and wife. Mrs. Anderson is a good teacher. The students are a little nervous, but they're happy. Mrs. Anderson is very funny, and her explanations are clear. It's a good class.

1. Mr. Anderson is ___*an English teacher, sick, etc.*_____.

2. Mrs. Anderson is not _____.

3. Mr. and Mrs. Anderson are _____.

4. The students are _____.

5. The English class is _____.

1-9 Summary: Basic Sentence Patterns with *Be*

(a)	SUBJECT + *BE* + NOUN I am *a student.*	The noun or pronoun that comes at the beginning of a sentence is called the "subject."
(b)	SUBJECT + *BE* + ADJECTIVE He is *intelligent.*	*Be* is a "verb." Almost all English sentences have a subject and a verb.
(c) (d)	SUBJECT + *BE* + A PLACE We are *in class.* She is *upstairs.*	Notice in the examples: There are three basic completions for sentences that begin with a *subject + the verb be:* • *a noun,* as in (a) • *an adjective,* as in (b) • *an expression of place,** as in (c) and (d)

*An expression of place can be a *preposition + noun,* or it can be one word: *upstairs.*

❑ **Exercise 43. Looking at grammar.** (Chart 1-9)
Write the form of *be* (*am, is,* or *are*) that is used in each sentence. Then write the grammar structure that follows *be*.

	BE	+	COMPLETION
1. We're students.	are	+	noun
2. Anna is in Rome.	is	+	place
3. I'm hungry.	am	+	adjective
4. Dogs are animals.	_____	+	_____
5. Jack is at home.	_____	+	_____
6. He's sick.	_____	+	_____
7. They're in class.	_____	+	_____
8. I'm a mechanic.	_____	+	_____
9. Gina is upstairs.	_____	+	_____
10. The peas are good.	_____	+	_____
11. Dan and I are nurses.	_____	+	_____
12. Nora is downstairs.	_____	+	_____
13. We aren't homesick.	_____	+	_____
14. They are astronauts.	_____	+	_____

Exercise 44. Listening. (Chapter 1)

Is and *are* are often contracted with nouns in spoken English. Listen to the sentences.
Practice saying them yourself. *Note:* *'s* and *'re* can be hard to hear.

1. Grammar is easy. → Grammar's easy.
2. My name is Josh.
3. My books are on the table.
4. My brother is 21 years old.
5. The weather is cold today.
6. The windows are open.
7. My money is in my wallet.

8. Mr. Smith is a teacher.
9. My parents are at work now.
10. The food is good.
11. Tom is sick today.
12. My roommates are from Chicago.
13. My sister is a student in high school.

❑ **Exercise 45. Looking at grammar.** (Chapter 1)

Choose the correct completion.

Example: My friend _____ from South Korea.
　　　　　a. he　　(b.) 's　　　c. Ø⋆

1. The test _____ easy.
　　a. are　　　　b. is　　　　　c. Ø

2. My notebook _____ on the table.
　　a. is　　　　b. are　　　　　c. Ø

3. My notebooks _____ on the table.
　　a. is　　　　b. are　　　　　c. Ø

4. Sue _____ a student.
　　a. is　　　　b. she　　　　　c. Ø

5. The weather _____ warm today.
　　a. is　　　　b. it　　　　　c. Ø

6. My friends _____ from Cuba.
　　a. are　　　　b. is　　　　　c. Ø

7. My book _____ on my desk.
　　a. it　　　　b. is　　　　　c. Ø

8. The teachers _____ in class.
　　a. is　　　　b. are　　　　　c. Ø

9. The teacher _____ nice.
　　a. 's　　　　b. are　　　　　c. Ø

10. Dinner _____ ready.
　　a. it　　　　b. is　　　　　c. Ø

⋆Ø = nothing

Part I. Read the paragraph. Look at new vocabulary with your teacher first.

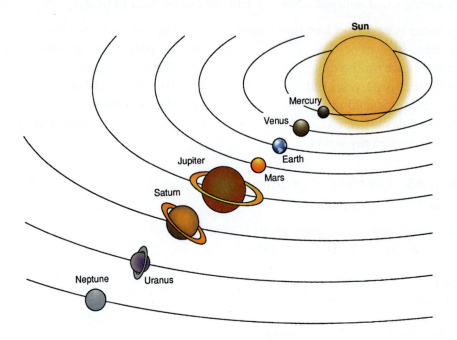

Venus

Venus is the second planet from the sun. It isn't big and it isn't small. It is between Earth and Mercury. It is an interesting planet. It is very bright at night. It is rocky and dusty. It is also hot. The temperature on Venus is 464 degrees Celsius or 867 degrees Fahrenheit.

Do you know these words?

bright
at night
rocky
dusty
temperature

Part II. Write a paragraph about Mars. Use the following information.

Facts:
- 4th (fourth) planet from the sun
- small
- between Earth and Jupiter
- red

- very rocky
- very dusty
- very cold (-55° C / -67° F)
- interesting?

Before you begin, look at the paragraph format.

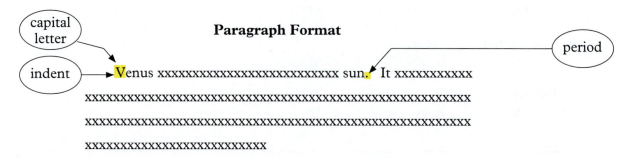

Part III. Editing check: Work individually or change papers with a partner. Check (✓) for the following:

1. ____ capital letter at the beginning of each sentence

2. ____ period at the end of each sentence

3. ____ paragraph indent

4. ____ a verb (for example, *is* or *are*) in every sentence

5. ____ correct spelling (use a dictionary or spell-check)

Chapter 2
Using Be and Have

❏ **Exercise 1. Warm-up.** (Chart 2-1)
Answer the questions.

    1. Is the weather nice today?   yes   no

    2. Are you in a classroom right now?   yes   no

    3. Are you hungry?   yes   no

2-1 Yes/No Questions with *Be*

QUESTION			STATEMENT			In a question, ***be*** comes in front of the subject.
BE +	SUBJECT		SUBJECT +	*BE*		
(a) *Am*	*I*	early?	*I*	*am*	early.	PUNCTUATION
(b) *Is*	*Ana*	a student?	*Ana*	*is*	a student.	A question ends with a question mark (?).
(c) *Are*	*they*	at home?	*They*	*are*	at home.	A statement ends with a period (.).

❏ **Exercise 2. Looking at grammar.** (Chart 2-1)
Complete the questions with ***am***, ***is***, or ***are***.

    1. _____ you tired?   6. _____ I a new student?

    2. _____ he late?   7. _____ they new students?

    3. _____ they here?   8. _____ you and Bill ready?

    4. _____ we early?   9. _____ Mr. Rivera sick?

    5. _____ she at home?   10. _____ Mr. and Mrs. Rivera sick?

❑   **Exercise 3. Looking at grammar.** (Chart 2-1)
Make questions.

1. A: _____*Is Mrs. Han a teacher?*_____
    B: Yes, Mrs. Han is a teacher.

2. A: _____
    B: Yes, carrots are vegetables.

3. A: _____
    B: Yes, Mr. Wang is absent today.

4. A: _____
    B: Yes, planets are big.

5. A: _____
    B: Yes, Amy and Mika are here today.

6. A: _____
    B: Yes, English grammar is fun.

7. A: _____
    B: Yes, I am ready for the next exercise.

❑   **Exercise 4. Listening.** (Chart 2-1)
Listen to the sentences. Write the words you hear.

Example: You will hear: A: Elena's absent today.
                            B: Is she sick?
            You will write: B: _____*Is*_____ she sick?

A: Elena's absent today.
B: _____ she sick?
       1
A: No.
B: _____ her husband sick?
       2
A: No.
B: _____ her children sick?
       3
A: No.
B: _____ she homesick?
       4
A: No.
B: So? What's the matter?
A: Her turtle _____ sick.
                   5
B: Are you serious? That's crazy!

a turtle

Exercise 5. Warm-up. (Chart 2-2)

Answer the questions. In b., both answers are possible. Which negative contraction do you prefer?

1. Is the classroom cold?
   a. Yes, it is.   b. No, it isn't. / No, it's not.

2. Are the chairs in the classroom comfortable?
   a. Yes, they are.   b. No, they aren't. / No, they're not.

2-2 Short Answers to Yes/No Questions

QUESTION		SHORT ANSWER	Spoken contractions are not used in short answers that begin with *yes*.
(a) **Is Kari** a student?	→	Yes, *she is*.	In (a): INCORRECT: Yes, she's.
	→	No, *she's not*.	
	→	No, *she isn't*.	
(b) **Are they** at home?	→	Yes, *they are*.	In (b): INCORRECT: Yes, they're.
	→	No, *they aren't*.	
		No, *they're not*.	
(c) **Are you** ready?	→	Yes, *I am*.	In (c): INCORRECT: Yes, I'm.
	→	No, *I'm not*.*	

Am and *not* are not contracted.

❏ **Exercise 6. Looking at grammar.** (Chart 2-2)

Make questions and give short answers.

1. A: _____*Are you tired?*_____
   B: _____*No, I'm not.*_____ (I'm not tired.)

2. A: _____*Is Alma in your class?*_____
   B: _____*Yes, she is.*_____ (Alma is in my class.)

3. A: _____
   B: _____ (I'm not homesick.)

4. A: _____
   B: _____ (Kareem is homesick.)

5. A: _____
   B: _____ (Kara isn't here today.)

6. A: _____
   B: _____ (The students in this class are smart.)

7. A: _____

   B: _____ (The chairs in this room aren't comfortable.)

8. A: _____

   B: _____ (I'm not single.)

9. A: _____

   B: _____ (We're married.)

❑ **Exercise 7. Let's talk: pairwork.** (Chart 2-2)
Work with a partner. Ask and answer questions. You can look at your book before you speak. When you speak, look at your partner.

Example: dolphins: intelligent/dumb
PARTNER A: Are dolphins intelligent?
PARTNER B: Yes, they are.
　　　　　OR
PARTNER A: Are dolphins dumb?
PARTNER B: No, they aren't.

a dolphin

PARTNER A	PARTNER B
1. a mouse: big/little	1. diamonds: expensive/cheap
2. lemons: sweet/sour	2. your grammar book: light/heavy
3. the world: flat/round	3. butterflies: beautiful/ugly
4. the weather: cool today/warm today	4. English grammar: easy/difficult
5. your dictionary: with you/at home	5. turtles: fast/slow
6. your shoes: comfortable/uncomfortable	6. the floor in this room: clean/dirty

❑ **Exercise 8. Looking at grammar.** (Charts 2-1 and 2-2)
Complete the conversations with your own words.

1. A: _____*Are*_____ you a student at this school?

   B: Yes, _____*I am*_____.

   A: _____ you from _____?

   B: No, _____ from _____.

2. A: Are you a/an _____?

   B: No, _____ not. I'm a/an _____.

3. A: Are _____ expensive?

    B: Yes, _____ .

    A: Is _____ expensive?

    B: No, _____ .

4. A: _____ Vietnam and Cambodia countries in Asia?

    B: Yes, _____ are.

    A: _____ a country in South America?

    B: Yes, _____ is.

    A: _____ a country in Africa?

    B: No, _____ not. It's a country in _____ .

❑ **Exercise 9. Warm-up.** (Chart 2-3)
Choose the correct answer for each question.

> On your head   No, they aren't

A: Are my glasses in the kitchen?

B: _____ .
    ₁

A: Where are they?

B: _____ !
    ₂

glasses

2-3 Questions with *Be:* Using *Where*

Where asks about place. *Where* comes at the beginning of the question, in front of *be*.

	QUESTION		SHORT ANSWER (LONG ANSWER)
	BE + SUBJECT		
(a)	*Is* *the book* on the table?	→	Yes, *it is*. (*The book is on the table.*)
(b)	*Are* *the books* on the table?	→	Yes, *they are*. (*The books are on the table.*)
	WHERE + *BE* + SUBJECT		
(c)	*Where* *is* *the book?*	→	*On the table.* (*The book is on the table.*)
(d)	*Where* *are* *the books?*	→	*On the table.* (*The books are on the table.*)

❏ **Exercise 10. Looking at grammar.** (Chart 2-3)
Choose the correct question for each response.

Question	**Response**
1. a. Is Sami absent? b. Where is Sami?	At home.
2. a. Where are the boxes? b. Are the boxes in the closet?	Yes, they are.
3. a. Are you outside? b. Where are you?	No, I'm not.
4. a. Is the mail on the kitchen counter? b. Where is the mail?	On the kitchen counter.

❏ **Exercise 11. Looking at grammar.** (Chart 2-3)
Make questions.

1. A: _____*Is Sara at home?*_____

    B: Yes, she is. (Sara is at home.)

2. A: _____*Where is Sara?*_____

    B: At home. (Sara is at home.)

3. A: _____

    B: Yes, it is. (Cairo is in Egypt.)

4. A: _____

    B: In Egypt. (Cairo is in Egypt.)

5. A: _____

    B: Yes, they are. (The students are in class today.)

6. A: _____

    B: In class. (The students are in class today.)

7. A: _____

    B: On Main Street. (The post office is on Main Street.)

8. A: _____

    B: Yes, it is. (The train station is on Grand Avenue.)

9. A: _____

    B: Over there. (The bus stop is over there.)

10. A: _____

    B: At work. (Ali and Jake are at work now.)

❏ **Exercise 12. Let's talk: pairwork.** (Chart 2-3)

Work with a partner. Ask and answer questions. Use **where**. You can look at your book before you speak. When you speak, look at your partner.

Example:
PARTNER A: Where is your pen?
PARTNER B: It's in my hand. (*or any other true answer*)

PARTNER A	PARTNER B
1. your money	1. your wallet
2. your books	2. your glasses or sunglasses
3. your coat	3. your family
4. your pencil	4. your apartment
5. (*name of a classmate*)	5. (*names of two classmates*)
6. your hometown	6. your hometown
7. (*name of a city in the world*)	7. (*name of a country in the world*)

❏ **Exercise 13. Warm-up.** (Chart 2-4)

Check (✓) the true sentences.

1. _____ I have a dictionary on my desk.

2. _____ Many students have backpacks.

3. _____ My teacher has a cell phone.

4. _____ Her cell phone has a case.

5. _____ The classroom has a globe.

a globe

2-4 Using *Have* and *Has*

	SINGULAR			PLURAL					
(a)	*I*	*have*	a pen.	(f)	*We*	*have*	pens.	I / you / we / they	+	*have*
(b)	*You*	*have*	a pen.	(g)	*You*	*have*	pens.			
(c)	*She*	*has*	a pen.	(h)	*They*	*have*	pens.			
(d)	*He*	*has*	a pen.					she / he / it	+	*has*
(e)	*It*	*has*	blue ink.							

❑ **Exercise 14. Looking at grammar.** (Chart 2-4)

Complete the sentences with *have* or *has*.

trucks

a van

1. You _____ a bike.

2. I _____ a bike.

3. She _____ a small car.

4. They _____ trucks.

5. We _____ trucks.

6. You and I _____ bikes.

7. The business _____ a van.

8. He _____ a motorcycle.

9. Radek _____ a motorcycle.

10. The Molinas _____ two motorcycles.

❑ **Exercise 15. Looking at grammar.** (Chart 2-4)

Choose the correct answer.

1. We   has / (have)   a daughter.

2. Venita   has / have   two daughters.

3. She   has / have   twin daughters.

4. The Leons are grandparents. They   has / have   one grandchild.

5. Hiro   has / have   an interesting job. He's a journalist.

6. You   has / have   a good job too.

7. You and I   has / have   good jobs.

8. I   has / have   a laptop computer.
    It   has / have   a small screen.

9. Samir is a website designer. He
    has / have   a laptop and a desktop.

10. A laptop   has / have   a battery.

11. Laptops   has / have   batteries.

a desktop   a laptop

❑ **Exercise 16. Vocabulary and grammar.** (Chart 2-4)
Complete each sentence with *have* or *has* and words from the box.

backaches	a fever	a sore throat
the chills	✓ a headache	a stomachache
a cold	high blood pressure	toothaches
coughs		

1. Mr. Kasim ___has a headache___ .

2. The patients _____ .

3. I _____ .

4. Mrs. Ramirez _____ .

5. You _____ .

6. The workers _____ .

7. Olga _____ .

8. You _____ .

9. Alan _____ .

10. They _____ .

Exercise 17. Let's talk: pairwork. (Chart 2-4)

Complete the conversations with a partner. You can look at your book before you speak. When you speak, look at your partner. Use this model.

Partner A: How _____?

Partner B: Not so good. _____.

Partner A: That's too bad.

Example: Jamal? . . . a toothache.
PARTNER A: How's Jamal?
PARTNER B: Not so good. He has a toothache.
PARTNER A: That's too bad. Your turn now.

1. you? . . . a headache.
2. you? . . . a sore tooth.
3. your mother? . . . a sore back.
4. Mr. Park? . . . a backache.

5. your parents? . . . colds.
6. the patients? . . . stomachaches.
7. your little brother? . . . a sore throat.
8. Mrs. Luna? . . . a fever.

Exercise 18. Looking at grammar. (Charts 1-1 and 2-4)

Rewrite the paragraph. Change "I" to "he." You will also need to change the verbs in **bold**.

Dr. Lee

    I **am** a doctor. I **am** 70 years old, so I **have** many years of experience. I **have** many patients. Some are very sick. I **have** a clinic downtown. I also **have** patients at the hospital. It is hard work, and I **am** often very tired. But I **am** also happy. I help many people.

_____*He is a doctor.*_____

_____

_____

_____

_____*He helps many people.*_____

Exercise 19. Looking at grammar. (Charts 1-1, 1-2, and 2-4)

Part I. Complete the sentences with *is* or *has*.

I have a college roommate, Tia. She . . .

1. ____*is*____ from a small town.
2. _____ nice.
3. _____ a motorcycle.
4. _____ a smart phone.
5. _____ smart.
6. _____ homework every night.

7. _____ homesick.
8. _____ a large family.
9. _____ quiet.
10. _____ a boyfriend.
11. _____ a pet bird at home.
12. _____ serious.

Part II. Complete the sentences with *are* or *have*.

The two students in the room next to us . . .

1. _____ a TV.

2. _____ two computers.

3. _____ noisy.

4. _____ messy.

5. _____ from a big city.

6. _____ busy.

7. _____ a lot of friends.

8. _____ friendly.

9. _____ parties on weekends.

10. _____ low grades.

❏ **Exercise 20. Warm-up.** (Chart 2-5)
Complete each sentence with a word from the box.

Her	His	My	Their

1. _____ name is Evita.

2. _____ name is Paulo.

| Her | His | My | Their |

3. _____ name is Natalie.

4. _____ names are Natalie and Paulo.

2-5 Using *My, Your, Her, His, Our, Their*

SINGULAR	PLURAL	SUBJECT FORM	POSSESSIVE FORM
(a) **I** have a book. *My* book is red.	(e) **We** have books. *Our* books are red.	I → my	
(b) **You** have a book. *Your* book is red.	(f) **You** have books. *Your* books are red.	you → your	
(c) **She** has a book. *Her* book is red.	(g) **They** have books. *Their* books are red.	she → her	
(d) **He** has a book. *His* book is red.		he → his we → our they → their	

I *possess* a book. = I *have* a book. = It is *my* book.
My, your, her, his, our, and *their* are called "possessive adjectives." They come in front of nouns.

❑ **Exercise 21. Looking at grammar.** (Chart 2-5)
Complete each sentence with a word from the box.

| her | his | my | our | their | your |

1. You're next. It's _____*your*_____ turn.

2. Susana's next. It's _____ turn.

her	his	my	our	their	your

3. Bruno and Maria are next. It's _____ turn.

4. My aunt is next. It's _____ turn.

5. I'm next. It's _____ turn.

6. The children are next. It's _____ turn.

7. You and Mohamed are next. It's _____ turn.

8. Marcos and I are next. It's _____ turn.

9. Bill's next. It's _____ turn.

10. Mrs. Sung is next. It's _____ turn.

❑ **Exercise 22. Vocabulary and grammar.** (Chart 2-5)
Complete the sentences with the information on the ID cards.

What information do you know about this person from his ID card?

1. _____ last name is _____.

2. _____ first name is _____.

3. _____ middle initial is _____.

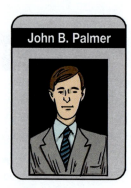

John B. Palmer

What information do the ID cards give you about Don and Kathy Johnson?

4. _____ zip code is _____.

5. _____ area code is _____.

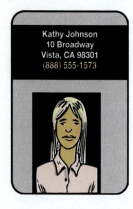

Kathy Johnson
10 Broadway
Vista, CA 98301
(888) 555-1573

Don Johnson
10 Broadway
Vista, CA 98301
(888) 555-1573

Dr. Diane Ellen Nelson
4/12/80

What do you know
about Dr. Nelson?

6. _____ birthdate is _____.

7. _____ birthday is _____.

8. _____ middle name is _____.

Write about yourself.

9. _____ first name is _____.

10. _____ last name is _____.

11. _____ middle name is _____.

12. _____ middle initial is _____.

13. _____ area code is _____.

14. _____ phone number is _____.

15. _____ zip code is _____.

16. _____ birthday is _____.

April

Sun.	Mon.	Tues.	Wed.	Thurs.	Fri.	Sat.
				1	2	3
4	5	6	7	8	9	10
11	12	13	14	15	16	17
18	19	20	21	22	23	24
25	26	27	28	29	30	

❑ **Exercise 23. Vocabulary: pairwork.** (Chart 2-5)
Work with a partner. Look at the vocabulary. Put a check (✓) beside the words you know.
Ask your partner about the ones you don't know. Your teacher can help you. The picture
on the next page shows clothes and jewelry.

Vocabulary Checklist		
COLORS	CLOTHES	JEWELRY
___ black	___ belt	___ bracelet
___ blue, dark blue, light blue	___ blouse	___ earrings
___ blue green	___ boots	___ necklace
___ brown, dark brown, light brown	___ coat	___ ring
___ gold	___ dress	___ watch
___ gray, dark gray, light gray	___ gloves	
___ green, dark green, light green	___ hat	
___ orange	___ jacket	
___ pink	___ jeans	
___ purple	___ pants	
___ red	___ sandals	
___ silver	___ shirt	
___ tan, beige	___ shoes	
___ white	___ skirt	
___ yellow	___ socks	
	___ suit	
	___ sweater	
	___ tie, necktie	
	___ T-shirt	

❑ **Exercise 24. Looking at grammar.** (Chart 2-5)
Complete the sentences with *my, your, her, his, our,* or *their*.

1. Malena has on* a blouse. _____*Her*_____ blouse is light blue.

2. Tomas has on a shirt. _____ shirt is yellow and brown.

3. I have on jeans. _____ jeans are blue.

4. Kiril and Oleg have on boots. _____ boots are brown.

5. Diana and you have on dresses. _____ dresses are red.

---

* *has on* and *have on* = wear (clothes)

6. Salma and I have on sweaters. _____ sweaters are green.

7. You have on shoes. _____ shoes are dark brown.

8. Nora has on a skirt. _____ skirt is black.

9. Leo has on a belt. _____ belt is white.

10. Sashi and Akira have on socks. _____ socks are gray.

11. Arturo has on pants. _____ pants are dark blue.

12. I have on earrings. _____ earrings are gold.

❑ **Exercise 25. Listening.** (Charts 2-4 and 2-5)

Listen to the sentences. Write the words you hear.

Example: You will hear: She has on boots.
You will write: _____*She has*_____ on boots.

Anna's clothes

1. _____ boots _____ zippers.

2. _____ a raincoat.

3. _____ raincoat _____ buttons.

4. _____ small.

5. _____ sweater _____ long sleeves.

6. _____ earrings on _____ ears.

7. _____ silver.

8. _____ on jeans.

9. _____ jeans _____ pockets.

an earring

a sweater

a raincoat

jeans

boots with
zippers

❑ **Exercise 26. Looking at grammar.** (Charts 2-4 and 2-5)

Complete the sentences. Use *have* or *has* and *my, your, her, his, our,* or *their*.

1. You _____*have*_____ a big family. _____*Your*_____ family is nice.

2. You and Tina _____ many cousins. _____ cousins are friendly.

3. I _____a brother. _____ brother is in college.

4. William _____ a sister. _____ sister is a doctor.

5. Lisa _____ a twin sister. _____ sister is disabled.

6. Iman and Amir are married. They _____ a baby. _____ baby is six months old.

7. Anton and I _____ a son. _____ son is seven years old.

8. Pietro and Julieta _____ a daughter. _____ daughter is ten years old.

9. I _____ an adopted brother. _____ brother is thirty.

10. Lidia is single. She _____ a brother. _____ brother is single too.

❑ **Exercise 27. Reading and grammar.** (Chapter 1 and Charts 2-4 and 2-5)
Part I. Read the story and answer the questions. Look at new vocabulary with your teacher first.

One Big Happy Family

Kanai is 13 years old. She has a big family. She has four sisters and five brothers. Kanai and her siblings are adopted. They are from several different countries. She likes her brothers and sisters. They have a good time. They are always busy. Kanai's parents are busy too. Her mother is an airline pilot. She goes away overnight fifteen days a month. Kanai's dad is a stay-at-home father. He has a lot of work, but the older kids are helpful. Kanai's parents love children. They are one big happy family.

Do you know these words?
sibling
adopted
pilot
overnight
stay-at-home father

1. Kanai is a girl.   yes   no

2. Only the girls are adopted.   yes   no

3. Kanai's father is home a lot.   yes   no

4. Her mother is home every night.   yes   no

Part II. Complete the sentences with *her*, *his*, or *their*. One sentence has two possible answers.

1. Kanai is adopted. _____ brothers and sisters are adopted too.

2. Her parents are busy. _____ mother is an airline pilot. _____ father is a stay-at-home dad.

3. She has nine siblings. _____ family is very large.

4. Kanai's dad is very busy. _____ children are helpful.

Part III. Complete the story with ***is, are, has,*** or ***have.***

One Big Happy Family

Kanai _____ 13 years old. She _____ a big family. She
                    1   2

_____ four sisters and five brothers. Kanai and her siblings are adopted.
      3

They _____ from several different countries. She likes her brothers and
             4

sisters. They _____ a good time. They _____ always busy.
                       5   6

Kanai's parents _____ busy too. Her mother _____ an airline pilot.
                        7   8

She _____ away overnight fifteen days a month. Kanai's dad _____
              9   10

a stay-at-home father. He _____ a lot of work, but the older kids are helpful.
                                  11

Kanai's parents love children. They are one big happy family.

❑ ## Exercise 28. Warm-up. (Chart 2-6)
Match the sentences to the pictures.

Picture A   Picture B

1. This is my wallet. ____   2. That is your wallet. ____

2-6 Using *This* and *That*

(a) I have a book in my hand. **This book** is red.	*this* book = the book is near me.
(b) I see a book on your desk. **That book** is blue.	*that* book = the book is not near me.
(c) **This** is my book.	
(d) **That** is your book.	
(e) **That's** her book.	CONTRACTION: *that is = that's*
(f) **This is** ("**This's**") her book.	In spoken English, *this is* is usually pronounced as *"this's."* It is not used in writing.

❑ **Exercise 29. Looking at grammar.** (Chart 2-6)

Complete the sentences with *this* or *that*.

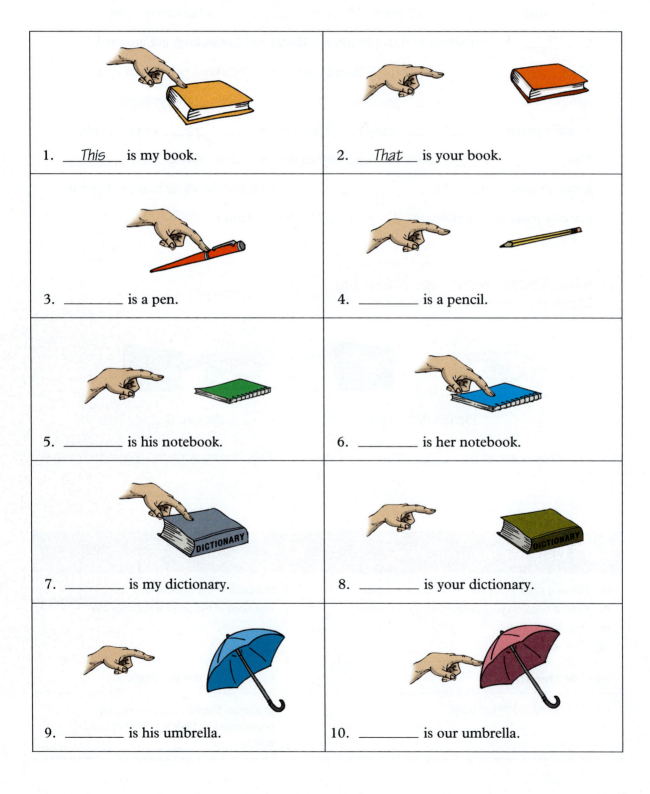

1. ___This___ is my book.

2. ___That___ is your book.

3. _____ is a pen.

4. _____ is a pencil.

5. _____ is his notebook.

6. _____ is her notebook.

7. _____ is my dictionary.

8. _____ is your dictionary.

9. _____ is his umbrella.

10. _____ is our umbrella.

Exercise 30. Let's talk: pairwork. **(Chart 2-6)**

Part I. Work with a partner. Take turns. Make a sentence with ***this*** or ***that*** for each picture.

Example:
Partner A: That is a backpack.
            Your turn.

a backpack

PARTNER A	PARTNER B
1. a credit card	2. a wallet
3. a credit card	4. a checkbook
5. a business card	6. a computer bag

Part II. Put items from a school bag, a bookbag, or a purse on a desk or table. Put some near you and some at a distance. Point to them, and your partner will make sentences with ***this*** or ***that***.

❏ **Exercise 31. Warm-up.** (Chart 2-7)
Match the sentences to the pictures.

Picture A

Picture B

1. Those are my keys. _____

2. These are your keys. _____

2-7 Using *These* and *Those*

(a) My books are on my desk. **These** are my books.		
(b) Your books are on your desk. **Those** are your books.		

SINGULAR		PLURAL
this	→	*these*
that	→	*those*

❏ **Exercise 32. Looking at grammar.** (Chart 2-7)
Complete the sentences with *these* or *those*.

1. _____ are my books.

2. _____ are your pencils.

3. _____ are his boots.

4. _____ are her shoes.

5. _____ are your hats.

6. _____ are their jackets.

❏ **Exercise 33. Vocabulary and grammar.** (Charts 2-6 and 2-7)
Look at the vocabulary in the picture. Choose the correct verb.

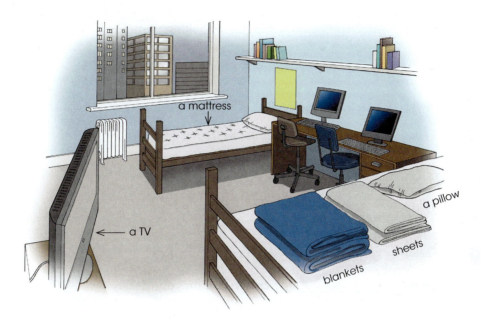

In our dorm room

1. This ⓘⓢ/ are my pillow.

2. That is / are your pillow.

3. Those sheets is / are for you.

4. These blankets is / are for me.

5. That TV is / are broken.

6. This chair is / are new.

7. Those mattresses is / are soft.

8. This mattress is / are uncomfortable.

❏ **Exercise 34. Looking at grammar.** (Charts 2-6 and 2-7)
Complete the sentences. Use the words in parentheses.

1. (*This, These*) _____*This*_____ pencil belongs to Alex.

   (*That, Those*) _____*That*_____ pencil belongs to Olga.

2. (*This, These*) _____ notepads belong to me.

   (*That, Those*) _____ notepad belongs to Kate.

3. (*This, These*) _____ coat is waterproof.

   (*That, Those*) _____ coats are not.

4. (*This, These*) _____ sunglasses belong to me.

   (*That, Those*) _____ sunglasses belong to you.

5. (*This, These*) _____ pillows are soft.

   (*That, Those*) _____ pillows are hard.

6. (*This, These*) _____ exercise is easy.

   (*That, Those*) _____ exercises are hard.

7. (*This, These*) _____ eraser is on my desk.

   (*That, Those*) _____ erasers are on your desk.

❏ **Exercise 35. Let's talk: pairwork.** (Charts 2-6 and 2-7)
Work with a partner. Make a sentence for each picture using ***this***, ***that***, ***these***, or ***those***.
Take turns.

Examples:
PARTNER A: That is a cap.
                   Your turn now.

 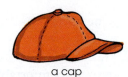

a cap

PARTNER B: These are caps.
                   Your turn now.

caps

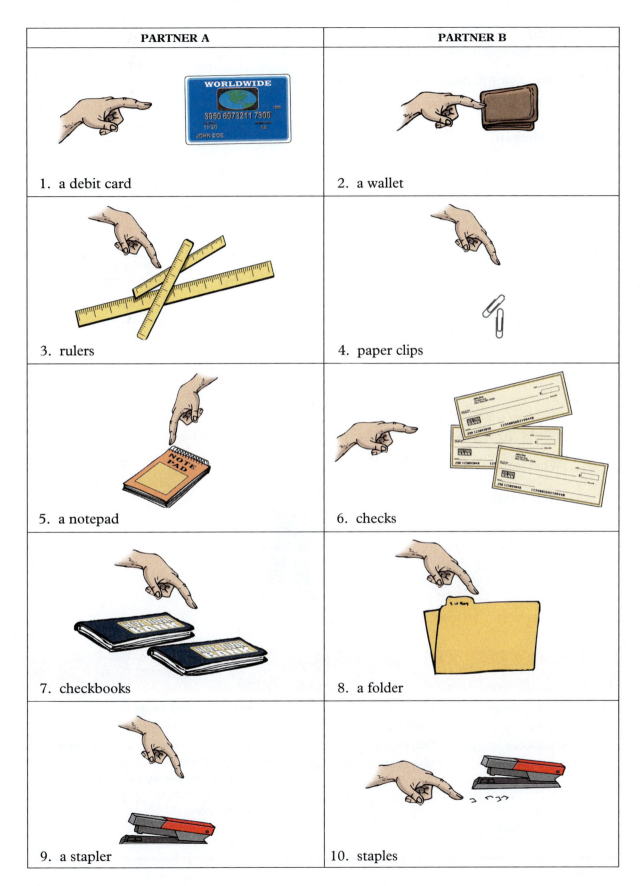

PARTNER A	PARTNER B
1. a debit card	2. a wallet
3. rulers	4. paper clips
5. a notepad	6. checks
7. checkbooks	8. a folder
9. a stapler	10. staples

□ **Exercise 36. Listening.** (Charts 2-6 and 2-7)

Listen to the sentences. Write the words you hear.

Example: You will hear: Those are clean dishes.

You will write: ___*Those are*___ clean dishes.

In the kitchen

1. _____ my coffee cup.

2. _____ your dessert.

3. _____ our plates.

4. _____ sponges _____ wet.

5. _____ dishcloths _____ dry.

6. _____ frying pan _____ dirty.

7. _____ frying pan _____ clean.

8. _____ salt shaker _____ empty.

sponges

□ **Exercise 37. Warm-up.** (Chart 2-8)

Answer the questions.

1. What is that? _____

2. Who is that? _____

a beetle

Tim

2-8 Asking Questions with *What* and *Who* + *Be*

(a) **What is** this (thing)?	It's a pen.	**What** asks about things.
(b) **Who is** that (man)?	That's Mr. Lee.	**Who** asks about people.
(c) **What are** those (things)?	They're pens.	Note: In questions with **what** and **who**,
(d) **Who are** they?	They're Mr. and Mrs. Lee.	• **is** is followed by a singular word.
		• **are** is followed by a plural word.
(e) **What's** this?		CONTRACTIONS:
(f) **Who's** that man?		what is = what's
		who is = who's

☐ **Exercise 38. Looking at grammar.** (Chart 2-8)

Complete the questions with *what* or *who* and *is* or *are*.

1. A: _____*Who is*_____ that woman?
   B: She's my sister. Her name is Sonya.

2. A: _____ those things?
   B: They're erasers.

3. A: _____ that?
   B: That's Ms. Walenski.

4. A: _____ this?
   B: That's my new camera. It's really small.

5. A: _____ those people?
   B: I'm not sure, but I think they're new students from Thailand.

6. A: _____ your name?
   B: Anita.

7. A: _____ your grammar teacher?
   B: Mr. Walker.

8. A: _____ your favorite teachers?
   B: Mr. Walker and Ms. Rosenberg.

9. A: _____ an only child?
   B: It's a child with no brothers or sisters.

10. A: _____ bats?
    B: They're animals with wings. They fly at night. They're not birds.

bats

❑ **Exercise 39. Vocabulary and speaking: pairwork.** (Chart 2-8)

Part I. Work with a partner. Write the names of the parts of the body on the pictures below. Use the words from the box.

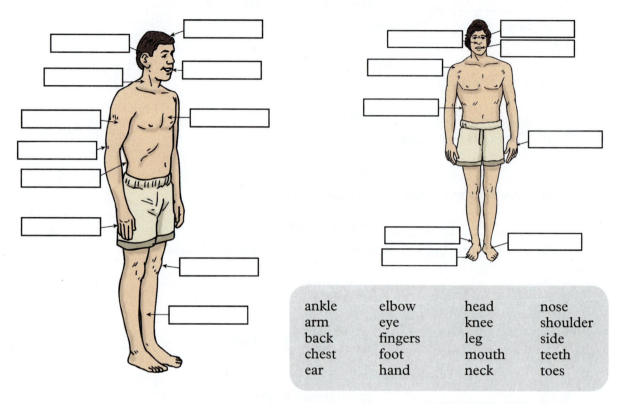

ankle	elbow	head	nose
arm	eye	knee	shoulder
back	fingers	leg	side
chest	foot	mouth	teeth
ear	hand	neck	toes

Part II. With your partner, take turns asking questions with ***this, that, these,*** and ***those.*** *Note:* Both partners can ask about both pictures.

Example:
PARTNER A: What is this?
PARTNER B: This is his leg. (*to Partner A*) What are those?
PARTNER A: Those are his fingers.

❑ **Exercise 40. Let's talk: class activity.** (Chart 2-8)

Your teacher will ask questions. Answer with ***this, that, these,*** and ***those.*** Close your book for this activity.

Example: hand
TEACHER: What is this? (*The teacher indicates her or his hand.*)
STUDENT: That is your hand.
          OR
TEACHER: What is that? (*The teacher indicates a student's hand.*)
STUDENT: This is my hand.

1. nose	3. arm	5. legs	7. foot	9. fingers
2. eyes	4. elbow	6. knee	8. shoulder	10. ears

Exercise 41. Check your knowledge. (Chapter 2)
Correct the mistakes.

has
1. She ~~have~~ a headache.

2. What are that?

3. Roberto he is a student in your class?

4. I am have a backache.

5. This is you dictionary. I my dictionary is at home.

6. Where my keys?

7. I am a sore throat.

8. He's father is from Cuba.

9. This books are expensive.

10. Where is the teachers?

11. A: Are you tired?

    B: Yes, I'm.

❏ **Exercise 42. Looking at grammar.** (Chapter 2)
Choose the correct completion.

1. Carla _____ a grammar book.
   a. have   b. is   (c.) has

2. This floor _____.
   a. dirty is   b. dirty   c. is dirty

3. _____ yellow.
   a. A banana are   b. A banana is   c. Bananas is

4. Lucas is _____ engineer.
   a. a   b. an   c. Ø

5. _____ books are really expensive.
   a. Those   b. They   c. This

6. Give this to Kathleen. It is _____ math book.
   a. she   b. an   c. her

7. That is _____.
   a. a mistakes   b. mistakes   c. a mistake

8. PABLO: _____ is your apartment?
   BLANCA: It's on Forest Street.
   a. What   b. Where   c. Who

9. YOKO: _____ these?
   GINA: My art books. I'm taking an art history class.
   a. What are   b. Who are   c. What is

10. MALIK: Are you hungry?
    LAYLA: Yes, _____.
    a. I'm   b. I'm not   c. I am

11. TINA: _____ that?
    LUIS: That's Paul Carter.
    a. Who's   b. What's   c. Where's

12. PAUL: _____ in your class?
    ERIC: No.
    a. Mr. Kim   b. Is Mr. Kim   c. Mr. Kim is he

❑ **Exercise 43. Looking at grammar.** (Chapter 2)
Complete the sentences with **am, is,** or **are.** Use **not** if necessary.

1. Apples _____ vegetables.

2. An apple _____ a kind of fruit.

3. I _____ from the United States.

4. We _____ human beings.

5. Balls _____ square.

6. Chickens _____ birds, but bats _____ birds.

7. Lemons _____ sweet. They _____ sour.

8. Soccer _____ a sport.

9. Soccer and basketball _____ sports.

10. Africa _____ a country. It _____ a continent.

❑ **Exercise 44. Looking at grammar.** (Chapter 2)
Complete the conversations with any words that make sense.

1. A: Where _____ your book?

   B: Hiroko _____ it.

   A: Where _____ your notebooks?

   B: Nasir and Angela _____ them.

2. A: _____ this?

   B: It _____ a picture of my family.

   A: _____ this?

   B: That's _____ father.

   A: _____ they?

   B: My brother and sister.

3. A: What's _____?

   B: I don't know. Ask the teacher.

   A: What's _____?

   C: It's _____.

4. A: Where _____?

   B: He's _____.

   A: Where _____?

   B: They're _____.

❑ **Exercise 45. Grammar and writing.** (Chapter 2)
Part I. Complete the sentences in the composition by Carlos.

My name _____*is*_____ Carlos. ____*I am* OR *I'm*____ from Mexico.
                1   2

_____ a student. _____ twenty years old.
        3   4

My family lives in Mexico City. _____ father _____ a
                                           5   6

businessman. _____ fifty-one years old. _____ mother
                       7   8

_____ an accountant. _____ forty-nine years old.
        9   10

I _____ two sisters and one brother. The names of my sisters
           11

_____ Rosa and Patricia. Rosa _____ a teacher.
        12   13

_____ twenty-eight years old. Patricia _____ a student.
        14   15

_____ eighteen years old. My brother _____ an engineer. His
                16   17
name _____ Pedro. He is married. He _____ two children.
            18   19

   I live in a dormitory. _____ a tall building on Pine Street. My address
                                    20

_____ 3225 Pine St. I live with my roommate. _____ name is
        21   22

Bob. _____ from Chicago. _____ nineteen years old.
              23   24

   I like my classes. They _____ interesting. I like _____
                                    25   26

classmates. _____ friendly.
                    27

Part II. Write about yourself. Follow the style below. Use your own paper.

PARAGRAPH I: **Information about you**:
              your name, hometown, age (*optional*)

PARAGRAPH II: **Information about your parents (if they are alive)**:
              their ages, jobs

PARAGRAPH III: **Information about other family or people in your life**:
              your siblings: names, ages, jobs OR
              your husband/wife: name, job OR
              your roommate/partner/friend: name, job

PARAGRAPH IV: **Additional information**:
              your home (apartment/dormitory/house): I live in a/an ____.
              your classes
              your classmates

Part III. Editing check: Work individually or change papers with a partner. Check (✓) for
the following:

1. ____ capital letter at the beginning of each sentence

2. ____ capital letter at the beginning of a person's name

3. ____ period at the end of each sentence

4. ____ paragraph indents

5. ____ a verb in every sentence

6. ____ correct use of **be** and **have**

7. ____ correct spelling (use a dictionary or computer spell-check)

Chapter 3
Using the Simple Present

☐ **Exercise 1. Warm-up.** (Chart 3-1)
Read the paragraph. Write the verb forms for *take*, *post*, and *share*.

I often take videos of my family and friends. I post them online. I share them with my family and friends. My brother Mario is a science teacher. He takes videos of his students and their experiments. He posts them online. He shares them with his classes.

take	*post*	*share*
1. I _____	3. I _____	5. I _____
2. Mario _____	4. He _____	6. He _____

3-1 Form and Basic Meaning of the Simple Present Tense

I *talk*. You *talk*. He *talk**s***. She *talk**s***. It *rain**s***. We *talk*. They *talk*.	The verb after 3rd person singular (**she**, **he**, **it**) has a final **-s**: *talk**s***.

		SINGULAR	PLURAL
	1st person:	I *talk*	we *talk*
	2nd person:	you *talk*	you *talk*
	3rd person:	she *talks*	they *talk*
		he *talks*	
		it *rains*	

(a) I *eat* breakfast **every morning**. (b) Olga *speaks* English **every day**. (c) We *sleep* **every night**. (d) They *go* to the beach **every weekend**.	The simple present tense expresses habits. In (a): Eating breakfast is a habit, a usual activity. *Every morning* = Monday morning, Tuesday morning, Wednesday morning, Thursday morning, Friday morning, Saturday morning, and Sunday morning.

 She wakes up every morning at 7:00.	 He shaves every morning.

Exercise 2. Looking at grammar. (Chart 3-1)
Complete the sentences with *speak* or *speaks*.

1. Martin _____ English.

2. I _____ German.

3. Erika _____ several languages.

4. Her husband _____ Thai and Vietnamese.

5. My friends and I _____ a little Persian.

6. My friends _____ Arabic.

7. They _____ Arabic fluently.

8. You _____ Spanish well.

9. You and I _____ Spanish well.

10. We _____ it well.

11. You and Peter _____ it well.

❑ **Exercise 3. Let's talk: pairwork.** (Chart 3-1)
Part I. Look at the list of habits. Check (✓) your habits every morning. Put them in order. What do you do first, second, third, etc.? Write them on the lines.

HABITS		MY HABITS EVERY MORNING
____ eat breakfast	1.	*I turn off the alarm clock.*
____ go to class	2.	
____ put on my clothes	3.	
____ drink a cup of coffee/tea	4.	
____ shave	5.	
____ put on my make-up	6.	
____ take a shower/bath	7.	
____ get up	8.	
____ pick up my books	9.	
____ walk to the bathroom	10.	
____ watch TV	11.	
____ look in the mirror	12.	
✓ turn off the alarm clock	13.	
____ go to the kitchen/the cafeteria	14.	
____ brush/comb my hair	15.	

_____ say good-bye to someone

_____ brush my teeth

_____ do exercises

_____ wash my face

16. _____

17. _____

18. _____

19. _____

Part II. Work with a partner. Talk about your habits every morning. Close your book for this activity.

❑ **Exercise 4. Listening.** (Chart 3-1)

Listen to the sentences. Choose the verbs you hear.

1. (wake)	wakes		6. watch	watches
2. wake	wakes		7. take	takes
3. get	gets		8. take	takes
4. go	goes		9. take	takes
5. do	does		10. talk	talks

❑ **Exercise 5. Looking at grammar.** (Chart 3-1)

Choose the correct completion.

1. My mother and father _____*eat*_____ breakfast at 7:00 every day.
   eat / eats

2. My mother _____ tea with her breakfast.
   drink / drinks

3. I _____ a bath every morning.
   take / takes

4. My sister _____ a shower.
   take / takes

5. I _____ English with my friends.
   study / studies

6. We _____ to school together every morning.
   walk / walks

7. Class _____ at 9:00 every day.
   begin / begins

8. It _____ at 12:00 for lunch.
   stop / stops

9. We _____ in the cafeteria.
   eat / eats

10. You _____ your lunch from home every day.
    bring / brings

11. My friends and I _____ home at 3:00 every afternoon.
    go / goes

12. You and Jamal _____ to the library after school every day.
    go / goes

Which sentence is true for you?

1. I always do my homework.
2. I usually do my homework.

3. I sometimes do my homework.
4. I never do my homework.

3-2 Frequency Adverbs

100%	*always*	(a)	Ivan *always* eats breakfast.
	usually	(b)	Maria *usually* eats breakfast.
	often	(c)	They *often* watch TV.
50%	*sometimes*	(d)	We *sometimes* watch TV.
	seldom	(e)	Sam *seldom* drinks milk.
	rarely	(f)	Rita *rarely* drinks milk.
0%	*never*	(g)	I *never* drink milk.

SUBJECT +
{
always
usually
often
sometimes
seldom
rarely
never
}
+ VERB

The words in this list are called "frequency adverbs." They come between the subject and the simple present verb.*

OTHER FREQUENCY EXPRESSIONS

(h) I drink tea
{
once *a day*.
two times / twice *a day*.
three times *a day*.
four times *a day*.
etc.
}

We can express frequency by saying how many times something happens
a day.
a week.
a month.
a year.

(i) I see my grandparents three times *a week*.

(j) I see my aunt once *a month*.

(k) I see my cousin Sam twice *a year*.

(l) I see my doctor every *year*.

Every is singular. The noun that follows (e.g., *morning*) must be singular.

INCORRECT: *every mornings*

* Some frequency adverbs can also come at the beginning or at the end of a sentence. For example:
   Sometimes I get up at seven. I **sometimes** get up at seven. I get up at seven **sometimes**.
   Also: See Chart 3-3, for the use of frequency adverbs with *be*.

Complete each sentence with a word from the box.

| always | often | never | rarely | sometimes | usually |

	SUN.	MON.	TUES.	WED.	THURS.	FRI.	SAT.
1. Ana _____ drinks tea with lunch.	☕	☕	☕	☕	☕	☕	☕
2. Kenji _____ drinks tea with lunch.		☕	☕	☕	☕	☕	☕
3. Clara _____ drinks tea with lunch.			☕	☕	☕	☕	☕
4. Igor _____ drinks tea with lunch.					☕	☕	☕
5. Sonya _____ drinks tea with lunch.							☕
6. Sami _____ drinks tea with lunch.							

❑   **Exercise 8. Looking at grammar.** (Chart 3-2)
Write "S" over the subject and "V" over the verb in each sentence. Rewrite the sentences, adding the given frequency adverbs.

1. always   S V
            I eat breakfast in the morning.

           _____*I always eat breakfast*_____ in the morning.

2. never   I eat carrots for breakfast.

           _____ for breakfast.

3. seldom   I watch TV in the morning.

           _____ in the morning.

4. sometimes   I have dessert after dinner.

           _____ after dinner.

5. usually   Kiri eats lunch at the cafeteria.

           _____ at the cafeteria.

6. often   We listen to music after dinner.

           _____ after dinner.

7. always   The students speak English in class.

           _____ in class.

❏ **Exercise 9. Let's talk: class activity.** (Chart 3-2)

Your teacher will ask you to talk about your morning, afternoon, and evening activities. Close your book for this activity.

Tell me something you...

1. always do in the morning.
2. never do in the morning.
3. sometimes do in the morning.
4. usually do in the afternoon.
5. seldom do in the afternoon.
6. never do in the afternoon.
7. often do in the evening.
8. sometimes do in the evening.
9. rarely do in the evening.
10. sometimes do on weekends.

❏ **Exercise 10. Looking at grammar.** (Chart 3-2)

Use the information in the chart to complete the sentences.

	SUN.	MON.	TUES.	WED.	THURS.	FRI.	SAT.
Hamid	🚌	🚌	🚌	🚌	🚌	🚌	🚌
Yoko							🚌
Victoria		🚌	🚌	🚌	🚌	🚌	🚌
Pavel			🚌	🚌	🚌	🚌	🚌
Mr. Wu							
Mrs. Cook					🚌	🚌	🚌

How often do the people in the chart take the bus during the week?

1. Hamid takes the bus _____*seven times*_____ a week. That means he _____*always*_____ takes the bus.

2. Yoko takes the bus _____ a week. That means she _____ takes the bus.

3. Victoria takes the bus _____ a week. That means she _____ takes the bus.

4. Pavel takes the bus _____ a week. That means he _____ takes the bus.

5. Mr. Wu _____ takes the bus.

6. Mrs. Cook takes the bus _____ a week. That means she _____ takes the bus.

Exercise 11. Warm-up. (Chart 3-3)

Choose the correct answer. What do you notice about the placement of the verb and the frequency adverb?

1. It *often rains* here.   yes   no
2. It *sometimes snows*.   yes   no
3. It *is often* cold here.   yes   no
4. It *is sometimes* hot.   yes   no

3-3 Position of Frequency Adverbs

SUBJECT + **BE** +	FREQUENCY ADVERB	Frequency adverbs come after the simple present tense forms of **be**: **am**, **is**, and **are**.
I am You are He is She is + It is We are They are	**always** **usually** **often** **sometimes** + late. **seldom** **rarely** **never**	
SUBJECT +	FREQUENCY ADVERB + OTHER SIMPLE PRESENT VERBS	Frequency adverbs come before all simple present verbs except **be**.
Tom +	**always** **usually** **often** **sometimes** + **comes** late. **seldom** **rarely** **never**	

❏ **Exercise 12. Looking at grammar.** (Chart 3-3)

Add the frequency adverbs to the sentences.

1. always   Anita is on time for class. → *Anita is always on time for class.*
2. always   Anita comes to class on time. → *Anita always comes to class on time.*
3. often   Liliana is late for class.
4. often   Liliana comes to class late.
5. never   It snows in my hometown.
6. never   It is very cold in my hometown.
7. usually   Hiroshi is at home in the evening.
8. usually   Hiroshi stays at home in the evening.
9. seldom   Thomas studies at the library in the evening.
10. seldom   His classmates are at the library in the evening.
11. sometimes   I skip breakfast.
12. rarely   I have time for a big breakfast.

Part I. Check (✓) the boxes to describe your activities after 5:00 P.M.

	ALWAYS	USUALLY	OFTEN	SOMETIMES	RARELY	NEVER
1. eat dinner						
2. go to a movie						
3. go shopping						
4. go swimming						
5. spend time with friends						
6. go to class						
7. be at home						
8. watch videos or DVDs						
9. study English						
10. send emails						
11. surf the Internet						
12. drink coffee after 9:00						
13. be in bed at ten o'clock						
14. go to bed late						

Part II. Exchange books with a partner. Your partner will tell the class two things about your evening.

Example: (Carlos) is usually at home. He sometimes sends emails.
(Olga) sometimes drinks coffee after 9:00 P.M. She usually goes to bed late.

❑ **Exercise 14. Writing.** (Chart 3-3)
Write about a typical day in your life, from the time you get up in the morning until you go to bed. Use the following words to show the order of your activities: ***then, next, at . . . o'clock, after that, later.***

Writing sample: I usually get up at 7:30. I shave, brush my teeth, and take a shower. Then I put on my clothes and go to the student cafeteria for breakfast. After that, I go back to my room. I sometimes watch the news on TV. At 8:15, I leave the dormitory. I go to class. My class begins at 8:30. I'm in class from 8:30 to 11:30. After that, I eat lunch. I usually have a sandwich and a cup of tea for lunch. (Continue until you complete your day.)

❑ **Exercise 15. Warm-up: listening.** (Chart 3-4)
Listen to the words. Decide if they have one syllable or two.

1. eat	one	two		4. pushes	one	two
2. eats	one	two		5. sleeps	one	two
3. push	one	two		6. fixes	one	two

3-4 Spelling and Pronunciation of Final -es

		SPELLING	PRONUNCIATION	
-sh	(a) push →	push**es**	push/əz/	Ending of verb: **-sh, -ch, -ss, -x**.
-ch	(b) teach →	teach**es**	teach/əz/	Spelling: add **-es**.
-ss	(c) kiss →	kiss**es**	kiss/əz/	Pronunciation: /əz/.
-x	(d) fix →	fix**es**	fix/əz/	

❑ **Exercise 16. Looking at grammar.** (Chart 3-4)
Use the correct form of the given verbs to complete the sentences.

1. brush   Arianna _____ *brushes* _____ her hair every morning.

2. teach   Alex _____ English.

3. fix   Pedro _____ his breakfast every morning.
                He makes eggs and toast.

4. drink   Sonya _____ tea every afternoon.

5. watch   Joon Kee often _____ television at night.

6. kiss   Viktor always _____ his children goodnight.

7. wear   Tina usually _____ jeans to class.

8. wash   Eric seldom _____ dishes.

9. walk   Jenny _____ her dog twice each day.

10. stretch,   When Jack gets up in the morning, he _____
    yawn   and _____.

❏ **Exercise 17. Listening.** (Chart 3-4)

Listen to the sentences and choose the verbs you hear.

1. teach ⟨teaches⟩   6. watch   watches

2. teach   teaches   7. brush   brushes

3. fix   fixes   8. brush   brushes

4. fix   fixes   9. wash   washes

5. watch   watches   10. wash   washes

❏ **Exercise 18. Looking at grammar.** (Charts 3-1 and 3-4)

Complete the sentences. Use the words from the box and add *-s* or *-es*. Practice reading the story aloud. Work with a partner or in small groups.

brush	get	take	wash
cook	✓ leave	turn	watch
fall	read	sit	

Laura _____*leaves*_____ her office every night at 5:00 and _____ on a
                    1   2

bus to go home. She has the same schedule every evening. She _____ dinner
                                                                               3

and then _____ down to eat at 6:00. After she _____ the
              4   5

dishes, she _____ on the TV. She usually _____ the news and
                 6   7

then a movie. At 9:00, she _____ a shower. She always _____
                                8   9

her teeth after her shower. Then she picks up a book and _____ in bed for a
                                                               10

while. She usually _____ asleep before 10:00.
                        11

❏ **Exercise 19. Warm-up.** (Chart 3-5)

What kind of ending does each verb have? Put the verbs from the box in the correct column.

b**uy**	f**ly**	pl**ay**	stu**dy**

CONSONANT + *-y*   VOWEL + *-y*

_____   _____

_____   _____

3-5 Adding Final -s/-es to Words That End in -y

(a)	*cry*	→	*cries*	ENDING OF VERB: consonant + -*y*
	try	→	*tries*	SPELLING: change **y** to *i*, add -*es*
(b)	*pay*	→	*pays*	ENDING OF VERB: vowel + -*y*
	enjoy	→	*enjoys*	SPELLING: add -*s*

❏ **Exercise 20. Looking at grammar.** (Chart 3-5)
Complete the chart with the correct form of each verb.

1. I try.	He _____*tries*_____ .
2. We study.	She _____ .
3. They say.	It _____ .
4. I enjoy games.	Ann _____ games.
5. You worry a lot.	My mother _____ a lot.
6. We pay bills.	Gina _____ bills.
7. You stay awake.	Paul _____ awake.
8. We fly.	A bird _____ .
9. Students buy books.	My brother _____ books.
10. I play music. ♪♪	My friend _____ music.

❏ **Exercise 21. Looking at grammar.** (Chart 3-5)
Complete each sentence with the simple present form of a verb from the box.

buy	cry	pay	stay
carry	employ	✓ play	study

1. Monique likes sports. She _____*plays*_____ tennis and soccer several times a week.

2. The school cafeteria is cheap. Rob _____ his lunch there every day.

3. My company is big. It _____ 2,000 people.

4. Elizabeth is always tired. Her new baby _____ during the night.

5. Mr. Garcia travels every week. He _____ in small hotels.

6. Some airplanes are very big. A large airplane _____ 400 to 500 passengers.

7. I usually pay with a debit card, but my husband _____ in cash.

8. Zara is a medical student. She _____ every night and on weekends.

❏ **Exercise 22. Warm-up.** (Chart 3-6)
Read the information about Milos and complete the chart.

Milos is a college student. He **has** a part-time job. He **does** the breakfast dishes at his dorm. Then he **goes** to class.

HAVE	DO	GO
I **have**	I **do**	I **go**
you **have**	you **do**	you **go**
he _____	he _____	he _____
she _____	she _____	she _____
it _____	it _____	it _____
we **have**	we **do**	we **go**
they **have**	they **do**	they **go**

3-6 Irregular Singular Verbs: *Has, Does, Goes*

(a) I *have* a book. (b) He *has* a book.	she he } + *has* /hæz/ it	**Have**, **do**, and **go** have irregular forms for 3rd person singular: have → has do → does go → goes
(c) I *do* my work. (d) She *does* her work.	she he } + *does* /dəz/ it	
(e) They *go* to school. (f) She *goes* to school.	she he } + *goes* /gowz/ it	Note that final **-s** is pronounced /z/ in these verbs.

❏ **Exercise 23. Looking at grammar.** (Chart 3-6)
Use the correct form of the given verbs to complete the sentences.

1. do   Pierre always ____*does*____ his homework.

2. do   We always _____*do*_____ our homework.

3. have   Yoko and Hamid _____ their books.

4. have   Mrs. Chang _____ a car.

5. go   Andy _____ to school every day.

6. do   Sara seldom _____ her homework.

7. do   We _____ exercises in class every day.

8. go, go   Roberto _____ downtown every weekend. He and his wife

                             _____ shopping.

9. play   My friends often _____ volleyball at the beach.

□ **Exercise 24. Listening.** (Chart 3-6)

Listen to the story. Complete the sentences with *is*, *has*, *does*, or *goes*.

Marco _____*is*_____ a student. He _____*has*_____ an unusual schedule. All of his
                  1   2

classes are at night. His first class _____ at 6:00 P.M. every day. He takes a break
                                          3

from 7:30 to 8:00. Then he _____ classes from 8:00 to 10:00.
                                   4

He leaves school and _____ home at 10:00. After he _____ dinner,
                                  5   6

he watches TV. Then he _____ his homework from midnight to 3:00 or 4:00 in
                                   7

the morning.

Marco _____ his own computer at home. When he finishes his homework,
                           8

he usually goes on the Internet. He often stays at his computer until the sun comes up.

Then he _____ a few exercises, _____ breakfast, and _____ to
                  9   10   11

bed. He sleeps all day. Marco thinks his schedule _____ great, but his friends
                                                           12

think it _____ strange.
        13

❑ **Exercise 25. Looking at grammar.** (Charts 3-1 → 3-6)
Complete the sentences with the words in parentheses. Use the simple present tense. Pay special attention to singular and plural and to the spelling of final **-s/-es**.

1. The students (*ask, often*) _____ *often ask* _____ questions in class.

2. Pablo (*study, usually*) _____ at the library every evening.

3. Olga (*bite*) _____ her fingernails when she is nervous.

4. Donna (*cash*) _____ a check at the bank once a week.

5. Sometimes I (*worry*) _____ about my grades at school. Sonya

   (*worry, never*) _____ about her grades. She (*study*)

   _____ hard.

6. Ms. Fernandez and Mr. Anderson (*teach*) _____ at the local high school.

   Ms. Fernandez (*teach*) _____ math.

7. Birds (*fly*) _____. They (*have*) _____ wings.

8. A bird (*fly*) _____. It (*have*) _____ wings.

9. Emilio (*do, always*) _____ his homework. He (*go, never*)

   _____ to bed until his homework is finished.

10. Mr. Cook (*say, always*)* _____ hello to his neighbor.

11. Ms. Chu (*pay, always*)* _____ attention in class. She (*answer*)

    _____ questions. She (*listen*) _____ to the

    teacher. She (*ask*) _____ questions.

❑ **Exercise 26. Let's talk: game.** (Charts 3-1 → 3-6)
Part I. Your teacher will assign you a verb from the list. Make a sentence with that verb. Walk around the room. Say your sentence to other students. Listen to other students say their sentences.

1. eat	4. brush	7. get up	10. do	13. put on
2. go	5. have	8. watch	11. listen to	14. carry
3. drink	6. study	9. speak	12. wash	15. kiss

Part II. Work in teams of five to eight students. Write as many sentences as you can remember. Each team will have one paper. The team with the most correct sentences wins.

---

*Pronunciation of **says** = /sɛz/. Pronunciation of **pays** = /peyz/.

❏ **Exercise 27. Let's talk: pairwork.** (Charts 3-1 → 3-6)
Work with a partner. Use frequency adverbs like *sometimes, rarely*, etc.

Part I. Yuri, Levi, and Peter do many things in the evening. How often do they do the things in the list? Pay attention to final *-s*.

Example: Yuri rarely/seldom does homework.

	YURI	LEVI	PETER
DO HOMEWORK	once a week	6 days a week	every day
SURF THE INTERNET	every day	once a week	once a month
WATCH TV	3–4 days a week	3–4 days a week	3–4 days a week
READ FOR PLEASURE	5 days a week	5 days a week	5 days a week
GO TO BED EARLY	once a week	5–6 nights a week	6–7 nights a week

Part II. For homework, write ten sentences about the activities of Yuri, Levi, and Peter.

❏ **Exercise 28. Looking at grammar.** (Charts 3-1 → 3-6)
Add *-s* or *-es* where necessary.

Abdul and Pablo

(1) My friend Abdul live͜s in an apartment near school. (2) He walk to school almost every day. (3) Sometimes he catch a bus, especially if it's cold and rainy outside. (4) Abdul share the apartment with Pablo. (5) Pablo come from Venezuela. (6) Abdul and Pablo go to the same school. (7) They take English classes. (8) Abdul speak Arabic as his first language, and Pablo speak Spanish. (9) They communicate in English. (10) Sometimes Abdul try to teach Pablo to speak a little Arabic, and Pablo give Abdul Spanish lessons. (11) They laugh a lot during the Arabic and Spanish lessons. (12) Abdul enjoy his roommate, but he miss his family back in Saudi Arabia.

❏ **Exercise 29. Speaking and writing: pairwork.** (Charts 3-1 → 3-6)
Work with a partner. Tell your partner five to ten things you do every morning. Use the list you made in Exercise 3. Your partner will also give you information about his/her morning. Take notes. Then write a paragraph about your partner's morning activities. Pay special attention to the use of final *-s/-es*. Ask your partner to read your paragraph and to check your use of final *-s/-es*.

❏ **Exercise 30. Warm-up.** (Chart 3-7)
Which sentences are true for you?

1. I like to speak English.   yes   no

2. I need to learn English.   yes   no

3. I want to speak English fluently.   yes   no

3-7 Like To, Want To, Need To

VERB + INFINITIVE	
(a) I **like** **to travel**. It's fun.	**Like**, **want**, and **need** can be followed by an infinitive.
(b) I **want** **to travel**. I have vacation time next month.	infinitive = **to** + the base form of the verb.*
(c) I **need** **to travel** for my job. I have no choice.	**Need to** is stronger than **want to**. **Need to** = necessary, important.

* The base form of a verb = a verb without -s, -ed, or -ing. Examples of the base form of a verb: *come, help, answer, write.* Examples of infinitives: *to come, to help, to answer, to write.* The base form is also called the simple form of a verb.

❏ **Exercise 31. Looking at grammar.** (Chart 3-7)
Make complete sentences. Pay attention to the final **-s** ending on singular verbs.

1. Maya \ need \ study   _Maya needs to study._

2. We \ want \ go home   _____

3. Bill and I \ like \ eat sweets   _____

4. You \ need \ speak more quietly   _____

5. She \ like \ talk on the phone   _____

6. Her friends \ like \ text   _____

7. They \ need \ save money   _____

8. He \ want \ travel   _____

❏ **Exercise 32. Reading and grammar.** (Charts 3-1 → 3-7)
Part I. Read the story.

A Wonderful Cook

Roberto is a wonderful cook. He often tries new recipes. He likes to cook for friends. He frequently invites my girlfriend and me to dinner. When we arrive, we go to the kitchen. He usually has three or four pots on the stove. He makes a big mess when he cooks. We like to watch him, and he wants to tell us about each recipe. His dinners are delicious. After dinner, he needs to clean the kitchen. We want to help him because we want him to invite us back soon.

Part II. Complete each sentence with a word from the box.

help	invite	is	like	likes to	wash

1. Roberto _____ a great cook.

2. He _____ try new recipes.

3. He likes to _____ friends to dinner.

4. After dinner, he needs to _____ the pots, and his friends

   _____ him.

5. His friends _____ his food.

☐ **Exercise 33. Let's talk: game.** (Chart 3-7)

Work in teams. What do you know about mosquitoes? Choose the correct answer.
The team with the most correct answers wins.*

1. They like to look for food during the day.	yes	no
2. They like to look for food at night.	yes	no
3. They need to lay their eggs in water.	yes	no
4. They like to travel.	yes	no
5. They need to sleep in water.	yes	no
6. Male mosquitoes need to bite.	yes	no
7. Female mosquitoes need to bite.	yes	no

☐ **Exercise 34. Warm-up.** (Chart 3-8)

Which sentences are true for you?

1. a. I like vegetables.   b. I don't like vegetables.

2. a. I drink tea.   b. I don't drink tea.

3. a. I eat meat.   b. I don't eat meat.

---

*See *Let's Talk: Answers*, p. 501.

3-8 Simple Present Tense: Negative

(a)	**I**	**do not**	drink coffee.	NEGATIVE: *I* *You* *We* *They* } + **do not** + *main verb*
	You	**do not**	drink coffee.	
	We	**do not**	drink coffee.	
	They	**do not**	drink coffee.	

NEGATIVE: *I* *You* *We* *They* } + **do not** + *main verb*

He *She* *It* } + **does not** + *main verb*

(b)	**He**	**does not**	drink coffee.
	She	**does not**	drink coffee.
	It	**does not**	drink coffee.

Do and **does** are called "helping verbs."

Notice in (b): In 3rd person singular, there is no **-s** on the main verb, **drink**; the final **-s** is part of the helping verb, **does**.

INCORRECT: *She does not drinks coffee.*

(c) I ***don't*** drink coffee.
He ***doesn't*** drink coffee.

CONTRACTIONS: **do not** = **don't**
does not = **doesn't**

People usually use contractions when they speak.
People often use contractions when they write.

❏ **Exercise 35. Looking at grammar.** (Chart 3-8)
Choose the correct verb.

1. We   does not / (do not)   have a TV.

2. She   does not / do not   like milk.

3. They   does not / do not   play soccer.

4. I   does not / do not   understand.

5. It   does not / do not   rain much here.

6. You   does not / do not   understand.

7. He   doesn't / don't   work hard.

8. You   doesn't / don't   need help.

9. They   doesn't / don't   live here.

10. She   doesn't / don't   speak English.

11. We   doesn't / don't   have time.

12. I   doesn't / don't   study every day.

Exercise 36. Looking at grammar. (Chart 3-8)

Use the given words to make negative sentences. Use contractions.

1. like, not   Ingrid _____*doesn't like*_____ tea.

2. like, not   I _____*don't like*_____ tea.

3. know, not   Mary and Jim are strangers. Mary _____ Jim.

4. speak, not   I _____ French.

5. need, not   It's a nice day today. You _____
your umbrella.

an umbrella

6. live, not   Dogs _____ long.

7. have, not   A dog _____ a long life.

8. have, not   We _____ class every day.

9. have, not   This city _____ nice weather in the summer.

10. snow, not   It _____ in Bangkok in the winter.

11. rain, not   It _____ every day.

❏ **Exercise 37. Let's talk: pairwork.** (Chart 3-8)

Work with a partner. Make two sentences about each picture.

Example:
PARTNER A: Isabel takes showers. She doesn't take baths.
　　　　　Your turn now.
PARTNER B: Omar has a dog. He doesn't have a cat.
　　　　　Your turn now.

YES   NO

1. (Isabel \ take)
showers
baths

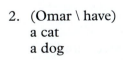

2. (Omar \ have)
a cat
a dog

YES		NO

      YES   NO   

3. (I \ drink)
tea
coffee

4. (Rob and Ed \ live)
an apartment
a house

5. (Julia \ drive)
a new car
an old car

6. (I \ play)
soccer
tennis

7. (Mr. Ortiz \ teach)
English
French

8. (we \ use)
typewriters
computers

9. (Inga \ watch)
news reports
old movies

10. (Marco \ study)
history
physics

Exercise 38. Let's talk: game. (Chart 3-8)

Sit in a circle. Use any of the verbs from the box. Make sentences with **not**.

Example: like
STUDENT A: I don't like bananas.
STUDENT B: (*Student A*) doesn't like bananas. I don't have a dog.
STUDENT C: (*Student A*) doesn't like bananas. (*Student B*) doesn't have a dog.
    I don't play baseball.

have	like	need	play	read	speak

Continue around the circle. Each time, repeat the information of your classmates before you say your sentence. If you have trouble, your classmates can help you. Your teacher will be the last one to speak.

Exercise 39. Looking at grammar. (Chart 3-8)

Use verbs from the box to complete the sentences. Make all of the sentences negative by using **does not** or **do not**. You can use contractions (**doesn't/don't**). Some verbs may be used more than one time.

do	eat	make	shave	speak
drink	go	put on	smoke	

1. Ricardo _____ *doesn't go* _____ to school every day.

2. My roommates are from Japan. They _____ Spanish.

3. Roberto has a beard. He _____ in the morning.

4. We _____ to class on Sunday.

5. Camilla is healthy. She _____ cigarettes.

6. Nadia and Anton always have lunch at home. They _____ in the cafeteria.

7. Sometimes I _____ my homework in the evening. I watch TV instead.

8. My sister likes tea, but she _____ coffee.

9. Hamid is a careful writer. He _____ spelling mistakes when he writes.

10. Sometimes Julianna _____ her shoes when she goes outside. She likes to go barefoot.

❏ **Exercise 40. Looking at grammar.** (Charts 1-6, 1-7, and 3-8)
Complete the chart with the correct form of the given verbs.

SIMPLE PRESENT: *BE*	SIMPLE PRESENT: *EAT*
1. I _____*am not*_____ hungry.	1. I _____*do not eat*_____ meat.
2. You _____ hungry.	2. You _____ meat.
3. She _____ hungry.	3. She _____ meat.
4. We _____ hungry.	4. We _____ meat.
5. It _____ hungry.	5. It _____ meat.
6. They _____ hungry.	6. They _____ meat.
7. He _____ hungry.	7. He _____ meat.
8. Raj _____ hungry.	8. Raj _____ meat.
9. You and I _____ hungry.	9. You and I _____ meat.

❏ **Exercise 41. Looking at grammar.** (Charts 1-6, 1-7, and 3-8)
Choose the correct verb.

1. I   am not / do not   late.
2. They   are not / do not   drink coffee.
3. He   is not / does not   do his homework.
4. You   are not / do not   poor.
5. She   is not / does not   do her homework.
6. The key   is not / does not   work.
7. It   is not / does not   in the car.
8. I   am not / do not   like vegetables.
9. We   are not / do not   live here.
10. We   are not / do not   citizens.

❏ **Exercise 42. Let's talk: class activity.** (Charts 1-6, 1-7, and 3-8)
Part I. Use the given words to make true sentences for each pair.

Example: a. Grass \ be blue.
              b. Grass \ be green
STUDENT A: Grass isn't blue.
STUDENT B: Grass is green.

Example: a. Dogs \ have tails

               b. People \ have tails.

STUDENT C: Dogs have tails.

STUDENT D: People* don't have tails.

1. a. A restaurant \ sell shoes.
   b. A restaurant \ serve food.

2. a. People \ wear clothes.
   b. Animals \ wear clothes.

3. a. A child \ need love, food, and care.
   b. A child \ need a driver's license.

4. a. Refrigerators \ be hot inside.
   b. Refrigerators \ be cold inside.

5. a. A cat \ have whiskers.
   b. A bird \ have whiskers.

whiskers

Part II. Make true sentences.

6. Doctors in my country \ be expensive.
7. A bus \ carry people from one place to another.
8. It \ be cold today.
9. English \ be an easy language to learn.
10. People in this city \ be friendly.
11. It \ rain a lot in this city.

❏ **Exercise 43. Warm-up.** (Chart 3-9)

What do you notice about the questions with **have** and **need?**

Are you okay?
Are you sick?
Do you have a fever?
Do you need a doctor?

---

*People is a plural noun. It takes a plural verb.

3-9 Simple Present Tense: Yes/No Questions

	DO/DOES + SUBJECT + MAIN VERB		QUESTION FORMS, SIMPLE PRESENT

	DO/DOES +	SUBJECT +	MAIN VERB
(a)	*Do*	*I*	*work?*
(b)	*Do*	*you*	*work?*
(c)	*Does*	*he*	*work?*
(d)	*Does*	*she*	*work?*
(e)	*Does*	*it*	*work?*
(f)	*Do*	*we*	*work?*
(g)	*Do*	*they*	*work?*

QUESTION FORMS, SIMPLE PRESENT

Do I
Do you
Does he
Does she   } + *main verb* (base form)
Does it
Do we
Do they

Notice in (c), (d), and (e): The main verb in the question does not have a final **-s**. The final **-s** is part of **does**.

INCORRECT: Does she works?

(h) **Am I** late?	When the main verb is a form of **be**, **do** is NOT used. See Chart 2-1, p. 28, for question forms with **be**.
(i) **Are you** ready?	
(j) **Is he** a teacher?	
(k) **Are we** early?	
(l) **Are they** at home?	
(m) **Are you** a student?	
INCORRECT: Do you be a student?	

QUESTION	SHORT ANSWER	
(n) **Do** you *like* fish? →	Yes, I *do*. No, I *don't*.	**Do, don't, does,** and **doesn't** are used in the short answers to yes/no questions in the simple present.
(o) **Does** Liam *like* fish? →	Yes, he *does*. No, he *doesn't*.	

(p) Brad *does* his homework.	Note that **do** can also be a main verb, as in (p) and (q).
(q) **Does** Brad *do* his homework?	

❏ **Exercise 44. Looking at grammar.** (Chart 3-9)

Make questions. Choose the correct answer.

1. A: *like \ you \ tea*   *Do you like tea?*
   B: (a.) Yes, I do.
       b. Yes, I like.

2. A: *speak \ Anita \ Italian* _____
   B: a. Yes, she does.
       b. Yes, she speaks.

3. A: *speak \ Thomas and Sierra \ Arabic* _____
   B: a. No, they don't.
       b. No, they don't speak.

4. A: *rain \ it \ in April* _____
   B: a. Yes, it does.
       b. Yes, it rains.

5. A: *do \ he \ his homework* _____
   B: a. No, he doesn't.
       b. No, he doesn't do.

6. A: *do \ you \ your homework* _____
   B: a. No, I don't.
       b. No, I don't do.

7. A: *have \ they \ enough money* _____
   B: a. Yes, they do.
       b. Yes, they have.

❑ **Exercise 45. Speaking and grammar: pairwork.** (Charts 2-1, 2-2, and 3-9)

Part I. Work with a partner. Take turns making questions and giving short answers. Use the names of your classmates in the questions. *Note: Part I* is speaking practice. Do not write the answers until *Part II.*

Example:
PARTNER A: _____
PARTNER B: _____ (He is in class today.)
PARTNER A: Is Ali in class today?
PARTNER B: Yes, he is.

Example:
PARTNER B: _____
PARTNER A: _____ (She doesn't speak Spanish.)
PARTNER B: Does Akiko speak Spanish?
PARTNER A: No, she doesn't.

1. PARTNER A: _____
      PARTNER B: _____ (He speaks English in class every day.)

2. PARTNER B: _____
      PARTNER A: _____ (She comes to class every day.)

3. PARTNER A: _____
      PARTNER B: _____ (They're in class today.)

4. PARTNER B: _____
      PARTNER A: _____ (He wears jeans every day.)

5. PARTNER A: _____
      PARTNER B: _____ (They aren't from Australia.)

6. PARTNER B: _____

       PARTNER A: _____ (They don't have dictionaries on their desks.)

7. PARTNER A: _____

       PARTNER B: _____ (They speak English.)

Part II. Now write the questions and answers in your book.

❏ **Exercise 46. Vocabulary and speaking.** (Chart 3-9)
Part I. Check (✓) the activities you do at least once a week.

1. ____ take a nap
2. ____ take a break
3. ____ take a shower
4. ____ take a bath
5. ____ take a bus/train/taxi

6. ____ make breakfast
7. ____ make lunch
8. ____ make dinner
9. ____ make a snack
10. ____ make my bed

11. ____ do my homework
12. ____ do the dishes
13. ____ do the laundry

Part II. Walk around the room. Ask questions using these phrases. For each question, find someone who can answer **yes**. *Note:* Remember to change **my** to **your**.

Example:
To STUDENT A: Do you take a nap in the afternoon?
    STUDENT A: No.
To STUDENT B: Do you take a nap in the afternoon?
    STUDENT B: Yes.
To STUDENT C: Do you make your bed every day?
    STUDENT C: Yes.

❏ **Exercise 47. Looking at grammar.** (Chapters 1 and 2; Charts 3-1 and 3-7 → 3-9)
Complete each sentence with the correct form of the given verb. Use the full form or contractions for the negative.

Part I. Statement Forms

LIVE	*BE*
1. I _____live_____ here.	I _____am_____ here.
2. They _____ here.	They _____ here.
3. He _____ here.	He _____ here.
4. You _____ here.	You _____ here.
5. She _____ here.	She _____ here.
6. We _____ here.	We _____ here.

Part II. Negative Forms

7. They ____*do not / don't live*____ here.   They _____*are not / aren't*_____ here.

8. I _____ here.   I _____ here.

9. She _____ here.   She _____ here.

10. You _____ here.   You _____ here.

11. He _____ here.   He _____ here.

12. We _____ here.   We _____ here.

Part III. Question Forms

13. ____*Do*____ you ____*live*____ here?   ____*Are*____ you here?

14. _____ they _____ here?   _____ they here?

15. _____ he _____ here?   _____ he here?

16. _____ we _____ here?   _____ we here?

17. _____ she _____ here?   _____ she here?

❏ **Exercise 48. Let's talk: game.** (Charts 2-1 and 3-9)
Work in teams. Complete the sentences with *is, are, do,* or *does.* Answer the questions with *yes* or *no.* The team with the most correct answers wins.

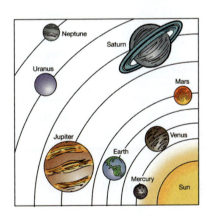

1. ____*Does*____ the moon go around the Earth?   (yes)   no

2. _____ the sun go around the Earth?   yes   no

3. _____ the planets go around the sun?   yes   no

4. _____ the sun a planet?   yes   no

5. _____ stars planets?   yes   no

6. _____ Venus hot?   yes   no

7. _____ Neptune easy to see?   yes   no

8. _____	Jupiter windy?	yes	no
9. _____	Venus and Mercury go around the sun?	yes	no
10. _____	Saturn and Uranus have moons?	yes	no

❏ **Exercise 49. Warm-up.** (Chart 3-10)
Match the questions with the correct answers.

1. Where is the lost-and-found? ____
2. Is the lost-and-found office in this building? ____
3. What is in this building? ____

a. The lost-and-found.
b. Yes, it is.
c. Down the hall.

3-10 Simple Present Tense: Asking Information Questions with *Where* and *What*

(WHERE/ WHAT)	+ DO/ DOES	+ SUBJECT	+ MAIN VERB		SHORT ANSWER	(a) = a yes/no question (b) = an information question
(a)	**Do**	they	*live*	in Miami? →	**Yes**, they do. **No**, they don't.	**Where** asks for information about a place.
(b) **Where**	**do**	they	*live*?	→	**In Miami**.	The form of yes/no questions and information questions is the same: **Do/Does** + subject + main verb
(c)	**Does**	Gina	*live*	in Rome? →	**Yes**, she does. **No**, she doesn't.	
(d) **Where**	**does**	Gina	*live*?	→	**In Rome**.	
(e)	**Do**	they	*need*	help? →	**Yes**, they do. **No**, they don't.	**What** asks for information about a thing.
(f) **What**	**do**	they	*need*?	→	**Help**.	
(g)	**Does**	Lee	*need*	help? →	**Yes**, he does. **No**, he doesn't.	
(h) **What**	**does**	Lee	*need*?	→	**Help**.	

❏ **Exercise 50. Looking at grammar.** (Chart 3-10)
Make questions.

1. A: _____*Does Hana eat lunch in the cafeteria every day?*_____
   B: Yes, she does. (Hana eats lunch in the cafeteria every day.)

2. A: _____*Where does Hana eat lunch every day?*_____
   B: In the cafeteria. (Hana eats lunch in the cafeteria every day.)

3. A: _____
   B: Rice. (She eats rice for lunch every day.)

4. A: _____
   B: At the post office. (Alfonso works at the post office.)

5. A: _____
   B: Yes, he does. (Alfonso works at the post office.)

6. A: _____
   B: Yes, I do. (I live in an apartment.)

7. A: _____
   B: In an apartment. (I live in an apartment.)

8. A: _____
   B: Popcorn. (Hector likes popcorn for a snack.)

9. A: _____
   B: At the University of Toronto. (Ming goes to school at the University of Toronto.)

10. A: _____
    B: Biology. (Her major is biology.)

11. A: _____
    B: To class. (I go to class every morning.)

12. A: _____
    B: In class. (The students are in class right now.)

❑ **Exercise 51. Let's talk: pairwork.** (Chart 3-10)
Work with a partner. Ask and answer questions with *where*.

Example: live
→ Where do you live?

PARTNER A	PARTNER B
1. live	1. buy your clothes
2. eat lunch every day	2. go on weekends
3. go after class	3. sit during class
4. study at night	4. eat dinner
5. go to school	5. do your homework
6. buy school supplies	6. go on vacation

❑ **Exercise 52. Reading.** (Chart 3-10)
Read the story and answer the questions.

Opposite Roommates

I have two roommates. One of them, Fernando, is always neat and clean. He washes his clothes once or twice a week. My other roommate, Matt, is the opposite of Fernando. For example, Matt doesn't change the sheets on his bed. He keeps the same sheets week after week. He never washes his clothes. He wears the same dirty jeans every day. He doesn't care if his clothes smell! Fernando's side of the room is always neat. He makes his bed, hangs up his clothes, and puts everything away. Matt's side of the room is always a mess. He doesn't make his bed, hang up his clothes, or put things away. What habits do you think I prefer?

1. What are some of Fernando's habits?
2. What are some of Matt's habits?
3. Who is a good roommate for you? Why?

❑ **Exercise 53. Let's talk: class activity.** (Chart 3-10)

Ask your teacher questions to get more information about each person's life.* Decide who has the best life and why.

Example:

STUDENT A: Where does Antonio live?
   TEACHER: On a boat.
STUDENT B: What does Lena do?
   TEACHER: She teaches skiing.
STUDENT C: What pets does Lisa have?
   TEACHER: She has a snake.

Continue asking questions until your chart is complete.

	Where does she/he live?	What does he/she do?	Where does she/he work?	What pets does he/she have?
ANTONIO	on a boat			
LENA		teaches skiing		
KANE			at a jewelry store	
LISA				a snake
JACK				

❑ **Exercise 54. Warm-up.** (Chart 3-11)

Answer the questions.

1. What time does Alberto's alarm clock go off? _____

2. When does Alberto get out of bed? _____

8:00 A.M.

8:30 A.M.

*Teacher: See *Let's Talk: Answers*, p. 501.

88 CHAPTER 3

3-11 Simple Present Tense: Asking Information Questions with *When* and *What Time*

| QUESTION* + DO/ + SUBJECT + MAIN | | | | | SHORT ANSWER | *When* and *what time* |
WORD *DOES* VERB						ask for information about time.
(a) **When**	do	you	go	to class? →	**At nine o'clock.**	
(b) **What time**	do	you	go	to class? →	**At nine o'clock.**	
(c) **When**	does	Anna	eat	dinner? →	**At six P.M.**	
(d) **What time**	does	Anna	eat	dinner? →	**At six P.M.**	

(e) **What time** do you **usually** go to class?	The frequency adverb usually comes immediately after the subject in a question: Question word + **does/do** + subject + **usually** + main verb

Where, when, what, what time, who, and *why* are examples of question words.

❑ **Exercise 55. Looking at grammar.** (Chart 3-11)
Make questions.

1. A: *When/What time do you eat breakfast?*
   B: At 7:30. (I eat breakfast at 7:30 in the morning.)

2. A: *When/What time do you usually eat breakfast?*
   B: At 7:00. (I usually eat breakfast at 7:00.)

3. A: _____
   B: At 6:45. (I usually get up at 6:45.)

4. A: _____
   B: At 6:30. (Maria usually gets up at 6:30.)

5. A: _____
   B: At 8:15. (The movie starts at 8:15.)

6. A: _____
   B: Around 11:00. (I usually go to bed around 11:00.)

7. A: _____
   B: At 12:30. (I usually eat lunch at 12:30.)

8. A: _____
   B: At 5:30. (The restaurant opens at 5:30.)

9. A: _____

B: At 9:05. (The train leaves at 9:05.)

10. A: _____

B: Between 6:30 and 8:00. (I usually eat dinner between 6:30 and 8:00.)

11. A: _____

B: At a quarter after eight. (Classes begin at a quarter after eight.)

12. A: _____

B: At 10:00 P.M. (The library closes at 10:00 P.M. on Saturday.)

❑ **Exercise 56. Let's talk: interview.** (Chart 3-11)

Walk around the room. Ask a question beginning with **when** or **what time**. Write the answer and your classmate's name. Then ask another classmate a different question with **when** or **what time**. Share a few of your answers with the class.

Example: eat breakfast
STUDENT A: When/What time do you eat breakfast?
STUDENT B: I usually eat breakfast around seven o'clock.

ACTIVITY	NAME	ANSWER
1. wake up		
2. usually get up		
3. eat breakfast		
4. leave home in the morning		
5. usually get to class		
6. eat lunch		
7. get home from school		
8. have dinner		
9. usually study in the evening		
10. go to bed		

Use the information about Professor Vega to make questions and answers.

1. *be \ he \ a physics teacher*

    _____Is he a physics teacher?_____

    _____No, he isn't._____

2. *what \ teach \ he*

    _____What does he teach?_____
    _____He teaches Psychology 101 and_____
    _____Child Psychology 205._____

> **Professor Vega**
>
> *Office hours:*
> Tuesday and Thursday
> 3:00 - 4:00
>
> *Classes:*
> Psychology 101, Room 213
> 9:00 - 10:00 daily
>
> Child Psychology 205, Room 201
> 11:00 - 12:50
> Tuesday and Thursday

3. *teach \ he \ Psychology 102*

    _____ ? _____

4. *where \ teach \ he \ Child Psychology 205*

    _____ ? _____

5. *be \ he \ in his office \ every day*

    _____ ? _____

6. *be \ he \ in his office \ at 9:00*

    _____ ? _____

7. *teach \ he \ at 7:00 A.M.*

    _____ ? _____

8. *what time \ leave \ he \ the office on Tuesdays and Thursdays*

    _____ ? _____

9. *be \ he \ a professor*

    _____ ? _____

❑ **Exercise 58. Looking at grammar.** (Chapter 3)

Complete the questions in the conversations. Use *is, are, does,* or *do*.

CONVERSATION 1:

A: What time _____does_____ the movie start?
            1

B: Seven-fifteen. _____ you want to go with us?
                   2

A: Yes. What time _____ it now?
                    3

B: Almost seven o'clock. _____ you ready to leave?
                          4

A: Yes, let's go.

CONVERSATION 2:

A: Where _____ my keys to the car?
          5

B: I don't know. Where _____ you usually keep them?
                        6

A: In my purse. But they're not there.

B: Are you sure?

A: Yes. _____ you see them?
         7

B: No. _____ they in one of your pockets?
        8

A: I don't think so.

B: _____ your husband have them?
    9

A: No. He has his own set of car keys.

B: Well, good luck!

A: Thanks.

CONVERSATION 3:

A: _____ you go to school?
    10

B: Yes.

A: _____ your brother go to school too?
    11

B: No, he works full-time.

A: Where _____ he work?
          12

B: At a hotel.

A: _____ he happy?
    13

B: Yes, he loves his job.

❏ **Exercise 59. Check your knowledge.** (Chapter 3)
Correct the mistakes.

lives
1. Niko ~~live~~ in Greece.

2. Lisa comes usually to class on time.

3. Diego use his cell phone often.

4. Amira carry a notebook computer to work every day.

5. She enjoy her job.

6. Miguel don't like milk. He never drink it.

7. Tina doesn't speaks Chinese. She speakes Spanish.

8. You a student?

9. Does your roommate sleeps with the window open?

10. Where your parents live?

11. What time is your English class begins?

12. Olga isn't need a car. She have a bicycle.

13. I no speak English.

14. Omar speak English every day.

15. A: Do you like strong coffee?

    B: Yes, I like.

❏ **Exercise 60. Looking at grammar.** (Chapter 3)
Make questions. Use your own words.

1. A: _____ ?
   B: No, I don't.

2. A: _____ ?
   B: Yes, I am.

3. A: _____ ?
   B: In an apartment.

4. A: _____ ?
   B: Six-thirty.

5. A: _____ ?

   B: Monday.

6. A: _____ ?

   B: No, he doesn't.

7. A: _____ ?

   B: No, she isn't.

8. A: _____ ?

   B: South of the United States.

9. A: _____ ?

   B: Yes, it is.

10. A: _____ ?

    B: Yes, they do.

11. A: _____ ?

    B: In Southeast Asia.

12. A: _____ ?

    B: Yes, I do.

❏ **Exercise 61. Speaking and writing: pairwork.** (Chapter 3)

Part I. Work with a partner. Take turns asking about things you have and don't have (for example, a car, a computer, a pet, children, a TV set, a briefcase, etc.). Take notes.

Example:
PARTNER A: Do you have a car?
PARTNER B: No.
PARTNER A: Do you have a computer?
PARTNER B: Yes, but it's not here. It's in my country.
Etc.

Part II. Take turns asking about things you like and don't like.

Example:
PARTNER B: Do you like pizza?
PARTNER A: Yes.
PARTNER B: Do you like the music of (name of a group or singer)?
PARTNER A: No, I don't.
Etc.

Part III. Write about your partner.

- Give a physical description.
- Write about things this person has and doesn't have.
- Write about things this person likes and doesn't like.

Here is some vocabulary to help you describe your partner.

HAIR TYPE	HAIR COLOR		EYE COLOR
straight	brown	blond	brown
curly	black	dark	blue
wavy	red	light	green
bald			gray

straight   curly   wavy   bald

Writing sample:

   My partner is Jin. He is very tall. He has brown eyes and black hair, and he has a nice smile. He is very friendly.

   Jin has an apartment near school. He doesn't have a car, but he has a bike. He rides his bike to school. He has a laptop computer. His family doesn't live here. He talks to them by video a few times a week.

   He is often homesick. He likes to watch movies from his country in the evening. He enjoys comedy and drama. He likes many kinds of music. He listens to music on his cell phone. He doesn't really like the food here. He likes spicy food. The food here is not spicy. Unfortunately, he is not a good cook, so he doesn't cook much. He likes to eat with his friends. They are good cooks.

Part IV. Editing check: Work individually or change papers with a partner. Check (✓) for the following:

1. _____ capital letter at the beginning of each sentence

2. _____ capital letter at the beginning of a person's name

3. _____ period at the end of each sentence

4. _____ paragraph indents

5. _____ a verb in every sentence

6. _____ correct use of *doesn't* or *isn't* in negative sentences

7. _____ correct spelling (use a dictionary or spell-check)

Chapter 4
Using the Present Progressive

❏ **Exercise 1. Warm-up.** (Chart 4-1)
Complete the sentences with the given words.

David

Nancy

happy/sad

1. David is _____.

2. Nancy is _____.

laughing/crying

He is _____.

She is _____.

4-1 *Be* + *-ing*: the Present Progressive	
am + ***-ing*** (a) I ***am sitting*** in class right now. ***is*** + ***-ing*** (b) Rita ***is sitting*** in class right now. ***are*** + ***-ing*** (c) You ***are sitting*** in class right now.	In (a): When I say this sentence, I am in class. I am sitting. I am not standing. The action (sitting) is happening right now, and I am saying the sentence at the same time.
	am, ***is***, ***are*** = helping verbs ***sitting*** = the main verb
	am, ***is***, ***are*** + ***-ing*** = the present progressive*

* The present progressive is also called the "present continuous."

Complete the sentences with the correct form of *be* (*am, is,* or *are*).

Right now . . .

1. it _____*is*_____ raining outside.

2. we _____ sitting in the college library.

3. you _____ writing.

4. some students _____ studying.

5. I _____ looking out the window.

6. two women _____ waiting for a bus.

7. they _____ talking.

8. a bus _____ coming.

❏ **Exercise 3. Looking at grammar.** (Chart 4-1)

Complete each sentence with the present progressive of the verb in *italics.*

1. *stand*   She _____*is standing*_____.

2. *sleep*   You _____.

3. *read*   He _____.

4. *eat*   I _____.

5. *help*   We _____.

6. *play*   They _____.

7. *snow*   It _____.

❏ **Exercise 4. Let's talk: class activity.** (Chart 4-1)

Your teacher will act out some verbs. Answer questions about these actions. Close your book for this activity.

Example: read
TEACHER: (*acts out reading*) I am reading. What am I doing?
STUDENT: You are reading.

1. write   4. count
2. sit   5. wave
3. stand   6. look at the ceiling

❑   **Exercise 5. Let's talk: pairwork.** (Chart 4-1)

Work with a partner. Take turns describing the pictures. Use the present progressive form of the verbs from the box.

Example:
PARTNER A: The woman is driving a car.
PARTNER B: (*points to the picture*)
PARTNER A: Your turn.

fish	get on (a bus)	laugh	sing	swim
fix (a computer)	kick (a soccer ball)	read	sleep	walk

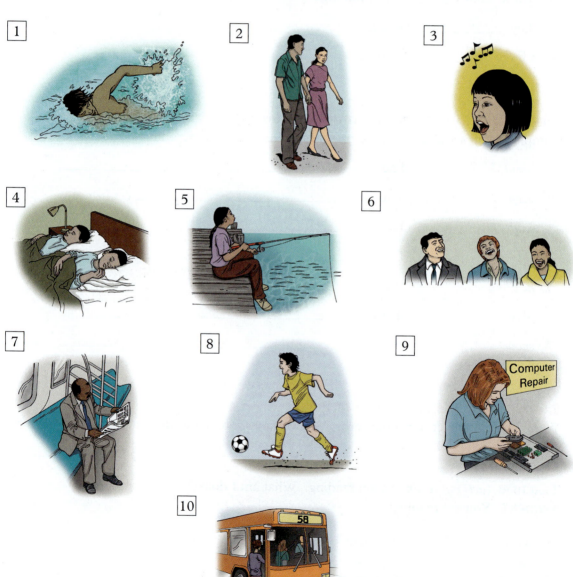

9 Computer Repair

❏ **Exercise 6. Let's talk: class activity.** (Chart 4-1)
Act out the directions your teacher gives you. Describe the actions using the present progressive. Continue the action during the description. Close your book for this activity.

Example:

TEACHER TO STUDENT A:	Please smile. What are you doing?
STUDENT A:	I'm smiling.
TEACHER TO STUDENTS A + B:	Please smile. (*Student A*), what are you and (*Student B*) doing?
STUDENT A:	We're smiling.
TEACHER TO STUDENT B:	What are you and (*Student A*) doing?
STUDENT B:	We're smiling.
TEACHER TO STUDENT C:	What are (*Student A* and *Student B*) doing?
STUDENT C:	They're smiling.
TEACHER TO STUDENT B:	What is (*Student A*) doing?
STUDENT B:	He/She is smiling.

1. Stand up.
2. Sit down.
3. Sit in the middle of the room.
4. Stand in the back of the room.
5. Stand between (_____) and (_____).
6. Touch your desk.
7. Look at the ceiling.
8. Hold up your right hand.
9. Hold up your left hand.
10. Clap your hands.

❏ **Exercise 7. Listening.** (Chart 4-1)
Read the story. Then listen to each sentence and look at the picture of Tony. Circle the correct answer. Compare your answers with your classmates' answers.

   Tony is not a serious student. He is lazy. He doesn't go to class much. He likes to sit in the cafeteria. Sometimes he sits alone, and sometimes he visits with friends from his country. He is in the cafeteria right now. What is he doing?

Example: Tony is talking on his cell phone.   (yes)   no

1. yes   no
2. yes   no
3. yes   no
4. yes   no
5. yes   no

6. yes   no
7. yes   no
8. yes   no
9. yes   no
10. yes   no

❑ **Exercise 8. Warm-up.** (Chart 4-2)
Answer the questions.

| count | ride | sleep | stop |

1. Which verb ends in a consonant + -e? _____
2. Which verb ends in two consonants? _____
3. Which verb ends in two vowels + one consonant? _____
4. Which verb ends in one vowel + one consonant? _____

4-2	**Spelling of** *-ing*	

	END OF VERB →	*-ING* FORM
RULE 1	A CONSONANT* + -e →	DROP THE -e AND ADD -ing
	smil**e** →	smi**ling**
	wri**te** →	wri**ting**
RULE 2	ONE VOWEL* + ONE CONSONANT →	DOUBLE THE CONSONANT AND ADD -ing**
	s**it** →	s**itting**
	r**un** →	r**unning**
RULE 3	TWO VOWELS + ONE CONSONANT →	ADD -ing; DO NOT DOUBLE THE CONSONANT
	r**ead** →	r**eading**
	r**ain** →	r**aining**
RULE 4	TWO CONSONANTS →	ADD -ing; DO NOT DOUBLE THE CONSONANT
	sta**nd** →	sta**nding**
	pu**sh** →	pu**shing**

*Vowels = *a, e, i, o, u.* Consonants = *b, c, d, f, g, h, j, k, l, m, n, p, q, r, s, t, v, w, x, y, z.*
**Exception to Rule 2: Do not double *w, x,* and *y. snow → snowing; fix → fixing; say → saying*

❑ **Exercise 9. Looking at spelling.** (Chart 4-2)
Write the *-ing* form of the given verbs.

1. take _____*taking*_____
2. come _____
3. dream _____
4. bite _____
5. hit _____
6. rain _____
7. hurt _____
8. plan _____
9. bake _____
10. snow _____
11. study _____
12. stop _____

❑ **Exercise 10. Looking at spelling.** (Chart 4-2)

Your teacher will act out a sentence. On a separate piece of paper, write the word that ends in *-ing*. Close your book for this activity.

Example: wave
TEACHER: (*waves*) I'm waving.
STUDENT: (*writes*) _____*waving*_____

1. smile	4. sit	7. write	10. sneeze
2. read	5. eat	8. fly	11. cut a piece of paper
3. drink	6. clap	9. sleep	12. cry

❑ **Exercise 11. Looking at grammar.** (Chart 4-2)

Complete the sentences. Use the present progressive form of the verbs from the box.

call	charge	eat	search	send	wait

At work

1. People are standing in the lobby. They _____*are waiting*_____ for the elevator.

2. A secretary _____ an email to the staff.

3. A customer is using an office phone. He _____ his office.

4. Several people are in the lunchroom. They _____ lunch.

5. A manager has his cell phone on his desk. He _____ his battery.

6. An employee needs information. She _____ the Internet.

❑ **Exercise 12. Warm-up.** (Chart 4-3)

Choose the correct completion.

1. The birds   are / aren't   flying.
2. They   are / aren't   sitting on a telephone wire.
3. A car   is / isn't   driving by.

4-3 Present Progressive: Negatives

(a) I **am not** sleeping. I am awake.	Present progressive negative:
(b) Ben **isn't** listening. He's daydreaming.	am is } + **not** + **-ing** are
(c) Mr. and Mrs. Silva **aren't** watching TV. They're reading.	

Ben

Mr. and Mrs. Silva

❏ **Exercise 13. Looking at grammar.** (Chart 4-3)
Make two sentences about each situation, one negative and one affirmative. Use the present progressive.

Example: Sandra: standing up / sitting down

Sandra _____*isn't standing up.*_____

She __*'s sitting down.*_____

SITUATION 1:
Otto: watching TV / talking on the phone

Otto _____

He _____

SITUATION 2:
Anita: listening to music / playing soccer

Anita _____

She _____

SITUATION 3:
Sofia and Bruno: reading / eating lunch

Sofia and Bruno _____

They _____

SITUATION 4:
Ted: making photocopies / fixing the photocopy machine

Ted _____

He _____

❑ **Exercise 14. Looking at grammar.** (Chart 4-3)
Part I. Read the paragraph.

Jamal is a car mechanic. He owns a car repair business. He is very serious and works very hard.

Right now Jamal is at work. What is he doing? Check (✓) the phrases that make sense.

1. __✓__ talk to customers
2. _____ play soccer in a park
3. _____ change the oil in a car
4. _____ watch a movie in a theater
5. _____ put on a new tire

6. _____ answer the office phone
7. _____ give a customer a bill
8. _____ repair an engine
9. _____ eat at a restaurant
10. _____ replace a windshield wiper

windshield wipers

Part II. Make true sentences about Jamal.

1. _____ *He is talking to customers.* _____

2. _____ *He isn't playing soccer in a park.* _____

3. _____

4. _____

5. _____

6. _____

7. _____

8. _____

9. _____

10. _____

❏ **Exercise 15. Let's talk.** (Chart 4-3)

Work in small groups. Take turns making sentences about the people in the list. Say what they are doing right now and what they are not doing right now.

Example: a neighbor
→ Mrs. Martinez is working in her office right now.
→ She is not working in her garden.

1. someone in your family
2. your favorite actor, writer, or sports star
3. a friend from childhood
4. a classmate
5. the leader of your country

❏ **Exercise 16. Warm-up.** (Chart 4-4)

Choose the correct answer.

1. Are you lying on a bed?
   a. Yes, I am.   b. No, I'm not.

2. Is your teacher dancing?
   a. Yes, he/she is.   b. No, he/she isn't.

3. Are the students in your class singing?
   a. Yes, they are.   b. No they aren't.

4-4 Present Progressive: Questions

	QUESTION			SHORT ANSWER (LONG ANSWER)	
	BE + SUBJECT + *-ING*				
(a)	*Is*	Marta	*sleeping*?	→ Yes, *she is*.	(She's sleeping.)
				→ No, *she's not*.	(She's not sleeping.)
				→ No, *she isn't*.	(She isn't sleeping.)
(b)	*Are*	you	*watching* TV?	→ Yes, *I am*.	(I'm watching TV.)
				→ No, *I'm not*.	(I'm not watching TV.)
	QUESTION WORD + BE + SUBJECT + *-ING*				
(c) *Where*	*is*	Marta	*sleeping*?	→ *In bed*.	(She's sleeping in bed.)
(d) *What*	*is*	Ted	*watching*?	→ *A movie*.	(Ted is watching a movie).
(e) *Why*	*are*	you	*watching* TV?	→ *Because I like this program*.	(I'm watching TV because I like this program.)

Exercise 17. Looking at grammar. (Chart 4-4)
Make questions.

    1. A: _____*Is the teacher helping*_____ students?

       B: Yes, she is. (The teacher is helping students.)

    2. A: _____?

       B: Yes, he is. (Ivan is talking on his phone.)

    3. A: _____?

       B: No, I'm not. (I'm not sleeping.)

    4. A: _____ TV?

       B: No, they aren't. (The students aren't watching TV.)

    5. A: _____ outside?

       B: No, it isn't. (It isn't raining outside.)

    6. A: _____?

       B: Yes, he is. (John is riding a bike.)

❏ **Exercise 18. Vocabulary and speaking: pairwork.** (Chart 4-4)
Part I. Work with a partner. Check (✓) the expressions you know. Your teacher will explain the ones you don't know.

do	*make*	*take*
____ do the dishes	____ make breakfast	____ take a nap
____ do the laundry	____ make a bed	____ take a shower
____ do homework	____ make a phone call	____ take a bath
____ do the ironing	____ make a mess	____ take a test
		____ take a break
		____ take medicine

Part II. With your partner, take turns asking and answering questions about the pictures. Find the differences. You can look at your book before you speak. When you speak, look at your partner. Partner A: Use the pictures on p. 107. Partner B: Use the pictures in Let's Talk: Answers, p. 501.

Example:

PARTNER A	PARTNER B
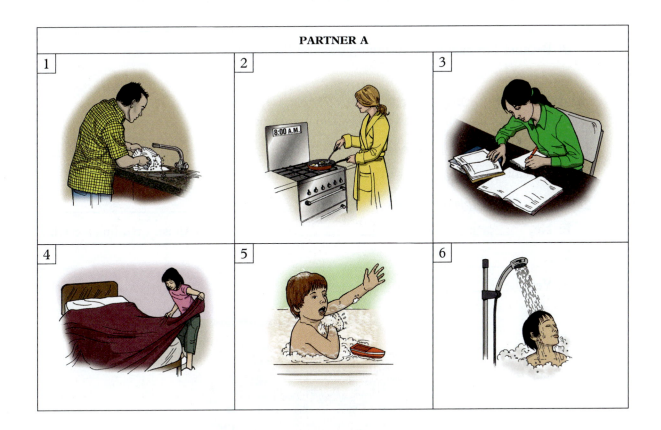	

PARTNER A: Is the girl in your picture taking a test?
PARTNER B: No, she isn't.
PARTNER A: What is she doing?
PARTNER B: She's taking a break.

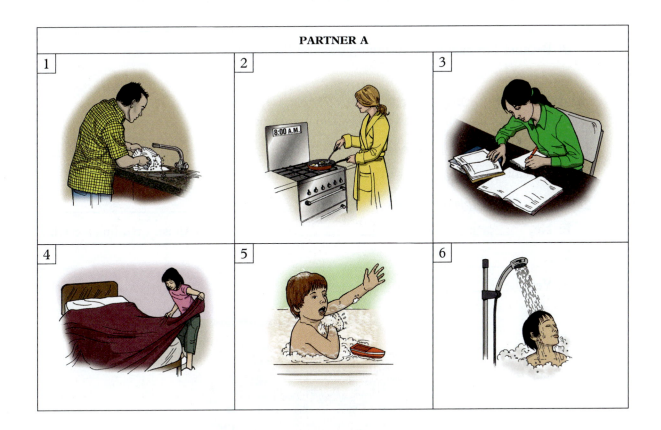

❏ **Exercise 19. Looking at grammar.** (Chart 4-4)
Make questions with *where*, *why*, and *what*.

1. A: _____*What are you reading?*_____

    B: My grammar book. (I'm reading my grammar book.)

2. A: _____

    B: Because we're doing an exercise. (I'm reading my grammar book because we're doing an exercise.)

3. A: _____

    B: A sentence. (I'm writing a sentence.)

4. A: _____

    B: In the back of the room. (Yoshi is sitting in the back of the room.)

5. A: _____

    B: In a hotel. (I'm staying in a hotel.)

6. A: _____

    B: Jeans and a sweatshirt. (Jonas is wearing jeans and a sweatshirt today.)

7. A: _____

    B: Because I'm happy. (I'm smiling because I'm happy.)

❏ **Exercise 20. Looking at grammar.** (Chart 4-4)
Make questions. Give short answers to yes/no questions.

1. A: What _____*are you writing?*_____

    B: A thank-you note. (I'm writing a thank-you note.)

2. A: _____*Is Ali reading a book?*_____

    B: No, _____*he isn't / he's not.*_____ (Ali isn't reading a book.)

3. A: _____

    B: Yes, _____ (Magda is eating lunch.)

4. A: Where _____

   B: At the Sunrise Café. (She's eating lunch at the Sunrise Café.)

5. A: _____

   B: No, _____ (Sam isn't drinking a cup of coffee.)

6. A: What _____

   B: A glass of lemonade. (He's drinking a glass of lemonade.)

7. A: _____

   B: No, _____ (The girls aren't playing in the street.)

8. A: Where _____

   B: In the park. (They're playing in the park.)

9. A: Why _____

   B: Because they don't have school today. (They're playing in the park because they
   don't have school today.)

10. A: _____

    B: Yes. (The girls are playing together.)

11. A: _____?

    B: No. (A parent isn't watching them.)

❏ **Exercise 21. Warm-up.** (Chart 4-5)
Answer the questions with *yes* or *no*.

1. Do you eat breakfast every day?
2. Do you talk on the phone every day?
3. Do you study English every day?
4. Are you eating breakfast right now?
5. Are you talking on the phone right now?
6. Are you studying English right now?

4-5 Simple Present Tense vs. the Present Progressive

	SIMPLE PRESENT	PRESENT PROGRESSIVE
	The simple present expresses habits or usual activities. Common time words are **every day**, **every year**, **every month**, **often**, **sometimes**, and **never**. The simple present uses **do** and **does** in negatives and questions.	The present progressive expresses actions that are happening right now, while the speaker is speaking. Common time words are **now**, **right now**, and **today**. The present progressive uses **am**, **is**, and **are** in negatives and questions.
STATEMENT	I *talk* You *talk* He, She, It *talks* } *every day*. We *talk* They *talk*	I *am talking* You *are talking* He, She, It *is talking* } *now*. We *are talking* They *are talking*
NEGATIVE	I *don't talk*. You *don't talk*. He, She, It *doesn't talk*. We *don't talk*. They *don't talk*.	I *am not talking*. You *are not talking*. He, She, It *is not talking*. We *are not talking*. They *are not talking*.
QUESTION	*Do* I *talk*? *Do* you *talk*? *Does* he, she, it *talk*? *Do* we *talk*? *Do* they *talk*?	*Am* I *talking*? *Are* you *talking*? *Is* he, she it *talking*? *Are* we *talking*? *Are* they *talking*?

❏ **Exercise 22. Looking at grammar.** (Chart 4-5)
Choose the correct completion.

1. Mari is working   (now.)   every day.

2. Mari works at a pharmacy   now.   every day.

3. I am working   today.   every day.

4. It's snowing   now.   every day.

5. You are making breakfast   today.   every day.

6. You make breakfast   right now.   every day.

7. We eat vegetables   right now.   every day.

8. We are eating outside   right now.   every day.

Complete the sentences with the correct form of the words in parentheses.

1. Ahmed (*talk*) _____talks_____ to his classmates every day in class.

   Right now he (*talk*) _____is talking_____ to Yoko. He (*talk, not*)

   _____ to his friend Omar right now.

2. It (*rain*) _____ a lot in this city, but it (*rain, not*) _____

   right now. The sun (*shine*) _____. (*it, rain*) _____

   a lot in your hometown?

3. Hans and Anna (*sit*) _____ next to each other in class every day, so they often

   (*help*) _____ each other with their grammar exercises. Right now Anna (*help*)

   _____ Hans with an exercise on verbs.

4. Roberto (*cook*) _____ his own dinner every evening. Right now he

   is in his kitchen. He (*cook*) _____ rice and beans.

   (*he, cook*) _____ meat for his dinner tonight too? No,

   he is a vegetarian. He (*eat, never*) _____ meat. (*you, eat*)

   _____ meat? (*you, be*) _____ a vegetarian?

❑ **Exercise 24. Listening.** (Chart 4-5)

Listen to each sentence. Choose the correct completion.

Examples: You will hear: Pedro is sleeping late . . .
             You will choose: (now)   every day

1. now   every day
2. now   every day
3. now   every day
4. now   every day
5. now   every day
6. now   every day
7. now   every day
8. now   every day

❏ **Exercise 25. Let's talk: pairwork.** (Chart 4-5)

Work with a partner. Take turns asking and answering questions about Isabel's activities. Use the present progressive and the simple present.

Example: check her phone for messages
PARTNER A: Is Isabel checking her phone for messages?
PARTNER B: Yes, she is.
PARTNER A: Does she check her phone for messages every day?
PARTNER B: Yes, she does.
PARTNER A: Your turn now.

drink tea	ride her bike	take a walk
listen to music	say "hi" to her neighbor	talk on her phone
play her guitar	write a report	text
play tennis	swim	watch TV

Exercise 26. Looking at grammar. (Chart 4-5)
Complete each question with <u>all</u> the correct answers.

a teacher	at school	early	sick	study	studying	work

1. a. Are you _____ *a teacher / early / studying / at school / sick* _____?

   b. Do you _____ *work / study* _____?

angry	a dancer	cook	dance	driving	ready	understand

2. a. Do you _____?

   b. Are you _____?

a problem	help	here	new	raining	ready	true	work

3. a. Is it _____?

   b. Does it _____?

❑ **Exercise 27. Looking at grammar.** (Chart 4-5)
Complete the sentences with **Do**, **Does**, **Is**, or **Are**.

On the subway

1. _____ *Do* _____ you have your ticket?

2. _____ *Is* _____ your ticket in your wallet?

3. _____ the train usually leave on time?

4. _____ the train on time?

5. _____ the tickets cheap?

6. _____ you looking at a map?

7. _____ you have enough money?

8. _____ the train here?

9. _____ we have extra time?

10. _____ the train leaving?

11. _____ the conductor check for tickets?

Listen to the conversation. Complete the sentences with the words you hear.

Example: You will hear: Are you doing an exercise?

You will write: ___*Are you doing*___ an exercise?

A: What are you doing? _____ on your English paper?
1

B: No. _____. _____ an email to my sister.
2   3

A: _____ to her often?
4

B: Yes, but I _____ a lot of emails to anyone else.
5

A: _____ to you often?
6

B: No, but she _____ me a lot.
7

❏ **Exercise 29. Looking at grammar.** (Chart 4-5)

Complete the sentences with the correct form of the words in parentheses.

1. A: Tom is on the phone.

   B: (*he, talk*) ___*Is he talking*___ to his wife?

   A: Yes.

   B: (*he, talk*) ___*Does he talk*___ to her often?

   A: Yes, he (*talk*) ___*talks*___ to her every day during his lunch break.

2. A: I (*walk*) _____ to school every day. I (*take, not*) _____
   _____ the bus. (*you, take*) _____ the bus?

   B: No, I don't.

3. A: Selena is in the hallway.

   B: (*she, talk*) _____ to her friends?

   A: No, she isn't. She (*run*) _____ to her next class.

4. A: I (*read*) _____ the newspaper every day.

   B: (*you, read*) _____ it online?

   A: No, I don't. I (*read, not*) _____ it online.

5. A: What (*you, read*) _____ right now?

   B: I (*read*) _____ my grammar book.

6. A: (*you, want*) _____ your coat?

   B: Yes.

   A: (*be, this*) _____ your coat?

   B: No, my coat (*hang*) _____ in the closet right now.

Exercise 30. Reading and grammar. (Chart 4-5)

Part I. Read the paragraph. Look at new vocabulary with your teacher first.

Reni's Job

    Reni is a server at a restaurant. She works long hours, and the restaurant pay is minimum wage. She earns extra money from tips. Reni is an excellent server. She is friendly and fast. Customers leave her good tips. Fifteen percent is average, but often she gets twenty percent. Today Reni is working an extra shift. A co-worker is sick, so Reni is taking her hours. Reni is feeling tired at the moment, but she is also happy because the tips are good. She is earning a lot of extra money today.

> *Do you know these words?*
> server
> minimum wage
> tips
> average
> shift
> co-worker

Part II. Complete the sentences with **Is, Do,** or **Does.**

1. _____*Is*_____ Reni a good server?

2. _____ the restaurant pay Reni a lot of money?

3. _____ customers leave her good tips?

4. _____ Reni work extra hours every day?

5. _____ Reni working extra hours today?

6. _____ she happy today?

7. _____ she earning extra money?

8. _____ she usually get good tips?

9. _____ servers earn a lot of money from tips?

Part III. Discuss possible answers to these questions.

1. In your opinion, what are some important qualities for a restaurant server? Check (✓) the items.

    _____ fast   _____ formal

    _____ friendly   _____ speaks other languages

    _____ talkative   _____ smiles a lot

    _____ polite   _____ has a good memory

2. Do customers leave tips at restaurants in your country? If yes, what percentage is an average tip? Do you like to leave tips?

3. What is more important for you at a restaurant: the food or the service?

4. In some countries, a usual workday is eight hours, and a usual workweek is 40 hours. What is the usual workday and workweek in your country?

❑ **Exercise 31. Warm-up.** (Chart 4-6)
Read the sentences. What do you notice about the verbs in red?

Right now, I am waiting at a bus stop. I see an ambulance. I hear a siren. A car and a motorcycle are stopping. The ambulance is going fast.

4-6 Non-Action Verbs Not Used in the Present Progressive

	Some verbs are NOT used in the present progressive. They are called "non-action verbs."
(a) I'm hungry **right now**. I **want** an apple. INCORRECT: *I am wanting an apple.*	In (a): **Want** is a non-action verb. *Want* expresses a physical or emotional need, not an action.

(b) I **hear** a siren. **Do** you **hear** it too?
  INCORRECT: *I'm hearing a siren.*
       Are you hearing it too?
	In (b): **Hear** is a non-action verb. *Hear* expresses a sensory experience, not an action.

NON-ACTION VERBS

dislike	hear	believe
hate	see	know
like	smell	think (*meaning* believe)*
love	taste	understand
need		
want		

*Sometimes *think* is used in progressive verbs. See Chart 4-8 for a discussion of *think about* and *think that*.

❑ **Exercise 32. Looking at grammar.** (Chart 4-6)
Complete the sentences. Use the simple present or the present progressive form of the verbs in parentheses.

1. Alicia is in her room right now. She (*listen*) _____*is listening*_____ to a podcast.

   She (*like*) _____*likes*_____ the podcast.

2. It (*snow*) _____ right now. It's beautiful! I (*like*)

   _____ this weather.

3. I (*know*) _____ Jessica Santos. She's in my class.

4. The teacher (*talk*) _____ to us right now. I (*understand*)

   _____ everything she's saying.

5. Emilio is at a restaurant right now. He (*eat*) _____ dinner. He

   (*like*) _____ the food. It (*taste*) _____ good.

6. Sniff-sniff. I (*smell*) _____ gas. (*you, smell*) _____ it?

7. Taro (*tell*) _____ us a story right now. I (*believe*)

_____ his story.

8. Ugh! Someone (*smoke*) _____ a cigar. It (*smell*)

_____ terrible! I (*hate*) _____ cigars.

9. Look at Mr. Gomez. He (*hold*) _____

a kitten in his hand. He (*love*) _____ the kitten.

Mr. Gomez (*smile*) _____ .

❑ **Exercise 33. Let's talk: interview.** (Chart 4-6)
Ask two students each question. Write their answers in the chart. Share some of their answers with the class.

QUESTION	STUDENT A	STUDENT B
1. What \ you \ like?		
2. What \ babies \ around the world \ like?		
3. What \ you \ want?		
4. What \ children around the world \ want?		
5. What \ you \ love?		
6. What \ teenagers around the world \ love?		
7. What \ you \ dislike or hate?		
8. What \ people around the world \ dislike or hate?		
9. What \ you \ need?		
10. What \ elderly people around the world \ need?		

❑ **Exercise 34. Warm-up.** (Chart 4-7)
Complete the sentences with the given phrases.

1. *am looking at / am watching*

   a. I _____ my cell phone. It is 10:00 P.M.

   b. I _____ a movie. It is very funny.

2. *hear / am listening to*

   a. I _____ the teacher carefully. She is explaining

   grammar to me.

   b. Shh! I _____ a noise. Maybe someone is downstairs!

4-7 *See, Look At, Watch, Hear,* and *Listen To*

SEE, LOOK AT, and *WATCH*	In (a): **see** = a non-action verb. Seeing happens
(a) I **see** many things in this room.	because my eyes are open. Seeing is a physical reaction, not a planned action.
(b) I**'m looking at** the clock. I want to know the time.	In (b): **look at** = an action verb. Looking is a planned or purposeful action. Looking happens for a reason.
(c) Bob **is watching** TV.	In (c): **watch** = an action verb. I *watch* something for a long time, but I *look at* something for a short time.
HEAR and *LISTEN TO*	In (d): **hear** = a non-action verb. Hearing is an unplanned act. It expresses a physical reaction.
(d) I'm in my apartment. I'm trying to study. I **hear** music from the next apartment. The music is loud.	
(e) I'm in my apartment. I'm studying. I have an iPod. I**'m listening to** music. I like to listen to music when I study.	In (e): **listen** (**to**) = an action verb. Listening happens for a purpose.

❑ **Exercise 35. Let's talk: class activity.** (Chart 4-7)
Your teacher will ask you questions. Close your book for this activity.

Example:
TEACHER: Look at the floor. What do you see?
STUDENT: I see shoes/dirt/etc.

1. What do you see in this room? Now look at something. What are you looking at?
2. Turn to p. 107 of this book. What do you see? Now look at one thing on that page. What are you looking at?
3. Look at the board. What do you see?
4. What programs do you like to watch on TV?
5. What sports do you like to watch?

6. What animals do you like to watch when you go to the zoo?
7. What do you hear at night in the place where you live?
8. What do you listen to when you go to a concert?
9. What do you listen to when you are at home?

Exercise 36. Looking at grammar. (Chart 4-7)
Complete the sentences. Use the simple present or the present progressive form of the verbs in parentheses.

SITUATION 1:

I (*sit*) _____*am sitting*_____ in class right now. I (*sit, always*)
1
_____*always sit*_____ in the same seat every day. Rashid is my partner
2
today. We (*do*) _____ a pairwork exercise. Right now we (*speak*)
3
_____ English. We both (*know*) _____
4   5
French, so sometimes we (*speak*) _____ French to each other. Of
6
course, our teacher (*want*) _____ us to speak English.
7

Sandro is in the corner of the room. He (*work, not*) _____.
8
He (*look*) _____ around the room. Kim (*check*)
9
_____ the answer key in his grammar book. Francisco
10
(*stare*) _____ at the clock. Abdullah (*smile*)
11
_____. Lidia (*tap*) _____ her foot. Hans
12   13
(*chew*) _____ gum.
14

SITUATION 2:

The person on the bench in the picture on page 120 is Caroline. She's an accountant.

She (*work*) _____ for the government. She (*have*) _____ an
1   2
hour for lunch every day. She (*eat, often*) _____ lunch in the
3
park. She (*bring, usually*) _____ a sandwich and some fruit
4
with her to the park. She (*sit, usually*) _____ on a bench, but
5
sometimes she (*sit*) _____ on the grass and (*watch*) _____
6   7
people and animals. She (*sees, often*) _____ joggers and squirrels. She
8
(*relax*) _____ when she eats at the park.
9

Right now I (*look*) _____ at the picture of Caroline. She (*be, not*)
10
_____ at home in the picture. She (*be*) _____ at the park. She
11   12
(*sit*) _____ on a bench. She (*eat*) _____ her
13   14
lunch. A jogger (*run*) _____ on a path through the park. A squirrel
15
(*sit*) _____ on the ground in front of Caroline. The squirrel
16
(*eat*) _____ a nut. Caroline (*watch*) _____
17   18
the squirrel. She (*watch, always*) _____ squirrels
19
when she eats lunch in the park. Some ducks (*swim*) _____
20
in the pond in the picture, and some birds (*fly*) _____ in
21
the sky. A police officer (*ride*) _____ a horse. He (*ride*)
22
_____ a horse through the park every day. Near Caroline, a family
23
(*have*) _____ a picnic. They (*go*) _____ on a picnic
24   25
every week.

❏ **Exercise 37. Warm-up.** (Chart 4-8)
Do you agree or disagree with each sentence? Circle *yes* or *no*.

    1. I think about my parents every day.   yes   no

    2. I am thinking about my parents right now.   yes   no

    3. I think that it is difficult to be a good parent.   yes   no

4-8 Think About and Think That

	THINK +	ABOUT + A NOUN	In (a): Ideas about my family are in my mind every day.
(a) I	think	about my family every day.	In (b): My mind is busy now. Ideas about grammar are in my mind right now.
(b) I	am thinking	about grammar right now.	

	THINK +	THAT + A STATEMENT	In (c): In my opinion, Emma is lazy. I believe that Emma is lazy. People use **think that** when they want to say (to state) their beliefs. The present progressive is often used with **think about**. The present progressive is almost never used with **think that**.
(c) I	think	that Emma is lazy.	
(d) Ed	thinks	that I am lazy.	
(e) I	think	that the weather is nice.	
			INCORRECT: I am thinking that Emma is lazy.

(f) I *think that* Marco is a nice person.	Examples (f) and (g) have the same meaning. People often omit *that* after *think*, especially in speaking.
(g) I *think* Marco is a nice person.	

❏ **Exercise 38. Grammar and speaking.** (Chart 4-8)
Use *I think that* to give your opinion. Share a few of your opinions with the class.

1. English grammar is easy / hard / fun / interesting.

    _____*I think that English grammar is interesting.*_____

2. People in this city are friendly / unfriendly / kind / cold.

    _____

3. The food at (*name of a place*) is delicious / terrible / good / excellent / awful.

    _____

4. Baseball / football / soccer / golf is interesting / boring / confusing / etc.

    _____

❏ **Exercise 39. Writing and speaking.** (Chart 4-8)
Complete the sentences with your own words. Share a few of your completions with the class.

1. I think that the weather today is _____

2. I think my classmates are _____

3. Right now I'm thinking about _____

4. In my opinion, English grammar is _____

5. In my opinion, soccer is _____

6. I think that my parents are _____

7. I think this school is _____

8. I think about _____ often.

9. I think that _____

10. In my opinion, _____

❏ **Exercise 40. Let's talk: game.** (Charts 4-5 → 4-8)
Work in small groups. One person will think about an animal or a food. The other students will ask questions and try to guess the answer.

Example: animal
STUDENT A: I'm thinking about an animal
STUDENT B: Is it big?
STUDENT A: No.
STUDENT C: Does it have wings?
STUDENT A: Yes.
STUDENT D: Is it a mosquito?
STUDENT A: Yes!

Another student chooses an animal or food.

❏ **Exercise 41. Reading.** (Chart 4-5 → 4-8)
Read the paragraph and the statements. Circle "T" for true and "F" for false.

Sleep: How Much Do People Need?

    Adults need about eight hours of sleep a night. Some need more and some need less, but this is an average amount. Newborn babies need the most sleep, about 14 to 16 hours every 24 hours. They sleep for about four hours. Then they wake up, eat, and then sleep again. As babies grow, they need a little less sleep, about 10 to 14 hours. Here is an interesting fact. Teenagers also need about 10 to 14 hours of sleep a night. Some people think teenagers sleep a lot because they are lazy. Actually, their bodies are changing, so they need a lot of rest. How much sleep do you get every night? Is it enough?

1. Everyone needs eight hours of sleep a night.   T   F

2. Newborn babies sleep 14 to 16 hours and then wake up.   T   F

3. Teenagers need a lot of sleep.   T   F

4. Teenagers and adults need the same amount of sleep.   T   F

❏ **Exercise 42. Looking at grammar.** (Chapter 4)
Choose the correct completion.

1. Lola and Pablo _____ TV right now.
   a. watch   b. watching   ⓒ are watching

2. A: _____ you writing to your parents?
   B: No. I'm studying.
   a. Are   b. Do   c. Don't

3. I _____ like to write letters.
   a. no   b. don't   c. am not

4. A: Jack has six telephones in his apartment.
   B: I _____ you. No one needs six telephones in one apartment.
   a. am believe   b. am not believing c. don't believe

5. When I want to know the time, I _____ a clock.
   a. see   b. look at   c. watch

6. A: Do you know Fatima?
   B: Yes, I do. I _____ she is a very nice person.
   a. am thinking   b. thinking   c. think

7. Where _____ Boris? Upstairs or downstairs?
   a. does   b. is   c. lives

8. Oh, no! Paul _____. He is allergic to cats.
   a. is sneezing   b. doesn't sneeze   c. sneezes

9. A: You look sad.
   B: Yes, I _____ about my family back in my country. I miss them.
   a. think   b. am thinking   c. thinking

❏ **Exercise 43. Check your knowledge.** (Chapter 4)
Correct the mistakes.

       raining   *don't*
1. It's ~~rainning~~ today. I ~~no~~ like the rain.

2. I like New York City. I am thinking that it is a wonderful city.

3. Does Abdul be sleeping right now?

4. Why you are going downtown today?

5. I am liking flowers. They are smelling good.

6. Bill at a restaurant right now. He usually eat at home, but today he eatting dinner at a restaurant.

7. Alex is siting at his desk. He writting a letter.

8. Where do they are sitting today?

❏ **Exercise 44. Reading and writing.** (Chapter 4)

Part I. Read the paragraph. Look at new vocabulary with your teacher first.

A Sleepless Night

Mila is in bed. It is 3:00 A.M. She is very tired, but she isn't sleeping. She is thinking about medical school. She is worrying about her final exams tomorrow. She needs to pass because she wants to be a doctor. She is tossing and turning in bed. She wants a few more days to study. She is thinking about possible test questions. She is wide-awake. She isn't going back to sleep tonight.

> *Do you know these words?*
>
> medical school
> final exams
> pass
> toss and turn
> wide-awake

Part II. Imagine it is 3:00 A.M. You are in bed, and you are wide-awake. You are having a sleepless night. What are you thinking about? Write a paragraph. Use both simple present and present progressive verbs.

Part III. Editing check: Work individually or change papers with a partner. Check (✓) for the following:

1. _____ paragraph indent

2. _____ capital letter at the beginning of each sentence

3. _____ period at the end of each sentence

4. _____ a verb in every sentence

5. _____ use of present progressive for activities right now

6. _____ correct spelling (use a dictionary or spell-check)

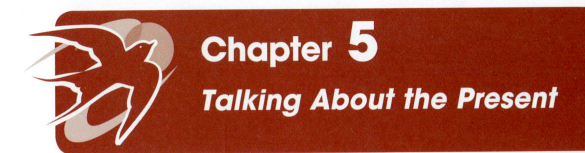

Chapter 5
Talking About the Present

☐ **Exercise 1. Warm-up.** (Chart 5-1)
Match the questions to the pictures.

Picture A	Picture B	Picture C

It's 11:00.	It's Saturday.	It's July.
1. What month is it?	2. What time is it?	3. What day is it?

5-1 Using *It* to Talk About Time

QUESTION		ANSWER	
(a) What day is it?	→	*It's* Monday.	In English, people use *it* to express (to talk about) time.
(b) What month is it?	→	*It's* September.	
(c) What year is it?	→	*It's* (2014).	
(d) What's the date today?	→	*It's* September 15th.	
	→	*It's* the 15th of September.	
(e) What time is it?	→	*It's* 9:00.*	
	→	*It's* nine.	
	→	*It's* nine o'clock.	
	→	*It's* 9:00 A.M.	

*American English uses a colon (two dots) between the hour and the minutes: 9:00 A.M. British English uses one dot: 9.00 A.M.

Exercise 2. Looking at grammar. (Chart 5-1)
Make questions. Begin each question with **What**.

1. A: _____*What day is it?*_____

   B: It's Tuesday.

2. A: _____

   B: It's March 14th.

3. A: _____

   B: (It's) ten-thirty.

4. A: _____

   B: (It's) March.

5. A: _____

   B: (It's) six-fifteen.

6. A: _____

   B: (It's) Wednesday.

7. A: _____

   B: (It's) the 1st of April.

8. A: _____

   B: (It's) 2014.

9. A: _____

   B: It's 7:00 A.M.

Sun	Mon	Tues	Wed	Thurs	Fri	Sat
				1	2	3
4	5	6	7	8	9	10
11	12	13	14	15	16	17
18	19	20	21	22	23	24
25	26	27	28	29	30	31

a calendar page

□ **Exercise 3. Warm-up.** (Chart 5-2)
Which answers are true for you? Complete item 3 with the time your English class meets.

1. I go to school

____ on Monday.

____ on Tuesday.

____ on Wednesday.

____ on Thursday.

____ on Friday.

____ on Saturday.

____ on Sunday.

2. I have class

____ in the morning.

____ in the evening.

____ at night.

3. I have class from _____ to _____.

                           (time)   (time)

5-2 Prepositions of Time

AT	(a) We have class **at** one o'clock. (b) I have an appointment with the doctor **at** 3:00.	**at** + a specific time on the clock
	(c) We sleep **at** night.	**at** + *night*
IN	(d) My birthday is **in** October. (e) I was born **in** 1989. (f) We have class **in** the morning. (g) Bob has class **in** the afternoon. (h) I study **in** the evening.	**in** + a specific month **in** + a specific year **in** + *the morning* **in** + *the afternoon* **in** + *the evening*
ON	(i) I have class **on** Monday(s). (j) I was born **on** October 31. (k) I was born **on** October 31, 1991.	**on** + a specific day of the week **on** + a specific date
FROM . . . TO	(l) We have class **from** 1:00 **to** 2:00.	**from** (a specific time) **to** (a specific time)

□ **Exercise 4. Looking at grammar.** (Chart 5-2)
Complete the sentences with prepositions of time.

1. *We have class . . .*

   a. ____*at*____ ten o'clock.

   b. _____ ten _____ eleven.

   c. _____ the morning and _____ the afternoon.

2. *I study . . .*

    a. _____ the evening.

    b. _____ night.

3. *I was born . . .*

    a. _____ May.

    b. _____ 1990.

    c. _____ May 21.

    d. _____ May 21, 1990.

4. a. The post office isn't open _____ Sundays.

    b. It's open _____ 8:00 A.M. _____ 5:00 P.M., Monday through Saturday.

    c. The post office closes _____ 5:00 P.M.

❏ **Exercise 5. Let's talk: pairwork.** (Chart 5-2)
Complete the sentences with information about your partner. Share some of your partner's answers with the class.

1. When do you eat breakfast?

    a. I eat breakfast in _____*the morning*_____ .

    b. I eat breakfast at _____ .

    c. I eat breakfast from _____ to _____ .

2. When do you study?

    a. I study at _____ .

    b. I study in _____ .

    c. I study on _____ .

    d. I study from _____ to _____ .

3. Tell about the time of your birth.

    a. I was born in _____ .

    b. I was born on _____ .

    c. I was born at _____ .

Exercise 6. Listening and grammar. (Chart 5-2)

Part I. Listen to each description. Write the name of the person.

Example: You will hear: I was born in June. I go to class in the morning.
My name is . . .

You will write: ___Lisa___

| June 2, 1992 7:00 A.M. | June 24, 1985 1:00 P.M. | July 7, 1997 7:00 P.M. | July 24, 1990 11:00 A.M. |

Lisa   Marta   Shen   Ron

1. _____   3. _____

2. _____   4. _____

Part II. Use the information in the pictures to complete the sentences.

1. I was born _____ July. I was born _____ July 7. My name is

   _____.

2. I was born _____ 1985. I was born _____ June 24, 1985. My name

   is _____.

3. I go to class _____ the morning. I go to class _____ 7:00. My name

   is _____.

4. Hi, my name is _____. I was born _____ July. I was born

   _____ July 24. I go to class _____ the morning.

Exercise 7. Warm-up. (Chart 5-3)

Which answers are true for you?

A: In your hometown, how's the weather in the summer?

B: It's sunny / cloudy / rainy / cold / hot / windy.

A: What's the weather like in the winter?

B: It's sunny / cloudy / rainy / cold / hot / windy.

5-3 Using *It* and *What* to Talk About the Weather

(a) ***It's*** sunny today. (b) ***It's*** hot and humid today. (c) ***It's*** a nice day today.	In English, people usually use ***it*** when they talk about the weather.
(d) ***What's the weather like*** in Istanbul in January? (e) ***How's the weather*** in Moscow in the summer? (f) ***What's the temperature*** in Bangkok today?	People commonly ask about the weather by saying *What's the weather like?* OR *How's the weather?* ***What*** is also used to ask about the temperature.

❏ **Exercise 8. Let's talk: pairwork.** (Chart 5-3)

How's the weather today? Choose *yes* or *no*. Share your answers with a partner. Do you and your partner agree? Report some of your answers to the class.

1. hot	yes	no	8. sunny	yes	no
2. warm	yes	no	9. nice	yes	no
3. cool	yes	no	10. clear	yes	no
4. chilly	yes	no	11. partly cloudy	yes	no
5. cold	yes	no	12. humid★	yes	no
6. freezing	yes	no	13. windy	yes	no
7. below freezing	yes	no	14. stormy	yes	no

❏ **Exercise 9. Let's talk: small groups.** (Chart 5-3)

Change the Fahrenheit (F) temperatures to Celsius★★ (C) by choosing temperatures from the box. Then describe the temperature in words.

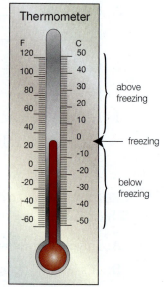

38°C	24°C	✓10°C	0°C	−18°C

	FAHRENHEIT	CELSIUS	DESCRIPTION
1.	50°F	*10°C*	*cool, chilly*
2.	32°F		
3.	100°F		
4.	75°F		
5.	0°F		

★*humid* = hot and wet
★★*Celsius* is also called "Centigrade."

Read the chart and follow the instructions.

"Approximate" means "close but not exact." Here is a fast way to get an
approximate number when you convert from one temperature system to another.[*]

• To change **Celsius to Fahrenheit**: DOUBLE THE CELSIUS NUMBER AND ADD 30.

Examples: 12°C × 2 = 24 + 30 =   54°F (Exact numbers: 12°C = 53.6°F)
         20°C × 2 = 40 + 30 =   70°F (Exact numbers: 20°C = 68°F)
         35°C × 2 = 70 + 30 = 100°F (Exact numbers: 35°C = 95°F)

• To change **Fahrenheit to Celsius**: SUBTRACT 30 FROM THE FAHRENHEIT NUMBER
AND THEN DIVIDE BY 2.

Examples: 60°F − 30 = 30 ÷ 2 = 15°C. (Exact numbers: 60°F = 15.6°C.)
         80°F − 30 = 50 ÷ 2 = 25°C. (Exact numbers: 80°F = 26.7°C.)
         90°F − 30 = 60 ÷ 2 = 30°C. (Exact numbers: 90°F = 32.2°C.)

---

[*]To get exact numbers, use these formulas: C = 5/9 (°F − 32) OR F = 9/5 (°C) + 32.

Change the temperatures from Celsius to Fahrenheit and from Fahrenheit to Celsius.
Calculate the <u>approximate</u> numbers.

1. 22°C _____*22°C = approximately 74°F (22°C x 2 = 44 + 30 = 74°F)*_____

2.   2°C _____

3. 30°C _____

4. 16°C _____

5. 25°F _____

6. 70°F _____

7. 100°F _____

❑ **Exercise 11. Let's talk: interview.** (Chart 5-3)
Interview your classmates about their hometowns. Ask questions about the name of the hometown, its location, its population, its weather, and its average temperature in a particular month (of your choice). Share some of their answers with the class.

Example:
STUDENT A: What's your hometown?
STUDENT B: Athens.
STUDENT A: Where is it?
STUDENT B: In southeastern Greece near the Aegean Sea.
STUDENT A: What's the population of Athens?
STUDENT B: Almost four million.
STUDENT A: What's the weather like in Athens in May?
STUDENT B: It's mild. Sometimes it's a little rainy.
STUDENT A: What's the average temperature in May?
STUDENT B: The average temperature is around 21° Celsius.

Write down the information you get here.

NAME	Spyros			
HOMETOWN	Athens			
LOCATION	SE Greece			
POPULATION	almost 4 million			
WEATHER	mild in May, around 21°C, in the mid-seventies Fahrenheit			

❏ **Exercise 12. Warm-up.** (Chart 5-4)

Complete the sentences.

1. There is / isn't a whiteboard in this room.

2. There are / aren't computers in this room.

3. There are _____ students in this room.
   (number)

5-4 *There + Be*

THERE + BE +	SUBJECT +	PLACE
(a) **There** **is**	**a bird**	in the tree.
(b) **There** **are**	**four birds**	in the tree.

There + be is used to say that something exists in a particular place.

Notice: The subject follows *be*:

  there + is + singular noun
  there + are + plural noun

(c) **There's** a bird in the tree.

(d) **There're** four birds in the tree.

CONTRACTIONS:

  there + is = there's
  there + are = there're

❏ **Exercise 13. Looking at grammar.** (Chart 5-4)

Complete the sentences with *is* or *are*. Then choose *yes* or *no*. Compare your answers with your classmates' answers.

1. There _____ is _____ a grammar book on my desk.   yes   no

2. There _____ are _____ many grammar books in this room.   yes   no

3. There _____ comfortable chairs in this classroom.   yes   no

4. There _____ a nice view from the classroom window.   yes   no

5. There _____ interesting places to visit in this area.   yes   no

6. There _____ a good place to eat near school.   yes   no

7. There _____ fun activities to do on weekends in this area.   yes   no

8. There _____ difficult words in this exercise.   yes   no

❏ **Exercise 14. Let's talk: pairwork.** (Chart 5-4)

Work with a partner. Complete each sentence with words from the box or your own words. You can look at your book before you speak. When you speak, look at your partner.

a book	a map	a notebook
books	papers	notebooks
tall buildings	a park	restaurants
a bulletin board	a pen	a sink
a calendar	a pencil	stores
chairs	a pencil sharpener	students
a chalkboard	people	a teacher
a clock	a picture	a whiteboard
a coffee shop	pictures	a window
desks	a post office	windows
light switches		

1. PARTNER A: There is . . . on this desk.
   PARTNER B: There are . . . on that desk.

2. PARTNER A: There are . . . on that wall.
   PARTNER B: There is . . . on this wall.

3. PARTNER A: There are . . . in this room.
   PARTNER B: There is also . . . in this room.

4. PARTNER A: There is . . . near our school.
   PARTNER B: There are also . . . near our school.

❏ **Exercise 15. Let's talk: small groups.** (Chart 5-4)

First, everyone in your group puts two or three objects (e.g., a coin, some keys, a pen, a dictionary) on a table in the classroom. Then take turns describing the items on the table. Begin with *There is* and *There are*.

Example:
STUDENT A: There are three dictionaries on the table.
STUDENT B: There are some keys on the table.
STUDENT C: There is a pencil sharpener on the table.

❏ **Exercise 16. Listening.** (Chart 5-4)

Listen to each sentence. Choose the word you hear. *Note:* You will hear contractions for *There is* and *There are*.

Example: You will hear: There're several windows in this room.
            You will choose: There's   (There're)

1. There's   There're   5. There's   There're
2. There's   There're   6. There's   There're
3. There's   There're   7. There's   There're
4. There's   There're   8. There's   There're

❑ **Exercise 17. Warm-up.** (Chart 5-5)
Answer the questions.

1. Is there an elevator in this building?   yes   no

2. Are there stairs in this building?   yes   no

5-5 *There + Be:* Yes/No Questions

QUESTION		SHORT ANSWER
BE + *THERE* + *SUBJECT*		
(a) **Is** **there** **an apple** in the refrigerator? →		Yes, **there is**.
→		No, **there isn't**.
(b) **Are** **there** **eggs** in the refrigerator? →		Yes, **there are**.
→		No, **there aren't**.

❑ **Exercise 18. Let's talk: pairwork.** (Chart 5-5)
Work with a partner. Ask questions about the refrigerator in the picture. Use the nouns in the list. Begin with **Is there** or **Are there**.

Example: a piece of cheese
PARTNER A: Is there a piece of cheese in the refrigerator?
PARTNER B: Yes, there is.
PARTNER A: Your turn now.

Example: onions
PARTNER B: Are there onions in the refrigerator?
PARTNER A: No, there aren't.
PARTNER B: Your turn now.

PARTNER A	PARTNER B
1. a carton of eggs	1. strawberries
2. a loaf of bread	2. oranges
3. apples	3. a bottle of orange juice
4. a cube of butter	4. a bowl of rice
5. potatoes	5. a bag of flour
6. vegetables	6. pickles

❏ **Exercise 19. Let's talk: small groups.** (Chart 5-5)

Take turns asking and answering questions about this city. Begin with *Is there* or *Are there*. If the answer is "I don't know," ask someone else.

Example: a zoo
STUDENT A: Is there a zoo in (*name of this city*)?
STUDENT B: Yes, there is. / No, there isn't.
STUDENT B: (*to Student C*) Is there an airport near (*name of this city*)?
STUDENT C: I don't know.
STUDENT B: (*to Student D*) Is there an airport near (*name of this city*)?
STUDENT D: Yes, there is. / No, there isn't.
Etc.

1. a zoo
2. an airport
3. lakes
4. good restaurants
5. a good Chinese restaurant
6. an art museum
7. an aquarium
8. interesting bookstores
9. a subway system
10. public swimming pools
11. a good public transportation system
12. a movie theater

❏ **Exercise 20. Let's talk: class activity.** (Chart 5-5)

Solve the puzzle. *Teacher's Note:* See *Let's Talk: Answers,* p. 502, to answer your students' questions.

The Romero family needs to decide where to stay for their summer vacation. They want a hotel with everything in the list below. Your teacher has information about several hotels. Ask her/him questions using the list. Then write *yes* or *no* in the correct column of the chart. Which hotel has everything that the Romeros want?

List:

a swimming pool   hiking trails   ocean-view rooms
a beach   horses to ride

Example:
STUDENT A: Is there a swimming pool at Hotel 1?
  TEACHER: Yes, there is.
STUDENT B: Are there hiking trails at Hotel 3?
  TEACHER: Yes, there are.

	A SWIMMING POOL	A BEACH	HIKING TRAILS	HORSES	OCEAN-VIEW ROOMS
HOTEL 1	yes				
HOTEL 2		yes			
HOTEL 3			yes		
HOTEL 4				yes	
HOTEL 5					yes

❏ **Exercise 21. Warm-up.** (Chart 5-6)
Answer the questions.

1. How many students are there at this school?
2. How many people are there in your country?
3. How many people are there on the earth?

5-6 *There + Be:* **Asking Questions with** *How Many*

QUESTION					SHORT ANSWER
HOW MANY +	SUBJECT +	ARE +	THERE +	PLACE	
(a) *How many*	*chapters*	*are*	*there*	in this book? →	Fifteen. (There are 15 chapters in this book.)
(b) *How many*	*provinces*	*are*	*there*	in Canada? →	Ten. (There are ten provinces in Canada.)

(c) How many words do you see?	Notice: The noun that follows *how many* is plural.
INCORRECT: *How many word do you see?*	

❏ **Exercise 22. Let's talk: class activity.** (Chart 5-6)
Ask and answer questions about this classroom. Use *How many* and the given words.

Example: desks
STUDENT A: How many desks are there in this room?
STUDENT B: Thirty-two. OR There are thirty-two desks in this room.
STUDENT A: That's right. OR No, I count thirty-three desks.

1. windows	3. students	5. women	7. grammar books
2. laptops	4. teachers	6. men	8. dictionaries

❏ **Exercise 23. Let's talk: pairwork.** (Chart 5-6)
Work with a partner. Ask questions. Begin with *How many*.

Example: days in a week
PARTNER A: How many days are there in a week?
PARTNER B: Seven. OR There are seven days in a week.
PARTNER A: Right. There are seven days in a week. Your turn now.

PARTNER A	PARTNER B
1. chapters in this book	1. pages in this book
2. doors in this room	2. people in this room
3. floors in this building	3. letters in the English alphabet (26)
4. states in the United States (50)	4. provinces in Canada (10)
5. countries in North America (3)	5. continents in the world (7)

□ **Exercise 24. Warm-up.** **(Chart 5-7)**

Guess the person. Notice the prepositions in red.

Who am I?

1. I live **in** London.
2. I live **on** Downing Street.
3. I live **at** 10 Downing Street.

5-7 Prepositions of Place

(a) My book is **on** *my desk*.	In (a): *on* = a preposition *my desk* = object of the preposition *on my desk* = a prepositional phrase
(b) Ned lives **in** *Miami*. 　　　　**in** *Florida*. 　　　　**in** *the United States*. 　　　　**in** *North America*.	A person lives **in** a city, a state, a country, a continent.
(c) Meg lives **on** *Hill Street*.	**on** a street, avenue, road, etc.
(d) She lives **at** *4472 Hill Street*.	**at** a street address
(e) My father is **in** *the kitchen*.	In (e): **in** is used with rooms: **in** *the kitchen*, **in** *the classroom*, **in** *the hall*, **in** *my bedroom*, etc.
(f) Ivan is **at** *work*. (g) Yoko is **at** *school*. (h) Olga is **at** *home*.	**At** + *work, school, home* expresses activity: In (f): Ivan is working at his office (or other place of work). In (g): Yoko is a student. She is studying. (Or, if she is a teacher, she is teaching.) In (h): Olga is doing things at her home.
(i) Siri is **in** *bed*. (j) Tim is **in** *class*. (k) Mr. Lee is **in** *the hospital*. (l) Paul is **in** *jail/prison*.	**In** + *bed, class, hospital, jail* has these special meanings: In (i): Siri is resting or sleeping *under* the covers. In (j): Tim is studying (or teaching). In (k): Mr. Lee is sick. He is a patient. In (l): Paul is a prisoner. He is not free to leave. NOTE: American English = *in the hospital* 　　　　British English = *in hospital*

❏ **Exercise 25. Looking at grammar.** (Chart 5-7)
Complete the sentences with *in*, *on*, or *at*.

Write about Alonso.

1. Alonso lives _____ Canada.

2. He lives _____ Toronto.

3. He lives _____ Lake Street.

4. He lives _____ 5541 Lake Street _____ Toronto, Canada.

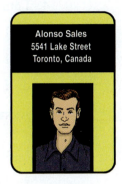

Alonso Sales
5541 Lake Street
Toronto, Canada

Write about Dr. Eng.

5. Dr. Eng lives on _____.

6. He lives in _____.

7. He lives at _____.

Dr. John Eng
342 First Street
Miami, Florida

Write about yourself.

8. I live _____.
　　　　　　　(name of country)

9. I live _____.
　　　　　　　(name of city)

10. I live _____.
　　　　　　　(name of street)

11. I live _____.
　　　　　　　(street address)

Exercise 26. Game. (Chart 5-7)

Work in teams. Complete the sentences with *in*, *on*, or *at*. Then guess the person, building, or company. Use words from the box. The team with the most correct answers wins.

Alexandria Pyramids	Facebook	Nike
Apple	Giza Pyramids	president of the U.S.
Boeing	Louvre Museum	prime minister of Canada
Eiffel Tower	Microsoft	vice president of the U.S.

1. I am a building.

   a. I am _____ Paris.

   b. I am _____ Anatole Avenue.

   c. I am _____ 5 Anatole Avenue.

   ANSWER: _____

2. I am a person.

   a. I live _____ Ottawa.

   b. I live _____ 24 Sussex Drive.

   c. I live _____ Sussex Drive.

   ANSWER: _____

3. I am a building.

   a. I am _____ Pyramid Street.

   b. I am _____ 124 Pyramid Street.

   c. I am _____ Egypt.

   ANSWER: _____

4. I am a company.

   a. I am _____ Oregon.

   b. I am _____ Bowerman Drive.

   c. I am _____ One Bowerman Drive.

   ANSWER: _____

5. I am a person.

   a. I live _____ Pennsylvania Avenue.

   b. I live _____ 600 Pennsylvania Avenue N.W.

   c. I live _____ the United States.

   ANSWER: _____

6. I am a company.

   a. I am _____ Illinois.

   b. I am _____ 100 North Riverside Plaza.

   c. I am _____ Chicago.

   ANSWER: _____

❏ ## Exercise 27. Looking at grammar. (Chart 5-7)

Complete the sentence with *at* or *in*.

Rachel isn't . . .

1. _____ her bedroom.

2. _____ bed.

3. _____ work.

4. _____ prison.

5. _____ home.

6. _____ jail.

7. _____ class.

8. _____ Africa.

9. _____ the hall.

10. _____ the hospital. She's well now.

Exercise 28. Looking at grammar. (Chart 5-7)
Complete the sentences with *at* or *in*.

1. When I was _____ work yesterday, I had an interesting phone call.

2. Poor Anita. She's _____ the hospital again for more surgery.

3. Mr. Gow is a teacher, but he isn't _____ school today. He's sick, so he is

   _____ home.

4. Last year at this time, Eric was _____ Vietnam. This year he's _____ Spain.

5. There's a fire extinguisher _____ the hall.

6. There are thirty-seven desks _____ our classroom.

7. Rob is _____ jail. He's going to be _____ prison for a long time.

8. Our hotel rooms are on the same floor. I'm _____ 501 and you're _____ 505.

9. Singapore is _____ Asia.

10. The kids are _____ the kitchen. They're making dinner for us!

11. A: Is Jennifer _____ home?

    B: No, she's still _____ class.

12. A: Where's Jack?

    B: He's _____ his room.

    A: What's he doing?

    B: He's _____ bed. He has a headache.

Exercise 29. Warm-up. (Chart 5-8)
Answer the questions.

Right now . . .

1. who is in front of you?
2. who is behind you?
3. who is beside you?
4. who is far away from the teacher?
5. who is in the middle of the room?
6. who is near the door?

5-8 More Prepositions of Place: A List

above	beside	in back of	in the middle of	on
around	between	in the back of	inside	on top of
at	far (away) from	in front of	near	outside
behind	in	in the front of	next to	under
below				

(a) The book is *beside* the cup.
(b) The book is *next to* the cup.
(c) The book is *near* the cup.

(d) The book is *between* two cups.

(e) The book is *far away from* the cup.

(f) The cup is *on* the book.
(g) The cup is *on top of* the book.

(h) The cup is *under* the book.

(i) The cup is *above* the book.

(j) The hand is *around* the cup.

(k) The man is *in back of* the bus.
(l) The man is *behind* the bus.

(m) The man is *in the back of* the bus.

(n) The man is *in front of* the bus.
In (k), (l), and (n): the man is *outside* the bus.

(o) The man is *in the front of* the bus.

(p) The man is *in the middle of* the bus.
In (m), (o), and (p): the man is *inside* the bus.

❑ **Exercise 30. Looking at grammar.** (Chart 5-8)
Describe the pictures by completing the sentences with prepositional expressions of place.

1. The apple is ____*on / on top of*____ the plate.

2. The apple is _____ the plate.

3. The apple is _____ the plate.

4. The apple is _____ the glass.

5. The apple isn't near the glass. It is _____ the glass.

6. The apple is _____ the glass.

7. The apple is _____ two glasses.

8. The hand is _____ the glass.

9. 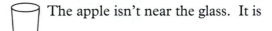 The dog isn't inside the car. The dog is _____ the car.

10. The dog is in _____ of the car.

11.  The dog is in _____ of the car.

12. The dog is in _____ of the car.

13. The dog is in _____ of the car.

❏ **Exercise 31. Let's talk: pairwork.** (Charts 5-4 → 5-8)

Work with a partner. Ask and answer questions about the picture. Use the questions below and the words from the box to help you.

Questions: *Where is the . . . ?* OR *Where are the . . . ?* OR *How many . . . are there?*

Examples:

PARTNER A: Where is the bird?
PARTNER B: The bird is on the table.
PARTNER A: Your turn to ask.

PARTNER B: How many birds are there?
PARTNER A: There is one bird.
PARTNER B: Your turn to ask.

bikes	butterflies	guitar	river
bird	clouds	mountains	train
boat	fish	knife	trees
boots	fishing pole	picnic bench	
bridge	flowers	picnic table	

❑ Exercise 32. Listening. (Chart 5-8)

 Listen to the statements about the picture on p. 144. Choose "T" for true and "F" for false.

Example: You will hear: A bike is in the water.

You will choose: T   Ⓕ

1. T	F	6. T	F	11. T	F
2. T	F	7. T	F	12. T	F
3. T	F	8. T	F	13. T	F
4. T	F	9. T	F	14. T	F
5. T	F	10. T	F	15. T	F

❑ Exercise 33. Let's talk: pairwork. (Chart 5-8)

Work with a partner. Choose a small object (a pen, pencil, coin, etc.). Give and follow directions. You can look at your book before you speak. When you speak, look at your partner.

Example: (*a small object such as a coin*)
PARTNER A (*book open*):   Put it on top of the desk.
PARTNER B (*book closed*): (*Partner B puts the coin on top of the desk.*)

1. Put it on your head.
2. Put it above your head.
3. Put it between your fingers.
4. Put it near me.
5. Put it far away from me.
6. Put it under your book.
7. Put it below your knee.
8. Put it in the middle of your grammar book.

Change roles.
9. Put it inside your grammar book.
10. Put it next to your grammar book.
11. Put it on top of your grammar book.
12. Put it in front of me.
13. Put it behind me.
14. Put it in back of your back.
15. Put it in the back of your grammar book.
16. Put your hand around it.

❑ **Exercise 34. Vocabulary and grammar.** **(Chapters 4 and 5)**

Part I. Work in pairs or as a class. Answer the questions. (Alternate questions if working in pairs.) Use the vocabulary from the box to help you.

burn	a bowl / a bowl of salad	meat / a piece of meat
eat dinner	a candle	a plate
have a steak for dinner	a cup / a cup of coffee	a restaurant
hold a knife and a fork	a fork	a saucer
	a glass / a glass of water	a spoon
	a knife	a steak
	a vase of flowers	a table
		a server

1. What is Jill doing?
2. What do you see on the table?
3. What is Jill holding in her right hand? in her left hand?
4. What is in the bowl?
5. What is on the plate?

6. What is in the cup?
7. What is burning?
8. Is Jill eating breakfast?
9. Is Jill at home? Where is she?
10. What is she cutting?

Part II. Complete the sentences.

1. Jill is sitting _____ a table.

2. There is a candle _____ the table.

3. There is coffee _____ the cup.

4. Jill _____ holding a knife _____ her right hand.

5. She's eating _____ a restaurant.

6. She _____ eating at home.

7. She _____ eating breakfast.

❏ **Exercise 35. Vocabulary and grammar.** (Chapters 4 and 5)

Part I. Work in pairs or as a class. Answer the questions. (Alternate questions if working in pairs.) Use the vocabulary from the box to help you.

read a book	the circulation desk
study at the library	a librarian
take notes	a shelf (singular)
	shelves (plural)★

1. What is Jon doing?
2. What do you see in the picture?
3. Is Jon at home? Where is he?

4. Is Jon reading a newspaper?
5. Where is the librarian standing?
6. Is Jon right-handed or left-handed?

Part II. Complete the sentences.

1. Jon is studying _____ the library.

2. He is sitting _____ a table.

3. He is sitting _____ a chair.

4. His legs are _____ the table.

5. There are books _____ the shelves.

6. Jon is writing _____ a piece of paper.

7. He's taking notes _____ a piece of paper.

8. He _____ reading a newspaper.

9. The librarian _____ standing _____ the circulation desk.

10. Another student is sitting _____ Jon.

★See Chart 6-6, p. 174, for information about nouns with irregular plural forms.

□ **Exercise 36. Vocabulary and grammar.** (Chapters 4 and 5)

Part I. Work in pairs or as a class. Answer the questions. (Alternate questions if working in pairs.) Use the vocabulary from the box to help you.

cash a check	a bank teller	a man (singular)
stand in line	a counter	men (plural)★
	a line	people (plural)★
		a woman (singular)
		women (plural)★

1. What is Megan doing?
2. Is Megan at a store? Where is she?
3. What do you see in the picture?
4. Who is standing behind Megan, a man or a woman?
5. Who is standing at the end of the line, a man or a woman?
6. How many men are there in the picture?
7. How many women are there in the picture?
8. How many people are there in the picture?
9. How many people are standing in line?

Part II. Complete the sentences.

1. Megan is _____ a bank.

2. Four people _____ standing in line.

3. Megan is standing _____ the counter.

4. The bank teller is standing _____ the counter.

5. A woman _____ standing _____ Megan.

6. Megan _____ standing _____ the end _____ the line.

7. A man _____ standing _____ the end _____ the line.

8. A businessman _____ standing _____ the woman in the skirt and the man with the beard.

★See Chart 6-6, p. 174, for information about nouns with irregular plural forms.

❑ **Exercise 37. Warm-up.** (Chart 5-9)
These sentences have the same meaning. Which speaker sounds more polite to you?

I want some coffee.

I would like some coffee.

5-9 *Would Like*

(a) I'm thirsty. I *want* a glass of water. (b) I'm thirsty. I *would like* a glass of water.	Examples (a) and (b) have the same meaning, but ***would like*** is usually more polite than ***want***. *I would like* is a nice way of saying *I want*.

(c) *I would like*
You would like
She would like
He would like } a glass of water.
We would like
They would like
	Notice in (c):
	    There is no final ***-s*** on ***would***.
	    There is no final ***-s*** on ***like***.

(d) CONTRACTIONS
    I'd = *I would*
    you'd = *you would*
    she'd = *she would*
    he'd = *he would*
    we'd = *we would*
    they'd = *they would*
	Would is often contracted with pronouns in both speaking and writing.
	In speaking, ***would*** is usually contracted with nouns too.
	WRITTEN: Ray would like to come.
	SPOKEN: "Ray'd like to come."

WOULD LIKE + INFINITIVE (e) I *would like* *to eat* a sandwich.	Notice in (e): ***would like*** can be followed by an infinitive.
WOULD + SUBJECT + *LIKE* (f) *Would* you *like* some tea?	In a question, ***would*** comes before the subject.
(g) Yes, I *would*. (I would like some tea.)	***Would*** is used alone in short answers to questions with ***would like***. It is not contracted in short answers.

Exercise 38. Grammar. (Chart 5-9)

Change the sentences to *would like*.

1. **Dan wants** a cup of coffee.

   → ____*Dan would like*_____ a cup of coffee.

2. **He wants** some sugar in his coffee.

   → ____*He would like*_____ some sugar in his coffee.

3. **Hassan and Eva want** some coffee too.

   → _____ some coffee too.

4. **They want** some sugar in their coffee too.

   → _____ some sugar in their coffee too.

5. **I want to thank** you for your help.

   → _____ you for your help.

6. **My friend wants to thank** you too.

   → _____ you too.

7. **My friends want to thank** you too.

   → _____ you too.

❑ **Exercise 39. Let's talk: class activity.** (Chart 5-9)

Your teacher will ask you questions. Answer the questions. Close your book for this activity.

1. Who's hungry right now? (_____), are you hungry? What would you like?
2. Who's thirsty? (_____), are you thirsty? What would you like?
3. Who's sleepy? What would you like to do?
4. What would you like to do this weekend?
5. What would you like to do after class today?
6. What would you like to have for dinner tonight?
7. What countries would you like to visit?
8. What cities would you like to visit in (*the United States, Canada, etc.*)?
9. What languages would you like to learn?
10. Pretend that you are a host at a party at your home and your classmates are your guests. Ask them what they would like to eat or drink.
11. Think of something fun to do tonight or this weekend. Use *would you like* and invite a classmate to join you.

❏ **Exercise 40. Warm-up.** (Chart 5-10)
What is the difference in meaning between these sentences?

I like chocolate.

I would like some chocolate.

5-10	*Would Like* vs. *Like*	
(a) I *would like to go* to the zoo.	In (a): ***I would like to go to the zoo*** means *I want to go to the zoo.* ***Would like*** indicates that I want to do something now or in the future.	
(b) I *like to go* to the zoo.	In (b): ***I like to go to the zoo*** means *I enjoy the zoo.* ***Like*** indicates that I always, usually, or often enjoy something.	

❏ **Exercise 41. Listening.** (Chart 5-10)

Listen to the sentences and choose the verbs you hear. Some sentences have contractions.

Example: You will hear: I'd like some tea.

You will choose: like   ⟨'d like⟩

1. like   'd like
2. like   'd like
3. like   'd like
4. likes   'd like
5. like   'd like

6. likes   'd like
7. like   'd like
8. like   'd like
9. like   'd like
10. like   'd like

Discuss possible completions for the sentences. Use your own words.

1. I need to _____ every day.

2. I want to _____ today.

3. I like to _____ every day.

4. I would like to _____ today.

5. I don't like to _____ every day.

6. I don't want to _____ today.

7. Do you like to _____?

8. Would you like to _____?

9. I need to _____ and _____ today.

10. _____ would you like to _____ this evening?

❑ **Exercise 43. Let's talk: pairwork.** (Charts 5-9 and 5-10)
Work in pairs. Ask and answer questions. You can look at your book before you speak. When you speak, look at your partner.

Example:
PARTNER A: Do you like apples?
PARTNER B: Yes, I do. OR No, I don't.
PARTNER A: Would you like an apple right now?
PARTNER B: Yes, I would. OR Yes, thank you. OR No, but thank you for asking.
PARTNER A: Your turn now.

PARTNER A	PARTNER B
1. Do you like coffee? Would you like a cup of coffee?	1. Do you like chocolate? Would you like some chocolate right now?
2. Do you like to watch movies? Would you like to go to a movie with me later today?	2. Do you like to go shopping? Would you like to go shopping with me later today?
3. What do you like to do on weekends? What would you like to do this weekend?	3. What do you like to do in your free time? What would you like to do in your free time tomorrow?
4. What do you need to do this evening? What would you like to do this evening?	4. Do you like to travel? What countries would you like to visit?

□ **Exercise 44. Vocabulary and grammar.** (Chapters 4 and 5)

Part I. Work in pairs or as a class. Answer the questions. (Alternate questions if working in pairs.) Use the vocabulary from the box to help you.

the date	a bank	first name/given name
sign a check★	cash	middle initial
sign her name	a check	last name/family name/surname
write a check		name and address

1. What is Mary doing?
2. What is Mary's address?
3. What is Mary's full name?
4. What is Mary's middle initial?
5. What is Mary's last name?

6. How much money does Mary want?
7. What is in the upper-left corner of the check?
8. What is in the lower-left corner of the check?
9. What is the name of the bank?

Part II. Complete the sentences.

1. Mary is writing a _____.

2. She is signing _____ name.

3. The date on the check is _____.

4. Mary lives _____ 3471 Tree Street.

5. Mary lives _____ Chicago, Illinois.

6. Mary is writing a check for _____.

★*Check* (American English) is spelled *cheque* in British and Canadian English. The pronunciation of *check* and *cheque* is the same.

❑ **Exercise 45. Vocabulary and grammar.** (Chapters 4 and 5)

Part I. Work in pairs or as a class. Answer the questions. (Alternate questions if working in pairs.) Use the vocabulary from the box to help you.

cook	(in the) kitchen	bread
cook dinner	a list/a grocery list	butter
make dinner	a pepper shaker	coffee
taste (food)	a pot	an egg
	a refrigerator	pepper
	a salt shaker	salt
		a stove
		a clock

1. What is Dave doing?
2. What do you see in the picture?
3. Where is Dave?
4. Is Dave tasting his dinner?
5. Is Dave a good cook?

6. Where is the refrigerator?
7. What is on the refrigerator?
8. Is the food on the stove hot or cold?
9. Is the food in the refrigerator hot or cold?

Part II. Complete the sentences.

1. Dave is making dinner. He's _____ the kitchen.

2. There is a pot _____ the stove.

3. The stove is _____ the refrigerator.

4. There is a grocery list _____ the refrigerator door.

5. Dave needs _____ to the grocery store.

6. A salt shaker and a pepper shaker are _____ the stove.

7. There is hot food _____ top _____ the stove.

8. There is cold food _____ the refrigerator.

❑ **Exercise 46. Vocabulary and grammar.** (Chapters 4 and 5)

Part I. Work in pairs or as a class. Answer the questions. (Alternate questions if working in pairs.) Use the vocabulary from the box to help you.

sing	a cat	a living room
sit on a sofa/a couch	a dog	a rug
sleep	a fish	a singer
swim	a fishbowl	a TV set/a television set
watch TV/television	a floor	
	a lamp	

1. What are Nate and Lisa doing?

2. What do you see in the picture?

3. Are Nate and Lisa in the kitchen? Where are they?

4. Where is the lamp?

5. Where is the rug?

6. Where is the dog?

7. Where is the cat?

8. Is the cat walking? What is the cat doing?

9. What is the dog doing?

10. What is on top of the TV set?

11. Is the fish watching TV?

12. What is on the TV screen? What are Nate and Lisa watching?

Part II. Complete the sentences.

1. Nate and Lisa _____ watching TV. They like _____ watch TV.

2. They _____ sitting _____ a sofa.

3. They _____ sleeping.

4. There is a rug _____ the floor.

5. A dog _____ sleeping _____ the rug.

6. A cat _____ sleeping _____ the sofa.

❑   **Exercise 47. Let's talk: game.** (Chapters 4 and 5)
Work in teams. Make sentences about the picture. Every sentence needs to have a preposition. Use the vocabulary from the box to help you. One team member writes the sentences on paper. Your teacher will give you a time limit. The team with the most grammatically correct sentences wins.

draw a picture	a clock	a piece of paper
talk on the phone	a calendar	a telephone book
talk to (someone)	a heart	a wall
talk to each other	a phone/a telephone	
	a picture	
	a picture of a mountain	

Nick   Kate

❑   **Exercise 48. Looking at grammar.** (Chapters 4 and 5)
Choose the correct completion.

1. Jack lives _____ China.
   a. in   b. at   c. on

2. I need _____ a new notebook.
   a. buy   b. to buy   c. buying

3. _____ a cup of tea?
   a. Would you like   b. Do you like   c. Are you like

4. There _____ twenty-two desks in this room.
   a. be   b. is   c. are

5. Pilots sit _____ an airplane.
   a. in front of   b. in the front of   c. front of

6. I live _____ 6601 Fourth Avenue.
   a. in   b. on   c. at

156 CHAPTER 5

7. The students _____ do their homework.
    a. don't want   b. aren't wanting   c. don't want to

8. _____ a TV in Marisa's bedroom?
    a. Are there   b. There   c. Is there

❏ **Exercise 49. Check your knowledge.** (Chapter 5)
Correct the mistakes.

1. Do you want ^{to}∧ go downtown with me?

2. There's many problems in big cities today.

3. I'd like see a movie tonight.

4. We are needing to find a new apartment soon.

5. Mr. Rice woulds likes to have a cup of tea.

6. How many students there are in your class?

7. What day it is today?

8. I am like to leave right now.

9. How the weather in Kenya?

10. The teacher would like to checking our homework now.

❏ **Exercise 50. Looking at grammar.** (Chapters 4 and 5)
Complete the sentences with your own words. Use your own paper.

1. I need ____ because ____.

2. I want ____ because ____.

3. I would like ____.

4. Would you like ____?

5. Do you like ____?

6. There is ____.

7. There are ____.

8. I'm listening to ____,
    but I also hear ____.

9. I'm looking at ____,
    but I also see ____.

10. I'm thinking about ____.

11. I think that ____.

12. In my opinion, ____.

13. How many ____ are
    there ____?

14. Is there ____?

15. Are there ____?

❑ **Exercise 51. Reading and writing.** (Chapters 4 and 5)

Part I. Read the sample paragraph. <u>Underline</u> the verbs.

A Happy Dream

    I am walking alone in a big field of flowers. There are thousands of colorful flowers around me. The air smells very sweet. The sun is shining, and the sky is bright blue. There are some tall trees, and the wind is gently blowing. Birds are singing in the trees. I am feeling very calm. I have no worries. My life is very peaceful. I would like to stay here forever. I don't want to wake up.

Part II. Write about a dream that you remember that describes a place. It can be a happy or a sad dream. If you can't remember a dream, imagine one. Use present verbs.

Include this information:

  1. Where are you?
  2. What are you doing?
  3. Describe the place. What is there around you?
  4. How are you feeling?

Part III. Editing check: Work individually or change papers with a partner. Check (✓) for the following:

  1. ____ paragraph indent

  2. ____ capital letter at the beginning of each sentence

  3. ____ period at the end of each sentence

  4. ____ a verb in every sentence

  5. ____ correct use of prepositions of place

  6. ____ use of present progressive for activities right now

  7. ____ *there is* + singular noun

  8. ____ *there are* + plural noun

  9. ____ correct spelling (use a dictionary or spell-check)

Chapter 6
Nouns and Pronouns

❏ **Exercise 1. Warm-up.** (Chart 6-1)

Work in small groups. Make lists of things that belong to each category. Compare your lists with other groups' lists. All of the words you use in this exercise are called "nouns."

1. Name clothing you see in this room. (*shirt*, etc.)

2. Name kinds of fruit. (*apple*, etc.)

3. Name things you drink. (*coffee*, etc.)

4. Name parts of the body. (*head*, etc.)

5. Name kinds of animals. (*horse*, etc.)

6. Name famous cities in the world* (*Paris, Tokyo*, etc.)

7. Name languages.* (*English*, etc.)

8. Name school subjects. (*history*, etc.)

6-1 Nouns: Subjects and Objects

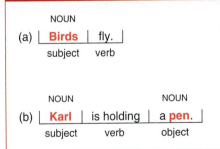

(a) **Birds** fly. *subject verb*	A NOUN is used as the SUBJECT of a sentence. A NOUN is used as the OBJECT of a verb.* In (a): **Birds** is a NOUN. It is used as the subject of the sentence.
(b) **Karl** is holding a **pen**. *subject verb object*	In (b): **pen** is a NOUN. It has the article **a** in front of it; **a pen** is used as the object of the verb **is holding**. Objects are NOUNS, and they come after a verb.

*Some verbs can be followed by an object. These verbs are called transitive verbs (*v.t.* in a dictionary). Some verbs cannot be followed by an object. These verbs are called intransitive verbs (*v.i.* in a dictionary).

---

*The names of cities and languages begin with capital letters.

❏ **Exercise 2. Looking at grammar.** (Chart 6-1)

Check (✓) the words that are nouns.

1. ____ eat
2. _✓_ dog
3. ____ nice
4. ____ math
5. ____ write
6. ____ have

7. ____ flowers
8. ____ juice
9. ____ ears
10. ____ Paris
11. ____ great
12. ____ English

❏ **Exercise 3. Looking at grammar.** (Chart 6-1)

For each sentence, write the object or write "no object."

NOUN

1. Cats catch mice. What do cats catch?   object = _____*mice*_____

2. Cats purr. What do cats do?   object = _____*no object*_____

3. Mice like cheese. What do mice like?   object = _____

4. Mice don't like people. Who don't mice like?   object = _____

5. Cats and mice have whiskers. What do cats and mice have?   object = _____

6. Cats sleep a lot. What do cats do?   object = _____

7. Cats scratch furniture. What do cats scratch?   object = _____

❏ **Exercise 4. Looking at grammar.** (Chart 6-1)

Check (✓) the sentences that have objects. Underline the objects.

1. a. _✓_ I am writing an email.
   b. _✓_ I am writing an email right now.
   c. ____ I am writing right now.

2. a. ____ Students memorize vocabulary.
   b. ____ Some students memorize every day.
   c. ____ Some students memorize vocabulary every day.

3. a. ____ The printer needs paper.
   b. ____ The printer needs ink and paper.
   c. ____ The printer has problems.

4. a. ____ The company is hiring.

   b. ____ The company is hiring workers.

   c. ____ The company is hiring today.

5. a. ____ Babies cry.

   b. ____ Babies cry frequently.

   c. ____ Babies cry loudly.

❑ **Exercise 5. Warm-up.** (Chart 6-2)
Complete each sentence with a preposition that describes the picture. Are the words in the box nouns, verbs, or adjectives?

above	across	in	on	under

1. The man is _____ the ground.

2. The man is _____ the plane.

3. The plane is _____ the sky.

6-2 Nouns as Objects of Prepositions

	NOUN			NOUN	
(a)	**Birds**	fly	in	the **sky**.	
	subject	verb	prep.	object of prep.	

A NOUN is also used as the OBJECT OF A PREPOSITION.

In (a): **in** is a PREPOSITION (prep.). The noun **sky** (with the article *the* in front) is the OBJECT of the preposition **in**.
In the sky is a PREPOSITIONAL PHRASE. (*phrase =* a group of words)

	NOUN		NOUN		NOUN
(b)	**Karl**	is holding	a **pen**	in	his **hand**.
	subject	verb	object	prep.	object of prep.

In (b): notice that the prepositional phrase comes after the noun it refers to.

INCORRECT: *Karl is holding in his hand a pen.*

SOME COMMON PREPOSITIONS

about	between	for	near	to
across	by	from	of	under
at	during	in	on	with

Exercise 6. Looking at grammar. (Chart 6-2)
Check (✓) the phrases that have prepositions. <u>Underline</u> the noun that is the object of each preposition.

1. ____ right now

2. ____ at noon

3. ____ on the counter

4. ____ in my closet

5. ____ some salt and pepper

6. ____ two days a week

7. ____ under the chair

8. ____ with a broom

a broom

Exercise 7. Looking at grammar. (Chart 6-2)
<u>Underline</u> the prepositions. Circle the object of each preposition.

1. a. A tutor helps Sari <u>with</u> her (homework.)

   b. A tutor helps Sari on Tuesday afternoons.

   c. A tutor helps Sari in the library.

2. a. The teacher erases the board.

   b. The teacher erases the board after class.

   c. The teacher erases the board with an eraser.

3. a. Elin cleans windows.

   b. Elin cleans in the afternoons.

   c. Elin cleans five days a week.

4. a. I do my homework in the library.

   b. I do my homework every weekend.

   c. I do my homework with my friends.

5. a. Birds fly during the day.

   b. Birds live in nests.

   c. Birds sit on eggs.

□ **Exercise 8. Looking at grammar.** (Charts 6-1 and 6-2)
Write the noun(s) for each sentence. Describe the grammatical structure of the sentences as shown in the examples.

Examples: Alicia studies chemistry. Noun(s): _____Alicia, chemistry_____

Alicia	studies	chemistry.	(none)	(none)
subject	verb	object of verb	preposition	object of prep.

The kids are playing in the park. Noun(s): _____kids, park_____

The kids	are playing	(none)	in	the park.
subject	verb	object of verb	preposition	object of prep.

1. Kids like candy. Noun(s): _____

subject	verb	object of verb	preposition	object of prep.

2. Dayo lives in Africa. Noun(s): _____

subject	verb	object of verb	preposition	object of prep.

3. The sun is shining. Noun(s): _____

subject	verb	object of verb	preposition	object of prep.

4. Lev is reading books about movies and filmmaking. Noun(s): _____

subject	verb	object of verb	preposition	object of prep.

5. Dara doesn't eat chicken or beef. Noun(s): _____

subject	verb	object of verb	preposition	object of prep.

6. Monkeys and birds eat fruit and insects. Noun(s): _____

subject	verb	object of verb	preposition	object of prep.

❑ **Exercise 9. Warm-up.** (Chart 6-3)

Do you agree or disagree with each sentence? Circle *yes* or *no*.

1. I cook delicious meals.		yes	no
2. I like raw vegetables.		yes	no
3. Fresh fruit is expensive.		yes	no

6-3 Adjectives with Nouns

(a) I don't like **cold** weather. adj. + noun (b) Alex is a **happy** child. adj. + noun (c) The **hungry** boy has a **fresh** apple. adj. + noun adj. + noun	An ADJECTIVE (adj.) describes a noun. In grammar, we say that adjectives modify nouns. The word *modify* means "change a little." Adjectives give a little different meaning to a noun: *cold weather, hot weather, nice weather, bad weather.* Adjectives come in front of nouns.
(d) The *weather is cold*. noun + be + adj.	Reminder: An adjective can also follow **be**; the adjective describes the subject of the sentence. (See Chart 1-7, p. 16.)

COMMON ADJECTIVES

beautiful - ugly	good - bad	angry	hungry
big - little	happy - sad	bright	important
big - small	large - small	busy	intelligent
boring - interesting	long - short	delicious	interesting
cheap - expensive	noisy - quiet	exciting	kind
clean - dirty	old - new	famous	lazy
cold - hot	old - young	favorite	nervous
dangerous - safe	poor - rich	free	nice
dry - wet	sour - sweet	fresh	ripe
easy - hard	strong - weak	healthy	serious
easy - difficult		honest	wonderful

❑ **Exercise 10. Looking at grammar.** (Chart 6-3)

Circle the nouns. <u>Underline</u> the adjectives. Draw an arrow from each adjective to the noun it describes.

1. Jake has an <u>expensive</u> (bike.)

2. My sister has a beautiful house.

3. We often eat at an Italian restaurant.

4. Valentina sings her favorite songs in the shower.

5. Olga likes American hamburgers.

6. You like sour apples, but I like sweet fruit.

❏ **Exercise 11. Let's talk: small groups.** (Chart 6-3)

Work in small groups. Take turns adding adjectives to the sentences. Use any adjectives that make sense. Think of at least three possible adjectives to complete each sentence.

1. I don't like _____*cold / hot / wet / rainy / bad / etc.*_____ weather.

2. Do you like _____ food?

3. I admire _____ people.

4. _____ people make me angry.

5. Pollution is a/an _____ big problem.

6. I had a/an _____ experience yesterday.

7. I don't like _____ cities.

8. I had a/an _____ dinner last night.

❏ **Exercise 12. Let's talk: small groups.** (Chart 6-3)

Part I. Complete each sentence with the name of a country and the adjective that goes with it.

1. Food from _____*China*_____ is _____*Chinese*_____ food.

2. Food from _____*Mexico*_____ is _____ food.

3. Food from _____ is _____ food

4. Food from _____ is _____ food.

5. Food from _____ is _____ food.

6. Food from _____ is _____ food.

7. Food from _____ is _____ food.

8. Food from _____ is _____ food.

Part II. What is the favorite ethnic food in your group? Give an example of this kind of food. Then find out the most popular ethnic food in other groups.

Example: Favorite ethnic food?
GROUP A: Italian
Example: An example of Italian food?
GROUP A: spaghetti

Favorite ethnic food in our group: _____

An example of this kind of food: _____

Part III. Working as a class, make a list of adjectives of nationality.

Choose <u>all</u> the correct completions for each sentence.

> | he | him | it |
> |------|------|----|
> | she | her | |

1. I understand _____.

2. You don't understand _____.

3. _____ understands us.

6-4 Subject Pronouns and Object Pronouns

SUBJECT PRONOUNS	OBJECT PRONOUNS	SUBJECT — OBJECT
(a) *I* speak English.	Bob knows *me*.	I — me
(b) *You* speak English.	Bob knows *you*.	you — you
(c) *She* speaks English.	Bob knows *her*.	she — her
(d) *He* speaks English.	Bob knows *him*.	he — him
(e) *It* starts at 8:00.	Bob knows *it*.	it — it
(f) *We* speak English.	Bob talks to *us*.	we — us
(g) *You* speak English.	Bob talks to *you*.	you — you
(h) *They* speak English.	Bob talks to *them*.	they — them
(i) I know *Tony*. *He* is a friendly person.	A pronoun has the same meaning as a noun. In (i): *He* has the same meaning as *Tony*.	
(j) I like *Tony*. I know *him* well.	In (j): *Him* has the same meaning as *Tony*. In grammar, we say that a pronoun "refers to" a noun. The pronouns *he* and *him* refer to the noun *Tony*.	
(k) I have *a red book*. *It* is on my desk.	Sometimes a pronoun refers to a *noun phrase*. In (k): *It* refers to the whole phrase *a red book*.	

❏ **Exercise 14. Looking at grammar.** (Chart 6-4)
Complete the sentences with the correct subject and object pronouns.

1. Jack loves Janey. _____*He*_____ loves _____*her*_____ very much.

2. Janey loves Jack. _____ loves _____ very much.

3. Janey and Jack love their daughter, Mia. _____ love _____ very much.

4. Janey and Jack love their son, Todd. _____ love _____ very much.

5. Todd loves his little sister, Mia. _____ loves _____ very much.

6. Janey loves her children. _____ loves _____ very much.

7. Jack loves his children. _____ loves _____ very much.

8. Janey and Jack love Todd and Mia. _____ love _____ very much.

❑ **Exercise 15. Looking at grammar.** (Chart 6-4)
Choose the correct answers.

1. Rita has a book. (She)/ It   bought   her /(it)   last week.

2. I know the new students, but Franco doesn't know   him / them   yet.

3. Where are my keys? Are   they / them   in your purse?

4. Ary is in Canada.   She / Her   is studying at a university.

5. Bert lives in my dorm. I eat breakfast with   he / him   every morning.

6. Sandra is my neighbor. I talk to   she / her   every day.   She / Her   and   I / me
   have interesting conversations.

7. I have two pictures on my bedroom wall. I like   it / them.   It / They   are beautiful.

8. Zola and I have a dinner invitation. Mr. and Mrs. Soto want   we / us   to come to
   dinner at their house.

9. Min has a new car.   He / It   is a convertible.

10. My husband and I have a new car.   We / Us   got   it / him   last month.

❑ **Exercise 16. Let's talk: interview.** (Chart 6-4)
Interview your classmates. Find someone who can answer *yes* to a question. Then ask the
follow-up question using the appropriate object pronoun.

Example:
STUDENT A: Do you send emails?
STUDENT B: No, I don't.
STUDENT A: (*Ask another student.*) Do you send emails?
STUDENT C: Yes, I do.

Follow-up question:
STUDENT A: When do you send **them**?
STUDENT C: I send **them** all day.

1. Do you do your homework?
   When do you . . . ?

2. Do you visit friends?
   When do you . . . ?

3. Do you read newspapers or magazines?
   When do you . . . ?

4. Do you talk to (*name of classmate*)?
   When do you . . . ?

5. Do you watch TV?
   When do you . . . ?

6. Do you buy groceries?
   When do you . . . ?

7. Do you wear boots?
   When do you . . . ?

8. Do you use a laptop computer?
   When do you . . . ?

❏ **Exercise 17. Looking at grammar.** (Chart 6-4)
Complete the sentences with the correct pronouns.

1. A: Do you know Zuri and Obi?

   B: Yes, _____ I _____ do. I live near _____ them _____ .

2. A: Is the chemical formula for water H_3O?

   B: No, _____ isn't. _____ is H_2O.

3. A: Do Julia and you want to come to the movie with us?

   B: Yes, _____ would. Julia and _____ would like to go to the movie

   with _____ .

4. A: Do Mr. and Mrs. Kelly live in the city?

   B: No, _____ don't. _____ live in the suburbs. I visited

   _____ last month.

5. A: Do you know how to spell "Mississippi"?

   B: Sure! I can spell _____. _____ is easy to spell.

6. A: Is Paul Peterson in your class?

   B: Yes, _____ is. I sit next to _____ .

❏ **Exercise 18. Listening.** (Chart 6-4)
Listen to the sentences. Notice that the "h" in **her** and **him** is often dropped in spoken English. The "th" in **them** can also be dropped. **Him** and **them** may sound the same.

1. Renata knows Oscar. She knows him very well.
2. Where does Shelley live? Do you have her address?
3. There's Vince. Let's go talk to him.
4. There are Dave and Lois. Let's go talk to them.

5. I'm looking online for JoAnne's phone number. What's her last name again?

6. I need to see our airline tickets. Do you have them?

❑ **Exercise 19. Listening.** (Charts 1-5 and 6-4)

Listen to each conversation and write the words you hear.

Example: You will hear: How is Mr. Park doing?

You will write: How _____*is*_____ Mr. Park doing?

You will hear: Great! I see him every week at the office.

You will write: Great! I see _____*him*_____ every week at the office.

1. A: Mika and _____ downtown this afternoon. Do you want to

   come _____?

   B: I don't think so, but thanks anyway. Chris and _____ to

   the library. _____ study for our test.

2. A: Hi, Abby. How do you like your new apartment?

   B: _____ great. I have a new roommate too. She's very nice.

   A: What's _____ name?

   B: Rita Lopez. Do you _____?

   A: No, but I know _____ brother. He's in my math class.

3. A: Do you see Mike and George very much?

   B: Yes, I see _____ often. We play video games at my house.

   A: Who usually wins?

   B: Mike. We never beat _____!

How many? Choose the correct number.

1. cup		one	two or more
2. class		one	two or more
3. countries		one	two or more
4. knives		one	two or more
5. radio		one	two or more

6-5 Nouns: Singular and Plural Forms

	SINGULAR	PLURAL	
(a)	one pen one apple one cup one elephant	two pen**s** three apple**s** four cup**s** five elephant**s**	To make the plural form of most nouns, add **-s**.
(b)	baby city	bab**ies** cit**ies**	End of noun: *consonant* + **-y** Plural form: change **y** to **i**, add **-es**
(c)	boy key	boy**s** key**s**	End of noun: *vowel* + **-y** Plural form: add **-s**
(d)	wife thief	wi**ves** thie**ves**	End of noun: **-fe** or **-f** Plural form: change **f** to **v**, add **-s** or **-es**
(e)	dish match class box	dish**es** match**es** class**es** box**es**	End of noun: **-sh, -ch, -ss, -x** Plural form: add **-es** Pronunciation: /əz/
(f)	tomato potato	tomato**es** potato**es**	End of noun: *consonant* + **-o** Plural form: add **-es**
	zoo radio	zoo**s** radio**s**	End of noun: *vowel* + **-o** Plural form: add **-s**

❏ **Exercise 21. Looking at grammar.** (Chart 6-5)
Complete the sentences. Use the plural form of the words in the boxes. Use each word only once.

Part I.

baby	city	cowboy	key	party
✓ boy	country	dictionary	lady	tray

1. Mr. and Mrs. Novak have one daughter and two sons. They have one girl and two _____boys_____ .

2. The students in my class come from many _____.

3. Women give birth to _____.

4. My money and my _____ are in my pocket.

5. I know the names of many _____ in the United States and Canada.

6. I like to go to _____ because I like to meet and talk to people.

7. People carry their food on _____ in a cafeteria.

8. We always check our _____ when we write compositions.

9. Good evening, _____ and gentlemen.

10. _____ ride horses.

Part II.

| knife | leaf | life | thief | wife |

11. It is fall. The _____ are falling from the trees.

12. Sue and Ann are married. They have husbands. They are _____.

13. We all have some problems in our _____.

14. Police officers catch _____.

15. Please put the _____, forks, and spoons on the table.

Part III.

bush	glass	sandwich	tomato
class	match	sex	zoo
dish	potato	tax	

16. Steve drinks eight _____ of water every day.

17. There are two _____: male and female.

18. Please put the _____ and the silverware on the table.

19. All citizens pay money to the government every year. They pay their _____.

20. I can see trees and _____ outside the window.

21. I want to light the candles. I need some _____.

22. When I make a salad, I use lettuce and _____.

23. Sometimes Pam has a hamburger and French-fried _____ for dinner.

24. Some animals live all of their lives in _____.

25. Mehmet is a student. He likes his _____.

26. We often eat _____ for lunch.

❏ **Exercise 22. Listening.** (Chart 6-5)

Choose the word you hear.

1. toy	(toys)		6. box	boxes
2. table	tables		7. package	packages
3. face	faces		8. chair	chairs
4. hat	hats		9. edge	edges
5. office	offices		10. top	tops

❑ **Exercise 23. Listening.** (Chart 6-5)

Listen to each sentence. Circle the word you hear.

1. desk   (desks)
2. place   places
3. sandwich   sandwiches
4. sentence   sentences
5. apple   apples

6. exercise   exercises
7. piece   pieces
8. rose   roses
9. bush   bushes
10. college   colleges

a rose

a rose bush

❑ **Exercise 24. Grammar and speaking.** (Chart 6-5)

Write the correct ending. Write Ø if no ending is necessary. Then decide if you agree or disagree with the sentence. Share some of your answers with a partner or the class. Remember: *a* = *one*.

1. I like banana _s_, strawberry _ies_, and peach _es_ .   yes   no

2. I eat a banana_____ every day.   yes   no

3. My favorite animals are elephant_____.   yes   no

4. A baby elephant_____ is cute.   yes   no

5. Baby_____ are cute.   yes   no

6. The grammar exercise_____ in this book are easy.   yes   no

7. A ride on a motorcycle_____ is fun.   yes   no

8. A ride on an airplane_____ is comfortable.   yes   no

9. This exercise_____ is easy.   yes   no

10. Cockroach_____ are ugly, and they scare me.   yes   no

a cockroach

❏ **Exercise 25. Warm-up.** (Chart 6-6)

Write *a* before the singular nouns.

1. a. _____ child

   b. _____ children

2. a. _____ teeth

   b. _____ tooth

3. a. _____ foot

   b. _____ feet

6-6 Nouns: Irregular Plural Forms

	SINGULAR	PLURAL	EXAMPLES
(a)	child	children	Mr. Smith has one *child*. Mr. Cook has two **children**.
(b)	foot	feet	I have a right *foot* and a left *foot*. I have two **feet**.
(c)	man	men	I see a *man* on the street. I see two **men** on the street.
(d)	mouse	mice	My cat sees a *mouse*. Cats like to catch **mice**.
(e)	tooth	teeth	My *tooth* hurts. My **teeth** are white.
(f)	woman	women	There's one *woman* in our class. There are ten **women** in your class.
(g)	sheep	sheep	Annie drew a picture of one *sheep*. Tommy drew a picture of two **sheep**.
(h)	fish	fish	Bob has an aquarium. He has one *fish*. Sue has an aquarium. She has seven **fish**.
(i)	(none)*	people	There are fifteen **people** in this room. (Notice: *People* does not have a final **-s**.)

* ***People*** is always plural. It has no singular form.

❑ **Exercise 26. Looking at grammar.** (Chart 6-6)

Complete the sentences with the correct form of the noun in each picture.

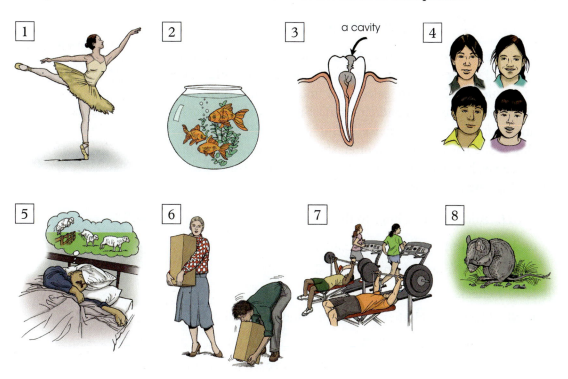

1. The dancer is standing on one _____. After a dance, her _____ are sore.

2. There are three _____ in the bowl. One _____ is blowing bubbles.

3. The dentist is checking my _____. One _____ has a cavity.

4. Janine has four _____. I have one _____.

5. Sometimes, I have trouble sleeping, so I count _____. One _____, two _____, . . . one hundred _____. Oh, no, I'm still awake!

6. This _____ is strong. This _____ is weak.

7. Are _____ stronger than _____, or are _____ stronger than _____?

8. There is a _____ in my bedroom wall. There are _____ under my house.

❏ **Exercise 27. Reading and grammar.** (Charts 6-5 and 6-6)

Part I. Read the story. Look at new vocabulary with your teacher first.

An Online Shopper

Tara likes to buy clothes online. She lives far away from stores and shopping malls. She knows many good online sites. She frequently checks for sales. She finds shirts, pants, and jackets for her husband and children. She buys skirts, dresses, warm coats, and hats for herself. But she doesn't get shoes online. She has big feet and often shoes don't fit. Sometimes she returns her purchases. For Tara, the best websites have free shipping for returns.

> *Do you know these words?*
> malls
> sales
> purchases
> free shipping

Part II. Add plural endings to the nouns. Write Ø for "no ending."

1. Tara shops at online site_____.

2. She lives far away from mall_____.

3. She checks website_____ for sale_____.

4. She like to buy clothes for her husband_____ and child_____.

5. She buys jacket_____, skirt_____, shirt_____, dress_____, and coat_____.

6. She doesn't buy shoe_____ online because she has big f_____.

7. Tara likes website_____ with free shipping for return_____.

❏ **Exercise 28. Looking at grammar.** (Charts 6-1 → 6-6)

A *complete sentence* is a group of words that has a subject and a verb. An *incomplete sentence* is a group of words that does not have a subject and a verb.

If the words are a complete sentence, change the first letter to a capital letter and add final punctuation (a period or a question mark). If the words are an incomplete sentence, write "NC" to mean "not complete."

1. M̸onkeys like bananas.

2. in my garden → *NC*

3. D̸o you like sour apples?

4. this class ends at two o'clock

5. teaches English

6. my mother works

7. in an office

8. my mother works in an office

9. does your brother have a job

10. does not work

11. my sister lives in an apartment

12. has a roommate

13. the apartment has two bedrooms

14. a small kitchen and a big living room

15. on the third floor

❏ **Exercise 29. Looking at grammar.** (Charts 6-1 → 6-6)
Choose the correct completion.

1. My sister and I live together. Our parents often call or visit _____.
   a. us   b. them   c. we   d. they

2. Dan has a broken leg. I visit _____ every day.
   a. he   b. him   c. them   d. it

3. Maya and I are good friends. _____ spend a lot of time together.
   a. They   b. You   c. We   d. She

4. Our kids enjoy the zoo. We often take _____ to the zoo.
   a. it   b. they   c. them   d. him

5. Cristina drives an old car. She takes good care of _____.
   a. her   b. them   c. it   d. him

6. Mark and _____ don't know Mr. Sung.
   a. I   b. me   c. us   d. them

7. Ms. Vargas is a lawyer in Chicago. Do you know _____?
   a. them   b. it   c. him   d. her

8. Ahmed lives near Yoko and _____.
   a. I   b. me   c. he   d. she

9. My sister and a friend are visiting me. _____ are visiting here for two days.
   a. She   b. They   c. We   d. Them

10. Do _____ have the correct time?
    a. you   b. them   c. him   d. her

❏ **Exercise 30. Warm-up.** (Chart 6-7)
Complete the sentences.

Who does this book belong to?

1. STUDENT A: It's his book   OR   It's his.
2. STUDENT B: It's her book.   OR   It's hers.
3. STUDENT C: It's your book.   OR   It's yours.
4. STUDENT D: It's our book.   OR   It's _____.
5. STUDENT E: It's their book.   OR   It's _____.

Do you know this exception?

6. It's my book.   OR   It's _____.

6-7 Possessive Pronouns: *Mine, Yours, His, Hers, Ours, Theirs*

	POSSESSIVE ADJECTIVE	POSSESSIVE PRONOUN	
(a) This book belongs to me. It is *my* book. It is *mine*.			A POSSESSIVE ADJECTIVE is used in front of a noun: *my* book.
	my your her his our their	mine yours hers his ours theirs	
(b) That book belongs to you. It is *your* book. It is *yours*.			
(c) That book is *mine*. INCORRECT: *That is mine book.*			A POSSESSIVE PRONOUN is used alone, without a noun following it, as in (c).

❏ **Exercise 31. Looking at grammar.** (Chart 6-7)
Write or say the correct possessive pronoun.

1. It's your money. It's _____.

2. It's our money. It's _____.

3. It's her money. It's _____.

4. It's their money. It's _____.

5. It's his money. It's _____.

6. It's my money. It's _____.

7. The money belongs to Matt. It's _____.

8. The money belongs to Elena. It's _____.

9. The money belongs to Matt and Elena. It's _____.

10. The money belongs to Stuart and me. It's _____.

□ **Exercise 32. Looking at grammar.** (Charts 2-5, 6-2, 6-4, and 6-7)
Complete the sentences. Use object pronouns, possessive adjectives, and possessive pronouns.

1. *I* own this book.

    a. This book belongs to _____*me*_____.

    b. This is _____*my*_____ book.

    c. This book is _____*mine*_____.

2. *They* own these books.

    a. These books belong to _____.

    b. These are _____ books.

    c. These books are _____.

3. *You* own that book.

    a. That book belongs to _____.

    b. That is _____ book.

    c. That book is _____.

4. *She* owns this pen.

    a. This pen belongs to _____.

    b. This is _____ pen.

    c. This pen is _____.

5. *He* owns that pen.

    a. That pen belongs to _____.

    b. That is _____ pen.

    c. That pen is _____.

6. *We* own those books.

    a. Those books belong to _____.

    b. Those are _____ books.

    c. Those books are _____.

Write the correct completion.

1. Is this _____*your*_____ pen?
   <u>your / yours</u>

2. Please give this dictionary to Oksana. It's _____.
   <u>her / hers</u>

3. A: Don't forget _____ hat. Here.
   <u>your / yours</u>

   B: No, that's not _____ hat. _____ is green.
   <u>my / mine</u>   <u>My / Mine</u>

4. A: Please take this bouquet of flowers as a gift from me. Here. They're

   _____.
   <u>your / yours</u>

   B: Thank you. You're very thoughtful.

5. A: That car belongs to Mr. and Mrs. Townsend.

   B: No, that's not _____. _____ car is new.
   <u>their / theirs</u>   <u>Their / Theirs</u>

6. A: Malik and I really like _____ new apartment. It has lots of space.
   <u>our / ours</u>

   How do you like _____?
   <u>your / yours</u>

   B: _____ is small, but it's comfortable.
   <u>Our / Ours</u>

7. A: Excuse me. Is this _____ umbrella?
   <u>your / yours</u>

   B: I don't have an umbrella. Ask Jay. Maybe it's _____.
   <u>he / his</u>

8. A: This isn't _____ phone.
   <u>my / mine</u>

   B: Are you sure?

   A: Yes, I have a flip phone. This one belongs to Carla. _____ is a
   <u>Her / Hers</u>
   smartphone.

❑ **Exercise 34. Warm-up.** (Chart 6-8)
Choose all the grammatically correct sentences.

1. His bedroom is messy.
2. The boy his bedroom is messy.
3. The boy bedroom is messy.
4. The boy's bedroom is messy.

6-8 Possessive Nouns

		SINGULAR NOUN	POSSESSIVE FORM	To show that a person possesses something, add an apostrophe (') and -s to a singular noun.
(a)	My *friend* has a car. My **friend's** car is blue.	**friend**	**friend's**	POSSESSIVE NOUN, SINGULAR: *noun + apostrophe (') + -s*
(b)	The *student* has a book. The **student's** book is red.	**student**	**student's**	

		PLURAL NOUN	POSSESSIVE FORM	Add an apostrophe (') at the end of a plural noun (after the -s).
(c)	The *students* have books. The **students'** books are red.	**students**	**students'**	POSSESSIVE NOUN, PLURAL: *noun + -s + apostrophe (')*
(d)	My *friends* have a car. My **friends'** car is blue.	**friends**	**friends'**	

❏ **Exercise 35. Looking at grammar.** (Chart 6-8)
Complete the sentences with the correct nouns.

1. Rebecca's dress is very colorful.

   The _____dress_____ belongs to _____Rebecca_____.

2. Dave's car was expensive.

   The _____ belongs to _____.

3. Where is Samir's room?

   The _____ belongs to _____.

4. Is the doctor's office crowded?

   The _____ belongs to _____.

❏ **Exercise 36. Looking at grammar.** (Chart 6-8)
Choose the correct answer for each boldfaced noun.

1. My **teacher's** office is large.   one teacher   more than one
2. My **teachers'** office is large.   one teacher   more than one
3. The **nurses'** uniform is green.   one nurse   more than one
4. The **nurse's** uniform is green.   one nurse   more than one
5. My **friends'** work is interesting.   one friend   more than one
6. The **dentist's** schedule is busy.   one dentist   more than one

Exercise 37. Looking at grammar. (Chart 6-8)
Complete the sentences with your classmates' names.

1. _____ hair is short and straight.

2. _____ grammar book is on her desk.

3. _____ last name is _____.

4. I don't know _____ address.

5. _____ eyes are brown.

6. _____ shirt is blue.

7. _____ backpack is on the floor.

8. I need to borrow _____ pen.

❏ **Exercise 38. Game.** (Chart 6-8)
Work in teams. Complete the sentences with words from the box. You may use a word more than one time. The team with the most correct answers wins.

brother	father	son
children	mother	wife
daughter	sister	

Family relationships

1. My uncle is my father's _____.

2. My grandmother is my mother's _____.

3. My brother-in-law is my husband's _____.

4. My sister's _____ are my nieces and nephews.

5. My niece is my brother's _____.

6. My nephew is my sister's _____.

7. My aunt's _____ is my mother.

8. My wife's _____ is my mother-in-law.

9. My brother's _____ is my sister-in-law.

10. My father's _____ and _____ are my grandparents.

Complete the sentences. Use the correct possessive form of the given words.

1. I   a. This bookbag is _____*mine*_____ .

    Ava   b. That bookbag is _____*Ava's*_____ .

    I   c. _____*My*_____ bookbag is red.

    she   d. _____*Hers*_____ is green.

2. we   a. These books are _____ .

    they   b. Those books are _____ .

    we   c. _____ books are on the table.

    they   d. _____ are on the desk.

3. Don   a. This raincoat is _____ .

    Kate   b. That raincoat is _____ .

    he   c. _____ is light brown.

    she   d. _____ is light blue.

4. I   a. This notebook is _____ .

    you   b. That one is _____ .

    I   c. _____ has _____ name on it.

    you   d. _____ has _____ name on it.

5. Ray   a. _____ apartment is on Pine Street.

    we   b. _____ is on Main Street.

    he   c. _____ apartment has three rooms.

    we   d. _____ has four rooms.

6. I   a. This is _____ pen.

    you   b. That one is _____ .

    I   c. _____ is in _____ pocket.

    you   d. _____ is on _____ desk.

7. we   a. _____ car is a Chevrolet.

       they   b. _____ is a Volkswagen.

       we   c. _____ gets 17 miles to the gallon.

       they   d. _____ car gets 30 miles to the gallon.

8. Gabi   a. These books are _____ .

       Evan   b. Those are _____ .

       she   c. _____ are on _____ desk.

       he   d. _____ are on _____ desk.

❏ **Exercise 40. Listening.** (Chart 6-8)

Listen to each sentence and choose the word you hear.

Example: You will hear: Your dad's job sounds interesting.

            You will choose: dad

1. Mack	Mack's	5. friend	friend's
2. Mack	Mack's	6. friend	friend's
3. teacher	teacher's	7. manager	manager's
4. teacher	teacher's	8. cousin	cousin's

❏ **Exercise 41. Looking at grammar.** (Chart 6-8)

Add apostrophes where necessary.

     Brian's
1. ~~Brians~~ last name is Wolf.

2. Stefan likes to work late at night. → *(no change)*

3. My teachers give a lot of homework.

4. My teachers names are Ms. Cordova and Mr. Durisova.

5. My teachers first name is Ellen.

6. The teacher collected all the students test papers at the end of the class.

7. Nicole is a girls name.

8. Erica and Natalie are girls names.

9. Do you know Monicas brother?

10. Ryans friends visited him last night.

❏ **Exercise 42. Warm-up.** (Chart 6-9)
Choose the correct answer.

1. Who is that?
   a. It's Tom.
   b. It's Tom's.

2. Whose is that?
   a. It's Tom.
   b. It's Tom's.

6-9 Questions with *Whose*

(a) **Whose book** is this? → **Mine.** → It's **mine**. → It's **my** book. (b) **Whose books** are these? → **Rita's.** → They're **Rita's**. → They're **Rita's** books.	**Whose** asks about possession. **Whose** is often used with a noun (e.g., *whose book*), as in (a) and (b).
(c) **Whose** is this? (*The speaker is pointing to one book.*) (d) **Whose** are these? (*The speaker is pointing to some books.*)	**Whose** can be used without a noun if the meaning is clear, as in (c) and (d).
(e) **Who's** your teacher?	In (e): **Who's** = **who is** **Whose** and **who's** have the same pronunciation.

Whose is this? There's no name on it. Who's the artist?

❏ **Exercise 43. Looking at grammar.** (Chart 6-9)
Choose the correct answer.

1. Whose birthday is today?
   a. Audrey's.
   b. Audrey.

2. Who is on the phone?
   a. Audrey's.
   b. Audrey.

3. Who is working at the bakery?
   a. Allen.
   b. Allen's.

4. Whose bakery is the best?
   a. Allen.
   b. Allen's.

5. Who's going to join us for lunch?
   a. Toshi's.
   b. Toshi.

6. Whose dirty socks are on the floor?
   a. Julian's.
   b. Julian.

❏ **Exercise 44. Looking at grammar.** (Chart 6-9)
Complete the sentences with **Whose** or **Who's**.

1. _____ your roommate this year?

2. _____ pen is this?

3. _____ on the phone?

4. _____ that?

5. _____ is that?

6. _____ making so much noise?

❏ **Exercise 45. Listening.** (Chart 6-9)
Listen to each sentence. Choose **Whose** or **Who's**.

1. Whose	Who's	6. Whose	Who's
2. Whose	Who's	7. Whose	Who's
3. Whose	Who's	8. Whose	Who's
4. Whose	Who's	9. Whose	Who's
5. Whose	Who's	10. Whose	Who's

❏ **Exercise 46. Looking at grammar.** (Charts 2-6, 2-7, and 6-9)
Write the correct completion.

1. Whose watch ____*is*____ ____*this*____?
         is / are   this / these

2. Whose glasses _____ _____?
                 is / are   that / those

3. Whose hat _____ _____?
              is / are   that / those

4. Whose shoe _____ _____?
               is / are   this / these

5. Whose keys _____ _____?
               is / are   this / these

❏ **Exercise 47. Let's talk: pairwork.** (Chart 6-9)
Work with a partner. Touch or point to something in the classroom that belongs to someone and ask a question with **Whose**.

Example:
PARTNER A: (*points to a book*) Whose book is this?
PARTNER B: It's mine. / Mine. / It's my book.
PARTNER A: Your turn.

❑ **Exercise 48. Warm-up.** (Chart 6-10)
Choose the answer that describes the picture. Only one answer is correct.

a. Woman's Restroom
b. Women's Restroom

6-10 Possessive: Irregular Plural Nouns

(a) The ***children's*** *toys* are on the floor.	Irregular plural nouns (*children, men, women, people*) have an irregular plural possessive form. The apostrophe (') comes <u>before</u> the final **-s**.
(b) That store sells ***men's*** *clothing*.	REGULAR PLURAL POSSESSIVE NOUN: *the* **students'** *books*
(c) That store sells ***women's*** *clothing*.	IRREGULAR PLURAL POSSESSIVE NOUN:
(d) I like to know about other ***people's*** *lives*.	*the* **women's** *books*

❑ **Exercise 49. Looking at grammar.** (Charts 6-8 and 6-10)
Complete each sentence with the possessive form of the given noun.

These books belong to . . .

1. Maggie.   They're _____*Maggie's*_____ books.

2. my friend.   They're _____ books.

3. my friends.   They're _____ books.

4. the child.   They're _____ books.

5. the children.   They're _____ books.

6. the woman.   They're _____ books.

7. the women.   They're _____ books.

❏ **Exercise 50. Looking at grammar.** (Charts 6-8 and 6-10)
Complete each sentence with the possessive form of the given noun.

1. children   That store sells _____*children's*_____ books.

2. women   Vanessa and Angelina are _____ names.

3. person   A biography is the story of a _____ life.

4. people   Biographies are the stories of _____ lives.

5. students   _____ lives are busy.

6. brother   Do you know my _____ wife?

7. wife   Vanya fixed his _____ old

                sewing machine.

8. dog   My _____ name is Fido.

9. dogs   My _____ names are Fido and Rover.

10. men   Are Jim and Tom _____ names?

11. man, woman Chris can be a _____ nickname or a

                _____ nickname.

12. children   Our _____ school is near our house.

❏ **Exercise 51. Looking at grammar.** (Charts 6-8 and 6-10)
Choose the correct completion.

1. The ____ work hard.
   a. students   b. student's   c. students'

2. My ____ name is Honey.
   a. cats   b. cat's   c. cats'

3. My ____ are traveling in Spain.
   a. cousins   b. cousin's   c. cousins'

4. My ____ is meeting them in two weeks.
   a. uncle   b. uncle's   c. uncles'

5. The three ____ coats are in the closet.
   a. boys   b. boy's   c. boys'

6. The _____ is riding his bike.
   a. boys   b. boy   c. boys'

7. We have three _____ and one girl in my family.
   a. boys   b. boy's   c. boys'

8. Two of my _____ live near me.
   a. friends   b. friend's   c. friends'

9. My _____ names are Frank and Martin.
   a. friend   b. friend's   c. friends'

10. My best _____ name is Andy.
    a. friends   b. friend's   c. friends'

❑ **Exercise 52. Check your knowledge.** (Chapter 6)
Correct the mistakes.

1. Jamil a car has. → *Jamil has a car.*

2. Babys cry.

3. Kurt helps Justin and I.

4. Our teacher gives tests difficult.

5. Charlie is cutting with a lawnmower the grass.

6. Do you know Yuko roommate?

7. My roommate desk is always a mess.

8. There are nineteen peoples in my class.

9. Veronica and Victor have three childrens.

10. Excuse me. Where is the men room?

11. There is twenty classroom in this building.

12. Mr. Torro is our teacher. Me like he very much.

13. Does that store sell children toys?

14. Whose is book on the chair?

15. It is mine book.

a lawnmower

Part I. Read the paragraph. Look at the boldface words. Write "S" if the word is singular and "P" if it is plural.

                          S

      My favorite **store** is City Market. It is a grocery store. I like this store because it has many kinds of **groceries**. I can buy interesting **ingredients** there. I often cook **dishes** from my **country**. City Market has a big **selection** of rice and fresh **vegetables**. I like to buy fresh, not frozen, vegetables and meat, but the meat at City Market is expensive, so I don't buy much. The store is near my **house**, and I can walk to it. The **people** are friendly and helpful.

Part II. Where do you like to shop? It can be a grocery store, clothes store, online store, etc. Complete the sentences. Combine the sentences into a paragraph. Add a few extra details to make your writing more interesting. Begin with *My favorite store is . . . .*

1. My favorite store is _____ .

2. I like this store because it _____ .

3. I often/sometimes buy _____ .

4. I don't like to buy _____ .

5. The store is _____ .

Part III. Work individually or change papers with a partner. Check (✓) for the following:

1. _____ indented paragraph
2. _____ capital letter at the beginning of each sentence
3. _____ period at the end of each sentence
4. _____ a verb in every sentence
5. _____ correct use of *-s/-es/-ies* endings for plural nouns
6. _____ correct use of irregular plural forms
7. _____ correct spelling (use a dictionary or spell-check)

Chapter 7
Count and Noncount Nouns

❏ **Exercise 1. Warm-up.** (Chart 7-1)
Which of the following can you count? There is only one possibility.

1. ____ sugar bowl

2. ____ sugar

7-1 Nouns: Count and Noncount

	SINGULAR	PLURAL	
COUNT NOUN	*a book* *one book*	*books* *two books* *some books* *a lot of books*	**A COUNT NOUN** SINGULAR: *a* + noun, *one* + noun PLURAL: noun + *-s*
NONCOUNT NOUN	*mail* *some mail* *a lot of mail*	(no plural form)	**A NONCOUNT NOUN** SINGULAR: Do not use *a*. Do not use *one*. PLURAL: A noncount noun does not have a plural form.

COMMON NONCOUNT NOUNS

advice	mail	bread	pepper
furniture	money	cheese	rice
help	music	coffee	salt
homework	traffic	food	soup
information	vocabulary	fruit	sugar
jewelry	weather	meat	tea
luck	work	milk	water

❏ **Exercise 2. Looking at grammar.** (Chart 7-1)

Look at the *italicized* words. <u>Underline</u> the noun. Is it count or noncount?

1.	He is sitting on *a* <u>*chair*</u>.	(count)	noncount
2.	He is sitting on *old* <u>*furniture*</u>.	count	(noncount)
3.	She has *a coin*.	count	noncount
4.	She has *some money*.	count	noncount
5.	The street is full of *heavy traffic*.	count	noncount
6.	There are *a lot of cars* in the street.	count	noncount
7.	I know *a fact* about bees.	count	noncount
8.	I have *some information* about bees.	count	noncount
9.	The teacher gives us *a lot of homework*.	count	noncount
10.	We have *an easy assignment*.	count	noncount
11.	I like *classical music*.	count	noncount
12.	Would you like *some coffee?*	count	noncount
13.	Our school has *a big library*.	count	noncount
14.	We are learning *new vocabulary* every day.	count	noncount
15.	I need *some advice*.	count	noncount
16.	Peter has *a good job*.	count	noncount
17.	He likes *his work*.	count	noncount
18.	Margo wears *a lot of bracelets*.	count	noncount

❏ **Exercise 3. Vocabulary and grammar.** (Chart 7-1)

Describe the pictures. Add *-s* to the ends of the words if necessary or write Ø (no ending).

PICTURE	DESCRIPTION
	1. one ring *Ø*
	2. two ring *s*

PICTURE	DESCRIPTION
	3. three ring _s_
	4. some jewelry _∅_
	5. two letter _____
	6. one postcard _____
	7. some mail _____
	8. one couch _____
	9. two table _____
	10. some chair _____
	11. some furniture _____
	12. a. a lot of car _____ b. a lot of traffic _____
	13. a. a lot of money _____ b. a lot of coin _____

Work in small groups. List the noncount nouns. Find the count nouns that are close in meaning. Use *a/an* with the count nouns.

advice	desk	jewelry	music
assignment	fact	job	song
bracelet	furniture	✓ letter	suggestion
cloud	homework	✓ mail	weather
coin	information	money	work

	NONCOUNT	COUNT
1.	*mail*	*a letter*
2.		
3.		
4.		
5.		
6.		
7.		
8.		
9.		
10.		

❏ **Exercise 5.** **Looking at grammar.** (Chart 7-1)

Complete the nouns with **-s** or **Ø** (no article).

1. a house_____, one house_____, two house_____, a lot of house_____, some house_____

2. a car_____, one car_____, four car_____, a lot of car_____

3. water_____, some water_____, a lot of water_____

4. a computer_____, three computer_____, some computer_____, a lot of computer_____

❏ **Exercise 6.** **Game.** (Chart 7-1)

Work in teams. Complete the sentences with as many nouns as possible. Write the names of things you see in the classroom. The team with the most grammatically correct nouns wins.

I see . . .

1. a	3. five	5. a lot of
2. two	4. some	6. many

❑ **Exercise 7. Game.** (Chapter 6 and Chart 7-1)
Work in groups or individually. The object of the game is to fill in each list with nouns that belong to the category of that list. If possible, write one noun that begins with each letter of the alphabet. When you finish your lists, count the nouns you have. That is your score. Who has the highest score?

	LIST 1 Things in nature	LIST 2 Things you eat and drink	LIST 3 Animals and insects	LIST 4 Things for sale at (*name of a local store*)
A	air			
B	bushes			
C				
D				
E	earth			
F	fish			
G	grass			
H				
I	ice			
J				
K				
L	leaves			
M				
N				
O	ocean			
P	plants			
Q				
R	rain			
S	stars			
T	trees			
U				
V				
W	water			
X				
Y				
Z				
	Score: ___13___	Score: _____	Score: _____	Score: _____

Exercise 8. Warm-up (Chart 7-2)
Are the words in red correct or incorrect?

1. I work in an office.
2. It is in a hotel.
3. I take an elevator to the top floor.
4. I have an amazing view.

7-2 Using *A* vs. *An*

(a) **A dog** is **an animal**.	**A** and **an** are used in front of singular count nouns. In (a): **dog** and **animal** are singular count nouns.
(b) I work in **an office**. (c) Mr. Tang is **an old man**.	Use **an** in front of words that begin with the vowels *a, e, i,* and *o*: *an apartment, an elephant, an idea, an ocean.* In (c): Notice that **an** is used because the adjective (*old*) begins with a vowel and comes in front of a singular count noun (*man*).
(d) I have **an uncle**. COMPARE (e) He works at **a university**.	Use **an** if a word that begins with "u" has a vowel sound: *an uncle, an ugly picture.* Use **a** if a word that begins with "u" has a /yu/ sound: *a university, a usual event.*
(f) I need **an hour** to finish my work. COMPARE (g) I live in **a house**. He lives in **a hotel**.	In some words that begin with "h," the "h" is not pronounced. Instead, the word begins with a vowel sound and **an** is used: *an hour, an honor.* In most words that begin with "h," the "h" is pronounced. Use **a** if the "h" is pronounced.

❏ **Exercise 9. Looking at grammar.** (Chart 7-2)
Complete the sentences with *a* or *an*.

1. Lars is eating _____ apple.

2. Tia is eating _____ banana.

3. Alice works in _____ office.

4. I have _____ idea.

5. I have _____ good idea.

6. Ada is taking _____ easy class.

7. Cuba is _____ island near the United States.

8. _____ hour has sixty minutes.

9. _____ healthy person gets regular exercise.

10. Elsa is _____ honest worker.

11. Markus needs _____ math tutor.

12. Bashir has _____ exciting job. He is _____ pilot. He flies helicopters.

❏ **Exercise 10. Listening.** (Chart 7-2)

Listen to each sentence. Choose the word you hear.

Example: You will hear: I come from a small town.
         You will choose: ⓐ   an

1. a   an   6. a   an
2. a   an   7. a   an
3. a   an   8. a   an
4. a   an   9. a   an
5. a   an   10. a   an

❏ **Exercise 11. Warm-up** (Chart 7-3)

Answer the questions about the nouns in the box.

a bike	some cars	some motorcycles
some pollution	some traffic	a truck

1. Which nouns are count? _____

2. Which nouns are noncount? _____

3. Which nouns are singular count? _____

4. Which nouns are plural count? _____

Can you make a rule about when to use *some?*

7-3 Using *A/An* vs. *Some*

(a) I have **a** pen.	**A/An** is used in front of SINGULAR COUNT nouns. In (a): The word **pen** is a singular count noun.
(b) I have **some** pens.	**Some** is used in front of PLURAL COUNT nouns. In (b): The word **pens** is a plural count noun.
(c) I have **some** rice.	**Some** is used in front of NONCOUNT nouns.* In (c): The word **rice** is a noncount noun.

* Reminder: Noncount nouns do not have a plural form. Noncount nouns are grammatically singular.

❑ **Exercise 12. Looking at grammar.** (Chart 7-3)
Look at each noun and circle the correct word: *a, an,* or *some*. Then decide if the noun is singular count, plural count, or noncount.

			SINGULAR COUNT	PLURAL COUNT	NONCOUNT
1. a	an	(some) letters		✓	
2. a	an	(some) mail			✓
3. (a)	an	some letter	✓		
4. a	an	some table			
5. a	an	some tables			
6. a	an	some furniture			
7. a	an	some car			
8. a	an	some automobiles			
9. a	an	some buses			
10. a	an	some traffic			
11. a	an	some advice			
12. a	an	some egg			
13. a	an	some eggs			
14. a	an	some hour			
15. a	an	some minutes			

Exercise 13. Looking at grammar. (Chart 7-3)

Write each word from the box in the correct column.

| ✓ answer | computer | evening | ideas | uncle | word |
| ✓ boy | day | idea | mail | vocabulary | words |

a	*an*	*some*
boy	answer	

❑ **Exercise 14. Looking at grammar.** (Chart 7-3)

Complete each sentence with *a, an,* or *some*. Is each noun singular count or noncount?

I have . . .

1.	_____some_____ fruit.	singular count	(noncount)
2.	_____ apple.	singular count	noncount
3.	_____ money.	singular count	noncount
4.	_____ euro.	singular count	noncount
5.	_____ sandwich.	singular count	noncount
6.	_____ flour.	singular count	noncount
7.	_____ soup.	singular count	noncount
8.	_____ letter.	singular count	noncount
9.	_____ information.	singular count	noncount
10.	_____ water.	singular count	noncount
11.	_____ word.	singular count	noncount
12.	_____ homework.	singular count	noncount
13.	_____ problem.	singular count	noncount
14.	_____ answer.	singular count	noncount

Work in small groups. Complete the lists with nouns. You may use adjectives with the nouns. Share some of your answers with the class.

1. things you usually see in an apartment

   a. a _____

   b. an _____

   c. some _____ (*plural noun*)

   d. some _____ (*noncount noun*)

2. things you usually see in a classroom

   a. a _____

   b. an _____

   c. some _____ (*plural noun*)

   d. some _____ (*noncount noun*)

3. things you usually see outdoors

   a. a _____

   b. an _____

   c. some _____ (*plural noun*)

   d. some _____ (*noncount noun*)

❏ **Exercise 16. Looking at grammar.** (Chart 7-3)
Complete the sentences with *a*/*an* or *some*.

1. Marisol is wearing ____*some*____ silver jewelry. She's wearing

   ____*a*____ necklace and ____*some*____ earrings.

2. Amir and I are busy. I have _____ homework to do.

   He has _____ work to do.

3. Asha has _____ job. She is _____ teacher.

4. We have _____ table, _____ couch, and _____ chairs
   in our living room.

5. We have _____ furniture in our living room.

6. Natalie is listening to _____ music.

7. I'm hungry. I would like _____ orange.

8. The kids are hungry. They would like _____ fruit. They would also like _____ cheese.

9. I need _____ information about the bus schedule.

10. I have a problem. I need _____ advice.

❑ **Exercise 17. Let's talk: pairwork.** (Chart 7-3)
Work with a partner. Use *a, an*, or *some* with the given word. Partner A: Your book is open to this page. Partner B: Your book is open to *Let's Talk: Answers*, p. 502.

Example: desks
PARTNER A: a desks
PARTNER B: Again?
PARTNER A: some desks
PARTNER B: Right.

1. apple	6. word
2. apples	7. music
3. children	8. rice
4. old man	9. hour
5. men	10. island

Change roles.
Partner B: Your book is open to this page. Partner A: Your book is open to p. 502.

11. animal	16. university
12. animals	17. uncle
13. people	18. bananas
14. fruit	19. bread
15. egg	20. vocabulary

❑ **Exercise 18. Looking at grammar.** (Chart 7-3)
Use the given word to complete the sentence. Add *-s* to a count noun (or give the irregular plural form). Do not add *-s* to a noncount noun.

1. money   I need some _____*money*_____.

2. key   I see some _____*keys*_____ on the table.

3. man   Some _____*men*_____ are standing in the street.

4. flour   I need to buy some _____.

5. flower   Andy wants to buy some _____ for his mom.

6. information   I need some _____.

7. jewelry   Fred is looking for some _____ for his wife.

8. child   Some _____ are playing in the park.

9. homework   I can't go to the movie because I have some _____
to do.

10. advice   Could you please give me some _____?

11. suggestion   I have some _____ for you.

12. help   I need some _____ with my homework.

13. sandwich   We're hungry. We want to make some _____.

14. animal   I see some _____ in the picture.

15. banana   The monkeys are hungry. They would like some _____.

16. water   I'm thirsty. I would like some _____.

17. weather   We're having some hot _____ right now.

18. picture   I have some _____ of my family in my wallet.

19. rice, bean   I usually have some _____ and
_____ for dinner.

❑ **Exercise 19. Reading and grammar.** (Chart 7-3)

Part I. Read the story. Look at new vocabulary with your teacher first.

some ice cream

a coupon

> Do you know these words?
>
> on sale
> brand
> 20% off

A Coupon Shopper

    Beth likes to shop with coupons. Coupons help her save **some** money. She usually gets coupons from newspapers, online, or in **some** stores. Today she is shopping for paper products like toilet paper and tissue. She has **a** coupon for free toilet paper. It says "Buy one package—get one free." She also wants **some** rice and butter. She doesn't have **a** coupon for rice, but her favorite rice is on sale. She has **a** coupon for butter, but it is still expensive with the coupon. She is looking for a cheaper brand. She also has **some** "20% off" coupons for frozen food. Ice cream sounds good. She loves ice cream, and she thinks **a** 20% coupon is good. Beth is happy because she is saving **some** money today.

Part II. Write the noun in the story that follows each word in **bold**. Can you say why *a* or *some* is used for each noun?

1. some _____money_____

2. some _____

3. a _____

4. some _____

5. a _____

6. a _____

7. some _____

8. a _____

9. some _____

Part III. Answer the questions.

1. What do people generally buy with coupons?

2. Do people buy things they don't need when they shop with coupons?

3. Do you use coupons? Why or why not?

❏ **Exercise 20. Warm-up.** (Chart 7-4)
Answer the questions. Answers may vary.

1. What do you drink every day?

    a. _____ coffee

    b. _____ milk

    c. _____ tea

    d. _____ water

    e. _____ juice

2. What do you put your drink(s) in?

    a. _____ a cup

    b. _____ a glass

3. Which phrases sound OK to you?

    a. _____ a cup of coffee

    b. _____ a glass of water

    c. _____ a glass of coffee

    d. _____ a glass of tea

    e. _____ a cup of water

    f. _____ a cup of juice

7-4 Measurements with Noncount Nouns

(a) I'd like **some** water.	Units of measure are used with noncount nouns to express a specific quantity. Examples: *a glass of, a cup of, a piece of.*
(b) I'd like **a glass of** water.	In (a): **some water** = an unspecific quantity
(c) I'd like **a cup of** coffee.	In (b): **a glass of water** = a specific quantity
(d) I'd like **a piece of** fruit.	

COMMON EXPRESSIONS OF MEASURE

a bag of rice	a bunch of bananas	a jar of pickles
a bar of soap	a can of corn*	a loaf of bread
a bottle of olive oil	a carton of milk	a piece of cheese
a bowl of cereal	a glass of water	a sheet of paper
a box of candy	a head of lettuce	a tube of toothpaste

    bag   bar   bottle   box

    can   carton   jar   tube   bunch

* In British English: *a tin of corn*

❏ **Exercise 21. Vocabulary and grammar.** (Chart 7-4)

Complete the sentences. Use *a piece of, a cup of, a glass of, a bowl of*.

I'm hungry and thirsty. I'd like . . .

1. _____*a cup of*_____ coffee.

2. _____ bread.

3. _____ water.

4. _____ tea.

5. _____ cheese.

6. _____ soup.

7. _____ meat.

8. _____ wine.

9. _____ fruit.

10. _____ rice.

❏ **Exercise 22. Let's talk: pairwork.** (Chart 7-4)

Work with a partner. Look at the list of food and drinks. Check (✓) what you eat and drink every day. Add your own words to the list. Then tell your partner the usual <u>quantity</u> you have every day. Use *a piece of, two pieces of, a cup of, three cups of, a glass of, a bowl of*, or *one, two, a, some*, etc., in your answers. Share a few of your partner's answers with the class.

Example:

_✓_ egg

____ banana

____ coffee

_✓_ fruit

_____*ice cream*_____

_____*orange juice*_____

PARTNER A: I have one egg every day.
I usually eat two pieces of fruit.
I like a bowl of ice cream at night.
I drink a glass of orange juice every morning.

List of food and drinks:

____ egg

____ soup

____ fruit

____ bread

____ banana

____ apples

____ rice

____ ice cream

____ water

____ chicken

____ cheese

____ tea

_____

_____

_____

_____

_____

_____

□ **Exercise 23. Looking at grammar.** (Chart 7-4)

Complete the sentences with nouns.

1. I'm going to the store. I need to buy a carton of _____ *orange juice / milk / etc.* _____

2. I also need a tube of _____ and two bars of _____.

3. I need to find a can of _____ and a jar of _____.

4. I need to get a loaf of _____ and a box of _____.

5. I would like a head of _____ if it looks fresh.

6. Finally, I would like a couple of bottles of _____ and a jar of _____.

□ **Exercise 24. Game.** (Chart 7-4)

Work in teams. Make a list of everything in the picture by completing the sentence
I see . . . . Try to use numbers (e.g., ***three*** *spoons*) or other units of measure (e.g., ***a box***
of *candy*). Use ***a*** for singular count nouns (e.g., ***a*** *fly*). Your teacher will give you a time
limit. The team with the most correct answers wins.

Example: I see three spoons, a box of candy, a fly, etc.

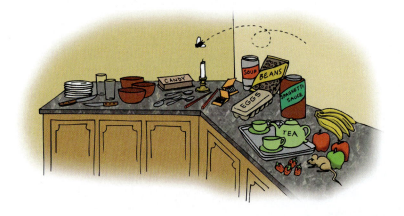

□ **Exercise 25. Let's talk: pairwork.** (Chart 7-4)

Work with a partner. Pretend that you are moving into a new apartment together. What
do you need? First, make a list. Then write the things you need and indicate quantity
(***two, some, a lot of***, etc.). List twenty to thirty things. Begin with ***We need***.

Example:
PARTNER A: a couch and two beds
PARTNER B: a can opener
PARTNER A: pots and pans
PARTNER B: bookcases
PARTNER A: paint
        Etc.

Possible answer: We need one couch and two beds, one can opener, some pots and pans, a
                  lot of bookcases, one can of paint, etc.

❏ **Exercise 26. Let's talk: pairwork.** (Chart 7-4)

Work with a partner. Complete the sentences with *a*, *an*, or *some* and the nouns.
Partner A: Your book is open to this page. Partner B: Your book is open to
Let's Talk: Answers, p. 502. Help your partner with the correct responses if necessary.

1. *I'm hungry. I'd like . . .*
   a. food.
   b. apple.
   c. sandwich.
   d. bowl of soup.

2. *I'm thirsty. I'd like . . .*
   a. glass of milk.
   b. water.
   c. cup of tea.

3. *I'm sick. I need . . .*
   a. medicine.
   b. ambulance.

4. *I'm cold. I need . . .*
   a. coat.
   b. hat.
   c. warm clothes.★
   d. heat.

5. *I'm tired. I need . . .*
   a. sleep.
   b. break.
   c. relaxing vacation.

Change roles.
Partner B: Your book is open to this page. Partner A: Your book is open to p. 502.

6. *I'm hungry. I'd like . . .*
   a. snack.
   b. fruit.
   c. orange.
   d. piece of chicken.

7. *I'm thirsty. I'd like . . .*
   a. juice.
   b. bottle of water.
   c. glass of iced tea.

8. *I'm sick. I need . . .*
   a. doctor.
   b. help.

9. *I'm cold. I need . . .*
   a. boots.
   b. blanket.
   c. hot bath.
   d. gloves.

10. *I'm tired. I need . . .*
    a. strong coffee.
    b. break.
    c. vacation.
    d. nap.

❏ **Exercise 27. Warm-up.** (Chart 7-5)

Which answers are true for you?

1. Do you eat much fruit?
   a. Yes, I eat a lot.   b. I eat a little.   c. No, I don't like fruit.

2. Do you eat many bananas?
   a. Yes, I eat a lot.   b. I eat a few.   c. No, I don't like bananas.

bananas

★*Clothes* is always plural. The word *clothes* does not have a singular form.

7-5 Using *Many, Much, A Few, A Little*

(a) I don't get **many** letters.	**Many** is used with PLURAL COUNT nouns.
(b) I don't get **much** mail.	**Much** is used with NONCOUNT nouns.
(c) Jan gets **a few** letters.	**A few** is used with PLURAL COUNT nouns.
(d) Ken gets **a little** mail.	**A little** is used with NONCOUNT nouns.

❏ **Exercise 28. Looking at grammar.** (Chart 7-5)

Complete the questions with **many** or **much**. Then give true answers. (If the answer is "zero," use "any" in the response.)

Example: How _____*much*_____ tea do you drink in a day?

Possible answers: I drink three cups. I drink one cup. I don't drink any tea. Etc.

1. How _____*much*_____ money do you have in your wallet?

2. How _____*many*_____ roommates do you have?

3. How _____ languages do you speak?

4. How _____ homework does your teacher usually assign?

5. How _____ tea do you drink in a day?

6. How _____ coffee do you drink in a day?

7. How _____ sentences are there in this exercise?

8. How _____ moons does the Earth have?

❏ **Exercise 29. Grammar and speaking: pairwork.** (Chart 7-5)

Complete the sentences with **many** or **much**. Then work with a partner. Ask about each item. Circle the answer your partner gives. Who has more items in their kitchen?

In your kitchen, do you have . . .

1. _____*much*_____ sugar?   Yes, I do.   No, I don't.

2. _____ paper bags?   Yes, I do.   No, I don't.

3. _____ flour?   Yes, I do.   No, I don't.

4. _____ salt?   Yes, I do.   No, I don't.

5. _____ spices?   Yes, I do.   No, I don't.

6. _____ olive oil?   Yes, I do.   No, I don't.

7. _____ butter?   Yes, I do.   No, I don't.

8. _____ dishwashing liquid?   Yes, I do.   No, I don't.

9. _____ cans of soup?   Yes, I do.   No, I don't.

10. _____ rolls of paper towels?   Yes, I do.   No, I don't.

❏ **Exercise 30. Looking at grammar.** (Chart 7-5)
Read the paragraph. Write *a little* or *a few* before each noun.

Andrew is having a party, but he has a problem. He doesn't like to cook. His cabinets and refrigerator are almost empty. His friends are very surprised. When they get to his house, they find out he has only . . . .

1. _____ eggs.

2. _____ juice.

3. _____ potatoes.

4. _____ fruit.

5. _____ meat.

6. _____ vegetables.

7. _____ butter.

8. _____ ketchup.

9. _____ pieces of chicken.

10. _____ cans of soup.

❏ **Exercise 31. Looking at grammar.** (Chart 7-5)
Part I. Change *a lot of* to *many* or *much*.

1. Daniel has a lot of problems. → *Daniel has many problems.*

2. I don't have a lot of money.

3. I don't put a lot of sugar in my coffee.

4. I have a lot of questions to ask you.

5. Pietro and Mia have a small apartment. They don't have a lot of furniture.

6. Lara is lazy. She doesn't do a lot of work.

7. I don't drink a lot of coffee.

8. Do you send a lot of text messages?

Part II. Change *some* to *a few* or *a little*.

1. I need some paper. → *I need a little paper.*

2. I usually add some salt to my food.

3. I have some questions to ask you.

4. Robert needs some help. He has some problems. He needs some advice.

5. I need to buy some clothes.

6. I have some homework to do tonight.

7. When I'm hungry in the evening, I usually eat some dark chocolate.

8. We usually do some speaking exercises in class every day.

❑ **Exercise 32. Let's talk: pairwork.** (Chart 7-5)

Work with a partner. Take turns asking and answering questions. Use the words from your list. Remember, you can look at your book before you speak. When you speak, look at your partner. Use this model.

    Partner A: How **much/many** _____ would you like?
    Partner B: I'd like **a little/a few**, please. Thanks.

Example: chicken
PARTNER A: How **much chicken** would you like?
PARTNER B: I'd like **a little**, please. Thanks.
PARTNER A: Your turn now.

Example: pencil
PARTNER B: How **many pencils** would you like?
PARTNER A: I'd like **a few**, please.
PARTNER B: Your turn now.

PARTNER A	PARTNER B
1. pen	1. salt
2. tea	2. banana
3. book	3. soup
4. apple	4. coffee
5. money	5. toy
6. help	6. cheese

❑ **Exercise 33. Let's talk: small groups.** (Charts 7-1, 7-3, and 7-5)

Work in small groups. Imagine you are all famous chefs. Create a dessert using the ingredients below. Give your recipe a name (it can be funny or strange). Tell the class about your dessert. Begin with *We need a little /a few / a lot of / two /some*. OR *We don't need any*.

1. ____ salt   7. ____ pieces of chocolate
2. ____ flour   8. ____ baking soda
3. ____ honey   9. ____ baking powder
4. ____ sugar   10. ____ eggs
5. ____ nuts   11. ____ cream
6. ____ coconut   12. ____ butter

other ingredients: _____

walnuts

❏ **Exercise 34. Warm-up.** (Chart 7-6)

Read the two conversations. In which conversation are Speaker A and Speaker B thinking about the same bedroom?

1. A: Where are the kids?

    B: I think they're hiding in a bedroom.

2. A: Where's Raymond?

    B: He's in the bedroom.

7-6 Using *The*

(a) A: Where's Max? B: He's in **the** *kitchen*.	A speaker uses **the** when the speaker and the listener have the same thing or person in mind. **The** shows that a noun is specific (not general).
(b) A: I have two pieces of fruit for us, an apple and a banana. What would you like? B: I'd like **the** *apple*, please.	In (a): Both A and B have the same kitchen in mind. In (b): When B says "the apple," both A and B have the same apple in mind.
(c) A: It's a nice summer day today. **The** *sky* is blue. **The** *sun* is hot. B: Yes, I really like summer.	In (c): Both A and B are thinking of the same sky (there is only one sky for them to think of) and the same sun (there is only one sun for them to think of).

(d) Nick has **a** *pen* and **a** *pencil*. **The** *pen* is blue. **The** *pencil* is yellow.	**The** is used with
	  • singular count nouns, as in (d).
	  • plural count nouns, as in (e).
	  • noncount nouns, as in (f).
	In other words, **the** is used with each of the three kinds of nouns.

(e) Nick has **some** *pens and pencils*. **The** *pens* are blue. **The** *pencils* are yellow.	

(f) Nick has **some** *rice* and **some** *cheese*. **The** *rice* is white. **The** *cheese* is yellow.	Notice in the examples: The speaker is using **the** for the second mention of a noun. When the speaker mentions a noun for a second time, both the speaker and listener are now thinking about the same thing.
	    First mention: I have **a** *pen*.
	    Second mention: **The** *pen* is blue.

❏ **Exercise 35. Looking at grammar.** (Chart 7-6)

Complete the sentences with **the** where necessary.

1. Elizabeth is standing outside. It is midnight.

    a. She's looking up at _____ sky.

    b. She sees _____ moon.

    c. She doesn't see _____ sun.

    d. _____ stars are very bright.

    e. _____ planets are difficult to find.

2. Rick and Lucy are looking for an apartment to rent. Right now they are standing in an old apartment. The kitchen has a lot of problems.

a. _____ refrigerator is broken.

b. _____ faucet doesn't turn on.

c. _____ ceiling has a leak.   a faucet

d. _____ window doesn't open.

e. _____ floor has a hole in it.

❑ **Exercise 36. Looking at grammar.** (Chart 7-6)
Complete the sentences with *the* or *a/an*.

1. I have ___*a*___ notebook and _____ grammar book. _____ notebook is brown. _____ grammar book is red.

2. Right now Maurice is sitting in class. He's sitting between _____ woman and _____ man. _____ woman is Graciela. _____ man is Mustafa.

3. Hana is wearing _____ ring and _____ necklace. _____ ring is on her left hand.

4. Brad and Angela are waiting for their plane to leave. Brad is reading _____ magazine. Angela is reading _____ newspaper online. When Angela finishes _____ newspaper and Brad finishes _____ magazine, they will trade.

5. In the picture below, there are four figures: _____ circle, _____ triangle, _____ square, and _____ rectangle. _____ circle is next to _____ triangle. _____ square is between _____ triangle and _____ rectangle.

circle   triangle   square   rectangle

6. I gave my friend _____ card and _____ flower for her birthday. _____ card wished her "Happy Birthday." She liked both _____ card and _____ flower.

❑ **Exercise 37. Let's talk: pairwork.** (Chart 7-6)
Work with a partner. Read the conversation aloud using *the* or *a/an*. After you finish speaking, write the answers.

A: Look at the picture below. What do you see?

B: I see _____ chair, _____ table, _____ window, and _____ plant.
    <u>1</u>   <u>2</u>   <u>3</u>   <u>4</u>

A: Where is _____ chair?
              <u>5</u>

B: _____ chair is under _____ window.
   <u>6</u>   <u>7</u>

A: Where is _____ plant?
              <u>8</u>

B: _____ plant is beside _____ chair.
   <u>9</u>   <u>10</u>

Change roles.

A: Do you see any people?

B: Yes. I see _____ man and _____ woman. _____ man is standing.
               <u>11</u>   <u>12</u>   <u>13</u>
   _____ woman is sitting down.
   <u>14</u>

A: Do you see any animals?

B: Yes. I see _____ dog, _____ cat, and _____ bird in _____ cage.
               <u>15</u>   <u>16</u>   <u>17</u>   <u>18</u>

A: What is _____ dog doing?
            <u>19</u>

B: It's sleeping.

A: How about _____ cat?
               <u>20</u>

B: _____ cat is watching _____ bird.
   <u>21</u>   <u>22</u>

Complete the sentences with *the* or *a/an*.

1. A: I need to go shopping. I need to buy _____ coat.

   B: I'll go with you. I need to get _____ umbrella.

2. A: Hi! Come in.

   B: Hi! _____ weather is terrible today! My umbrella is all wet.

   A: I'll take your umbrella and put it in _____ kitchen so it can dry.

3. A: Gloria has _____ great job. She builds websites. Her company gives her _____ new computer every year.

   B: Wow! She's lucky.

4. A: How much longer do you need to use _____ computer?

   B: Just five more minutes, and then you can have it.

5. A: I need _____ stamp for this letter. Do you have one?

   B: Right here.

6. A: Would you like _____ egg for breakfast?

   B: No thanks. I'll just have _____ glass of juice and some toast.

   some toast

   a toaster

7. A: Do you see my pen? I can't find it.

   B: There it is. It's on _____ floor.

   A: Oh. I see it. Thanks.

8. A: Could you answer _____ phone? Thanks.

   B: Hello?

❏ **Exercise 39. Game.** (Chart 7-6)
Work in teams. Answer the questions. One person on each team writes the answers. You have five minutes. The team with the most grammatically correct answers wins.

1. What's on the floor?
   _____*Some desks, a piece of gum, some dirt, a garbage can, etc.*_____

2. What's on the ceiling?

3. What's out in the hallway?

4. What's outside the window?

5. What's on the board (chalkboard, whiteboard, or bulletin board)?

❑ **Exercise 40. Warm-up.** (Chart 7-7)
Which sentence (a. or b.) is true for each statement?

1. Bananas are expensive right now.
   a. Only some bananas are expensive.
   b. Bananas in general are expensive.

2. The bananas are green.
   a. A specific group of bananas is green.
   b. Bananas in general are green.

7-7 Using Ø (No Article) to Make Generalizations

(a) **Ø** *Apples* are good for you. (b) **Ø** *Students* use **Ø** *pens* and **Ø** *pencils*. (c) I like to listen to **Ø** *music*. (d) **Ø** *Rice* is good for you.	No article (symbolized by **Ø**) is used to make generalizations with • plural count nouns, as in (a) and (b), and • noncount nouns, as in (c) and (d).
(e) Tim and Jan ate some fruit. ***The*** *apples* were very good, but ***the*** *bananas* were too old.	COMPARE: In (a), the word ***apples*** is general. It refers to all apples, any apples. No article (**Ø**) is used. In (e), the word ***apples*** is specific, so ***the*** is used in front of it. It refers to the specific apples that Tim and Jan ate.
(f) We went to a concert last night. ***The*** *music* was very good.	COMPARE: In (c), ***music*** is general. In (f), ***the music*** is specific.

❑ **Exercise 41. Looking at grammar.** (Chart 7-7)
Decide if the words in **bold** are general or specific.

1. The **eggs** are delicious.	general	specific
2. Are **eggs** healthy?	general	specific
3. Please pass the **salt**.	general	specific
4. I love **salt**!	general	specific
5. **Apples** have vitamin C.	general	specific
6. The **apples** have brown spots.	general	specific

❑ **Exercise 42. Looking at grammar.** (Chart 7-7)
Complete the sentences with ***the*** or **Ø** (no article).

1. Oranges are orange, and _____Ø_____ bananas are yellow.

2. Everybody needs _____ food to live.

3. We ate at a good restaurant last night. _____ food was excellent.

4. _____ salt tastes salty, and _____ pepper tastes hot.

5. _____ coffee has caffeine.

6. _____ coffee in the pot is fresh.

7. _____ pages in this book are full of grammar exercises.

8. _____ books have _____ pages.

9. I like _____ fruit. I also like _____ vegetables.

lettuce
a tomato   broccoli
celery

vegetables

❑ **Exercise 43. Listening.** (Charts 7-6 and 7-7)

Listen to each sentence. Decide if the given noun has a general or a specific meaning.

1. vegetables	(general)	specific
2. cats	general	specific
3. teacher	general	specific
4. bananas	general	specific
5. cars	general	specific
6. car	general	specific
7. computers	general	specific
8. park	general	specific

❑ **Exercise 44. Let's talk.** (Charts 7-3, 7-6, and 7-7)

Work in small groups or as a class. Choose the sentence that is closest in meaning to the given situation. Discuss the differences.

1. Mark is at an electronics store. There are five tablets. He buys one.
   a. He buys a tablet.
   b. He buys the tablet.

a tablet computer

2. Pat is at a music store. There is only one guitar on the shelf. She buys it.
   a. She buys a guitar.
   b. She buys the guitar.

3. Martha is at the library. There is one book about Nelson Mandela.
   a. She checks out the book about Nelson Mandela.
   b. She checks out a book about Nelson Mandela.

4. Misako walks outside and looks up at the sky.
   a. She sees the sun.
   b. She sees a sun.

5. Horses are my favorite animals.
   a. I love the horses.
   b. I love horses.

6. There are fifty cars in a parking lot. Ten cars are white.
   a. The cars in the parking lot are white.
   b. Some cars in the parking lot are white.

❏ **Exercise 45. Listening.** (Charts 7-1 → 7-7)

Listen to the sentences and write the words you hear. Use *a*, *an*, or *the*.

1. A: Do you have ____*a*____ pen?

   B: There's one on _____ counter in _____ kitchen.

2. A: Where are _____ keys to _____ car?

   B: I'm not sure. You can use mine.

3. A: Shh. I hear _____ noise.

   B: It's just _____ bird outside, probably _____ woodpecker.
   Don't worry.

4. A: Henry Jackson teaches at _____ university.

   B: I know. He's _____ English professor.

   A: He's also the head of _____ department.

5. A: Hurry! We're late.

   B: No, we're not. It's five o'clock, and we have _____ hour.

   A: No, we don't. It's six! Look at _____ clock.

   B: Oops. I need _____ new battery for my watch.

❏ **Exercise 46. Warm-up.** (Chart 7-8)

Which words can complete each sentence?

1. I have   some fruit / some oranges / any oranges.

2. I don't have   some fruit / any fruit / any oranges.

3. Do you have   some fruit / some oranges / any fruit / any oranges?

7-8 Using *Some* and *Any*

AFFIRMATIVE	(a) Vera has **some** money.	Use **some** in affirmative statements.
NEGATIVE	(b) Vera doesn't have **any** money.	Use **any** in negative statements.
QUESTION	(c) Does Vera have **any** money? (d) Does Vera have **some** money?	Use either **some** or **any** in a question.
(e) I don't have **any** money. (noncount noun) (f) I don't have **any** matches. (plural count noun)		**Any** is used with noncount nouns and plural count nouns.

Exercise 47. Looking at grammar. (Chart 7-8)
Complete the sentences with *some* or *any*.

1. Harry has ____*some*____ money.

2. I don't have ____*any*____ money.

3. Do you have __*some / any*__ money?

4. Do you need _____ help?

5. No, thank you. I don't need _____ help.

6. Kalil needs _____ help.

7. Diana usually doesn't get _____ mail.

8. We don't have _____ fruit in the apartment. We don't have _____

   apples, _____ bananas, or _____ oranges.

9. The house is empty. There aren't _____ people in the house.

10. I need _____ paper. Do you have _____ paper?

11. Heidi can't write a letter because she doesn't have _____ paper.

12. Sasha is getting along fine. He doesn't have _____ problems.

13. I need to go to the grocery store. I need to buy _____ food. Do you need to

    buy _____ groceries?

14. I'm not busy tonight. I don't have _____ homework to do.

15. I don't have _____ money in my wallet.

16. There are _____ beautiful flowers in my garden this year.

□ **Exercise 48. Let's talk: interview.** (Chart 7-8)
Walk around the room. Interview your classmates. Use this model.
   Student A: Do you have some/any ____?
   Student B: Yes, I have some ____. OR No, I don't have any ____.

1. pencils with erasers
2. notebook paper
3. money in your pocket
4. children

5. stepchildren
6. pets
7. worries
8. advice for me

Now share some of your answers with the rest of the class.

❏ **Exercise 49. Let's talk: small groups.** (Chart 7-8)

Work in small groups. You are at a mall. You have a gift card for your group. The amount is equal to the cost of a new computer. What do you want to buy for your group? What don't you want to buy? Add two more suggestions to the list.

camera	music CD	socks	video game
DVD	perfume	software	winter jacket
hat	pet	suitcase	_____
jewelry	shoe	summer clothes	_____

1. We want to buy some / a lot of / two . . . .

2. We don't want to buy any . . . .

❏ **Exercise 50. Looking at grammar.** (Chapters 6 and 7)

Complete the sentences with these words. If necessary, use the plural form.

bush	glass	✓match	strawberry
centimeter	homework	page	thief
dish	inch	paper	tray
edge	information	piece	valley
fish	knife	sex	weather
foot	leaf	size	woman

1. I want to light a candle. I need some _____*matches*_____.

2. _____ fall from the trees in autumn.

3. The application asked for my name, address, and _____: male or female.

4. Some _____, forks, and spoons are on the table.

5. I want to take the bus downtown, but I don't know the bus schedule. I need some _____ about the bus schedule.

6. I need to write a composition. I have a pen, but I need some _____.

7. Plates and bowls are called _____.

8. Married _____ are called wives.

9. There are a lot of trees and _____ in the park.

10. Ike is studying. He has a lot of _____ to do.

11. My dictionary has 437 _____.

12. This puzzle has 200 _____.

13. A piece of paper has four _____.

14. Mountains are high, and _____ are low.

15. When the temperature is around 35°C (77°F), I'm comfortable. But I don't like very hot _____.

16. _____ steal things: money, jewelry, cars, etc.

17. _____ are small, red, sweet, and delicious.

18. People carry their food on _____ at a cafeteria.

19. Sweaters in a store usually come in four _____: small, medium, large, and extra large.

20. In some countries, people usually use cups for their tea. In other countries, they use _____ for their tea.

21. Toshiro has five _____ in his aquarium.

22. There are 100 _____ in a meter.

23. There are 12 _____ in a foot.*

24. There are 3 _____ in a yard.*

❏ **Exercise 51. Check your knowledge.** (Chapter 7)
Correct the mistakes.

      some

1. I need ~~an~~ advice from you.

2. I don't like hot weathers.

3. I usually have a egg for breakfast.

4. Sun rises every morning.

5. The students in this class do a lot of homeworks every day.

6. How many language do you know?

7. I don't have many money.

8. Alexander and Carmen don't have some children.

9. A pictures are beautiful. You're a good photographer.

---

*1 inch = 2.54 centimeters; 1 foot = 30.48 centimeters; 1 yard = 0.91 meters

10. There isn't a traffic early in the morning.

11. I can't find any bowl for my soup.

❏ **Exercise 52. Let's talk.** (Chapter 7)
Imagine that a new shopping center is coming to your neighborhood. It will have a drugstore, a bank, and a grocery store. Decide what additional stores you want. Your teacher will help you with any vocabulary you don't know.

Part I. Choose any six businesses from the list and write their names in any of the five available spaces on Blueprint #1 on this page.

✓ a bank	✓ a grocery store	a post office
a bookstore	an ice-cream shop	a shoe store
a camera shop	an Internet café	a sports equipment store
✓ a drugstore	a laundromat	a vegetarian food store
a drycleaner's	a movie theater	a video rental store
an exercise gym	a music store	
a fast-food restaurant	a pet supply store	

Blueprint #1
(your business locations)

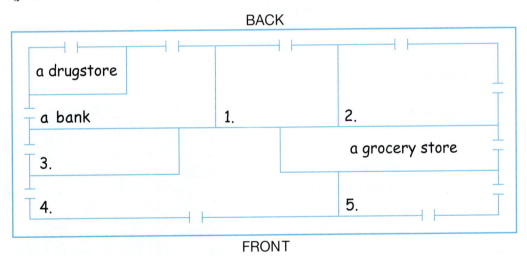

Part II. Work with a partner, but do not look at each other's blueprints. Ask your partner about the location of his/her new businesses. Write your partner's answers on your copy of Blueprint #2 on p. 222. Use this pattern:

Partner A: Is there **a/an** . . . ?
Partner B: Yes, there is. / No, there isn't.
Partner A: Where is **the** . . . ?
Partner B: It's next to / beside / in back of / in front of **the** . . . .

Example:

PARTNER A: Is there **an** exercise gym?
PARTNER B: No, there isn't.
PARTNER A: Is there **a** bank?
PARTNER B: Yes, there is.
PARTNER A: Where is **the** bank?
PARTNER B: It's in front of **the** drugstore.

Blueprint #2
(your partner's business locations)

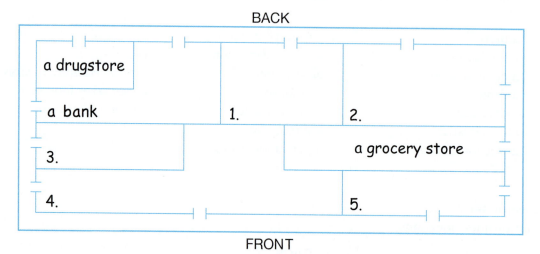

BACK

a drugstore
a bank   1.   2.
3.   a grocery store
4.   5.

FRONT

❑ **Exercise 53. Reading, grammar, and writing.** (Chapter 7)
Part I. Read the story.

A Day at the Park

It is a beautiful day. Some people are at a park. A woman is sitting on a blanket. She is having a picnic. A little girl nearby is smelling some flowers. An older man is standing near a pond. He is pointing at some toy boats. Two boys are riding their bikes. A man and a woman are sitting on a bench. The woman is knitting. The man is feeding some birds. Some ducks are swimming, and a cat wants to catch them. The cat is hungry.

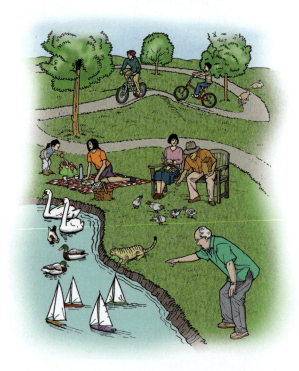

Part II. Write *a, an,* or *some* in front of each word according to the paragraph. Is the article usage clear to you?

1. _____ beautiful day

2. _____ people

3. _____ park

4. _____ woman

5. _____ blanket

6. _____ picnic

7. _____ little girl

8. _____ flowers

9. _____ older man

10. _____ pond

11. _____ toy boats

12. _____ man and _____ woman

13. _____ bench

14. _____ woman

15. _____ man

16. _____ birds

17. _____ ducks

18. _____ cat

19. _____ cat

Part III. Describe the picture. Begin with *It is a* _____ *day*. Make sure to use *a, an,* and *some*.

Part IV. Editing check: Work individually or change papers with a partner. Check (✓) for the following:

1. ____ indented paragraph

2. ____ capital letter at the beginning of each sentence

3. ____ period at the end of each sentence

4. ____ a verb in every sentence

5. ____ correct use of *a, an, some*

6. ____ *-s/-es* endings for plural nouns

7. ____ correct spelling (use a dictionary or spell-check)

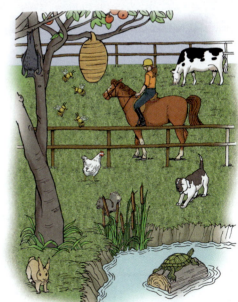

Chapter 8
Expressing Past Time, Part 1

□ **Exercise 1. Warm-up.** (Chart 8-1)
Read the statements and choose the answers.

1. I am tired now.   yes   no

2. I was tired two hours ago.   yes   no

3. Some students are absent today.   yes   no

4. Some students were absent yesterday.   yes   no

8-1 Using *Be:* Past Time

PRESENT TIME	PAST TIME
(a) I ***am*** in class ***today***.	(d) I ***was*** in class ***yesterday***.
(b) Alison ***is*** sick ***today***.	(e) Alison ***was*** sick ***yesterday***.
(c) My friends ***are*** at home ***today***.	(f) My friends ***were*** at home ***yesterday***.

SIMPLE PAST TENSE OF *BE*

SINGULAR	PLURAL
I was	**we were**
you were (one person)	**you were** (more than one person)
she was	**they were**
he was	
it was	

I
she
he   } + *was*
it

we
you   } + *were*
they

□ **Exercise 2. Looking at grammar.** (Chart 8-1)
Complete the sentences with ***was*** or ***were***.

TODAY   YESTERDAY

1. You are at school.   You ____*were*____ at home.

2. We are at school.   We _____ at home.

3. He is at school.   He _____ at home.

4. You and I are at school.   You and I _____ at home.

5. She is at school.   She _____ at home.

6. They are at school.   They _____ at home.

7. Brian and James are at school.   Brian and James _____ at home.

8. My parents are at school.   My parents _____ at home.

9. I am at school.   I _____ at home.

10. The teacher is at school.   The teacher _____ at home.

❑ **Exercise 3. Looking at grammar.** (Chart 8-1)
Change the sentences to past time.

1. Bashar is in class today. → *He was in class yesterday too.*

2. I'm in class today. → *I was in class yesterday too.*

3. Martina is at the library today.

4. We're in class today.

5. You're busy today.

6. I'm happy today.

7. The classroom is hot today.

8. Elise is in her office today.

9. Tony is in his office today.

10. Noor and Eli are in their offices today.

❑ **Exercise 4. Let's talk.** (Chart 8-1)
Part I. Think about yourself as a three-year-old child. Check (✓) the words that describe you best.

_____ quiet   _____ loud   _____ afraid

_____ shy   _____ smart   _____ friendly

_____ funny   _____ curious   _____ a troublemaker

Part II. Work with a partner. Tell your partner about yourself. Begin with *I was . . . .*

❏ **Exercise 5. Warm-up.** (Chart 8-2)
Choose the correct verb to make true sentences.

The weather

1. Last month, it   was / was not   nice.

2. The weekends   were / were not   sunny.

3. Yesterday, it   was / was not   hot.

8-2 Simple Past Tense of *Be:* Negative

(a) I **was not** in class yesterday. (b) I **wasn't** in class yesterday.	NEGATIVE CONTRACTIONS **was + not = wasn't** **were + not = weren't**
(c) They **were not** at home last night. (d) They **weren't** at home last night.	I she he } + wasn't we you } + weren't it they

---

❏ **Exercise 6. Looking at grammar.** (Chart 8-2)
Complete the sentences with **wasn't** or **weren't**.

Joe and JoAnn went on a trip. They were very happy because . . .

1. the airplane ride _____*wasn't*_____ long.

2. the trains _____ slow.

3. the hotel _____ expensive.

4. the restaurants _____ expensive.

5. the tourist areas _____ crowded.

6. the language _____ difficult.

7. the weather _____ cold.

❏ **Exercise 7. Grammar and speaking.** (Chart 8-2)
Use the given words to make true sentences. Share some of your answers with the class.

Yesterday at noon, I was/wasn't . . .

1. hungry.
2. tired.
3. at home.
4. at school.
5. with my family.

6. sick.
7. in the hospital.
8. on an airplane.
9. outdoors.
10. at the movies.

□ **Exercise 8. Listening.** (Charts 8-1 and 8-2)

Listen to the sentences. Choose the verbs you hear.

Example: You will hear: I was at school all day yesterday.
You will choose: (was)   wasn't

1.	was	wasn't
2.	was	wasn't
3.	was	wasn't
4.	was	wasn't
5.	was	wasn't
6.	was	wasn't
7.	were	weren't
8.	were	weren't
9.	were	weren't
10.	were	weren't

□ **Exercise 9. Warm-up: pairwork.** (Chart 8-3)

Work with a partner. Ask these questions.

Last night at midnight,

1. were you asleep?
2. were you on the phone?
3. was it quiet at your home?

8-3 Past of *Be:* Questions

YES/NO QUESTIONS		SHORT ANSWER	(LONG ANSWER)
(a) **Were you** in class yesterday? (be) + (subject)	→ →	**Yes, I was.** **No, I wasn't.**	(I was in class yesterday.) (I wasn't in class yesterday.)
(b) **Was Carlos** tired last night? (be) + (subject)	→	**Yes, he was.** **No, he wasn't.**	(He was tired last night.) (He wasn't tired last night.)
INFORMATION QUESTIONS		SHORT ANSWER	(LONG ANSWER)
(c) **Where were you** yesterday? Where + (be) + (subject)	→	**In class.**	(I was in class yesterday.)
(d) **When was Emily** sick? When + (be) + (subject)	→	**Last week.**	(She was sick last week.)

❏ **Exercise 10. Looking at grammar.** (Chart 8-3)

Make questions and give short answers. Use the words from the box.

> at the airport   in Iceland
> at the dentist   in the hospital
> ✓ at the library

1. (*you \ at home \ last night*)

    A: _____ *Were you at home last night?* _____

    B: No, _____ *I wasn't.* _____

    A: Where _____ *were you?* _____

    B: I _____ *was at the library.* _____

2. (*Mr. Gupta \ at work \ last week*)

    A: _____

    B: No, _____

    A: Where _____

    B: He _____

3. (*Oscar and Anya \ at the train station \ at midnight*)

    A: _____

    B: No, _____

    A: Where _____

    B: They _____

4. (*Gabriella \ at the gym \ yesterday afternoon*)

    A: _____

    B: No, _____

    A: Where _____

    B: She _____

5. (*you and your family \ in Canada \ last year*)

A: _____

B: No, _____

A: Where _____

B: We _____

Iceland

❏ **Exercise 11. Let's talk: class activity.** (Chart 8-3)

Think about your first day in this class. Check (✓) the words that describe your feelings that day. Then answer your teacher's questions.

Example: happy
    TEACHER: Were you happy the first day of class?
STUDENT A: Yes, I was happy.
STUDENT B: No, I wasn't happy.
    TEACHER: (*to Student C*) Tell me about (*Student A*) and (*Student B*).
STUDENT C: (*Student A*) was happy. (*Student B*) wasn't happy.

1. ____ excited

2. ____ scared/afraid

3. ____ nervous

4. ____ relaxed (not nervous)

5. ____ quiet

6. ____ talkative

❏ **Exercise 12. Let's talk: pairwork.** (Chart 8-3)

Work with a partner. Take turns making questions orally. After you finish, write the verbs.

SITUATION: You went on a roller coaster ride with a friend yesterday.

1. _____*Was*_____ it fun?

2. _____ it scary?

3. _____ you afraid?

4. _____ the ride long?

5. _____ you sick afterwards?

6. _____ your friend sick?

7. _____ you nervous?

8. _____ your friend nervous?

9. _____ the ride safe?

10. _____ you tired?

□ **Exercise 13. Looking at grammar.** (Chapter 2 and Chart 8-3)
Make questions and give short answers.

1. (*you \ in class \ yesterday*)

    A: _____*Were you in class yesterday?*_____

    B: Yes, _____*I was.*_____

2. (*Claire \ in class \ today*)

    A: _____*Is Claire in class today?*_____

    B: No, _____*she isn't.*_____ She's absent.

3. (*you \ tired \ last night*)

    A: _____

    B: Yes, _____ I went to bed early.

4. (*you \ hungry \ right now*)

    A: _____

    B: No, _____, but I'm thirsty.

5. (*the weather \ hot in New York City \ last summer*)

    A: _____

    B: Yes, _____ It was very hot.

6. (*the weather \ cold in Alaska \ in the winter*)

    A: _____

    B: Yes, _____ It's very cold.

7. (*Astrid and Mohammed \ here \ yesterday afternoon*)

    A: _____

    B: Yes, _____

8. (*the students \ in this class \ intelligent*)

    A: _____

    B: Of course _____ They are very intelligent!

9. (*Mr. Tok \ absent \ today*)

    A: _____

    B: Yes, _____

    A: Where _____

    B: _____

10. (*Tony and Benito \ at the party \ last night*)

A: _____

B: No, _____

A: Where _____

B: _____

11. (*Amy \ out of town \ last week*)

A: _____

B: Yes, _____

A: Where _____

B: _____

12. (*Mr. and Mrs. Sanchez \ in town \ this week*)

A: _____

B: No, _____ They're out of town.

A: Oh? Where _____

B: _____

❑   **Exercise 14. Let's talk: find someone who . . . .** (Charts 8-2 and 8-3)
Interview your classmates about their days in elementary school. Make questions with
was/**were**. Find people who can answer *yes* to your questions. Write down their names.

Example: you \ shy
STUDENT A: Were you shy?
STUDENT B: No, I wasn't.
STUDENT A: (*to Student C*) Were you shy?
STUDENT C: Yes, I was.

	FIRST NAME		FIRST NAME
1. you \ shy		7. you \ noisy	
2. you \ outgoing*		8. you \ athletic	
3. you \ talkative		9. you \ active	
4. you \ happy		10. you \ well-behaved	
5. you \ hardworking		11. you \ a serious student	
6. you \ quiet		12. you \ artistic	

*outgoing = not shy

Check (✓) your activities this morning. What do you notice about the verb endings?

Earlier today, I . . .

1. ____ washed my face.

2. ____ brushed my teeth.

3. ____ combed my hair.

4. ____ shaved.

8-4 Simple Past Tense: Using *-ed*

SIMPLE PRESENT	(a) I	*walk*	to school	*every day*.	*verb* + *-ed* = simple past tense
SIMPLE PAST*	(b) I	*walked*	to school	*yesterday*.	I you she he it we they } + walked (verb + *-ed*)
SIMPLE PRESENT	(c) Ann	*walks*	to school	*every day*.	
SIMPLE PAST	(d) Ann	*walked*	to school	*yesterday*.	

*For pronunciation of the simple past tense, see Appendix Chart A5-3, p. 488.

❏ **Exercise 16. Looking at grammar.** (Chart 8-4)
Complete the sentences orally. Use the simple past. Then write the answers.

1. Every day I walk to work. Yesterday I _____ *walked* _____ to work.

2. Every day I work. Yesterday I _____.

3. Every day Nabeel shaves. Yesterday Nabeel _____.

4. Every night Paula watches TV. Last night she _____ TV.

5. Every day you exercise. Last night you _____.

6. Every day people smile. Yesterday they _____.

7. Every week it rains. Last week it _____.

8. Every day we ask questions. Yesterday we _____ questions.

9. Every day I talk on the phone. Yesterday I _____ on the phone.

10. Every day Tomo listens to music. Yesterday he _____ to music.

❑ **Exercise 17. Let's talk: pairwork.** (Chart 8-4)

Work with a partner. Check (✓) all your activities yesterday. Tell your partner about them. Begin with **Yesterday I . . . .** Share a few of your partner's answers with the class.

1. ____ ask the teacher a question
2. ____ cook dinner
3. ____ wash some clothes
4. ____ listen to music on the radio
5. ____ use a computer
6. ____ stay home in the evening
7. ____ walk in a park

8. ____ watch TV
9. ____ work at my desk
10. ____ wait for a bus
11. ____ smile at several people
12. ____ talk on a cell phone
13. ____ dream in English
14. ____ dream in my language

❑ **Exercise 18. Looking at grammar.** (Chart 8-4)

Complete the sentences. Use the simple present or the simple past of the verbs from the box.

ask	erase	smile	walk
cook	✓ rain	stay	watch
dream	shave	wait	work

1. It often _____ *rains* _____ in the morning. It _____ *rained* _____ yesterday.

2. I _____ to school every morning. I _____ to school yesterday morning.

3. Sara often _____ questions. She _____ a question in class yesterday.

4. I _____ a movie on television last night. I usually _____ TV in the evening because I want to improve my English.

5. Mario _____ his own dinner yesterday evening. He _____ his own dinner every evening.

6. I usually _____ home at night because I have to study. I _____ home last night.

7. I have a job at the library. I _____ at the library every evening. I _____ there yesterday evening.

8. When I am asleep, I often _____. I _____ about

   my family last night.*

9. Linda usually _____ for the bus at a bus stop in front of her

   apartment building. She _____ for the bus there yesterday

   morning.

10. The teacher _____ some words from the board a couple of minutes

    ago. He used his hand instead of an eraser.

11. Our teacher is a warm, friendly person. She often _____ when she

    talks to us.

12. Rick doesn't have a beard anymore. He _____ it five days ago.

    Now he _____ every morning.

□ **Exercise 19. Vocabulary and listening.** (Chapter 3 and Chart 8-4)
The simple past tense ending can be difficult to hear. Listen to each sentence and choose
the verb you hear. Look at new vocabulary with your teacher first.

Example: You will hear: Jeremy loves soccer.

              You will choose: love   (loves)   loved

A soccer coach

1. work	works	worked
2. play	plays	played
3. play	plays	played
4. score	scores	scored
5. help	helps	helped
6. learn	learns	learned
7. watch	watches	watched
8. like	likes	liked
9. work	works	worked
10. work	works	worked

Do you know these words?

coach
tournament
score
goals

---

*The past of *dream* can be *dreamed* or *dreamt*.

Choose the correct time words to make true sentences.

1. I was at home   yesterday morning / one hour ago / yesterday evening.

2. I watched TV   last weekend / last night / yesterday afternoon.

3. I talked to someone in my family   last month / last week / an hour ago.

8-5 Past Time Words: *Yesterday, Last,* and *Ago*

PRESENT		PAST	Note the changes in time expressions from present to past.
today	→	yesterday	
this morning	→	yesterday morning	
this afternoon	→	yesterday afternoon	
this evening	→	yesterday evening	
tonight	→	last night	
this week	→	last week	

REFERENCE LIST: TIME EXPRESSIONS

YESTERDAY	*LAST*	*AGO*
(a) Bob was here . . . ***yesterday***. ***yesterday morning***. ***yesterday afternoon***. ***yesterday evening***.	(b) Sue was here . . . ***last night***. ***last week***. ***last weekend***. ***last month***. ***last year***. ***last spring***. ***last summer***. ***last fall***. ***last winter***. ***last Monday***. ***last Tuesday***. ***last Wednesday***. ***etc***.	(c) Tom was here . . . ***five minutes ago***. ***two hours ago***. ***three days ago***. ***a (one) week ago***. ***six months ago***. ***a (one) year ago***.

NOTICE

In (a): ***yesterday*** is used with *morning, afternoon,* and *evening.*

In (b): ***last*** is used with *night,* with long periods of time (*week, month, year*), with seasons (*spring, summer,* etc.), and with days of the week.

In (c): ***ago*** means "in the past." It follows specific lengths of time (e.g., *two minutes* + *ago, five years* + *ago*).

Exercise 21. Looking at grammar. (Chart 8-5)
Complete the sentences with *yesterday* or *last*.

1. *I worked in the university bookstore . . .*

   a. _____*last*_____ Friday.

   b. _____ week.

   c. _____ fall.

   d. _____ month.

   e. _____ year.

   f. _____ summer.

2. *I visited my cousins . . .*

   a. _____ night.

   b. _____ evening.

   c. _____ morning.

   d. _____ afternoon.

   e. _____ Sunday.

   f. _____ spring.

□ **Exercise 22. Looking at grammar.** (Chart 8-5)
Complete the sentences. Use a past time expression and *wasn't* or *weren't*.

1. I'm at home tonight, but _____*I wasn't at home last night.*_____

2. I am here today, but _____

3. Kaya is busy today, but _____

4. Mack and Carly are at work this afternoon, but _____

5. Ben is at the library tonight, but _____

6. You're here today, but _____

7. Dr. Ruckman is in her office this morning, but _____

8. It's cold this week, but _____

9. We're tired this evening, but _____

Use the information in the calendar to complete the sentences about Ken's activities.
Use a time expression from Chart 8-5.

JUNE						
Sunday	**Monday**	**Tuesday**	**Wednesday**	**Thursday**	**Friday**	**Saturday**
						1
2	3	4	5	6 *3:00 p.m. doctor/Dad*	7	8
9	10	11	12	13 *London*	14	15
Paris 16	*home* 17	*dance class/Ava* 18	*10:00 a.m. dentist movie/Sam* 19	20 TODAY	21	22
23	24	25	26	27	28	29
30						

Today is the 20th.

1. ___Three days ago___, Ken ___was___ at home.

2. _____, he _____ in Paris.

3. _____, he _____ in London.

4. _____, he _____ at the dentist.

5. _____, Ken and his dad _____ at the doctor.

6. _____, Ken and Sam _____ at a movie.

7. _____, Ken and Ava _____ at a dance class.

❑ **Exercise 24. Looking at grammar.** (Chart 8-5)
   Complete the sentences with your own words. Use **ago**.

   1. I'm in class now, but I was at home _____*ten minutes ago / two hours ago / etc.*_____

   2. I'm in class today, but I was absent from class _____

   3. I'm in this country now, but I was in my country _____

   4. I was in (*name of a city*) _____

   5. I was in elementary school _____

   6. I arrived in this city _____

   7. There is a nice park in this city. I was at the park _____

   8. We finished Exercise 16 _____

   9. I was home in bed _____

   10. It rained in this city _____

❑ **Exercise 25. Listening.** (Chart 8-5)
   Part I. Write the date.

   Today's date is _____ .

   Listen to the questions. Write the dates.

   1. _____   5. _____

   2. _____   6. _____

   3. _____   7. _____

   4. _____

   Part II. Write the time.

   Right now the time is _____ .

   Listen to the questions. Write the times.

   1. _____

   2. _____

   3. _____

❏ **Exercise 26. Warm-up.** (Chart 8-6)
Read the information about Jerry. Complete the sentences. Change the verbs in red to present time.

Last Night

Last night, Jerry ate dinner at 7:00. Then he did his homework for two hours. At 10:00, he went to bed.

Every Night

Every night, Jerry _____ dinner at 7:00. Then he _____
           1   2

his homework for two hours. At 10:00, he _____ to bed.
                                                  3

8-6 Simple Past Tense: Irregular Verbs (Group 1)

Some verbs do not have **-ed** forms. Their past forms are irregular.

PRESENT		SIMPLE PAST	
come	–	came	(a) I **come** to class **every day**.
do	–	did	(b) I **came** to class **yesterday**.
eat	–	ate	
get	–	got	(c) I **do** my homework **every day**.
go	–	went	(d) I **did** my homework **yesterday**.
have	–	had	
put	–	put	(e) Meg **eats** breakfast **every morning**.
see	–	saw	(f) Meg **ate** breakfast **yesterday morning**.
sit	–	sat	
sleep	–	slept	
stand	–	stood	
write	–	wrote	

❏ **Exercise 27. Vocabulary and speaking.** (Chart 8-6)
Practice using irregular verbs. Close your book for this activity.

Example: **come–came**
TEACHER: come–came. I come to class every day. I came to class yesterday. What did I do yesterday?
STUDENTS: (*repeat*) come–came. You came to class yesterday.

1. ***do–did*** We do exercises in class every day. We did exercises yesterday. What did we do yesterday?

2. ***eat–ate*** I eat lunch at 12:00 every day. Yesterday I ate lunch at 12:00. What did I do at 12:00 yesterday?

3. **get–got** I get up early every day. I got up early yesterday. What did I do yesterday? Did you get up early yesterday? What time did you get up?

4. **go–went** I go downtown every day. I went downtown yesterday. What did I do yesterday? Did you go downtown? Where did you go?

5. **have–had** I have breakfast every morning. I had breakfast yesterday morning. I had toast and fruit. What did I have yesterday morning? What did you have for breakfast yesterday morning?

6. **put–put** I like hats. I put on a hat every day. I put on a hat yesterday. What did I do yesterday?

7. **see–saw** I see my best friend every day. Yesterday I saw my best friend. What did I do yesterday? Did you see your best friend? Who did you see?

8. **sit–sat** I usually sit at my desk in the mornings. I sat at my desk yesterday morning. What did I do yesterday morning?

9. **sleep–slept** Sometimes I sleep for a long time at night. I slept for 10 hours last night. What did I do last night? Did you sleep for 10 hours last night? How many hours did you sleep last night?

10. **stand–stood** I stand at the bus stop every day. I stood at the bus stop yesterday. What did I do yesterday?

11. **write–wrote** I usually write in my journal every day. I wrote in my journal yesterday. What did I do yesterday? Did you write in your journal? What did you write about?

❑ **Exercise 28. Let's talk: pairwork.** (Chart 8-6)
Work with a partner. Take turns changing the sentences from the present to the past.

Example: I have class every day.
PARTNER A: I have class every day. I had class yesterday. Your turn now.

Example: Orlando gets mail from home every week.
PARTNER B: Orlando gets mail from home every week. Orlando got mail from home last week. Your turn now.

PARTNER A	PARTNER B
1. Lara gets some mail every day.	1. We have lunch every day.
2. They go to work every day.	2. I write emails to my parents every week.
3. The students stand in line at the cafeteria every day.	3. Jin comes to class late every day.
4. I see my friends every day.	4. I do my homework every day.
5. Hamid sits in the front row every day.	5. I eat breakfast every morning.
6. I sleep for eight hours every night.	6. Carlos puts his books in his briefcase every day.

❑ **Exercise 29. Looking at grammar.** (Charts 8-4 and 8-6)

Complete the sentences. Change the words in parentheses to the simple present, the present progressive, or the simple past. Pay attention to the spelling.

1. I (*get*) _____*got*_____ up at eight o'clock yesterday morning.

2. Ellie (*talk*) _____ to Barack on the phone last night.

3. Ellie (*talk*) _____ to Barack on the phone right now.

4. Ellie (*talk*) _____ to Barack on the phone every day.

5. Jim and I (*eat*) _____ lunch in the cafeteria two hours ago.

6. We (*eat*) _____ lunch in the cafeteria every day.

7. I (*go*) _____ to bed early last night.

8. My roommate (*study*) _____ Spanish last year.

9. Kate (*write*) _____ an email to her parents yesterday.

10. Kate (*write*) _____ an email to her parents every week.

11. Kate is in her room right now. She (*sit*) _____ at her desk.

12. Hanna (*do*) _____ her homework last night.

13. Yesterday I (*see*) _____ Fumiko at the library.

14. I (*have*) _____ a dream last night. I (*dream*)

_____ about my friends. I (*sleep*) _____

_____ for eight hours.

15. A strange thing (*happen*) _____ to me yesterday. I couldn't

remember my own telephone number.

16. My wife (*come*) _____ home around five every day.

17. Yesterday, she (*come*) _____ home at 5:15.

18. Our teacher (*stand*) _____ in the middle of the room

    right now.

19. Our teacher (*stand*) _____ in the front of the room yesterday.

20. Devon (*put*) _____ the butter in the refrigerator yesterday.

21. He (*put*) _____ the milk in the refrigerator every day.

22. Antonio usually (*sit*) _____ in the back of the room, but

    yesterday he (*sit*) _____ in the front row. Today, he (*be*)

    _____ absent. He (*be*) _____ absent

    two days ago too.

❑ **Exercise 30. Listening.** (Chart 8-6)

Listen to the beginning of each sentence. Choose the correct completion(s). There may be more than one correct answer.

Example: You will hear: He did . . .

You will choose: (a.) his homework.   (b.) a good job.   c. absent.

1. a. a chair.   b. some rice.   c. some numbers.

2. a. on the floor.   b. a man.   c. together.

3. a. late.   b. yesterday.   c. car.

4. a. an answer.   b. pretty.   c. a book.

5. a. a good grade.   b. last month.   c. a new truck.

6. a. a watch.   b. next to my parents.   c. at the bus stop.

❑ **Exercise 31. Warm-up.** (Chart 8-7)

Choose the verbs to make true sentences.

When my grandparents were in high school, they . . .

1. had / didn't have   computers.

2. ate / didn't eat   fast food.

8-7 Simple Past Tense: Negative

	SUBJECT	+	DID	+	NOT	+	MAIN VERB	
(a)	I		did		not		walk	to school yesterday.
(b)	You		did		not		walk	to school yesterday.
(c)	Tim		did		not		eat	lunch yesterday.
(d)	They		did		not		come	to class yesterday.

INCORRECT: *I did not walked to school yesterday.*
INCORRECT: *Tim did not ate lunch yesterday.*

I
you
she
he
it
we
they
} + **did not** + main verb*

Notice: The base form of the main verb is used with **did not**.

(e) I **didn't walk** to school yesterday.
(f) Tim **didn't eat** lunch yesterday.

NEGATIVE CONTRACTION
did + **not** = **didn't**

*EXCEPTION: **did** is NOT used when the main verb is **be**. See Charts 8-2 and 8-3.
  CORRECT: Dan *wasn't* here yesterday.
 INCORRECT: *Dan didn't be here yesterday.*

❏ **Exercise 32. Looking at grammar.** (Chart 8-7)
Complete the sentences. Use **not**.

TWO DAYS AGO	YESTERDAY
1. I got to school late.	I _____*didn't get*_____ to school late.
2. You got to school late.	You _____ school late.
3. She got to school late.	She _____ to school late.
4. They stayed home.	They _____ home.
5. We stayed home.	We _____ home.
6. She did her homework.	She _____ her homework.
7. You did your homework.	You _____ your homework.
8. We did our homework.	We _____ our homework.
9. I was sick.	I _____ sick.
10. They were sick.	They _____ sick.

❏ **Exercise 33. Let's talk: pairwork.** (Chart 8-7)

Work with a partner. Take turns using ***I don't . . . every day*** and ***I didn't . . . yesterday***.

Example: walk to school
PARTNER A: I don't walk to school every day. I didn't walk to school yesterday.
    Your turn now.

Example: listen to the radio
PARTNER B: I don't listen to the radio every day. I didn't listen to the radio yesterday.
    Your turn now.

PARTNER A	PARTNER B
1. eat breakfast	1. go to the library
2. watch TV	2. visit my friends
3. go shopping	3. see (*name of a person*)
4. read a newspaper	4. do my homework
5. study	5. get on the Internet

❏ **Exercise 34. Looking at grammar.** (Chart 8-7)

Complete the sentences. Change the words in parentheses to the simple present, present progressive, or simple past.

1. Jasmin (*come, not*) _____*didn't come*_____ to the meeting yesterday. She (*stay*)
   _____*stayed*_____ in her office.

2. I (*go*) _____ to a movie last night, but I (*enjoy, not*)
   _____ it. It (*be, not*) _____ very good.

3. Kay (*read*) _____ a magazine right now. She (*watch, not*)
   _____ TV. She (*like, not*) _____ to
   watch TV during the day.

4. A: (*Be*) _____ you sick yesterday?

   B: No, but my daughter (*feel, not*) _____ good, so I stayed
      home with her. She's fine now.

5. Toshi is a busy student. Sometimes he (*eat, not*) _____ lunch
   because he (*have, not*) _____ enough time between classes.
   Yesterday he (*have, not*) _____ time for lunch. He (*get*)
   _____ hungry during his afternoon class.

□ **Exercise 35. Let's talk: game.** (Chart 8-7)

Work in groups of six to eight students. Tell your group things you didn't do yesterday. Repeat the information from the other students in your group. The last person in the group repeats all the sentences.

Example: go

STUDENT A: I didn't go to the zoo yesterday.

STUDENT B: (*Student A*) didn't go to the zoo yesterday. I didn't have lunch in Beijing yesterday.

STUDENT C: (*Student A*) didn't go to the zoo yesterday. (*Student B*) didn't have lunch in Beijing yesterday. I didn't swim in the Pacific Ocean yesterday.
Etc.

Suggestions:

drive to	wake up	wear	talk to
walk to	swim	buy	use
eat	sing	study	fly to

□ **Exercise 36. Reading and grammar.** (Chart 8-7)

Read the story about Matt's morning. Then read the sentences that follow. If a sentence is true, do not change it. If it is not true, write a negative statement.

My Early Morning

Yesterday, my alarm clock didn't go off. I jumped out of bed and looked at the clock. I was late for work. I hurried to the kitchen and quickly prepared breakfast. I had some juice and toast. After breakfast, I put the dishes in the sink. I didn't have time to wash them. Then I quickly got dressed. Soon, I was ready. I walked to the bus. At the bus stop, I didn't recognize anyone. Then I looked at my watch. I was two hours early! I was half asleep when I jumped out of bed earlier and misread★ the time on my clock.

1. Matt's alarm clock went off. _____*Matt's alarm clock didn't go off.*_____

2. He got out of bed quickly. _____*(no change)*_____

3. He cooked a big breakfast. _____

4. He washed the dishes. _____

5. He got dressed in a hurry. _____

6. He saw his friends at the bus stop. _____

7. He was late for work. _____

8. It was time for work. _____

★*misread* = read incorrectly

Exercise 37. Warm-up. (Chart 8-8)
Answer the questions.

1. a. Do you wake up early every day?
   b. Did you wake up early today?

2. a. Do you eat breakfast every morning?
   b. Did you eat breakfast this morning?

8-8 Simple Past Tense: Yes/No Questions

DID + SUBJECT + MAIN VERB				SHORT ANSWER	(LONG ANSWER)
(a) *Did*	*Tess*	*walk*	to school? →	*Yes, she did.*	(She walked to school.)
			→	*No, she didn't.*	(She didn't walk to school.)
(b) *Did*	*you*	*come*	to class? →	*Yes, I did.*	(I came to class.)
			→	*No, I didn't.*	(I didn't come to class.)

❑ **Exercise 38. Let's talk: class activity.** (Chart 8-8)
Answer the simple past tense questions. Close your book for this activity.

Example:
  TEACHER: Did you work late last night?
STUDENT A: No, I didn't.
  TEACHER: (*Student A*), ask another student the same question.
STUDENT A: Did you work late last night?
STUDENT B: Yes, I did.
  TEACHER: (*Student B*), ask another student the same question.

Continue to the next question after three to five students have answered.

1. Did you walk home yesterday?

2. Did you come to class late today?

3. Did you wake up early today?

4. Did you eat meat for breakfast?

5. Did you drink coffee this morning?

6. Did you exercise today?

7. Did you play video games yesterday?

8. Did you text someone before 7:00 A.M.?

9. Did you make your bed this morning?

10. Did you wash the dishes this morning?

❏ **Exercise 39. Looking at grammar.** (Chart 8-8)

Make questions and give short answers.

1. A: _____*Did you walk downtown yesterday?*_____

   B: _____*Yes, I did.*_____ (I walked downtown yesterday.)

2. A: _____*Did it rain last week?*_____

   B: _____*No, it didn't.*_____ (It didn't rain last week.)

3. A: _____

   B: _____ (I ate lunch at the cafeteria.)

4. A: _____

   B: _____ (Mr. Kwan didn't go out of town last week.)

5. A: _____

   B: _____ (I had a cup of tea this morning.)

6. A: _____

   B: _____ (Ricardo and I went to a dance last night.)

7. A: _____

   B: _____ (Galina studied English in high school.)

8. A: _____

   B: _____ (Kirsten and Ali didn't do their homework.)

9. A: _____

   B: _____ (I saw Gina at dinner last night.)

10. A: _____

    B: _____ (I didn't dream in English last night.)

❏ **Exercise 40. Listening.** (Chart 8-8)

Listen to the questions. Write the words you hear.

Example: You will hear: Did you have your test already?

You will write: _____*Did you*_____ have your test already?

1. _____ do well on the test?

2. _____ finish the assignment?

3. _____ make sense?

4. _____ answer your question?

5. _____ need more help?

6. _____ understand the homework?

7. _____ explain the project?

8. _____ complete the project?

9. _____ do well?

10. _____ pass the class?

❏ **Exercise 41. Let's talk: find someone who . . . .** (Chart 8-8)

Interview your classmates. Make simple past questions with the given words. Find people who can answer *yes* and write their names.

Example: eat ice cream \ yesterday?
STUDENT A: Did you eat ice cream yesterday?
STUDENT B: No, I didn't. I didn't eat ice cream yesterday.
STUDENT A: (*Ask another student.*) Did you eat ice cream yesterday?
STUDENT C: Yes, I did. I ate ice cream yesterday. (*Write Student C's name.*)

ACTIVITY	FIRST NAME
1. eat rice \ yesterday?	
2. do homework \ last night?	
3. get an email \ yesterday?	
4. go shopping \ yesterday?	
5. sleep well \ last night?	
6. a. have coffee for breakfast \ this morning? b. put sugar in your coffee \ this morning?	
7. see a good movie \ last week?	
8. write in English \ today?	
9. sit on the floor \ yesterday?	
10. stand in line for something \ last week?	

❑ **Exercise 42. Listening.** **(Chart 8-8)**

In spoken English, speakers sometimes change or drop sounds. In questions, *did* and the pronoun that follows it can change.

Part I. Listen to the examples.

1. **Did you** ("dih-juh") see the news this morning?

2. A: Jim called.
   B: **Did he** ("dih-de") leave a message?

3. A: Julia called.
   B: **Did she** ("dih-she") leave a message?

4. **Did it** ("dih-dit") rain yesterday?

5. A: The kids are watching TV.
   B: **Did they** ("dih-they") finish their homework?

6. My keys aren't here. **Did I** ("dih-di") leave them in the car?

Part II. You will hear questions with *did* + *a pronoun.* Write the full forms.

Examples: You will hear: "Dih-dit" rain yesterday?
   You will write: _____*Did it*_____ rain yesterday?

   You will hear: "Dih-juh" come to class yesterday?
   You will write: _____*Did you*_____ come to class yesterday?

1. _____ finish the homework assignment?

2. _____ take a long time?

3. _____ hear my question?

4. _____ hear my question?

5. _____ speak loud enough?

6. _____ understand the information?

7. _____ understand the information?

8. _____ want more help?

9. _____ explain it okay?

10. _____ do a good job?

❑ **Exercise 43. Reading and grammar.** (Chart 8-8)
Read the story. Then write the questions the doctor asked Kevin and give Kevin's answers.

Kevin's Unhealthy Habits

Kevin didn't feel well. He went to see Dr. Benson. Dr. Benson checked him and asked him about his lifestyle. Kevin had several unhealthy habits: he slept very little, he didn't exercise, he ate unhealthy foods, and he smoked. He needed to change these habits. Kevin listened to the doctor, but he didn't change any habits. He went back to the doctor a month later. The doctor asked him several questions.

1. Dr. Benson: *you \ continue*

   ___*Did you continue*___ to smoke last month? Kevin: _____*Yes, I did.*_____

2. Dr. Benson: *you \ change*

   _____ your eating habits? Kevin: _____

3. Dr. Benson: *you \ exercise*

   _____? Kevin: _____

4. Dr. Benson: *you \ sleep*

   _____ more? Kevin: _____

5. Dr. Benson: *you \ think*

   _____ my advice was a joke? Kevin: _____

❑ **Exercise 44. Warm-up.** (Chart 8-9)

Which sentences are true for you?

1. ____ I sometimes drink water with dinner.

2. ____ I drank water with dinner last night.

3. ____ I think about my family every day.

4. ____ I thought about my family at midnight last night.

8-9	**Simple Past Tense: Irregular Verbs (Group 2)**	
bring – brought	drive – drove	run – ran
buy – bought	read – read*	teach – taught
catch – caught	ride – rode	think – thought
drink – drank		

*The simple past form of *read* is pronounced the same as the color *red*.

❑ **Exercise 45. Vocabulary and speaking.** (Chart 8-9)

Practice using irregular verbs. Close your book for this activity.

*Example: **teach–taught***

TEACHER: teach–taught. I teach class every day. I taught class yesterday. What did I do yesterday?

STUDENTS: (*repeat*) teach–taught. You taught class yesterday.

1. ***bring–brought*** I bring my book to class every day. I brought my book to class yesterday. What did I do yesterday?

2. ***buy–bought*** I buy apps for my phone. Yesterday, I bought an app for my phone. What did I do yesterday?

3. ***catch–caught*** On weekends, I go fishing. Sometimes, I catch fish. I caught a fish last week. Sometimes I catch a cold. Last week, I caught a bad cold. What did I do last week?

4. ***think–thought*** I often think about my family. I thought about my family yesterday. What did I do yesterday?

5. **REVIEW:** What did I bring to class yesterday? What did you bring yesterday? What did I buy yesterday? What did I catch last week? What did I think about yesterday? What did you think about yesterday?

6. ***run–ran*** Sometimes I'm late for class, so I run. Yesterday I was late, so I ran. What did I do yesterday?

7. ***read–read*** I like to read books. I read every day. Yesterday I read a book. What did I do yesterday? What did you read yesterday?

8. ***drink–drank*** I usually drink a cup of coffee in the morning. I drank a cup of coffee this morning. What did I do this morning? Did you drink a cup of coffee this morning? What do you usually drink in the morning? Do you drink the same thing every morning?

9. **drive–drove**   I usually drive my car to school. I drove my car to school this morning. What did I do this morning? Who has a car? Did you drive to school this morning?

10. **ride–rode**   Sometimes I ride the bus to school. I rode the bus yesterday morning. What did I do yesterday morning? Who rode the bus to school this morning?

11. **REVIEW:** I was late for class yesterday morning, so what did I do? What did I read yesterday? What did you read yesterday? Did you read a newspaper this morning? What did I drink this morning? What did you drink this morning? I have a car. Did I drive to school this morning? Did you? Did you ride the bus?

❏ **Exercise 46. Looking at grammar.** (Chart 8-9)
Complete each sentence with the correct form of the word in parentheses.

1. A: Why are you out of breath?

   B: I (*run*) _____ to class because I was late.

2. A: I (*ride*) _____ the bus to school yesterday. How did you get to school?

   B: I (*drive*) _____ my car.

3. A: Did you decide to change schools?

   B: I (*think*) _____ about it, but then I decided to stay here.

4. A: (*you, go*) _____ shopping yesterday?

   B: Yes. I (*buy*) _____ a new pair of shoes.

5. A: (*you, study*) _____ last night?

   B: No, I didn't. I was tired. I (*read*) _____ the news online and then

   (*go*) _____ to bed early.

6. A: Do you like milk?

   B: No. I (*drink*) _____ milk when I (*be*) _____ a child, but I don't like milk now.

7. A: Did you leave your dictionary at home?

   B: No. I (*bring*) _____ it to class with me.

8. Yesterday Sasha (*teach*) _____

   us how to say "thank you" in Japanese. Kim (*teach*)

   _____ us how to say "I love you"

   in Korean.

9. A: Did you enjoy your fishing trip?

   B: I had a wonderful time! I (*catch*)

   _____ a lot of fish.

Exercise 47. Let's talk: pairwork. (Chart 8-9)
Work with a partner. Take turns asking and answering simple past tense questions.

Example: think
PARTNER A: Did you think about me last night?
PARTNER B: Yes, I did. I thought about you last night. OR
                    No, I didn't. I didn't think about you last night.

PARTNER A	PARTNER B
1. drive	1. think
2. ride	2. drink
3. catch	3. read
4. teach	4. buy
5. bring	5. run

❏ **Exercise 48. Listening.** (Chart 8-9)
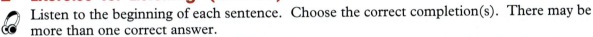
Listen to the beginning of each sentence. Choose the correct completion(s). There may be more than one correct answer.

Example: You will hear: He drank . . .
                    You will choose: (a.) some tea.   b. bread.   (c.) water.

1. a. last week.   b. a fish.   c. happy.
2. a. very fast   b. a house.   c. to the store.
3. a. books.   b. the kids.   c. the newspaper.
4. a. a story.   b. a bike.   c. a horse.
5. a. good.   b. some food.   c. a doctor.
6. a. people.   b. into town.   c. home.

❏ **Exercise 49. Writing.** (Charts 8-1 → 8-9)
Use the expressions from the list to write sentences about yourself. When did you do these things in the past? Use the simple past tense and past time expressions (*yesterday, two days ago, last week, etc.*) in all of your sentences. Use your own paper.

Example: go downtown with (*someone*)
Possible sentence: I went downtown with Marco two days ago.

1. arrive in (*this city*)
2. eat at a restaurant
3. buy (*something*)
4. have a cold
5. be in elementary school
6. drink a cup of coffee
7. talk to (*someone*) on the phone
8. study arithmetic
9. read a newspaper
10. play (soccer, a pinball machine, etc.)
11. see (*someone* or *something*)
12. think about (*someone* or *something*)
13. be born

Exercise 50. Warm-up. (Chart 8-10)
Which sentences are true for you?

1. _____ I sing in the shower every morning.

2. _____ I sang in the shower yesterday morning.

3. _____ I sometimes speak English in my dreams.

4. _____ I spoke English in my last dream.

8-10 Simple Past Tense: Irregular Verbs (Group 3)

break – broke	meet – met	sing – sang
fly – flew	pay – paid	speak – spoke
hear – heard	ring – rang	take – took
leave – left	send – sent	wake up – woke up

❏ **Exercise 51. Vocabulary and speaking.** (Chart 8-10)
Practice using irregular verbs. Close your book for this activity.

Example: ***break–broke***
   TEACHER: break–broke. Sometimes a person breaks an arm or a leg.
            I broke my arm five years ago. What happened five years ago?
   STUDENTS: (*repeat*) break–broke. You broke your arm.
   TEACHER: (*to Student A*) Did you ever* break a bone?
   STUDENT A: Yes. I broke my leg ten years ago.

1. ***fly–flew***   Sometimes I fly home in an airplane. I flew home in an airplane last month.
   What did I do last month? Did you fly to this city? When?

2. ***hear–heard***   I hear birds singing every morning. I heard birds singing yesterday.
   What did I hear yesterday? What did you hear when you woke up this morning?

3. ***pay–paid***   I pay the rent every month. I paid the rent last month. What did I do last
   month? Did you pay your rent last month?

4. ***send–sent***   I send my mom a gift every year on her birthday. I sent my mom a
   gift last year on her birthday. What did I do last year? When did you send a gift to
   someone?

5. ***leave–left***   I leave for school at 8:00 every morning. I left for school yesterday at
   8:00 A.M. What did I do at 8:00 A.M. yesterday? What time did you leave for class this
   morning?

6. ***meet–met***   I sometimes meet friends for lunch. Last month I met some friends for
   lunch. What did I do last month? Do you sometimes meet friends for lunch?

7. ***take–took***   I take my younger brother to the movies every month. I took my younger
   brother to the movies last month. What did I do last month? Who has a younger
   brother or sister? Where and when did you take him/her someplace?

---

*ever = at any time

8. ***wake–woke*** I usually wake up at six. This morning I woke up at six-thirty. What time did I wake up this morning? What time did you wake up this morning?

9. ***speak–spoke*** I speak to many students every day. Before class today, I spoke to (. . .). Who did I speak to? Who did you speak to before class today?

10. ***ring–rang*** I didn't turn my cell phone off when I went to bed last night. This morning, it rang at six-thirty and woke me up. What happened at six-thirty this morning? Who had a phone call this morning? What time did the phone ring?

11. ***sing–sang*** I sing in the shower every morning. I sang in the shower yesterday. What did I do yesterday? Do you ever sing in the shower? When was the last time?

12. ***break–broke*** Sometimes I break things. This morning I dropped a glass on the floor, and it broke. What happened this morning? When did you break something?

❏ ## Exercise 52. Looking at grammar. (Chart 8-10)
Complete the conversations. Use the correct form of the verbs from the box.

break	leave	ring	speak
fly	meet	send	take
hear	pay	sing	wake

1. A: What happened to your finger?

   B: I _____ it in a soccer game.

2. A: Who did you talk to at the director's office?

   B: I _____ to the secretary.

3. A: When did Jessica leave for Europe?

   B: She _____ for Europe five days ago.

4. A: Did you write Ted an email?

   B: No, but I _____ him a text.

5. A: Do you know Meg Adams?

   B: Yes. I _____ her a couple of weeks ago.

6. A: Why did you call the police?

   B: Because I _____ a burglar!

7. A: Where did you go yesterday?

   B: I _____ my son and daughter to the zoo.

8. A: What time did you get up this morning?

   B: 6:15.

   A: Why did you get up so early?

   B: The phone _____.

9. A: Did you enjoy the party?

   B: Yes, I had a good time. We _____ songs and danced. It was fun.

10. A: You look sleepy.

    B: I am. I _____ up before dawn this morning and never went back to sleep.

11. A: Did you give the painter a check?

    B: No. I _____ him in cash.

12. A: A bird _____ into our apartment yesterday through an open window.

    B: Really? What did you do?

    A: I caught it and took it outside.

❑ **Exercise 53. Let's talk: pairwork.** (Chart 8-10)

Work with a partner. Take turns asking and answering simple past tense questions.

Example: fly
PARTNER A: Did you fly to Paris last week?
PARTNER B: Yes, I did. I flew to Paris last week. OR
            No, I didn't. I didn't fly to Paris last week.

PARTNER A	PARTNER B
1. hear	1. fly
2. break	2. leave
3. take	3. speak
4. sing	4. wake up
5. ring	5. send
6. pay	6. meet

□ **Exercise 54. Listening.** (Chart 8-10)

Listen to the story. Then read each sentence and choose the correct answer.

A doctor's appointment

1. The man was at the doctor's office.	yes	no
2. He took some medicine.	yes	no
3. He was in bed for a short time.	yes	no
4. The man spoke to the nurse.	yes	no
5. He is feeling okay now.	yes	no

□ **Exercise 55. Warm-up.** (Chart 8-11)

Which sentences are true for you?

1. _____ I sometimes lose my keys.

2. _____ I lost my keys last week.

3. _____ I often wear jeans.

4. _____ I wore jeans yesterday.

8-11 Simple Past Tense: Irregular Verbs (Group 4)

begin – began	say – said	tell – told
find – found	sell – sold	tear – tore
lose – lost	steal – stole	wear – wore
hang – hung		

□ **Exercise 56. Vocabulary and speaking.** (Chart 8-11)

Practice using irregular verbs. Close your book for this activity.

Example: begin–began

TEACHER: begin–began. Our class begins at (9:00) every day. Class began at (9:00 this morning). When did class begin (this morning)?

STUDENTS: (*repeat*) begin–began. Class began at (9:00 this morning).

1. *lose–lost*   Sometimes I lose things. Yesterday I lost my keys. What did I lose yesterday?

2. *find–found*   Sometimes I lose things. And then I find them. Yesterday I lost my keys, but then I found them in my jacket pocket. What did I do yesterday?

3. *tear–tore*   If I make a mistake when I write a check, I tear the check up. Yesterday, I made a mistake when I wrote a check, so I tore it up and wrote a new check. What did I do yesterday?

4. *sell–sold*   People sell things that they don't need anymore. My friend has a new bike, so she sold her old bike. What did she do?

5. *hang–hung*   I like to hang pictures on my walls. This morning I hung a new picture in my bedroom. What did I do this morning?

6. *tell–told*   The kindergarten teacher likes to tell stories to her students. Yesterday she told a story about a little red train. What did the teacher do yesterday?

7. *wear–wore*   I wear a sweater to class every evening. Last night I also wore a jacket. What did I wear last night?

8. *steal–stole*   Thieves steal money and other things. Last month a thief stole my aunt's wallet. What did a thief do last month?

9. *say–said*   People usually say "hello" when they answer a phone. When my friend answered his phone this morning, he said "hello." What did he do this morning?

❏   **Exercise 57. Looking at grammar.** (Chart 8-11)
Complete the sentences with the correct form of the verbs from the box.

begin	hang	say	steal	tell
find	lose	sell	tear	wear

1. A: Did you go to the park yesterday?

   B: No. We stayed home because it _____ to rain.

   A: Oh, that's too bad.

2. A: Susie is in trouble.

   B: Why?

   A: She _____ a lie. Her mom and dad are upset.

   B: I'm sure she's sorry.

3. A: Did you find your sunglasses?

   B: No. I _____ them at the soccer game. I need to get some new ones.

4. A: Where's my coat?

   B: I _____ it up in the closet for you.

5. A: Where did you get that pretty shell?

   B: I _____ it on the beach.

shells

6. A: Do you still have your bike?

   B: No. I _____ it because I needed some extra money.

7. A: It's hot in here.

   B: Excuse me? What did you say?

   A: I _____, "It's hot in here."

8. A: Why did you take the bus to work this morning? Why didn't you drive?

   B: Because somebody _____ my car last night.

   A: Did you call the police?

   B: Of course I did.

9. A: Did you wear your blue jeans to the job interview?

   B: Of course not! I _____ a suit.

10. A: I wrote the wrong amount on the check, so I had to write a new check.

    B: What did you do with the first check?

    A: I _____ it into pieces.

❏ **Exercise 58. Let's talk: pairwork.** (Chart 8-11)
Work with a partner. Take turns asking and answering simple past tense questions.

Example: wear
PARTNER A: Did you wear slippers last night?
PARTNER B: Yes, I did. I wore slippers last night. OR
             No, I didn't. I didn't wear slippers last night.

PARTNER A	PARTNER B
1. hang	1. find
2. steal	2. sell
3. wear	3. lose
4. say	4. tell
5. begin	5. tear

Exercise 59. Listening. (Chart 8-11)

Listen to the story. Then read each sentence and choose the correct answer.

A wedding ring

1. The woman lost her mother's ring.	yes	no
2. Someone stole the ring.	yes	no
3. Her dog found the ring in the garden.	yes	no
4. Her mother wore the ring for a while.	yes	no
5. The woman was happy at the end of the story.	yes	no

❏ **Exercise 60. Looking at grammar.** (Chapter 8)

You went to a birthday party last night. A friend is asking you questions about it. Complete the sentences with *did*, *was*, or *were*.

1. _____ you go with a friend?

2. _____ your friends at the party?

3. _____ the party fun?

4. _____ many people there?

5. _____ you have a good time?

6. _____ there a birthday cake?

7. _____ you eat a piece of birthday cake?

8. _____ everyone sing "Happy Birthday"?

9. _____ you hungry?

10. _____ you bring a present?

a present

❏ **Exercise 61. Looking at grammar.** (Chapter 8)

Complete the sentences with *did*, *was*, or *were*.

1. I _____*did*_____ not go to work yesterday. I _____*was*_____ sick, so I stayed home.

2. Ray _____ not in his office yesterday. He _____ not go to work.

3. A: _____ Mr. Chan in his office yesterday?

   B: Yes.

   A: _____ you see him about your problem?

   B: Yes. He answered all my questions. He _____ very helpful.

4. A: _____ you at the meeting yesterday?

   B: Yes.

   A: _____ I miss anything?

   B: No. It _____ really short. The fire alarm went off right after it started.

      We _____ outside for the rest of the hour.

5. A: Where _____ you yesterday?

   B: I _____ at the zoo.

   A: _____ you enjoy it?

   B: Yes, but the weather _____ very hot. I tried to stay out of the sun.

      Most of the animals _____ in their houses or in the shade. The sun

      _____ too hot for them too. They _____ not want to be outside.

❏ **Exercise 62. Looking at grammar.** (Chapter 8)
Make questions.

A bad experience

1. A: _____ *Do you live in an apartment?* _____

   B: Yes, I do. (I live in an apartment.)

2. A: _____ *Do you have a roommate?* _____

   B: No, I don't. (I don't have a roommate.)

3. A: _____

   B: No, I don't. (I don't want a roommate.)

4. A: _____

   B: Yes, I did. (I had a roommate last year.)

5. A: _____

   B: No, it wasn't. (It wasn't a good experience.)

6. A: _____

   B: Yes, he was. (He was messy.)

      For example, he never picked up his dirty clothes. He never washed his dirty

      dishes. He was always late with his part of the rent.

7. A: _____

   B: No, he didn't. (He didn't help me clean.)

8. A: _____

   B: Yes, I was. (I was glad when he left.)

❏ **Exercise 63. Let's talk.** (Chapter 8)

Work in pairs or small groups. Read the facts about four people: Lara, Josh, Max, and Kira. They live in an apartment building on the same floor. Which apartment does each person live in? Use the clues to find out.

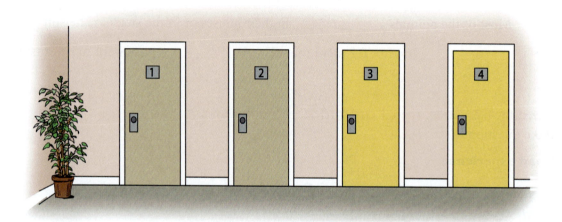

Clues:

1. Lara painted her door yellow.

2. Josh and Lara lived in the same neighborhood as children. Now they are next-door neighbors.

3. Max loves music. He works at a music store. His parents were musicians in a band.

4. Kira isn't very social. She didn't want neighbors on both sides, so she rented an end unit.

5. Lara moved into her apartment last year.

6. The first time Max played loud music, both Kira and Josh knocked on the walls. They told him to turn it down.

APARTMENT NUMBER	1	2	3	4
NAME				

Exercise 64. Check your knowledge. (Chapter 8)

Correct the mistakes.

                    stole   *s*

1. Someone ~~stealed~~ my bike two day ago.

2. Did you went to the party yesterday weekend?

3. I hear an interesting story yesterday.

4. The teacher not ready for class yesterday.

5. Did came Dennis to work last week?

6. Yesterday night I staied home and work on my science project.

7. A few students wasn't on time for the final exam yesterday.

8. Your fax came before ten minutes. Did you got it?

9. Did you the movie watch?

10. The store no have yellow bananas. I get some green ones.

11. Did you nervous about your test last week?

12. I didn't saw you at the party. Did was you there?

❏ **Exercise 65. Reading and writing.** (Chapter 8)

Part I. Read the story.

An Embarrassing Week

      Andy did some embarrassing things last week. For example, on Monday, he wore his slippers to work. He got on the bus and looked down at his feet. He felt very stupid and wanted to hide his feet.

      That night, he typed an email to his girlfriend. He told her he loved her. But he hit the wrong button and he sent the message to his boss. His girlfriend and his boss have the same first name. He didn't know until the next morning when she greeted him at work. She didn't look very happy.

      On Friday, he went to a nice restaurant with co-workers for lunch and ate a salad. After lunch he had a meeting. He talked a lot at the meeting. People gave him strange looks, but Andy didn't know why. Later he found out the reason. He had lettuce on his front teeth.

      Andy is hoping for a better week this week. He hid his slippers under the bed and put a mirror in his desk drawer. But he didn't tell his girlfriend about the email because he is still very embarrassed.

Part II. Write about something embarrassing that you did or something embarrassing that happened to you. Your title can be "An Embarrassing Week," "An Embarrassing Day," "An Embarrassing Night," "An Embarrassing Experience," etc. If you can't think of things, write about a family member or a friend.

1. First, write single sentences about one or more embarrassing things you or someone else did. Use simple past tense verbs.

2. Add details to make the story interesting. Answer these questions:

   Where and/or when did it happen?

   What did you think?

   How did you feel?

   What did you do next?

   Did you need to find a solution?

3. Put this information into one or more paragraphs.

Part III. Editing check: Work individually or change papers with a partner. Check (✓) for the following:

1. _____ indented paragraph

2. _____ capital letter at the beginning of each sentence

3. _____ period at the end of each sentence

4. _____ correct use of the simple past for a completed activity

5. _____ correct use of **didn't** and **wasn't** for simple past negatives

6. _____ correct spelling (use a dictionary or computer spell-check)

Chapter 9
Expressing Past Time, Part 2

❏ **Exercise 1. Warm-up.** (Chart 9-1)
Choose the correct answer for each question.

1. When did you get to school?
   a. Yes, I did.　　b. Downtown.　　c. At 11:00.

2. Where were you born?
   a. At midnight.　　b. In this city.　　c. Yes, I was.

9-1 Simple Past Tense: Using *Where, Why, When,* and *What Time*

QUESTION					SHORT ANSWER
(a)		*Did*	you	*go*	downtown?	→ Yes, I did. / No, I didn't.
(b)	*Where*	did	you	*go*?		→ **Downtown.**
(c)		Were	you		downtown?	→ Yes, I was. / No, I wasn't.
(d)	*Where*	were	you?			→ **Downtown.**
(e)		*Did*	you	*run*	because you were late?	→ Yes, I did. / No, I didn't.
(f)	*Why*	did	you	*run*?		→ **Because I was late.**
	Why	didn't	you	*walk*?		**Because I was late.**
(g)		*Did*	Ann	*come*	at six?	→ Yes, she did. / No, she didn't.
(h)	*When* ⎫					
	What time ⎭	did	Ann	*come*?		→ **At six.**

COMPARE	
(i) *What time* did Ann come? → **At six.** → **Seven o'clock.** → **Around 9:30.**	***What time*** usually asks for a specific time on a clock.
(j) *When* did Ann come? → **At six.** → **Friday.** → **June 15th.** → **Last week.** → **Three days ago.**	The answer to ***when*** can be various expressions of time.

❏ **Exercise 2. Looking at grammar.** (Chart 9-1)
Make simple past tense questions and answers about Rosa's vacation.

1. Where . . . go?
2. Why . . . go there?
3. When/What time . . . leave?

```
Rosa's travel plans
To Hawaii
For a vacation
Leave at 2:00 P.M.
```

1. A: _____*Where did Rosa go?*_____

   B: _____*She went to Hawaii.*_____

2. A: _____

   B: _____

3. A: _____

   B: _____

❏ **Exercise 3. Looking at grammar.** (Chart 9-1)
Make questions. Use *where, when, what time,* or *why*.

1. A: _____*Where did you go yesterday?*_____

   B: To the beach. (I went to the beach yesterday.)

2. A: _____

   B: Last month. (Mr. Chu arrived in Canada last month.)

3. A: _____

   B: At 7:05. (Their plane arrived at 7:05.)

4. A: _____

   B: Because I was tired. (I stayed home last night because I was tired.)

5. A: _____

   B: Because I stayed up the night before. (I was tired because I stayed up the night before.)

6. A: _____

   B: To Greece. (Sofia went to Greece for her vacation.)

7. A: _____

   B: Around midnight. (Lia finished her homework around midnight.)

8. A: _____

   B: Five weeks ago. (I came to this city five weeks ago.)

Exercise 4. Let's talk: interview. (Chart 9-1)

Walk around the room. Ask and answer questions using the simple past tense. Share some of your classmates' answers with the class.

Example: What time \ go to bed \ you \ last night?
STUDENT A: What time did you go to bed last night?
STUDENT B: I went to bed at 10:00 last night.

1. What time \ get up \ you \ this morning?
2. When \ finish \ you \ your homework \ last night?
3. Where \ be \ you \ at 10:00 last night?
4. Why \ choose \ you \ this school?
5. Why \ decide \ you \ to study English?
6. What time \ cook \ you \ dinner ?
7. Where \ cook \ you \ dinner?
8. What time \ walk \ you \ into this room?
9. Where \ buy \ you \ this book?
10. When \ buy \ you \ this book?

Exercise 5. Listening. (Chart 9-1)

Choose the correct answer for each question you hear. Use the information on the datebook pages.

Example: You will hear: Where did Isabel go?
            You will choose: a. At 1:00 P.M.   (b.) To the gym.   c. For an exercise class.

Marco's Day		Sabrina's Day		Bill's Day		Isabel's Day	
Mon.	April 4	Mon.	April 4	Mon.	April 4	Mon.	April 4
7:00 A.M.		12:00 Noon		10:00 A.M.		1:00 P.M.	
School		City Café		Dentist		Gym	
meeting with teacher		business meeting		check-up		exercise class	

1. a. At noon.   b. To the City Café.   c. Because she had a meeting.
2. a. At noon.   b. To the City Café.   c. Because she had a meeting.
3. a. To the gym.   b. For an exercise class. c. At 1:00 P.M.
4. a. To the gym.   b. For an exercise class. c. At 1:00 P.M.
5. a. To the gym.   b. For an exercise class. c. At 1:00 P.M.
6. a. Because he had a meeting. b. At 7:00 A.M.   c. To school.
7. a. Because he had a meeting. b. At 7:00 A.M.   c. To school.
8. a. To the dentist.   b. For a check-up.   c. At 10:00 A.M.
9. a. To the dentist.   b. For a check-up.   c. At 10:00 A.M.

Exercise 6. Looking at grammar. (Chart 9-1)
Complete the negative questions.

1. A: I didn't go to class yesterday.

   B: Why didn't ____*you go to class*_____?

   A: Because I was sick.

2. A: I didn't finish my homework.

   B: Why didn't _____?

   A: Because I didn't have enough time.

3. A: I didn't eat breakfast this morning.

   B: Why didn't _____?

   A: Because I wasn't hungry.

4. A: I didn't clean my apartment last week.

   B: Why didn't _____?

   A: Because I was too tired.

5. A: I didn't turn on my cell phone yesterday.

   B: Why didn't _____?

   A: Because I wanted to finish my work.

❑ **Exercise 7. Listening.** (Chart 9-1)

Listen to the questions. Choose the verb you hear: ***did*** or ***didn't***. *Note:* ***Did you*** can sound like "Did-ja." ***Did he*** can sound like "Dih-de."

Example: You will hear: Why didn't he help?

You will choose: did   (didn't)

1. did	didn't		5. did	didn't	
2. did	didn't		6. did	didn't	
3. did	didn't		7. did	didn't	
4. did	didn't		8. did	didn't	

❑ **Exercise 8. Warm-up.** (Chart 9-2)
Choose the correct answer.

What did you want?

a. Some help.   b. Yes, I did.   c. Yes, I was.   d. Mr. Harris.

9-2 Questions with *What*

What is used in a question when you want to find out about a thing. *Who* is used when you want to find out about a person. (See Chart 9-3 for questions with *Who*.)

(QUESTION + WORD)	HELPING + VERB	SUBJECT +	MAIN VERB		SHORT ANSWER	(LONG ANSWER)
(a)	*Did*	Carol	*buy*	a car? →	Yes, she did.	(*She bought a car.*)
(b) *What*	*did*	Carol	*buy*?	→	*A car.*	(*She bought a car.*)
(c)	*Is*	Fred	*holding*	a book? →	Yes, he is.	(*He's holding a book.*)
(d) *What*	*is*	Fred	*holding*?	→	*A book.*	(*He's holding a book.*)

S V O (e) Carol bought *a car*.	In (e): *a car* is the object of the verb.
O V S V (f) *What* did Carol buy?	In (f): *What* is the object of the verb.

❑ **Exercise 9. Looking at grammar.** (Chart 9-2)
Make questions.

1. A: _____*Did you buy a new TV?*_____

    B: Yes, I did. (I bought a new TV.)

2. A: _____*What did you buy?*_____

    B: A new TV. (I bought a new TV.)

3. A: _____

    B: Yes, she is. (Maya is carrying a suitcase.)

4. A: _____

    B: A suitcase. (Maya is carrying a suitcase.)

5. A: _____

    B: Yes, I do. (I see a plane.)

6. A: _____

    B: A plane. (I see a plane.)

7. A: _____

    B: No, I'm not. (I'm not afraid of mice.) Are you?

8. A: _____

    B: The map on the wall. (The teacher is talking about the map on the wall.)

9. A: _____

   B: Some soup. (Franco had some soup for lunch.)

10. A: _____

    B: Yes, he did. (Franco had some soup for lunch.)

11. A: _____

    B: A sandwich. (Franco usually eats a sandwich for lunch.)

12. A: _____

    B: No, he doesn't. (Franco doesn't like salads.)

❑ **Exercise 10. Let's talk: class activity.** (Chart 9-2)
Answer the questions your teacher asks you. Pronounce the verb endings clearly. Close your book for this activity.

Example: walk to the front of the room
   TEACHER: (*Student A*), walk to the front of the room.
STUDENT A: (*walks to the front of the room*)
   TEACHER: (*to Student B*) What did (*Student A*) do?
STUDENT B: She/He walked to the front of the room.
   TEACHER: (*to Student A*) What did you do?
STUDENT A: I walked to the front of the room.

1. smile
2. laugh
3. cough
4. sneeze
5. shave (*act out*)
6. erase the board
7. sign your name
8. open the door
9. close the door
10. ask a question
11. wash your hands (*act out*)
12. touch the floor
13. point at the door
14. fold a piece of paper
15. count your fingers
16. push (*something in the room*)
17. pull (*something in the room*)
18. yawn
19. pick up your pen
20. add two and two on the board

❑ **Exercise 11. Vocabulary and grammar.** (Chart 9-2)

Ask your teacher for the meaning of the given words. Begin your question with *What*.

Example: century
STUDENT: What does *century* mean?
TEACHER: *Century* means "100 years."

1. humid
2. awful
3. quiet

4. grocery store
5. pretty difficult
6. ill

7. murder
8. enjoy
9. old-fashioned

❑ **Exercise 12. Let's talk: class activity.** (Charts 9-1 and 9-2)

Ask your teacher questions to complete the chart with information about each person's day.★

SITUATION: All these women were absent from school yesterday. What did each person do? In your opinion, who had the best day?

Example:
STUDENT A: What time did Jenny wake up?
  TEACHER: 7:00 A.M.
STUDENT B: What did Jin eat for breakfast?
  TEACHER: Rice.

	wake up	**eat for breakfast**	**spend the day**	**go to bed**	**absent**
JENNY	*7:00 A.M.*				
JIN		*rice*			
JADA			*at the beach*		
JANICE				*10:00 P.M.*	
JULIANNA					*Because she needed to earn extra money for school tuition.*

❑ **Exercise 13. Listening.** (Charts 9-1 and 9-2)

Listen to the questions. Write the words you hear.

Example: You will hear: Where did they go?
           You will write: ____*Where did they*____ go?

1. _____ arrive?
2. _____ leave?
3. _____ want?
4. _____ study?

5. _____ say?
6. _____ move?
7. _____ move to?

★*Teacher:* See Let's Talk: Answers, p. 503.

❑ **Exercise 14. Warm-up.** (Chart 9-3)
Match each picture with the correct conversation.

Picture A

Picture B

1. A: Who did you pick up at the airport?
    B: My father.

2. A: Who picked you up at the airport?
    B: My father.

9-3 Questions with *Who* and *Whom*

QUESTION	ANSWER	
(a) **What** did they see? → **A boat.** (They saw a boat.) (b) **Who** did they see? → **Jay.** (They saw Jay.)		**What** is used to ask questions about *things*. **Who** is used to ask questions about *people*.
(c) **Who** did they see? → **Jay.** (They saw Jay.) (d) **Whom** did they see? → **Jay.** (They saw Jay.)		Examples (c) and (d) have the same meaning. **Whom** is used in formal English as the object of a verb or a preposition. In (c): **Who**, not **whom**, is usually used in everyday English. In (d): **Whom** is used in very formal English. **Whom** is rarely used in everyday spoken English.
(e) **Who(m)** did they see? → **Jay.** (They saw **Jay**.) (f) **Who** saw Jay? → **Ella.** (**Ella** saw Jay.) (g) **Who** lives there? → **Ed.** (**Ed** lives there.) (h) **Who** came? → **Eva.** (**Eva** came.) INCORRECT: *Who did come?*		In (e): **Who(m)** is the object of the verb. Usual question word order is used: *question word + helping verb + subject + main verb* In (f), (g), and (h): **Who** is the subject of the question. Usual question word order is NOT used. When **who** is the subject of a question, do NOT use **does, do,** or **did.** Do NOT change the verb in any way: the verb form in the question is the same as the verb form in the answer.

❏ **Exercise 15. Looking at grammar.** (Chart 9-3)
Work with a partner. Make questions orally with **who**. Then write the questions.

Example: The teacher saw Alan. The teacher talked to Alan. The teacher helped Alan.

→ a. ___*Who saw Alan*_____? The teacher.
→ b. ___*Who talked to Alan*_____? The teacher.
→ c. ___*Who helped Alan*_____? The teacher.
→ d. ___*Who did the teacher see*_____? Alan.
→ e. ___*Who did the teacher talk to*_____? Alan.
→ f. ___*Who did the teacher help*_____? Alan.

1. Alan called Yuko. Alan visited Yuko. Alan studied with Yuko.

   a. _____? Alan.

   b. _____? Alan.

   c. _____? Alan.

   d. _____? Yuko.

   e. _____? Yuko.

   f. _____? Yuko.

2. Ron talked to the kids. Ron watched the kids. Ron played with the kids.

   a. _____? Ron.

   b. _____? The kids.

   c. _____? Ron.

   d. _____? The kids.

   e. _____? Ron.

   f. _____? The kids.

❏ **Exercise 16. Looking at grammar.** (Chart 9-3)
Make questions. Answer the questions where necessary.

1. Astrid carried the baby.

   a. Who carried _____? Astrid.

   b. Who did _____? The baby.

2. The firefighter saved the woman.

    a. Who did _____? The woman.

    b. Who saved _____? The firefighter.

3. Professor Ramic taught the students.

    a. Who taught _____? _____.

    b. Who did _____? _____.

❑ **Exercise 17. Looking at grammar.** (Chart 9-3)
Make questions.

    1. A: _____

       B: Nina. (I saw Nina at the party.)

    2. A: _____

       B: Nina. (Nina came to the party.)

    3. A: _____

       B: Kenji. (I talked to Kenji.)

    4. A: _____

       B: Abbey. (Barak helped Abbey.)

    5. A: _____

       B: Barak. (Barak helped Abbey.)

    6. A: _____

       B: Barak and Abbey. (I invited Barak and Abbey.)

❑ **Exercise 18. Let's talk: pairwork.** (Charts 9-1 → 9-3)
Work with a partner. Finish this conversation between a parent and a teenager. Use your imagination. You can make it funny or serious. Perform your conversation for the class.

PARENT: Where did you go last night?

TEENAGER: _____
                                        1

PARENT: What did you do?

TEENAGER: _____
                                        2

PARENT: Who did you see?

TEENAGER: _____
                                        3

PARENT: Who saw you?

TEENAGER: _____
                                        4

PARENT: When did you get home?

TEENAGER: _____
                                        5

PARENT: Is there anything else you want to tell me?

TEENAGER: _____
                                        6

PARENT: You're grounded!⋆

⋆*to be grounded:* a type of punishment from a parent: the child stays at home and can't do activities with friends.

Listen to each question and choose the best answer.

Example: You will hear: Why was John late?
You will choose: a. Yesterday.   b. At the park.   (c.) Because he slept too long.

1. a. At midnight.   b. Because it was late.   c. With my parents.

2. a. Last month.   b. In a small town.   c. Because he was a
                                                        co-worker.

3. a. In a minute.   b. Some money.   c. John and Sarah.

4. a. At work.   b. At 10:00.   c. There was a party.

5. a. An apartment downtown.   b. Next week.   c. Because we like the city.

6. a. The bus.   b. Because her car   c. Maya did.
                            didn't start.

7. a. Because I didn't   b. My friends.   c. It was fun.
      have time.

❏ **Exercise 20. Game.** (Chart 9-3)
Work in teams. Choose two places from the list and write as many questions as you can for
each situation. Try to use a mix of *Wh*-questions: **When, Where, What time, Who,** and
Why. The team with the most grammatically correct questions wins.

Example: Your friend just got home from the shopping mall.
Possible questions: What did you buy? Where did you shop? Etc.

Your friend just got home from . . .

1. the shopping mall.   4. the dentist's office.   7. the hospital.
2. the library.   5. the train station.   8. a one-week vacation.
3. the airport.   6. the movies.   9. a soccer tournament.

❏ **Exercise 21. Warm-up.** (Chart 9-4)
Complete the sentences with your own words.

1. a. Right now a pack of gum costs _____.

   b. When I was a child, a pack of gum cost _____.

2. a. In restaurants, some chefs make _____ for dinner.

   b. The last time I cooked dinner, I made _____.

9-4 Simple Past Tense: Irregular Verbs (Group 5)

cost – cost	hit – hit	shut – shut
cut – cut	hurt – hurt	spend – spent
forget – forgot	lend – lent	understand – understood
give – gave	make – made	

❑ **Exercise 22. Vocabulary and speaking.** (Chart 9-4)

Practice using irregular verbs. Close your book for this activity.

*Example: **cost–cost***

TEACHER: cost–cost. Gasoline costs a lot of money. Yesterday, I bought gas for my car. It cost a lot of money. How much did it cost?

STUDENTS: (*repeat*) cost–cost. It cost a lot of money.

1. ***cost–cost*** I bought a jacket yesterday. I paid a lot for it. It cost (. . .). What did I buy yesterday? How much did it cost?

2. ***cut–cut*** (. . .) cuts vegetables when he/she makes a salad. Two nights ago, he/she made a salad and cut his/her finger with the knife. What happened two nights ago?

3. ***forget–forgot*** Sometimes I forget my wallet. Last night, I forgot it at a restaurant. What did I do last night?

4. ***give–gave*** People give gifts on birthdays. Last week, (. . .) had a birthday. I gave him/her (*something*). What did I do?

5. ***hit–hit*** When you play tennis, you hit the ball with a tennis racket. When you play table tennis, you hit the ball with a paddle. What do you do when you play tennis? What do you do when you play table tennis?

6. ***hurt–hurt*** When I have a headache, my head hurts. Yesterday I had a headache. My head hurt. How did my head feel yesterday? How does your head feel when you have a headache?

7. ***lend–lent*** I lend money to my friends if they need it. Yesterday I lent (*an amount of money*) to (. . .). What did I do?

8. ***make–made*** I know how to make ice cream! Last week I made chocolate ice cream for a birthday party. What did I do last week?

9. ***shut–shut*** I shut the garage door every night at 10:00 P.M. I shut it early last night. What did I do last night?

10. ***spend–spent*** I usually spend Saturdays with friends. But last Saturday, I spent the day with my parents. What did I do last Saturday?

11. ***understand–understood*** I don't always understand singers when they sing. But yesterday I listened to a new song, and I understood every word. What did I understand?

Complete each sentence. Use the correct form of the word in parentheses.

1. A: How much does a new car cost?

   B: It (*cost*) _____costs_____ a lot. New cars are expensive.

2. A: Did you get a ticket for the rock concert?

   B: No, it (*cost*) _____ too much.

3. A: Where's your history book?

   B: I (*give*) _____ it to Robert.

4. A: What happened?

   B: I had a car accident. I (*hit*) _____
   a telephone pole.

5. A: May I have your homework, please?

   B: I'm sorry, but I don't have it. I (*forget*) _____ it.

6. A: Did you eat breakfast?

   B: Yeah. I (*make*) _____ some scrambled eggs and toast for myself.

7. Eric (*shut*) _____ the window when he wakes up every morning.

8. Eric (*shut*) _____ the window when he woke up yesterday morning.

9. A: Did you enjoy going into the city to see a show?

   B: Yes, but I (*spend*) _____ a lot of money.

10. A: Do you have a calculator?

    B: Yes, but I (*lend*) _____ it to George.

11. A: Is that knife sharp?

    B: It's very sharp. It (*cut*) _____ everything easily.

12. A: Why are you wearing a cap on your head? It's so hot today.

    B: I went to a barber this morning. He (*cut*) _____ my hair too short.

    A: Let me see. Oh, it looks fine.

Exercise 24. Listening. (Chart 9-4)

Listen to the beginning of each sentence. Choose the correct completion(s). There may be more than one correct answer.

Example: You will hear: Kurt made . . .
You will choose: (a.) his lunch.   (b.) furniture.   c. in the morning.

1. a. the answer.   b. the conversation.   c. the teacher.

2. a. money.   b. to her house.   c. some furniture.

3. a. your hair?   b. some paper?   c. between?

4. a. tomorrow.   b. a tree.   c. an animal.

5. a. remember.   b. his appointment.   c. the question.

❏ **Exercise 25. Warm-up.** (Chart 9-5)

Which answers are true for you?

1. a. Right now I feel   fine / okay / tired / hungry.

    b. On the first day of class, I felt   fine / okay / nervous / scared.

2. a. My favorite sports team   wins / doesn't win   a lot of games.

    b. My favorite sports team   won / didn't win   its last game.

9-5 Simple Past Tense: Irregular Verbs (Group 6)

blow – blew	grow – grew	swim – swam
draw – drew	keep – kept	throw – threw
fall – fell	know – knew	win – won
feel – felt		

❏ **Exercise 26. Vocabulary and speaking.** (Chart 9-5).

Practice using irregular verbs. Close your book for this activity.

Example: ***fall–fell***
TEACHER: fall–fell. Rain falls. Leaves fall. Sometimes people fall. Yesterday I fell down.
         I hurt my knee. How did I hurt my knee
         yesterday?
STUDENTS: (*repeat*) fall–fell. You fell (down).

1. ***blow–blew***   The sun shines. Rain falls. Wind blows. Last week we had a storm. It rained hard, and the wind blew hard. Tell me about the storm last week.

2. ***draw–drew*** I draw once a week in art class. Last week I drew a picture of a mountain. What did I do in art class last week?

3. ***fall–fell*** Sometimes I fall down. Yesterday I fell down some steps outside my house. What happened to me yesterday?

4. ***feel–felt*** Sometimes I feel sleepy in class. I felt tired all day yesterday. How did I feel yesterday? How did you feel yesterday?

5. ***grow–grew*** Trees grow. Flowers grow. Vegetables grow. Usually I grow vegetables in my garden, but last year I grew only flowers. What did I grow in my garden last year?

6. ***keep–kept*** Now I keep my money in (*name of a local bank*). Last year I kept my money in (*name of another local bank*). Where did I keep my money last year?

7. ***know–knew*** This class knows a lot about English grammar. Last week, many students knew the answers to my questions. What did many students know last week?

8. ***swim–swam*** I swim in (*name of a lake, sea, ocean, or local swimming pool*) every summer. I swam in (*name of a lake, sea, ocean, or local swimming pool*) last summer. What did I do last summer?

9. ***throw–threw*** In baseball, the pitcher throws the ball. I like to play baseball. I like to throw the ball. Yesterday, when I played baseball, I was the pitcher. What did I do with the ball?

a pitcher

a batter

10. ***win–won*** You can win a game or lose a game. Last weekend (*name of a local sports team*) won a game/match against (*name of another team*). What did (*name of the local sports team*) do last weekend? Did they win or lose?

❑ **Exercise 27. Looking at grammar.** (Chart 9-5)
Complete the sentences. Use the simple past form of the verbs from the box.

blow	fall	grow	know	throw
draw	feel	keep	swim	win

1. A: Did you enjoy your tennis game with Jackie?

   B: Yes, but I lost. Jackie _____.

2. A: How did you break your leg?

   B: I _____ down on the ice on the sidewalk.

3. A: Did you give the box of candy to your girlfriend?

   B: No, I didn't. I _____ it and ate it myself.

4. A: That's a nice picture.

   B: I agree. Tanya _____ it. She's a good artist.

5. A: Your daughter is so tall!

   B: I know. She _____ a lot last year.

6. A: I burned my finger.

   B: Did you put ice on it?

   A: No. I _____ on it.

7. A: Did you finish the test?

   B: No. I _____ all of the answers, but I ran out of time.

8. A: Did you have fun at the beach?

   B: Lots of fun. We _____ in the ocean.

9. A: What's the matter? You sound like you have a frog in your throat.

   B: I think I'm catching a cold. I _____ okay yesterday, but I don't feel very good today.

10. A: How did you break the window, Tommy?

    B: Well, I _____ a ball to Julie, but it missed Julie and hit the window instead.

❏ **Exercise 28. Listening.** (Chart 9-5)

Listen to the beginning of each sentence. Choose the correct completion(s). There may be more than one correct answer.

Example: You will hear: Tim knew . . .
You will choose: (a.) my father.   b. a ball.   (c.) the answer.

1. a. tomorrow.	b. on a car.	c. in the park.
2. a. the game.	b. a prize.	c. lost.
3. a. on the paper.	b. a picture.	c. with a pencil.
4. a. happy.	b. in the morning.	c. excited.
5. a. a ball.	b. not.	c. a pillow.

❏ **Exercise 29. Warm-up.** (Chart 9-6)

Make true sentences for you.

1. Some people feed animals at the zoo.

   When I was a child, I   fed / didn't feed   animals at the zoo.

2. During storms, some kids hide in closets or under the bed.

   When I was a child, I   hid / didn't hide   during a storm.

9-6 Simple Past Tense: Irregular Verbs (Group 7)

become – became	build – built	hide – hid
bend – bent	feed – fed	hold – held
bite – bit	fight – fought	shake – shook

❑ **Exercise 30. Vocabulary and speaking.** (Chart 9-6)
Practice using irregular verbs. Close your book for this activity.

Example: **hold–held**
   TEACHER: hold–held. I often hold my book open when I teach. Yesterday I held my
      book open when we practiced grammar. What did I do with my book?
   STUDENTS: (*repeat*) hold–held. You held your book open.

1. **become–became**   Lilly got the flu last month. She became very sick. Now she is
   better. What happened when Lilly got the flu?
2. **bend–bent**   When I drop something, I bend over to pick it up. I just dropped my
   pen, and then I bent over to pick it up. What did I do?
3. **bite–bit**   Sometimes dogs bite people. Yesterday my friend's dog bit my hand when I
   petted it. What did the dog do?
4. **build–built**   I have some friends who know how to build houses. They built their
   own house next to the river. What did my friends do?
5. **feed–fed**   I have a (dog, cat, parrot, etc.). I have to feed it every day. Yesterday I fed
   it once in the morning and once in the evening. What did I do yesterday?
6. **fight–fought**   People fight in wars. People fight diseases. They fight for freedom.
   My country fought a war in (*year*). What did my country do in (*year*)?
7. **hide–hid**   I have a coin in my hand. Close your eyes while I hide it. Okay, open your
   eyes. I hid the coin. Where's the coin? Why don't you know?
8. **hold–held**   When it rains, I hold my umbrella above my head. Yesterday it rained.
   I held my umbrella above my head. What did I do yesterday?
9. **shake–shook**   People sometimes shake their finger or their head. Sometimes they
   shake when they're cold. Right now I'm shaking my (finger/head). What did I
   just do?

❑ **Exercise 31. Looking at grammar.** (Chart 9-6).
Complete the sentences. Use the past simple form of the verbs from the box.

become	build	hide
bend	feed	hold
bite	fight	shake

1. Many countries in the world _____*fought*_____ in World War II.

2. I need a new pair of glasses. I sat on my old glasses and

_____ them.

3. I _____ my husband's birthday present in the

closet yesterday. I didn't want him to find it.

4. Emma and Steve saved money. They didn't buy a bookcase for their new apartment.

They bought wood and _____ one.

5. The baby is sleeping peacefully. She's not hungry. Her mother _____

her before she put her in bed.

6. David is a Canadian citizen. Maria was born in Puerto Rico, but when she married

David, she _____ a Canadian citizen too.

7. Doug is a new father. He felt very happy when he _____ his baby in his

arms for the first time.

8. A: Ouch!

B: What's the matter?

A: I _____ my tongue.

9. When my dog got out of the lake, it _____

itself. Dogs always do that when they're wet.

❏ **Exercise 32. Listening.** (Chart 9-6)

Listen to the beginning of each sentence. Choose the correct completion(s). There may be more than one correct answer.

Example: You will hear: I bent . . .
            You will choose: ⓐ my arm.   b. a building.   c. the road.

1. a. the dog.   b. happy.   c. her baby.

2. a. next week.   b. usually.   c. a new house.

3. a. a stick.   b. my hand.   c. sad.

4. a. in the bedroom.   b. behind a tree.   c. their money.

5. a. some pens.   b. the classroom.   c. some papers.

❑ **Exercise 33. Warm-up.** (Chart 9-7)
Which completions are true for you?

1. *Before I ate breakfast this morning, I . . .*
   a. took a shower.
   b. washed my face.
   c. made tea.
   d. combed my hair.

2. *After I got to school today, I . . .*
   a. ate something.
   b. bought some coffee.
   c. did my homework.
   d. talked to friends.

9-7 *Before* and *After* in Time Clauses

S V (a) *I ate breakfast.* = a main clause	A clause is a group of words that has a subject and a verb.
S V (b) ***before** I went to class* = a time clause	A main clause is a complete sentence. Example (a) is a complete sentence. Example (b) is an incomplete sentence. It must be connected to a main clause, as in (c) and (d).
S V (c) | I ate breakfast | ***before** I went to class.* | main clause time clause	

S V
(d) | ***Before** I went to class,* | | I ate breakfast. |
       time clause   main clause
	A time clause begins with a time word such as ***before*** or ***after***:
	    before + S + V = a time clause
	    after + S + V = a time clause

(e) | We took a walk | ***after** we finished our work.* |
     main clause   time clause
 	
(f) | ***After** we finished our work,* | | *we took a walk.* |
      time clause   main clause
	A time clause can come after a main clause, as in (c) and (e). A time clause can come before a main clause, as in (d) and (f).* There is no difference in meaning between (c) and (d) or between (e) and (f).

(g) We took a walk | *after the movie.* |
            prep. phrase
 	
(h) I had a cup of coffee | *before class.* |
            prep. phrase
	Before and ***after*** don't always introduce a time clause. They are also used as prepositions followed by a noun object, as in (g) and (h). See Charts 1-8, p. 21, and 6-2, p. 161, for information about prepositional phrases.

* NOTE: When a time clause comes before the main clause, a comma is used between the two clauses. A comma is not used when the time clause comes after the main clause.

❑ **Exercise 34. Looking at grammar.** (Chart 9-7)
Put brackets around the main clause and the time clause in each sentence. Write "M" over the main clause and "T" over the time clause.

               T   *M*
1. **[**Before I ate the banana,**] [**I peeled it.**]**

2. We arrived at the airport before the plane landed.

3. I went to a movie after I finished my homework.

4. After the kids got home from school, they watched TV.

5. Before I moved to this city, I lived at home with my parents.

☐ **Exercise 35. Looking at grammar.** (Chart 9-7)
In the first pair of sentences, write "1" before the activity that happens first and "2" before the activity that happens second. Then choose the sentence(s) with the correct meaning.

1. __2__ Salman went to sleep.
   __1__ Salman watched a movie.
   - (a.) Before Salman went to sleep, he watched a movie.
   - b. Before Salman watched a movie, he went to sleep.

2. ____ We went home.
   ____ We left my uncle's house.
   - a. After we went home, we left my uncle's house.
   - b. After we left my uncle's house, we went home.

3. ____ I washed the dishes.
   ____ I put them away.
   - a. After I put the dishes away, I washed them.
   - b. Before I put the dishes away, I washed them.

4. ____ The lions chased the zebra.
   ____ The lions ate the zebra.
   - a. Before the lions ate the zebra, they chased it.
   - b. Before the lions chased the zebra, they ate it.
   - c. After the lions chased the zebra, they ate it.
   - d. After the lions ate the zebra, they chased it.

☐ **Exercise 36. Game.** (Chart 9-7)
Work in teams. Find all the incomplete sentences. Make them complete and add the correct punctuation. Your teacher will give you a time limit. The team with the most grammatically correct answers wins.

Example: Before my cell phone died last night
Possible answer: Before my cell phone died last night, I texted several friends.

1. After Jonas and Nora got married in Hawaii last June
2. We went to the zoo before we ate our lunch
3. The kids played soccer in the park
4. After you finished your homework last night
5. Vikram didn't eat before he took his medicine
6. Before I took my daughter to the dentist last week
7. After school started at the beginning of the year
8. Before Gino told me about his problems, I thought he was happy

❑ **Exercise 37. Let's talk: small groups.** (Chart 9-7)

Work in small groups. Combine the two ideas into one sentence by using **before** and **after** to introduce time clauses. Make four sentences for each item.

Example: I put on my coat. / I went outside.

STUDENT A: Before I went outside, I put on my coat.
STUDENT B: I put on my coat before I went outside.
STUDENT C: After I put on my coat, I went outside.
STUDENT D: I went outside after I put on my coat.

1. She ate breakfast. / She went to work.

2. He did his homework. / He went to bed.

3. We bought tickets. / We walked into the movie theater.

❏ **Exercise 38. Warm-up.** (Chart 9-8)
Do the sentences have the same or a different meaning?

1. When I got home from school, I ate a snack.

2. I ate a snack when I got home from school.

9-8 *When* in Time Clauses

(a) **When** *the rain stopped,* we took a walk. OR We took a walk *when the rain stopped*.	**When** can introduce a time clause. **when** + S + V = a time clause In (a): **When** the rain stopped is a time clause. In (b): Notice that the noun (*Tom*) comes before the pronoun (*he*).
(b) When **Tom** was a child, **he** lived with his aunt. OR **Tom** lived with his aunt *when* **he** *was a child.*	
COMPARE (c) *When did the rain stop?* = a question (d) *when the rain stopped* = a time clause	**When** is also used to introduce questions.* A question is a complete sentence, as in (c). A time clause is not a complete sentence, as in (d).

*See Charts 3-11, p. 89, and 9-1 for information about using *when* in questions.

❏ **Exercise 39. Looking at grammar.** (Chart 9-8)
Add a capital letter and a question mark to complete the sentences. Write "NC" to mean "not complete" if the group of words is a time clause and not a question.

1. a. when did Jim arrive → *W̷hen did Jim arrive?*

   b. when Jim arrived → *NC*

2. a. when you were in Iran

   b. when were you in Iran

3. a. when did the movie end

   b. when the movie ended

4. a. when Khalid and Bakir were at the restaurant on First Street

   b. when were Khalid and Bakir at the restaurant on First Street

5. a. when the museum opens

   b. when does the museum open

❑ **Exercise 40. Looking at grammar.** (Chart 9-8)
Make sentences by combining the ideas in Column A with those in Column B. Then change the position of the time clause.

Example: When the show ended,
   → When the show ended, people clapped.
   → People clapped when the show ended.

Column A	Column B
1. When the show ended,	a. when I dropped it.
2. When I was in Japan,	b. I closed my umbrella.
3. Elena bought some new shoes	c. when he was in high school.
4. I took a lot of photographs	✓ d. people clapped.
5. Adam was a soccer player	e. when she went shopping yesterday.
6. When the rain stopped,	f. I stayed in a hotel in Tokyo.
7. The mirror broke	g. when I was in Hawaii.

❑ **Exercise 41. Looking at grammar.** (Chart 9-8)
Use the given words to make (a) a simple past tense question and (b) a simple past tense clause. Use your own words to complete the sentence in (b).

1. When \ snow \ it

   a. _____ *When did it snow?* _____

   b. _____ *When it snowed, I built a snowman.* _____

2. When \ leave \ you

    a. _____

    b. _____

3. When \ feel homesick \ Thomas

    a. _____

    b. _____

4. When \ go out \ electricity

    a. _____

    b. _____

❑ **Exercise 42. Warm-up.** (Chart 9-9)
Complete the sentences with the correct time for you.

  1. Now I am studying grammar, but yesterday I wasn't studying grammar at

    _____.

  2. Now I am not sleeping, but last night, I was sleeping at _____.

9-9 Present Progressive and Past Progressive

PRESENT PROGRESSIVE (in progress right now) (a) It's 10:00 now. Boris *is sitting* in class.	The present progressive describes an activity in progress right now, at the moment of speaking. See Chart 4-1, p. 96. In (a): Right now it is 10:00. Boris began to sit before 10:00. Sitting is in progress at 10:00. (See next page.)
PAST PROGRESSIVE (in progress yesterday) (b) It was 10:00. Boris *was sitting* in class.	The past progressive describes an activity in progress at a particular time in the past. In (b): Boris began to sit in class before 10:00 yesterday. At 10:00 yesterday, sitting in class was in progress. (See next page.)

PRESENT PROGRESSIVE FORM: *AM, IS, ARE* + *-ING*
(c) It's 10:00. I   *am sitting* in class.
           Boris *is sitting*   in class.
           We   *are sitting* in class.
	The forms of the present progressive and the past progressive consist of *be* + *-ing*. The present progressive uses the present forms of *be*: *am*, *is*, and *are* + *-ing*.

PAST PROGRESSIVE FORM: *WAS, WERE* + *-ING* (d) It was 10:00. Boris *was sitting* in class. We *were sitting* in class.	The past progressive uses the past forms of *be*: *was* and *were* + *-ing*.

Boris *is sitting* in class right now at ten o'clock.

Boris *was sitting* in class yesterday at ten o'clock.

❑ **Exercise 43. Grammar and speaking: class activity.** (Chart 9-9)
Complete each sentence with the correct form of the verb in parentheses. Discuss the meaning of the phrase "in progress."

1. Paul started to eat dinner at 7:00. At 7:05, Kara came. Paul (*eat*)

_____ when Kara (*come*) _____ at 7:05.

2. Bobby was at home yesterday evening. His favorite program was on TV last night. It started at 8:00. It ended at 9:00. At 8:30, his friend Kristin called.

When Kristin (*call*) _____ at 8:30, Bobby (*watch*) _____

_____ TV.

3. Rosa played her guitar for an hour yesterday morning. She started to play her guitar at 9:30. She stopped at 10:30. Mike arrived at her apartment at 10:00.

At 10:00, Rosa (*play*) _____ her guitar.

❑ **Exercise 44. Let's talk: class activity.** (Chart 9-9)

Look at the picture. Use the past progressive to describe the activities that were in progress the night of the robbery.

SITUATION: Mr. and Mrs. Gold invited some friends to their house for the weekend. A thief stole Mrs. Gold's jewelry at midnight on Saturday. What were the guests doing at midnight?

❑ **Exercise 45. Warm-up.** (Chart 9-10)

Check (✓) all the sentences that match the picture.

While the teacher was talking,

1. _____ the fire alarm began to ring.

2. _____ a student fell asleep.

3. _____ a spider crawled into the room.

4. _____ a desk fell over.

5. _____ another teacher came into the room.

6. _____ the room caught fire.

9-10 Using *While* with Past Progressive

(a) The phone rang **while** *I was sleeping*. OR	*while* + *subject* + *verb* = *a time clause* *While I was sleeping* is a time clause. *while* = *during that time*
(b) **While** *I was sleeping*, the phone rang.*	A *while*-clause describes an activity that was in progress at the time another activity happened. The verb in a *while*-clause is often past progressive (e.g., *was sleeping*).

*NOTE: When a time clause comes before the main clause, a comma is used between the two clauses. A comma is not used when the time clause comes after the main clause.

❑ **Exercise 46. Let's talk: class activity.** (Chart 9-10)
Combine the sentences. Use *while*.

1. I was studying last night.
   Rita called.
   → *While I was studying last night,* Rita called.
   → *Rita called while I was studying last night.*

2. Someone knocked on my apartment door.
   I was eating breakfast yesterday.

3. I was cooking dinner last night.
   I burned my hand.

4. Yoko raised her hand.
   The teacher was talking.

5. A tree fell on my car.
   I was driving in a windstorm.

6. I was studying last night.
   A mouse suddenly appeared on my desk.

❑ **Exercise 47. Warm-up.** (Chart 9-11)
What word begins each time clause? What verb form is in each time clause?

1. a. While I was studying, the mouse appeared.

   b. The mouse appeared while I was studying.

2. a. When the mouse appeared, I was studying.

   b. I was studying when the mouse appeared.

9-11 Simple Past Tense vs. Past Progressive

(a) Jane **called** me yesterday. (b) I **talked** to Jane for an hour last night. (c) What time **did** you **get up** this morning?	The SIMPLE PAST describes activities or situations that began and ended at a particular time in the past (e.g., *yesterday, last night*).
(d) I **was studying** when Jane called me last night. (e) While I **was studying** last night, Jane called.	The PAST PROGRESSIVE describes an activity that was in progress (was happening) at the time another action happened. In (d) and (e): The studying was in progress when Jane called. **When** is commonly used with the simple past activity, as in (d).
2 1 (f) | I **opened** my umbrella | | when it **began** to rain. | main clause time clause	If both the time clause and the main clause in a sentence are simple past, it means that the action in the time clause happened first, and the action in the main clause happened second. In (f): First, it began to rain; second, I opened my umbrella.
COMPARE (g) When the phone **rang,** I **answered** it. (h) When the phone **rang,** I **was studying**.	In (g): First, the phone rang; second, I answered it. In (h): First, the studying was in progress; second, the phone rang.

❑ **Exercise 48. Let's talk: class activity.** (Chart 9-11)
Your teacher will ask you to perform and describe actions using *while*-clauses or *when*-clauses. Close your book for this activity.

Example: Erase the board. / Open the door.
    TEACHER: (*Student A*), please erase the board. What are you doing?
STUDENT A: (*erases the board*) I'm erasing the board right now.
    TEACHER: (*Student B*), would you please open the door?
STUDENT B: (*opens the door*)
    TEACHER: Thank you. You may both sit down. (*Student C*), will you please describe the two actions we saw?
STUDENT C: While (*Student A*) was erasing the board, (*Student B*) opened the door. OR (*Student A*) was erasing the board when (*Student B*) opened the door.

1. Write on the board. / Drop a book on the floor.
2. Walk around the room. / Say hello to (*Student A*).
3. Look out the window. / Take (*Student A*)'s grammar book.
4. Draw a picture on the board. / Ask (*Student A*) a question.

Exercise 49. Looking at grammar. (Chart 9-11)

Complete the sentences. Use the past progressive in the *while*-clauses. Use the simple past in the *when*-clauses.

1. While I (*wash*) ___was washing___ the dishes last night, I (*get*) _____got_____

   a phone call from my best friend.

2. When my best friend (*call*) _____ last night, I (*wash*) _____

   _____ the dishes.

3. My friend Jessica (*come*) _____ over while I (*eat*) _____

   _____ dinner last night.

4. I (*eat*) _____ dinner when my friend Jessica (*come*)

   _____ over last night.

5. My friend Ricardo (*come*) _____ when I (*stream*) _____

   _____ a movie on my computer last night. I (*invite*)

   _____ him to watch it with me.

6. I (*stream*) _____ a movie on my computer last night when my friend

   Ricardo (*come*) _____ over.

7. Jason (*wear*) _____ a suit and tie when I (*see*) _____

   him yesterday.

8. While I (*watch*) _____ TV in bed last night and (*relax*)

   _____ after a long day, my new puppy (*take*) _____

   my slippers.

❑ **Exercise 50. Speaking and writing: pairwork.** (Chart 9-11)
Part I. Work with a partner. Use the information about Bill Gates to make sentences with the simple past and past progressive. Use *while, when, before,* and *after.*

Example: 1967: entered Lakeside School
1968: wrote his first computer program
→ *In 1967, Bill Gates entered Lakeside School.*
→ *While he was studying at Lakeside, he wrote his first computer program.*

Bill Gates: a brief history

1955:	was born in Seattle, Washington
1967:	entered Lakeside School
1967–1973:	studied at Lakeside School
1968:	wrote his first computer program
1970:	started his first software company
1973:	graduated from Lakeside
1973–1977:	studied at Harvard University
1975:	began to design programs for personal computers
1975:	started Microsoft with Paul Allen
1975–2008:	led Microsoft
1977:	left Harvard University
1994:	got married to Melinda French
1996:	his first child was born
2008:	retired from Microsoft
2008:	became more active in the Bill and Melinda Gates Foundation

Part II. Make a timeline of seven to ten events in your partner's life. Write sentences with the simple past and past progressive. Use *while, when, before,* and *after.*

❑ **Exercise 51. Reading and listening.** (Charts 9-7 → 9-11)
Part I. Read the story about Steve Jobs. Look at new vocabulary with your teacher first.

Steve Jobs

Steve Jobs is another very famous computer person. He was also born in 1955. He grew up in Palo Alto, California. When he was in high school, he worked for electronics businesses in the summer. He also met Steve Wozniak. They became friends and business partners and built their first computer together.

Do you know these words?
electronics
design
fired
cancer
medical treatments
cure
turned + (*age*)

After he graduated from high school, he went to Reed College. He didn't study there very long, but he stayed in the area. He liked to visit the college's calligraphy—artistic handwriting—classes. He learned a lot about design and used it years later with his products.

Jobs, Wozniak, and Ron Wayne started Apple Computer in 1976. In 1985, Apple fired him, so he started NeXT Computer, Inc. While he was working at NeXT, he met Laurene Powell, and they got married.

In 1996, Apple bought NeXT and Jobs once again worked at Apple. Under Jobs, Apple became very successful. In 2001, it introduced the iPod. In 2007, it sold the first iPhone. Three years later, the iPad came out.

Unfortunately, while Jobs was working at Apple, he got cancer. Medical treatments didn't cure him. In 2011, ten months after he turned 56, Steve Jobs died.

Part II. Complete the sentences with *before, after, when,* or *while*.

1. _____ Steve Jobs was attending high school, he worked for electronics businesses in the summer.

2. _____ he finished high school, he attended Reed College for a short time.

3. _____ he was living near Reed College, he visited calligraphy classes.

4. _____ he began NeXT Computer Inc., Apple fired him.

5. _____ Steve Jobs was working at Apple, the company introduced the iPod, iPhone, and iPad.

6. _____ Steve Jobs turned 57, he died.

Part III. Complete the sentences with the verbs you hear.

1. Steve Jobs _____ born in 1955.

2. While he _____ up in Palo Alto, California, he _____ interested in computers.

3. Jobs and Wozniak _____ their first computer together.

4. After Jobs _____ from high school, he _____ to Reed College.

5. He _____ there very long, but he _____ in the area.

6. He _____ a lot about calligraphy, and it _____ him with the design of his products.

7. In 1985, Apple _____ him, so he _____ NeXT Computer, Inc.

8. While he _____ at NeXT, he _____ Laurene Powell, and they got married.

9. Under Jobs, Apple _____ very successful.

10. Unfortunately, while Jobs _____ at Apple, he _____ cancer.

11. Medical treatments _____ cure him, and Jobs _____ in 2011.

❏ **Exercise 52. Looking at grammar.** (Chart 9-11)
Complete the sentences. Use the simple past or the past progressive form of the verbs in parentheses.

1. While my cousin and I (*have*) _____ dinner at a restaurant last night, we (*see*) _____ a friend of mine. I (*introduce*) _____ her to my cousin.

2. When I (*hear*) _____ a knock at the door last night, I (*walk*) _____ to the door and (*open*) _____ it. When I (*open*) _____ the door, I (*see*) _____ my brother. I (*greet*) _____ him and (*ask*) _____ him to come in.

3. When my cousin and I (*play*) _____ a video game last night, my brother (*call*) _____ me. He (*be*) _____ on the highway, and his car (*be*) _____ out of gas. I (*buy*) _____ gas and (*take*) _____ it to him.

4. While I (*walk*) _____ to class yesterday morning, I (*see*) _____ Abdullah. We (*say*) _____ hello.

❏ **Exercise 53. Looking at grammar.** (Chapter 9)
Choose the best completion.

1. I was surfing the Internet. I heard a knock on the door. When I heard the knock on the door, I ____ it.
   a. open
   b. am opening
   c. opened
   d. was opening

2. A: When ____ you talk to Jake?
   B: Yesterday.
   a. do
   b. are
   c. did
   d. were

3. I _____ TV when Gina called last night. We talked for an hour.
    a. watch   c. am watching
    b. watched   d. was watching

4. Mike is in his bedroom right now. He _____ , so we need to be quiet.
    a. is sleeping   c. slept
    b. sleeps   d. was sleeping

5. Kate _____ tell us the truth yesterday. She lied to us.
    a. don't   b. doesn't   c. didn't   d. wasn't

6. I saw a fish while I _____ in the ocean yesterday.
    a. swim   c. were swimming
    b. was swimming   d. swimming

7. When I heard the phone ring, I _____ it.
    a. answer   c. answered
    b. am answering   d. was answering

8. A: _____ you go to concerts often?
   B: Yes. I go at least once a month.
    a. Do   b. Did   c. Was   d. Were

9. While I _____ dinner last night, I burned my finger.
    a. cooking   b. cook   c. was cooking   d. was cook

10. Where _____ after work yesterday?
    a. you went   b. you did go   c. did you went   d. did you go

❑ **Exercise 54. Looking at grammar.** (Chapters 8 and 9)
Complete the sentences with the past form of the verbs in parentheses.

Part I.

Yesterday (be) _____*was*_____ a terrible day. Everything (go) _____
                      1   2

wrong. First, I (oversleep) _____. My alarm clock (ring, not)
                            3

_____. I (wake) _____ up when I (hear)
       4   5

_____ a noise outside my window. It was 9:15. I (get) _____
       6   7

dressed quickly. I (run) _____ to class, but I (be) _____ late.
                         8   9

The teacher (be) _____ upset with me.
                 10

Part II.

During a break, I (*go*) _____ 11 outside. While I (*sit*)

_____ 12 under a tree near the classroom building, I (*see*)

_____ 13 a friend. I (*call*) _____ 14 to him. He (*join*)

_____ 15 me on the grass. We (*talk*) _____ 16 about our

classes. While we (*talk*) _____ 17 , I (*stand*) _____ 18 up,

(*step*) _____ 19 in a hole, and (*break*) _____ 20 my ankle.

Part III.

My friend (*drive*) _____ 21 me to the hospital. We (*go*) _____ 22

to the emergency room. After the doctor (*take*) _____ 23 X-rays of my ankle,

he (*put*) _____ 24 a cast on it.

I (*pay*) _____ 25 my bill. Then we (*leave*) _____ 26

the hospital. My friend (*take*) _____ 27 me home and (*help*)

_____ 28 me up the stairs to my apartment.

Part IV.

When we (*get*) _____ 29 to my apartment, I (*look*) _____ 30

for my key in my purse and in my pockets. There was no key.

I (*ring*) _____ the doorbell. My roommate (*be, not*) _____
             31   32

there, so I (*sit*) _____ down on the floor with my friend and (*wait*)
                         33

_____ for my roommate to get home.
          34

　　Finally, my roommate (*come*) _____ home. I (*eat*) _____
                                                         35   36

dinner quickly and (*go*) _____ to bed. While I (*sleep*) _____ ,
                                   37   38

I (*dream*) _____ that I broke my arm. I hope my dream doesn't come true!
                       39

❑　**Exercise 55. Check your knowledge.** (Chapter 9)
Correct the mistakes.

　　　　　　　　go
　1. Did you ~~went~~ downtown yesterday?

　2. Yesterday I speak to Ken before he leaves his office and goes home.

　3. I heared a good joke last night.

　4. When Pablo finished his work.

　5. I visitted my cousins in New York last month

　6. Where you did go yesterday afternoon?

　7. Ms. Wah was fly from Singapore to Tokyo last week.

　8. When I see my friend yesterday, he isn't speak to me.

　9. Why Mustafa didn't came to class last week?

10. Where you bought those shoes? I like them.

11. Mr. Adams teached our class last week.

12. Who you talk to?

13. Who did open the door? Jack openned it.

Part I. Read the paragraph. <u>Underline</u> the past verbs.

An Unforgettable Day

(1) I remember February 28, 2001 very clearly. It <u>was</u> 12:00 in the afternoon, and

(2) I was at home with my daughter. She was a year old, and we were having lunch.

(3) There was a lot of noise outside our apartment building because builders were putting

(4) on a new roof. Suddenly, I heard a very loud noise. The room began to move and

(5) didn't stop. It was an earthquake! I grabbed my daughter and got under the kitchen

(6) table. I told her everything was okay, but actually I felt afraid. The shaking lasted

(7) about 45 seconds, but it felt longer. My husband was traveling that day, and I wanted

(8) to talk to him. I tried to call him on his phone several times, but there was no cell

(9) service. I was nervous, and I wasn't thinking very clearly. Finally, after ten minutes,

(10) I remembered the Internet. I checked and saw a news story about a very strong

(11) earthquake. Before I finished the article, my husband called. He was driving when

(12) he felt the earthquake, so he stopped at a gas station and waited. He was fine. Some

(13) buildings fell down in our city, but fortunately no one died.

Part II. Write about a day you remember well. Begin with this sentence: ***I remember*** (*date*) ***very clearly***.

Include this information in your paragraph:

1. What happened on that day?
2. When did it happen?
3. Where were you?
4. What were you doing?

5. Were other people there? What were they doing?
6. How did you feel?
7. How did the day/event end?

Part III. Editing check: Work individually or change papers with a partner. Check (✓) for the following:

1. _____ indented paragraph
2. _____ capital letter at the beginning of each sentence
3. _____ period at the end of each sentence
4. _____ correct use of past progressive for an activity in progress
5. _____ correct use of simple past for a completed activity
6. _____ correct spelling (use a dictionary or computer spell-check)

Chapter 10
Expressing Future Time, Part 1

□ **Exercise 1. Warm-up.** (Chart 10-1)
Make the sentences true for you.

1. Yesterday I woke up at _____. Tomorrow I am going to wake up at _____.

2. Last night I ate dinner at _____. Tomorrow I am going to eat dinner at _____.

10-1 Future Time: Using *Be Going To*

(a) I **am going to go** downtown tomorrow. (b) Sue **is going to be** here tomorrow afternoon. (c) We **are going to come** to class tomorrow morning.	**Be going to** expresses (talks about) the future. FORM: **am** **is** } + **going to** + base form **are**
(d) I**'m not going to go** downtown tomorrow. (e) Joe **isn't going to be** at the meeting tomorrow. (f) We **aren't going to eat** dinner early tonight.	NEGATIVE: **be** + **not** + **going to**
(g) A: **Are** you **going to go** downtown tomorrow? B: No, I'm not. (h) A: **Is** Jim **going to be** at the meeting tomorrow? B: Yes, he is. (i) A: What time **are** we **going to eat** dinner tonight? B: At eight.	QUESTION: **be** + *subject* + **going to** A form of **be** is used in the short answer to a yes/no question with **be going to**, as in (g) and (h). (See Chart 2-2, p. 30, for information about short answers with **be**.)
(j) I'm **gonna** leave. (k) She's **gonna** stay.	In spoken English, *going to* is often pronounced "gonna." In formal written English, **going to** rather than *"gonna"* is used.

□ **Exercise 2. Looking at grammar.** (Chart 10-1)
Complete each sentence with the correct form of **be going to**.

Don't worry!

1. I am not late.   I ___*am going to be*___ on time.

2. We are not late.   We _____ on time.

3. She is not late.   She _____ on time.

4. You are not late.   You _____ on time.

5. They are not late.   They _____ on time.

6. Tim and I are not late.   Tim and I _____ on time.

7. Dr. Mason is not late.   Dr. Mason _____ on time.

8. Kyle and Sam are not late. Kyle and Sam _____ on time.

❑   **Exercise 3. Let's talk: pairwork.** (Chart 10-1)

Part I. Work with a partner. Which of the given activities are you going to do tomorrow?
Which ones are you not going to do tomorrow?

Example: go downtown
PARTNER A (*book open*):   Are you going to go downtown tomorrow?
PARTNER B (*book closed*): Yes, I am. I'm going to go downtown tomorrow. OR
                          No, I'm not. I'm not going to go downtown tomorrow.

1. get up before eight o'clock
2. take a shower
3. make your bed
4. do the dishes
5. take a test
6. make a phone call
7. get a haircut
8. make dinner
9. make a mess in the kitchen
10. watch TV in the evening
11. go to bed early

Change roles.
12. get up early
13. get some exercise
14. walk to school
15. take a nap
16. do your laundry
17. do some ironing
18. go shopping
19. eat dinner alone
20. have dessert
21. chat with friends online
22. take a bath

Part II. Write three activities your partner is going to do tomorrow. Write three activities you are not going to do.

❑ **Exercise 4. Looking at grammar.** (Chart 10-1)
Complete the sentences. Use *be going to* and the words from the box (or your own words).

call the manager	go to an Italian restaurant	take a sick day
call the police	go to the park	take it to the post office
get something to eat	lie down	take them to the laundromat
✓go to the bookstore	take dance lessons	try to see the dentist today

1. I need to buy a textbook. I _____ *am going to go to the bookstore.* _____

2. Grace is hungry. She _____

3. My clothes are dirty. I _____

4. I have a toothache. I _____

5. George has to mail a package. He _____

6. It's a nice day today. Molly and I _____

7. Amanda and I want learn how to dance. We _____

8. It's late at night. I hear a burglar! I _____

9. I feel terrible. I think I'm getting the flu. I _____

10. Ivan and Natasha want pizza. They _____

11. Dana lives in an apartment. There's a problem with the plumbing. She _____

_____

❏ **Exercise 5. Let's talk: interview.** (Chart 10-1)

Walk around the room. Ask and answer questions using *be going to*. Write down your classmates' names and their answers. Share some of their answers with the class.

Example: when \ go downtown
STUDENT A: When are you going to go downtown?
STUDENT B: Tomorrow afternoon. / In a couple of days. / Around noon. / Etc.

QUESTION	FIRST NAME	ANSWER
1. where \ go after class today		
2. what time \ get home tonight		
3. when \ eat dinner		
4. where \ eat dinner		
5. what time \ go to bed tonight		
6. what time \ get up tomorrow morning		
7. where \ be tomorrow morning		
8. when \ finish your English studies		
9. where \ live next year		
10. when \ take a trip and where \ go		

❏ **Exercise 6. Game.** (Chart 10-1)

Work in teams. Your teacher will ask you a question. Discuss the answer. Raise your hand when you are ready. The first team to give a correct answer gets a point. Close your book for this activity.

Example: You want to buy some tea. What are you going to do?
TEAM A STUDENT: I'm going to go to the grocery store.

1. You have a toothache. What are you going to do?
2. You need to mail a package. Where are you going to go?
3. Your clothes are dirty.
4. It's midnight. You're sleepy.
5. It's late at night. You hear a burglar.
6. You need to buy some groceries.
7. You want to go swimming.
8. You want to go fishing.
9. You want to buy a new coat.
10. You're hungry.
11. You have a headache.
12. It's a nice day today.
13. You need to cash a check.
14. You want some (pizza) for dinner.
15. You're reading a book. You don't know the meaning of a word.

❑ **Exercise 7. Warm-up.** (Chart 10-2)
Check all (✓) the sentences that have a future meaning.

1. _____ I am flying to Montreal tomorrow.

2. _____ My aunt and uncle are meeting me at the airport.

3. _____ They are going to have their 50th anniversary next week.

10-2 Using the Present Progressive to Express Future Time

(a) Sue	*is going to leave*	at 8:00 tomorrow.	Sometimes the present progressive is used to express future time.
(b) Sue	*is leaving*	at 8:00 tomorrow.	Examples (a) and (b) mean the same thing.
(c) We	*are going to drive*	to Toronto next week.	Examples (c) and (d) mean the same thing.
(d) We	*are driving*	to Toronto next week.	The present progressive is used for future meaning when the speaker is talking about plans that have already been made.

COMMON VERBS					
come	drive	go	meet	spend	stay
do	fly	leave	return	start	take

❑ **Exercise 8. Looking at grammar.** (Chart 10-2)
Rewrite the sentences using the present progressive.

A trip to Greece

1. My mother and I are going to leave for our trip at 10:00 tomorrow.

   My mother and I are leaving for our trip at 10:00 tomorrow.

2. We are going to fly to Athens. _____

3. We are going to spend a week there. _____

4. My father is going to meet us there. _____

5. He is going to take the train. _____

6. We are going to go sightseeing together. _____

7. I am going to come back by boat, and they are going to return by train.

   _____

❏ **Exercise 9. Listening.** (Chart 10-2)

Listen to each sentence. Decide if the meaning is present or future time.

Example: You will hear: We are meeting later this afternoon.
You will choose: present   (future)

1. present	future		5. present	future
2. present	future		6. present	future
3. present	future		7. present	future
4. present	future		8. present	future

❏ **Exercise 10. Let's talk: interview.** (Chart 10-2)

Walk around the room. Ask and answer questions using the present progressive. Write down your classmates' names and answers. Share some of their answers with the class.

Example: what \ do \ tonight
STUDENT A: What are you doing tonight?
STUDENT B: I'm staying home and watching a DVD.

QUESTION	FIRST NAME	ANSWER
1. where \ go \ after school		
2. what time \ have dinner		
3. when \ go \ to bed tonight		
4. what time \ get up \ tomorrow		
5. what \ do \ tomorrow		
6. what \ do \ this weekend		

❏ **Exercise 11. Listening.** (Charts 10-1 and 10-2)

Listen to each sentence. Choose the verb you hear.

Example: You will hear: It's going to rain tomorrow.
You will choose: (a.) is going to rain   b. is raining   c. rains

1. a. am going to leave	b. am leaving	c. leave
2. a. is going to start	b. is starting	c. starts
3. a. is going to come	b. is coming	c. comes
4. a. is going to call	b. is calling	c. calls
5. a. Are you going to study	b. Are you studying	c. Do you study
6. a. are going to have	b. are having	c. have
7. a. aren't going to go	b. aren't going	c. don't go
8. a. is going to eat	b. is eating	c. eats
9. a. is going to help	b. is helping	c. helps

❏ **Exercise 12. Let's talk: small groups.** (Charts 10-1 and 10-2)
Your group won a contest and received a lot of money. (As a class, decide on the amount.)
You can use it for one of the four situations. What are you going to do with the money?
Choose one situation and talk about your plans.

1. The money is to help other people. What are you going to do?
2. The money is to improve your school. What are you going to do?
3. The money is to make the world a better place. What are you going to do?
4. The money is for a wonderful vacation for your class. Where are you going to go and what are you going to do?

❏ **Exercise 13. Warm-up.** (Chart 10-3)
Choose the correct completion.

1. I studied English   last week / next week.
2. I am going to take a break   a few minutes ago / in a few minutes.
3. I did homework   last night / tomorrow night.

10-3 Words Used for Past Time and Future Time

PAST	FUTURE	
yesterday	tomorrow	PAST: It *rained* **yesterday**. FUTURE: It*'s going to rain* **tomorrow**.
yesterday morning yesterday afternoon yesterday evening last night	tomorrow morning tomorrow afternoon tomorrow evening tomorrow night	PAST: I *was* in class **yesterday morning**. FUTURE: I*'m going to be* in class **tomorrow morning**.
last week last month last year last weekend last spring last summer last fall last winter last Monday, etc.	next week next month next year next weekend next spring next summer next fall next winter next Monday, etc.	PAST: Mary *went* downtown **last week**. FUTURE: Mary *is going to go* downtown **next week**. PAST: Bob *graduated* from high school **last spring**. FUTURE: Ann *is going to graduate* from high school **next spring**.
. . . minutes ago . . . hours ago . . . days ago . . . weeks ago . . . months ago . . . years ago	in . . . minutes (from now) in . . . hours (from now) in . . . days (from now) in . . . weeks (from now) in . . . months (from now) in . . . years (from now)	PAST: I *finished* my homework **five minutes ago**. FUTURE: Pablo *is going to finish* his homework **in five minutes**.

❑ **Exercise 14. Looking at grammar.** (Chart 10-3)
Complete the sentences. Use *yesterday*, *last*, *tomorrow*, or *next*.

1. I went swimming _____*yesterday*_____ morning.

2. Alberto is going to go to the beach _____*tomorrow*_____ morning.

3. I'm going to take a trip _____ week.

4. Diana went to Miami _____ week for a short vacation.

5. We had a test in class _____ afternoon.

6. _____ afternoon we're going to look for a used car.

7. My friend bought a used car _____ Friday.

8. My sister is going to arrive _____ Tuesday.

9. My brother is going to enter the university _____ fall.

10. _____ spring I took a trip to San Francisco.

11. Mia is going to fly to London _____ month.

12. Zack lived in Tokyo _____ year.

13. I'm going to study at the library _____ night.

14. _____ night I watched TV.

15. _____ evening I'm going to go to a baseball game.

16. Mrs. Chang went to a basketball game _____ evening.

❑ **Exercise 15. Grammar and speaking.** (Chart 10-3)
Part I. Complete the questions with time expressions.

1. What did you do _____?

2. What are you going to do _____?

3. Where are you going to be in _____?

4. Where were you _____?

5. Where did you go last _____?

6. Where are you going to go next _____?

7. What are you going to do tomorrow _____?

8. What did you do yesterday _____?

Part II. Work with a partner. Ask and answer questions. Share a few of your partner's answers with the class.

❑ **Exercise 16. Looking at grammar.** (Chart 10-3)
Complete the sentences. Use the given time expressions with *ago* or *in*.

1. ten minutes   Class is going to end ____*in ten minutes.*_____

2. ten minutes   Hanan's class ended ____*ten minutes ago.*_____

3. an hour   The post office isn't open. It closed _____

4. an hour   Yoshi is going to call us _____

5. two months   I'm studying abroad now, but I'm going to be back home

    _____

6. two months   My wife and I took a trip to Morocco _____

7. a minute   Karen left _____

8. half an hour   I'm going to meet Peter at the coffee shop _____

9. one week   The new highway is going to open _____

10. a year   I was living in Korea _____

❑ **Exercise 17. Let's talk: pairwork.** (Chart 10-3)

Work with a partner. Change the sentences using *ago* or *in*. Use the calendar to calculate length of time. "Today" is September 9th.

1. Brad is going to leave his old job as a hotel chef on September 12th.

   → *Brad is going leave his old job in three days.*

2. He is going to start a new job as a chef at a famous restaurant on September 14th.

3. Brad graduated from cooking school in Paris on June 9th.

4. He is going to be in a cooking competition on September 23rd.

5. Brad began taking cooking classes in 2009.

6. He moved to Paris a year later.

7. Brad is going to cook for a TV show on September 30th.

8. Brad is going to marry his high school sweetheart on December 9th.

SEPTEMBER						
Sun.	Mon.	Tues.	Wed.	Thurs.	Fri.	Sat.
1	2	3	4	5	6	7
8	9	10	11	12	13	14
15	16	17	18	19	20	21
22	23	24	25	26	27	28
29	30					

❑ **Exercise 18. Listening.** (Chart 10-3)

Listen to the beginning of each sentence. Choose the correct completion.

Example: You will hear: Rudi is going to finish his work . . .

You will choose: a. five minutes ago. (b.) in five minutes.

1. a. one hour ago.   b. in one hour.

2. a. two weeks ago.   b. in two weeks.

3. a. one year ago.   b. in one year.

4. a. ten minutes ago.   b. in ten minutes.

5. a. a few minutes ago.   b. in a few minutes.

6. a. last spring.   b. next spring.

7. a. last summer.   b. next summer.

8. a. last weekend.   b. next weekend.

9. a. yesterday evening.   b. tomorrow evening.

❑ **Exercise 19. Let's talk: interview.** (Chart 10-3)

Walk around the room. Ask a different student each pair of questions. Write down the names of the students and their answers. Share some of their answers with the class.

Example: what \ do \ yesterday?
STUDENT A: What did you do yesterday?
STUDENT B: I stayed home and studied for a test.

Example: what \ do \ tomorrow?
STUDENT A: What are you going to do tomorrow?
STUDENT B: I'm going to go to a party with my friends.

QUESTION	FIRST NAME	ANSWERS
1. where \ go \ yesterday? where \ go\ tomorrow?		
2. who \ call \ last week? who \ call \ next week?		
3. who \ call \ yesterday? who \ call \ tomorrow?		
4. what \ watch on TV \ last week? what \ watch on TV \ next week?		
5. where \ live \ five years ago? where \ live \ in five years?		

❏ **Exercise 20. Looking at grammar.** (Chart 10-3)
Complete the sentences. Use *yesterday*, *last*, *tomorrow*, *next*, *in*, or *ago*.

1. I went to the zoo _____ *last* _____ week.

2. Yolanda Matos went to the zoo a week _____.

3. Charles Nelson is going to go to the park _____ Saturday.

4. We're going to go to the park _____ two days.

5. My kids went to the pool _____ morning.

6. My cousin is going to go to the circus _____ afternoon.

7. Kim Yang-Don graduated from Sogang University _____ spring.

8. We're going to have company for dinner _____ night.

9. We had company for dinner three days _____.

10. We're going to have dinner at our friends' house _____ two days.

11. _____ evening we're going to go to a concert.

12. _____ Friday I went to a party.

13. _____ afternoon the students took a test.

14. My stepsister arrived here _____ month.

15. She is going to leave _____ two weeks.

16. _____ year Kyoko is going to be a freshman in college.

❑ **Exercise 21. Warm-up.** (Chart 10-4)
Read the sentences and choose the correct number.

1. Dave left a couple of weeks ago.	two	five
2. JoAnn is going to get married in a few months.	one	four

10-4 Using *A Couple Of* or *A Few* with *Ago* (Past) and *In* (Future)

(a) Sam arrived here **one** (OR **a**) *year ago*. (b) Jack is going to be here *in **two** minutes*. (c) I talked to Ann ***three** days ago*.	Numbers are often used in time expressions with **ago** and **in**.
(d) I saw Carlos ***a couple of** months ago*. (e) He's going to return to Mexico *in **a couple of** months*. (f) I got a letter from Gina ***a few** weeks ago*. (g) I'm going to see Gina *in **a few** weeks*.	**A couple of** and **a few** are also commonly used. **A couple of** means "two." *A couple of months ago = two months ago* **A few** means "a small number, not a large number." *A few weeks ago = two, three, four,* or *five weeks ago*
(h) I began college last year. I'm going to graduate *in **two** **more** years*. My sister is almost finished with her education. She's going to graduate *in **a few more** months*.	Frequently, the word **more** is used in future time expressions that begin with **in**.

Exercise 22. Reading and speaking. (Chart 10-4)

Read the paragraph. Then, as a class, decide if the statements are true or false.

Love at First Sight?

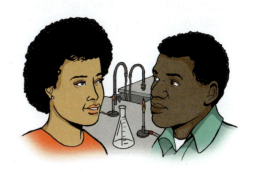

Ben and Jen met September 15, 2009. It was the first day of college for them. They were in chemistry class. Ben fell in love with Jen a few days later. Ben asked Jen to marry him on January 1. Jen gave him her answer a couple of days later. She wasn't sure, so she said "no." A couple of months later, she changed her mind. They got married a few months after that. A couple of years later they had their first child. They are very happy together.

1. Ben fell in love with Jen on September 16.	T	F
2. Jen told Ben "no" in January.	T	F
3. Jen changed her mind in March.	T	F
4. Ben and Jen got married in April.	T	F
5. They had their first child in 2013.	T	F

Exercise 23. Let's talk: small groups. (Chart 10-4)

Work in small groups. Take turns completing the sentences. Use information from your own life. Use the given words with **ago** or **in**. Use numbers (*one, two, three, ten, sixteen, etc.*) or the expressions **a couple of** or **a few**.

1. days   We studied Chapter 9 ___*a couple of days ago / three days ago / etc.*___

2. days   We're going to finish this chapter ___*in a few more days / in three or*___

        ___*four days / etc.*___

3. hours   I ate breakfast _____

4. hours   I'm going to eat lunch/dinner _____

5. minutes   We finished Exercise 22 _____

6. minutes   This class is going to end _____

7. years   I was born _____

8. years   My parents got married _____

9. weeks   I arrived in this city _____, and I'm going
   months
   years   to leave this city _____

❏ **Exercise 24. Looking at grammar.** (Chart 10-4)
Complete the sentences with your own words. Write about your life. For example, what did you do a few days ago? What are you going to do in a few days? Share some of your sentences with the class.

1. _____ a few days ago.

2. _____ in a few days.

3. _____ in a few more minutes.

4. _____ three hours ago.

5. _____ in four more hours.

6. _____ a couple of days ago.

7. _____ in a couple of months.

8. _____ many years ago.

9. _____ in a couple of minutes.

❏ **Exercise 25. Listening.** (Chart 10-4)
Listen to the sentences. Choose **same** if the sentence below has the same meaning. Choose **different** if the meaning is different.

Example: You will hear: Liam graduated from high school a few years ago.
You will read: Liam graduated from high school two years ago.
You will choose: (same)   different

1. Jean is going to leave in two days.   same   different

2. Lena is going to leave in three weeks.   same   different

3. We sold our house five years ago.   same   different

4. The phone rang five minutes ago.   same   different

5. Marc is going to be here in fifteen minutes.   same   different

❏ **Exercise 26. Warm-up.** (Chart 10-5)
Underline the time phrase in each sentence. Check (✓) the sentence that has a present meaning.

1. ____ I am working this morning.

2. ____ I worked this morning.

3. ____ I am going to work this morning.

10-5 Using *Today*, *Tonight*, and *This* + *Morning*, *Afternoon*, *Evening*, *Week*, *Month*, *Year*

PRESENT	Right now it's 10:00 A.M. We are in our English class. (a) We **are studying** English **this morning**.	today tonight this morning
PAST	Right now it's 10:00 A.M. Nancy left home at 9:00 to go downtown. She isn't at home right now. (b) Nancy **went** downtown **this morning**.	this afternoon These words this evening can express this week present, past, this weekend or future time. this month
FUTURE	Right now it's 10:00 A.M. Class ends at 11:00. After class today, I'm going to go to the bank. (c) I**'m going to go** to the bank **this morning**.	this year

❏ **Exercise 27. Looking at grammar.** (Chart 10-5)
Answer the questions orally or in writing (on a separate piece of paper).

1. What did you do earlier this year? → *I came to this city earlier this year.*
2. What are you doing this year?
3. What are you going to do this year?
4. What did you do earlier today?
5. What are you doing today, right now?
6. What are you going to do later today?
7. What did you do earlier this morning / afternoon / evening?
8. What are you going to do later this morning / afternoon / evening?

❏ **Exercise 28. Looking at grammar.** (Chart 10-5)
Choose <u>all</u> the correct time expressions.

1. What are you doing ____?
   a. this morning
   b. this week
   c. tonight
   d. this afternoon
   e. today

2. What did you do ____?
   a. this week
   b. this month
   c. today
   d. this year
   e. this evening

3. What are you going to do ____?
   a. this morning
   b. this weekend
   c. tonight
   d. this year
   e. today

Exercise 29. Let's talk: small groups. (Chart 10-5)
Work in small groups. Take turns being Student A and asking your classmates questions about future activities. Student A will ask two questions with **When**.

Example: go downtown
STUDENT A: When are you going to go downtown?
STUDENT B: This weekend. / Tomorrow morning. / In a couple of days. / Etc.
STUDENT A: When is (*Student B*) going to go downtown?
STUDENT C: He/She is going to go downtown this weekend.

1. have dinner
2. do your grammar homework
3. go shopping
4. go to (*name of a class*)
5. visit (*name of a place in this city*)
6. call (*name of a student*) on the phone

7. go to (*name of a restaurant*) for dinner
8. see your family again
9. buy a car
10. see (*name of a new movie*)
11. go to (*name of an event*)
12. take a vacation

❑   **Exercise 30. Let's talk: pairwork.** (Chart 10-5)
Work with a partner. Ask questions using the verbs from the box or your own words.

Example: tomorrow morning
PARTNER A: Are you going to come to class tomorrow morning?
PARTNER B: Yes, I am. OR No, I'm not.

Example: yesterday morning
PARTNER A: Did you eat breakfast yesterday morning?
PARTNER B: Yes, I did. OR No, I didn't.

buy	do	eat	send	visit
call	drink	get up	shop	wake up
come	drive	go	sleep	wash

1. last night
2. tomorrow night
3. tonight
4. tomorrow afternoon
5. yesterday afternoon
6. this afternoon
7. last Friday
8. next Friday
9. next week

Change roles.

10. last week
11. this week
12. yesterday morning
13. tomorrow morning
14. this morning
15. later today
16. a couple of hours ago
17. in a couple of hours
18. this evening

❑ **Exercise 31. Listening.** (Chart 10-5)

Listen to each sentence. Decide if the meaning is past, present, or future time.

Example: You will hear: The students are busy working on a project in the
classroom.

You will choose: past   (present)   future

1. past	present	future		6. past	present	future
2. past	present	future		7. past	present	future
3. past	present	future		8. past	present	future
4. past	present	future		9. past	present	future
5. past	present	future		10. past	present	future

❑ **Exercise 32. Warm-up.** (Chart 10-6)

Check (✓) the sentences with a future meaning.

1. _____ The test is going to be long.   3. _____ The test was long.

2. _____ The test is long.   4. _____ The test will be long.

10-6 Future Time: Using *Will*

AFFIRMATIVE STATEMENT	(a) Mike **will arrive** at 10:00 tomorrow. (b) Mike **is going to arrive** at 10:00 tomorrow.	Examples (a) and (b) have basically the same meaning.
	(c) CORRECT: Mike **will go** there. INCORRECT: *Mike will goes there.* INCORRECT: *Mike wills go there.*	The base form of a verb follows **will**. In (c): *goes* and *wills go* are NOT correct.
	(d) CORRECT: Mike **will arrive** at 10:00. INCORRECT: *Mike will arrives at 10:00.*	There is never a final **-s** on **will** for future time.
	(e) CORRECT: Mike **will go** there. INCORRECT: *Mike will to go there.*	**Will** is not followed by an infinitive with **to**. In (e): *will to go* is not correct.
CONTRACTIONS	(f) I will come. = **I'll** come. You will come. = **You'll** come. She will come. = **She'll** come. He will come. = **He'll** come. It will come. = **It'll** come. We will come. = **We'll** come. They will come. = **They'll** come.	**Will** is contracted to **'ll** with subject pronouns.* These contractions are common in both speaking and writing.
NEGATIVE STATEMENT	(g) Bob **will not be** here tomorrow. (h) Bob **won't be** here tomorrow.	NEGATIVE CONTRACTION **will** + **not** = **won't**

*__Will__ is also often contracted with nouns in speaking (but not in writing).
    WRITTEN: *Tom will be here at ten.*
    SPOKEN: *"Tom'll be here at ten."*

Exercise 33. Let's talk: class activity. (Chart 10-6)
Change the sentences by using **will** to express future time.

1. Mrs. Ortega is going to need some help tomorrow.
    → Mrs. Ortega will need some help tomorrow.
2. Lev and Olga are going to help her.
3. The train is going to be late.
4. Hurry up, or we're going to miss the beginning of the concert.
5. I'm not going to be at home this evening.
6. Kelly is going to wait for us at the bus stop.
7. Be careful with those scissors! You're going to hurt yourself!
8. You are going to have two science classes next term, not one.

❑ **Exercise 34. Let's talk: small groups.** (Chart 10-6)
Work in small groups. What is going to happen in the lives of your classmates in the
next 50 years? Make predictions about your classmates' futures. Share some of your
predictions with the class.

Example:
STUDENT A: Greta is going to become a famous research scientist.
STUDENT B: Ali will have a happy marriage and lots of children.
STUDENT C: Armando will live in a quiet place and write books.★
            Etc.

❑ **Exercise 35. Listening.** (Chart 10-6)

Part I. Listen to each pair of sentences and note the contractions with **will**.

1. a. The doctor will see you in a few minutes. OR
   b. The doctor'll see you in a few minutes.

2. a. Mom will be home late. OR
   b. Mom'll be home late.

3. a. Bob will pick us up. OR
   b. Bob'll pick us up.

Part II. Complete the sentences with the words you hear: **will** or **'ll**.

1. The nurse _____ give you some medicine.

2. Your headache _____ go away quickly.

3. The weather _____ be nice tomorrow.

4. Sorry, dinner _____ be late tonight.

★When two verbs are connected by *and*, the helping verbs **be going to** and **will** are usually not repeated.
  For example: *I'm going to lock the doors and ~~am going to~~ turn out the lights.*
              I'll lock the doors and ~~will~~ turn out the lights.

5. The bus _____ be here in a few minutes.

6. Dad _____ help you with your homework later.

7. The students _____ need more time for review.

□ **Exercise 36. Warm-up.** (Chart 10-7)
Answer the questions.

1. Will you be here next year?	Yes, I will. No, I won't.
2. Will you be a student next year?	Yes, I will. No, I won't.
3. Will you graduate next year?	Yes, I will. No, I won't.

10-7 Asking Questions with *Will*

QUESTION						ANSWER
(QUESTION WORD) +	*WILL* +	SUBJECT +	MAIN VERB			
(a)	*Will*	*Tom*	*come*	tomorrow?	→	**Yes, he will.** ★ **No, he won't.**
(b)	*Will*	*you*	*be*	at home tonight?	→	**Yes, I will.** ★ **No, I won't.**
(c) When	*will*	*Ann*	*arrive*?		→	**Next Saturday.**
(d) What time	*will*	*the plane*	*arrive*?		→	**Three-thirty.**
(e) Where	*will*	*you*	*be*	tonight?	→	**At home.**

*NOTE: *Will* is not contracted with a pronoun in a short answer. See Chart 2-2, p. 30, for information about the use of contractions in short answers.

□ **Exercise 37. Looking at grammar.** (Chart 10-7)
Make questions.

1. A: _____*Will you be at home tomorrow night?*_____

   B: Yes, _____*I will.*_____ (I'll be at home tomorrow night.)

2. A: _____*Will Mona be in class tomorrow?*_____

   B: No, _____*she won't.*_____ (Mona won't be in class tomorrow).

3. A: _____*When will you see Mr. Lu?*_____

   B: Tomorrow afternoon. (I'll see Mr. Lu tomorrow afternoon.)

4. A: _____

   B: Yes, _____ (The plane will be on time.)

5. A: _____

   B: Yes, _____ (Dinner will be ready in a few minutes.)

6. A: _____

   B: In a few minutes. (Dinner will be ready in a few minutes.)

7. A: _____

   B: Next year. (I'll graduate next year.)

8. A: _____

   B: At the community college. (Elyse will go to school at the community college next year.)

9. A: _____

   B: No, _____ (Jenna and Scott won't be at the party.)

10. A: _____

    B: Yes, _____ (Martin will arrive in Chicago next week.)

11. A: _____

    B: In Chicago. (Martin will be in Chicago next week.)

12. A: _____

    B: No, _____ (I won't be home early tonight.)

13. A: _____

    B: In a few minutes. (Dr. Fernandez will be back in a few minutes.)

14. A: _____

    B: Yes, _____ (We'll be ready to leave at 8:15.)

❑ **Exercise 38. Let's talk: pairwork.** (Chart 10-7)

Part I. Imagine you are visiting Paris. Check (✓) the fun things you will do on your trip.

Paris activities:

_____ visit the Eiffel Tower

_____ ride the elevator to the top

_____ drink coffee in a French café

_____ buy a painting from a street artist

_____ ride a boat on the Seine River

_____ see the *Mona Lisa* at the Louvre museum

_____ speak French

_____ buy some clothes at a designer shop

_____ eat dinner in an expensive French restaurant

_____ visit Notre Dame cathedral

_____ take a bus tour of Paris

_____ buy some French perfume

Part II. Work with a partner. Take turns asking and answering questions about your activities.

Example: visit the Eiffel Tower
PARTNER A: Will you visit the Eiffel Tower?
PARTNER B: Yes, I will. OR No, I won't.
PARTNER A: Your turn now.

PARTNER A	PARTNER B
1. visit the Eiffel Tower	1. ride the elevator to the top
2. drink coffee in a French café	2. buy a painting from a street artist
3. ride a boat on the Seine River	3. see the *Mona Lisa* at the Louvre museum
4. speak French	4. buy some clothes at a designer shop
5. eat dinner in an expensive French restaurant	5. visit Notre Dame cathedral
6. take a bus tour of Paris	6. buy some French perfume

❑ **Exercise 39. Listening.** (Chart 10-7)
You are going away on a dream vacation. Where would you like to visit? It can be a small town, a big city, a country, or a place far away from cities or towns. Write it down. Then listen to each question and write a short answer. Share a few of your answers.

Place: _____

1. _____

2. _____

3. _____

4. _____

5. _____

Exercise 40. Reading, listening, and speaking. (Chart 10-7)
Part I. Read the story. Then listen to the questions and choose the correct answers.

SITUATION: Samantha is a high school student. She is thinking about next year. New Year's is in one week. She wants to change some of her habits. She is making some New Year's resolutions.

Samantha's New Year's Resolutions

Samantha is a good student. She studies a lot, but she likes to go to parties on weekends. She wants to attend a good university, so next year she will study on weekends too. She has a healthy lifestyle, but sometimes she forgets to exercise. She will exercise four times a week. Now, she exercises only two times a week. She doesn't smoke, but she wants to lose a little weight. She will start a new diet next year. Samantha loves her grandmother, but she doesn't see her very much. Samantha misses her. Next year, she will visit her grandmother once a week. Samantha is planning a lot of changes, and she thinks she will be happier.

1. (Yes, she will.)   No, she won't.
2. Yes, she will.   No, she won't.
3. Yes, she will.   No, she won't.
4. Yes, she will.   No, she won't.
5. Yes, she will.   No, she won't.
6. Yes, she will.   No, she won't.
7. Yes, she will.   No, she won't.
8. Yes, she will.   No, she won't.

Part II. Imagine it is New Year's and you are making some resolutions. What are some things you are going to do/will do to improve yourself and your life this year? Make a list. Then share some of your ideas with the class.

Example: I will stop smoking.
         I am going to get more exercise.
         Etc.

❏ **Exercise 41. Listening.** (Chart 10-7)

Won't and *want* sound similar. Listen carefully to the sentences and choose the verbs you hear.

1. won't   (want)   5. won't   want
2. won't   want   6. won't   want
3. won't   want   7. won't   want
4. won't   want   8. won't   want

10-8 Verb Summary: Present, Past, and Future

	STATEMENT: AFFIRMATIVE	STATEMENT: NEGATIVE	QUESTION
SIMPLE PRESENT	I *eat* lunch every day. She *eats* lunch every day.	I *don't eat* lunch. She *doesn't eat* lunch.	*Do* you *eat* lunch? *Does* she *eat* lunch?
PRESENT PROGRESSIVE	I *am eating* lunch right now. She *is eating* lunch. They *are eating* lunch.	I*'m not eating* lunch. She *isn't eating* lunch. They *aren't eating* lunch.	*Am* I *eating* lunch? *Is* she *eating* lunch? *Are* they *eating* lunch?
SIMPLE PAST	He *ate* lunch yesterday.	He *didn't eat* lunch.	*Did* he *eat* lunch?
BE GOING TO	I *am going to eat* lunch tomorrow. She *is going to eat* lunch tomorrow. They *are going to eat* lunch tomorrow.	I*'m not going to eat* lunch tomorrow. She *isn't going to eat* lunch tomorrow. They *aren't going to eat* lunch tomorrow.	*Am* I *going to eat* lunch tomorrow? *Is* she *going to eat* lunch tomorrow? *Are* they *going to eat* lunch tomorrow?
WILL	He *will eat* lunch tomorrow.	He *won't eat* lunch tomorrow.	*Will* he *eat* lunch tomorrow?

❑ **Exercise 42. Looking at grammar.** (Chart 10-8)
Complete the sentences with the verbs in parentheses.

1. Right now Marta (*sit*) _____*is sitting*_____ at her desk.

2. She (*do, not*) _____ homework. She (*chat*) _____ online with her parents.

3. She (*chat*) _____ with them every week.

4. She (*chat, not*) _____ with them every day.

5. Her parents (*expect, not*) _____ to talk to her every day.

6. Last night Marta (*send*) _____ an email to her brother. Then she

   (*start*) _____ to text her sister.

7. While Marta was texting her sister, her phone (*ring*) _____ . It was her

   best friend.

8. Marta (*finish, not*) _____ the text. After she (*talk*)

   _____ to her friend, she (*go*) _____ to bed.

9. Tomorrow she (*call*) _____ her sister.

10. Marta (*chat, not*) _____ with her parents tomorrow.

11. (*you, chat*) _____ online with someone every day?

12. (*you, chat*) _____ online with someone yesterday?

13. (*you, chat*) _____ online with someone tomorrow?

□ **Exercise 43. Listening.** (Chart 10-8)

Listen to the sentences. Write the verbs you hear.

A restaurant meal

1. Bert _____ meat, eggs, or fish.

2. He's a vegetarian. He _____ meat. He _____

   _____ it as a child either.

3. His wife, Beth, _____ meat, but she isn't a vegetarian.

4. She _____ the taste of meat.

5. They _____ a new restaurant tomorrow.

6. It _____ last month, and online reviews _____ it is

   excellent.

7. Bert _____ probably _____ a dish with lots of vegetables.

8. Beth _____ vegetables for a main dish. She _____

   probably _____ for some type of fish.

9. _____ themselves?

10. _____ back to this restaurant?

10-9 Verb Summary: Forms of *Be*

	STATEMENT: AFFIRMATIVE	STATEMENT: NEGATIVE	QUESTION
SIMPLE PRESENT	I *am* from South Korea. He *is* from Egypt. They *are* from Venezuela.	I *am not* from Jordan. She *isn't* from Egypt. They *aren't* from Italy.	*Am* I from Chile? *Is* she from Greece? *Are* they from Kenya?
SIMPLE PAST	Ann *was* late yesterday. They *were* late yesterday.	She *wasn't* on time. They *weren't* on time.	*Was* she late? *Were* they late?
BE GOING TO	I *am going to be* on time. She *is going to be* on time. They *are going to be* on time.	I*'m not going to be* late. She *isn't going to be* late. They *aren't going to be* late.	*Am* I *going to be* on time? *Is* she *going to be* on time? *Are* they *going to be* on time?
WILL	He *will be* absent.	He *won't be* in class.	*Will* he *be* absent?

❏ **Exercise 44. Looking at grammar.** (Chart 10-9)
Complete the sentences with the verbs in parentheses.

1. I (*be*) _____ in class right now. I (*be, not*) _____ here yesterday.

    I (*be*) _____ absent yesterday. (*you, be*) _____ in class

    yesterday? (*Carmen, be*) _____ here yesterday?

2. Carmen and I (*be*) _____ absent from class yesterday. We (*be, not*) _____

    _____ here.

3. My friends (*be*) _____ at Fatima's apartment tomorrow evening. I (*be*)

    _____ there too. (*you, be*) _____ there? (*Akira, be*)

    _____ there?

4. A whale (*be, not*) _____ a fish. It (*be*) _____ a mammal.

    Dolphins (*be, not*) _____ fish either. They (*be*) _____ mammals.

a dolphin

a whale

❏ **Exercise 45. Looking at grammar.** (Charts 10-8 and 10-9)
Complete the questions with *Are* or *Do*.

SITUATION: Rebecca's daughter is starting fourth grade this morning. Her mother is asking her questions.

1. _____*Do*_____ you want to get there early?
2. _____*Are*_____ you excited?
3. _____ you have your notebook?
4. _____ you remember your teacher's name?
5. _____ you a little scared?
6. _____ you have your lunch money?
7. _____ you ready to go?
8. _____ you okay?
9. _____ you want me to be quiet?

❏ **Exercise 46. Looking at grammar.** (Charts 10-8 and 10-9)
Complete the sentences with *Were* or *Did*.

SITUATION: Jeff has a hard job and works long hours. He got home at 3:00 A.M. Now it's later in the morning, and his roommates are asking him questions.

1. _____ you at your office?
2. _____ you stay late?
3. _____ you have a lot of work?
4. _____ you busy?
5. _____ you tired when you got home?
6. _____ you feel tired?
7. _____ you drink a lot of coffee?
8. _____ you hungry at 3:00 A.M.?
9. _____ you go to bed late?

❏ **Exercise 47. Looking at grammar.** (Charts 10-8 and 10-9)
Complete the sentences with the verbs in parentheses. Give short answers to questions where necessary.

1. A: (*you, have*) _____*Do you have*_____ a car?
   B: No, I _____*don't*_____. I (*take*) _____*take*_____ the bus to work every day.

2. A: (*you, walk*) _____ to work yesterday?
   B: No, I _____. I (*ride*) _____ my motorcycle.

3. A: (*you, be*) _____ in class tomorrow?

   B: Yes, I _____. But I (*be, not*) _____ in class the day after tomorrow.

4. A: Where (*you, study, usually*) _____?

   B: In my room.

   A: (*you, go*) _____ to the library to study sometimes?

   B: No. I (*like, not*) _____ to study at the library.

5. A: (*Abby, call*) _____ you last night?

   B: Yes, she _____. We (*talk*) _____ for a few minutes.

   A: (*she, tell*) _____ you about her brother, Brian?

   B: No, she _____. She (*say, not*) _____ anything about him. Why?

   A: Brian (*be*) _____ in an accident.

   B: That's too bad. What happened?

   A: A dog (*run*) _____ in front of his bike. He (*see, not*)

   _____ a truck next to him, and he (*hit*) _____ it. It was an unfortunate accident.

   B: (*he, be*) _____ in the hospital now?

   A: No, he _____. He (*be*) _____ at home.

□ **Exercise 48. Check your knowledge.** (Chapter 10)

Correct the mistakes.

                 will you
1. When ~~you will~~ come?

2. Is Kiril will go to work tomorrow?

3. Will Gary to meet us for dinner tomorrow?

4. We went to a movie last evening.

5. What time you are going to come tomorrow?

6. My sister is going to meet me at the airport. My brother won't to be there.

7. Mr. Pang will sells his business and retires next year.

8. Do you will be in Venezuela next year?

9. I saw Jim three day ago.

10. *Formal written English:* I'm gonna graduate with a degree in chemistry.

❑ **Exercise 49. Listening, reading, writing, and speaking.** (Chapter 10)

Part I. Listen to the play. Then take turns reading the roles. Look at new vocabulary with your teacher first.

Jack and the Beanstalk

NARRATOR: Once upon a time* there was a boy named Jack. He lived with his mother in a small village.

MOTHER: We are very poor. We have no money. Our cow has no milk.

JACK: What are we going to do?

MOTHER: You'll go to the market and sell the cow.

NARRATOR: Jack left his home and met an old man on the road.

OLD MAN: I will buy your cow. I will pay you with beans. Here, these are magic beans.

NARRATOR: Jack took the beans home to his mother.

MOTHER: You stupid boy. We have nothing now. We are going to die.

NARRATOR: She threw the beans out the window. The next morning, Jack woke up and saw a huge beanstalk outside his window. It went into the clouds. He decided to climb it. At the top, he saw a castle. Inside the castle, there lived a giant and his wife. He went into the castle.

WIFE: What are you doing? My husband likes to eat boys for breakfast. You need to hide or he will eat you.

JACK: I'm so scared. Please help me.

> **Do you know these words?**
>
> | village | oven |
> |---|---|
> | magic beans | bones |
> | giant | axe |

a castle

a beanstalk

---

once upon a time = a long time ago

WIFE: Here, climb inside the oven. After breakfast, my husband will fall asleep.

GIANT: Fee-Fi-Fo-Fum,*
I smell the blood of an Englishman.
If he's alive or if he's dead,
I'll use his bones to make my bread.

Hmm. I smell a boy. Wife, are you going to feed me a boy for breakfast?

WIFE: No, I think the smell is the boy from last week. Here's your breakfast.

NARRATOR: The giant ate, counted his gold coins, and soon fell asleep. Jack got out of the oven, took a few gold coins, climbed down the beanstalk, and ran to his mother.

MOTHER: Oh, Jack. You saved us. Now we have money for food. But you are not going to go back to the castle. The giant will eat you.

NARRATOR: But Jack wanted more money. Soon he climbed the beanstalk. Again the giant's wife hid Jack in the oven. The giant had a hen. It laid golden eggs. After the giant fell asleep, Jack stole the hen.

a harp

a hen

MOTHER: What will we do with a hen? Why didn't you bring more gold coins? Jack, you have no sense.

JACK: Wait, mother. The hen is going to lay a golden egg. Watch.

NARRATOR: The hen laid a golden egg.

MOTHER: Oh, you wonderful boy! We will be rich.

NARRATOR: But Jack wanted more from the giant, so he went up the beanstalk one more time. This time, a golden harp was playing. It made beautiful music. Soon the giant went to sleep, and Jack took the harp. The giant heard a noise and woke up.

GIANT: I will catch you and eat you alive.

---

*Fee-Fi-Fo-Fum = words with no meaning. They help the second line rhyme.

NARRATOR: The giant ran after Jack. Jack climbed down the beanstalk. The giant followed. Jack took an axe and chopped down the stalk. The giant fell.

GIANT: Ahhhhhhhhhh!

JACK: The giant is dead.

MOTHER: Now we are safe. The harp will give us beautiful music. My sadness will go away. Our lives will be happy. You saved us!

NARRATOR: And they lived happily ever after.

Part II. Work in small groups. Complete the play below. Jack is now Jill. The giant is now a dragon. Make the lines silly, funny, or just different.

Jill and the Dragon

NARRATOR: Once upon a time there was a girl named Jill. She lived with her mother in a small village.

MOTHER: We are very poor. We have no money for food.

JILL: _____

MOTHER: _____

NARRATOR: Jill left her home and met a/an _____ on the road.

_____ : _____

NARRATOR: Jill took the _____ home to her mother.

MOTHER: _____

NARRATOR: She threw the _____ out the window. The next morning, Jill woke up and saw a huge _____ outside her window. It went into the clouds. She decided to climb it. At the top, she saw a castle. Inside the castle, there lived a fire-breathing dragon and his wife. He owned all the gold in the kingdom. Jill went into the castle.

a dragon

WIFE: _____

JILL: _____

WIFE: _____

DRAGON: _____

NARRATOR: Jill ran down the _____ with a few gold coins in her hands. Her clothes were a little burned, but she was safe.

MOTHER: _____

JILL: _____

NARRATOR: The next morning, Jill climbed up the _____ again. She carried a sack with her.

DRAGON: _____

WIFE: _____

DRAGON: _____

NARRATOR: Jill escaped from the castle with the sack full of gold coins. She ran down

the _____. The dragon tried to catch her. He jumped on the

_____, but when he breathed, the _____ caught
on fire. It burned to the ground. The dragon fell and died.

JILL: _____

MOTHER: _____

NARRATOR: And they lived happily ever after.

Part III. Editing check: Work individually or change papers with a partner. Check (✓) for the following:

1. ____ capital letter at the beginning of each sentence

2. ____ period at the end of each sentence

3. ____ use of **will** or **be going to** for a future activity

4. ____ use of past verbs for past activities

5. ____ correct use of time expressions with present, past, and future

6. ____ correct spelling (use a dictionary or spell-check)

Part IV. OPTION 1: Practice and perform your play for the class.

OPTION 2: Practice and perform "Jack and the Beanstalk" for the class.

Chapter 11
Expressing Future Time, Part 2

❏ **Exercise 1. Warm-up.** (Chart 11-1)
Which two sentences have the same meaning?

1. Jon might change jobs.

2. Jon will change jobs.

3. Jon may change jobs.

11-1 *May/Might* vs. *Will*

(a) It **may rain** *tomorrow*. (b) Anita **may be** at home *now*.	**May** + *verb* (base form) expresses a possibility in the future, as in (a), or a present possibility, as in (b).
(c) It **might rain** *tomorrow*. (d) Anita **might be** at home *now*.	**Might** has the same meaning as **may**. Examples (a) and (c) have the same meaning. Examples (b) and (d) have the same meaning.
(e) Tom **will be** at the meeting *tomorrow*. (f) Ms. Lee **may/might be** at the meeting *tomorrow*.	In (e): The speaker uses **will** because he feels sure about Tom's presence at the meeting tomorrow. In (f): The speaker uses **may/might** to say, "I don't know if Ms. Lee will be at the meeting, but it is possible."
(g) Ms. Lee **may/might not be** at the meeting *tomorrow*.	Negative form: **may/might** + **not** NOTE: Examples (f) and (g) have essentially the same meaning: Ms. Lee may or may not be at the meeting tomorrow.
INCORRECT: Ms. Lee may will be at the meeting tomorrow. *INCORRECT:* Ms. Lee might will be at the meeting tomorrow.	**May** and **might** are <u>not</u> used with **will**.

Exercise 2. Looking at grammar. (Chart 11-1)

Complete the sentences. Use **will** or **won't** if you are sure. Use **may** or **might** if you are not sure.

1. I _____ be in class next Monday.

   → *I **will be** in class next Monday.* = You're sure.

   → *I **will not** (**won't**) **be** in class next Monday.* = You're sure.

   → *I **may**/**might be** in class next Monday.* OR

   → *I **may**/**might not be** in class next Monday.* = It's possible, but you're not sure.

2. I _____ eat breakfast tomorrow morning.

3. I _____ be in class tomorrow.

4. I _____ get a text from a friend of mine tomorrow.

5. I _____ watch TV for a little while after dinner tonight.

6. We _____ have a grammar test tomorrow.

7. I _____ eat dinner at a restaurant tonight.

8. It _____ be cloudy tomorrow.

9. The sun _____ rise tomorrow morning.

10. I _____ choose a career in music after I finish school.

11. The population of the earth _____ continue to grow.

12. Cities _____ become more and more crowded.

13. We _____ live on other planets.

❑ **Exercise 3. Let's talk: small groups.** (Chart 11-1)

Work in small groups. Take turns completing the sentences about yourself and other people in the list.

I	a friend
you (name of a classmate)	a world leader
your teacher	a movie star
a member of your family	a famous athlete

1. In five years, _____ will _____.

2. Next year, _____ may not _____.

3. _____ might _____ tomorrow.

4. _____ might or might not _____ next week.

5. _____ won't _____ in 2025.

6. _____ might not _____ tomorrow.

7. Next year, _____ won't _____.

8. In 20 years, _____ may _____.

9. Next week, _____ may or may not _____.

10. _____ will _____ in a few years.

an athlete

❑ **Exercise 4. Writing and speaking.** (Chart 11-1)

Write two paragraphs. Use the given words in the paragraphs below. Use your own paper.

Paragraph 1: Write about your activities *yesterday*.
Paragraph 2: Write about your activities *tomorrow*. Include activities you **will** do and activities you **may** or **might** do.

Then show your paragraphs to a partner. Your partner will share some of your activities with the class.

PARAGRAPH 1.

I got up at _____ yesterday morning. After that, _____. Around _____ o'clock, _____. Later _____. At _____ o'clock, _____. Then _____. _____ a little later. Then at _____ o'clock _____.

PARAGRAPH 2.

I'm going to get up at _____ tomorrow morning. Then _____. After that, _____. Around _____ o'clock, _____. Later _____. At _____ o'clock, _____. Next, _____. _____ a little later. Then at _____ o'clock, _____.

❏ **Exercise 5. Warm-up.** (Chart 11-2)
Which answers are true for you? What do you notice about **may** and **maybe** in sentence c.?

1. *Tomorrow morning, . . .*
   a. I will go to school early.
   b. I won't go to school early.
   c. I may go to school early.

2. *Tomorrow night, . . .*
   a. I will go to the library.
   b. I won't go to the library.
   c. maybe I will go to the library.

11-2 *Maybe* (One Word) vs. *May Be* (Two Words)

(a) A: Will Jamal be in class tomorrow? B: I don't know. **Maybe. Maybe Jamal will be** in class tomorrow, and **maybe he won't**.	The adverb **maybe** (one word) means "possibly."
(b) | **Maybe** | Jamal | will be | here. adverb subject verb	**Maybe** comes in front of a subject and verb.
(c) | Jamal | **may be** | here tomorrow. subject verb	**May be** (two words) is used as the verb of a sentence.

❏ **Exercise 6. Looking at grammar.** (Chart 11-2)
Find the sentences where **maybe** is used as an adverb and where **may** is used as part of the verb. Choose the correct answer.

1. Maybe it will rain tomorrow.   (adverb)   verb

2. It may rain tomorrow.   adverb   (verb)

3. We may go to the art museum tomorrow.   adverb   verb

4. Maybe Jessica will come with us.   adverb   verb

5. She may have a day off tomorrow.   adverb   verb

6. It's cold and cloudy today. It may be cold and cloudy tomorrow.   adverb   verb

7. Maybe the weather will be warm and sunny this weekend.   adverb   verb

❑ **Exercise 7. Looking at grammar.** (Chart 11-2)
Complete the sentences with *maybe* or *may be*.

1. A: I _____*may be*_____ a little late tonight.

   B: That's okay. I won't worry about you.

2. A: Will you be here by seven o'clock?

   B: It's hard to say. _____*Maybe*_____ I'll be a little late.

3. A: It _____ cold tomorrow.

   B: That's okay. Let's go to the beach anyway.

4. A: Will the plane be on time?

   B: I think so, but it _____ a few minutes late.

5. A: Do you want to go to the park tomorrow?

   B: Sure. That sounds like fun.

   A: Let's talk to Carlos too. _____ he would like to go with us.

6. A: Where's Mr. Callis?

   B: Look in Room 506 down the hall. I think he _____ there.

   A: No, he's not there. I just looked in Room 506.

   B: _____ he's in Room 508.

❑ **Exercise 8. Let's talk.** (Chart 11-2)
Work in groups or as a class. The group leader or your teacher will ask you questions. Answer them by using *I don't know* + *maybe* or *may/might*. If you work in groups, choose a new leader where indicated.

Example:
TEACHER/LEADER: What are you going to do tonight?
      STUDENT: I don't know. Maybe I'll watch TV. / I may watch TV. / I might watch TV.

1. What are you going to do tonight?
2. What are you going to do tomorrow?
3. What are you going to do after class today?
4. What are you going to do this weekend?
5. What are you going to do this evening?

Choose a new leader.
6. Who is going to go shopping tomorrow? What are you going to buy?
7. Who is going to go out to eat tonight? Where are you going to go?
8. Who is going to watch TV tonight? What are you going to watch?
9. Who is going to get married? When?

Choose a new leader.

10. Who is going to leave class early? Why?

11. Is it going to rain tomorrow? What is the weather going to be like tomorrow?

12. Who is planning to go on a vacation? Where are you going to go?

13. Who wants to have a pet? What kind of pet are you going to get?

❏ **Exercise 9. Looking at grammar.** (Chart 11-2)
Rewrite the sentences. Use the words in parentheses.

1. Maybe I will study.

    a. (*might*) _____*I might study.*_____

    b. (*may*) _____*I may study.*_____

2. The teacher might give a test.

    a. (*maybe*) _____

    b. (*may*) _____

3. Maybe Natalie will be home early.

    a (*may*) _____

    b. (*might*) _____

4. She might be late.

    a. (*maybe*) _____

    b. (*may*) _____

5. It may rain tomorrow.

    a. (*maybe*) _____

    b. (*might*) _____

❏ **Exercise 10. Listening.** (Chart 11-2)

Listen to the sentences. Choose the use of *may* that you hear.

Example: You will hear: Maybe I'll see you tomorrow.
        You will choose: (*Maybe*)   *May* + verb

1. *maybe*	*may* + verb	5. *Maybe*	*May* + verb
2. *maybe*	*may* + verb	6. *Maybe*	*May* + verb
3. *Maybe*	*May* + verb	7. *maybe*	*may* + verb
4. *maybe*	*may* + verb	8. *Maybe*	*May* + verb

□ **Exercise 11. Looking at grammar.** (Chart 11-2)
Answer the questions. Use *maybe* or *may/might*.

1. A: Is Anthony going to come to the party?

   B: I don't know. _____*Maybe*_____.

2. A: What are you going to do tomorrow?

   B: I don't know. I _____*may / might*_____ go swimming.

3. A: Are Lilly and James going to get married?

   B: _____. Who knows?

4. A: Where is Robert?

   B: I don't know. He _____ be at his office.

5. A: Where is Robert?

   B: I don't know. _____ he's at his office.

6. A: I'd like to have a pet.

   B: What kind of pet would you like to get?

   A: I'm not sure. _____ I'll get

   a canary. Or _____ I'll get a snake.

   I _____ get a fish. Or I

   _____ get a turtle.

   B: What's wrong with a cat or dog?

a canary

□ **Exercise 12. Let's talk: pairwork.** (Charts 11-1 and 11-2)
Work with a partner. Use the phrases below to tell your partner about your activities
tomorrow. Use *will/won't, going to/not going to, maybe, may,* and *might*.

Example: go to a movie / go shopping
PARTNER A: I'm not going to go to a movie tomorrow. OR I might go shopping.
PARTNER B: I might go to a movie. OR Maybe I'll go shopping.

1. wake up early / sleep in
2. eat a big breakfast / eat a small breakfast
3. stay home / go to school
4. get some exercise in the afternoon / take a nap in the afternoon
5. do my homework in the evening / watch TV in the evening
6. eat an ice cream cone / eat vegetables
7. cook dinner / eat out
8. shop online / shop at a store

an ice
cream cone

9. clean my house (apartment, bedroom, car, kitchen) / read a book

10. visit a friend / visit a social networking site

❏ **Exercise 13. Listening.** (Charts 11-1 and 11-2)

Listen to each sentence. Choose the sentence that has the same meaning as the sentence you hear.

Example: You will hear: I might be absent tomorrow.
          You will choose: (a.) Maybe I will be absent.   b. I'm going to be absent.

1. a. Our plans will change.
   b. Our plans might change.

2. a. It is going to rain.
   b. Maybe it will rain.

3. a. We may finish this grammar book soon.
   b. We will finish this grammar book soon.

4. a. Maybe Henry will get good news tomorrow.
   b. Henry is going to get good news tomorrow.

5. a. The class may start on time.
   b. The class is going to start on time.

❏ **Exercise 14. Let's talk: pairwork.** (Charts 11-1 and 11-2)

Work with a partner. Check (✓) the boxes that describe your activities tomorrow. Show your answers to your partner. She/He will make sentences about you using **may, might,** or **maybe**. Share some of them with the class.

Example: eat lunch / go shopping, etc.

Possible sentences: (*to your partner*) You may eat lunch. You won't go shopping. Etc.
                  (*to the class*) She/He may eat lunch. She/He won't go shopping. Etc.

ACTIVITY	YES	NO	MAYBE
1. eat lunch			
2. go shopping			
3. send some emails			
4. watch TV			
5. talk on the phone			
6. play soccer			
7. read an English language newspaper			
8. look up information on the Internet			
9. have dinner with friends			
10. chat online			

❑ **Exercise 15. Warm-up.** (Chart 11-3)

<u>Underline</u> the time word in each sentence. What tense is used in the red clause? Does the clause have present or future meaning?

1. Before I go on vacation next week, I'm going to clean my apartment.

2. When I get home next month, my apartment will be clean.

11-3 Future Time Clauses with *Before, After,* and *When*

(a) *Before Ann goes to work tomorrow,* she will eat breakfast. INCORRECT: *Before Ann will go to work tomorrow, she will eat breakfast.* INCORRECT: *Before Ann is going to go to work tomorrow, she will eat breakfast.*	In (a): **Before Ann goes to work tomorrow** = a future time clause;* **she will eat breakfast** = main clause. A future time clause uses the SIMPLE PRESENT TENSE. *Will* OR *be going to* is used in the main clause.
(b) I'm going to finish my homework *after I eat dinner tonight.* (c) *When I go to New York next week,* I'm going to stay at the Hilton Hotel.	In (b): **after I eat dinner tonight** = a future time clause In (c): **When I go to New York next week** = a future time clause Notice: A comma follows a time clause when it comes at the beginning of a sentence.

*See Chart 9-7, p. 284, for more information about time clauses.

❑ **Exercise 16. Looking at grammar.** (Chart 11-3)

<u>Underline</u> the time clauses.

1. <u>After I get home tonight</u>, I'm going to email my parents.

2. Mr. Masri will finish his report before he leaves the office today.

3. I'll get some fresh fruit when I go to the grocery store tomorrow.

4. Before I go to bed tonight, I'm going to read a story to my little brother.

5. I'm going to look for a job with a computer company after I graduate next year.

❑ **Exercise 17. Looking at grammar.** (Chart 11-3)

Complete the sentences with the words in parentheses. Use **be going to** for the future.

1. Before I (*go*) _____*go*_____ to bed tonight, I (*watch*) _____*am going to watch*_____ my favorite show on TV.

2. I (*buy*) _____ a new coat when I (*go*) _____ shopping tomorrow.

3. After I (*finish*) _____ my homework this evening, I (*text*) _____ _____ my friends.

4. When I (*see*) _____ Eduardo tomorrow, I (*ask*) _____

   _____ him to join us for dinner this weekend.

5. Before I (*buy*) _____ my plane ticket to Australia, I (*check*) _____

   _____ websites for cheap airfares.

❏ **Exercise 18. Looking at grammar.** (Chart 11-3)
Write "1" before the first action and "2" before the second. Then write two sentences:
one with *before* and one with *after*. Use a form of *be going to* in the main clause.

1. __1__ I brush my teeth.

   __2__ I go to bed.

   a. _____ *I'm going to brush my teeth before I go to bed.* OR _____

      _____ *Before I go to bed, I'm going to brush my teeth.* _____

   b. _____ *After I brush my teeth, I'm going to go to bed.* OR _____

      _____ *I'm going to go to bed after I brush my teeth.* _____

2. _____ I go to sleep.

   _____ I turn off my cell phone.

   a. _____

   b. _____

3. _____ I spell-check the words.

   _____ I turn in my essay.

   a. _____

   b. _____

4. ____ The passengers get on the airplane.

____ The passengers go through security.

a. _____

b. _____

❏ **Exercise 19. Let's talk: class activity.** (Chart 11-3)
Your teacher will ask you questions. Give complete answers using time clauses. Close your book for this activity.

Example:
TEACHER: Who's going to go shopping later today?
STUDENT A: (*raises his/her hand*)
TEACHER: What are you going to do after you go shopping?
STUDENT A: After I go shopping, I'm going to go home. OR
I'm going to go home after I go shopping.
TEACHER: (*to Student B*) What is (*Student A*) going to do after he/she goes shopping?
STUDENT B: After (*Student A*) goes shopping, he/she is going to go home. OR
(*Student A*) is going to go home after he/she goes shopping.

1. Who's going to study tonight? What are you going to do after you study tonight?

2. Who else is going to study tonight? What are you going to do before you study tonight?

3. Who's going to watch TV tonight? What are you going to do before you watch TV?

4. Who else is going to watch TV tonight? What are you going to do after you watch TV?

5. (. . .), what are you going to do tomorrow? What are you going to do before you ____ tomorrow? What are you going to do after you ____ tomorrow?

6. Who's going out of town soon? Where are you going? What are you going to do when you go to (*name of place*)?

7. Who's going to eat dinner tonight? What are you going to do before you eat dinner? What are you going to do after you eat dinner? What are you going to have for dinner?

8. (. . .), what time are you going to get home today? What are you going to do before you get home? What are you going to do when you get home? What are you going to do after you get home?

❏ **Exercise 20. Let's talk.** (Chart 11-3)
Imagine that one day you will speak English fluently. What will you do? What won't you do? Make statements with **will** and **won't**. Work with a partner, in groups, or as a class.

When I speak English fluently, I . . .

1. need a dictionary.

2. think in English.

3. feel relaxed with native speakers.

4. dream in English.

5. have an accent.

6. translate from my language.

7. speak with my friends in English.

8. speak with my family in English.

❏ **Exercise 21. Speaking and writing: pairwork.** (Chart 11-3)

Part I. Read the writing sample and think about your own future. What are some special things that you would like to do in your life?

   In 2020, Hans is going to climb Mt. Everest. He's going to train for a couple of years first. Then he's going to climb with a group of people. When he gets to the top, he's going to put a flag from his country in the snow.

   In 2025, Hans is going to swim with dolphins. He is going to have an underwater video camera with him. After he takes the video, he will make a short movie for family and friends.

Write your plans in the chart. Also, write down the year. Then give it to your partner.

YEAR	ACTIVITY

Part II. Write about your partner's plans. Try to include some time clauses beginning with ***when, after,*** and ***before.*** Ask your partner questions about the activities to get more information.

❏ **Exercise 22. Warm-up.** (Chart 11-4)

Choose the correct verbs.

A: What are you going to do next weekend?

B: If I   have / will have   time, I   help / will help   you move to your new dorm room.

A: Wow! Great!

11-4 Clauses with *If*

(a)	**If it rains tomorrow,** | we will stay home. | *if*-clause main clause	An *if*-clause begins with **if** and has a subject and a verb. An *if*-clause can come before or after a main clause.
(b)	| We will stay home | **if it rains tomorrow.** | main clause *if*-clause	Notice: A comma follows an *if*-clause when it comes at the beginning of a sentence.
(c)	**If it rains** *tomorrow,* we won't go on a picnic.	The SIMPLE PRESENT is used in the *if*-clause to express future time. **Will** or **be going to** is used in the main clause.
(d)	I'm going to buy a new car next year **if I have** enough money. **If I don't have** enough money next year for a new car, I'm going to buy a used car.	

❑ **Exercise 23. Looking at grammar.** (Chart 11-4)
Choose the correct verbs.

SITUATION: Andrew is applying for a new job in New York City.

1. If Andrew   gets / will get   the job, he is going to move there.
2. If he   moves / is going to move   there, he is going to rent an apartment.
3. If he   rents / is going to rent   an apartment, he is going to need extra money.
4. If he   needs / will need   extra money, his parents will loan him some.
5. If his parents   loan / will loan   him money, he will be very grateful.

❑ **Exercise 24. Let's talk: pairwork.** (Chart 11-4)
Work with a partner. Ask and answer questions.
     Partner A: Ask a question that begins with ***What are you going to do . . . ?***
                 Your book is open.
     Partner B: Answer the question. Include the *if*-clause in your answer.
                 Your book is closed.

Example: . . . if the weather is nice tomorrow?
PARTNER A: What are you going to do if the weather is nice tomorrow?
PARTNER B: If the weather is nice tomorrow, I'm going to sit outside in the sun. OR
                 I'm going to sit outside in the sun if the weather is nice tomorrow.

1. . . . if the weather is cold tomorrow?
2. . . . if the weather is hot tomorrow?
3. . . . if you don't understand a question that I ask you?
4. . . . if you don't feel well tomorrow?
5. . . . if you go to (*name of a place in this city*) tomorrow?

Change roles.

   6. . . . if it snows tonight?

   7. . . . if you're hungry after class today?

   8. . . . if you don't study tonight?

   9. . . . if you lose your grammar book?

  10. . . . if someone steals your (*name of a thing: bike, wallet, etc.*)?

❑ **Exercise 25. Looking at grammar.** (Chart 11-4)
Complete the sentences with the words in parentheses. Use **be going to** or **will** for the future.

  1. If Malik (*be*) _____ *is* _____ in class tomorrow, I (*ask*) _____ *am going to / will ask* _____

     him to join us for coffee after class.

  2. If the weather (*be*) _____ nice tomorrow, I (*go*) _____

     _____ to Central Park with my friends.

  3. I (*stay, not*) _____ home tomorrow if the weather (*be*)

     _____ nice.

  4. If I (*feel, not*) _____ well tomorrow, I (*go, not*) _____

     _____ to work.

  5. Masako (*stay*) _____ in bed tomorrow if she (*feel, not*)

     _____ well.

  6. We (*stay*) _____ with my aunt and uncle if we (*go*) _____

     _____ to Miami next week.

  7. If my friends (*be*) _____ busy tomorrow, I (*go*) _____

     to a movie by myself.

❑ **Exercise 26. Listening.** (Chart 11-4)
Listen to the questions. Answer each question in a complete sentence. Remember, **going to** may sound like **gonna**.

  1. _____

  2. _____

  3. _____

  4. _____

□ **Exercise 27. Reading and speaking.** (Charts 11-1 → 11-4)

Part I. Read the story and answer the questions. Look at new vocabulary with your teacher first.

Life in 100 Years

> *Do you know these words?*
>
> magazine
> prediction
> ambulance
> tunnel

In December of 1900, *Ladies Home Journal*, an American magazine, published an article titled "What May Happen in the Next Hundred Years." There were 29 predictions about life in the year 2000. Below are some of them.

Cars will be cheaper and stronger than horses. They will do the work of two horses or more. Police, ambulance drivers, and street cleaners will use cars instead of horses. People won't see horses on the streets.

Big cities won't have streetcars. In the future, if people need to go somewhere, they will travel below or high above the ground. Subways and tunnels will have moving stairways, and they will carry people up or down.

There will be no C, X, or Q in the English alphabet because these sounds are not necessary. In the future, people will spell by sound. First, newspapers will do this. After people see this change, they will do the same.

A final prediction: English will be the number one language in the world and Russian will be number two.

1. Which predictions came true?
2. Which ones did not?
3. Are there any predictions you think are silly or strange?

Part II. Work in small groups. Make some predictions for 100 years from now. Use *will*, *may*, *maybe*, or *might*.

□ **Exercise 28. Warm-up.** (Chart 11-5)

Choose the correct time word for each sentence.

1. Before I go to the beach, I put on sunscreen.   every day   tomorrow

2. Before I go to the beach, I am going to put on   every day   tomorrow
   sunscreen.

11-5 Expressing Future and Habitual Present with Time Clauses and If-Clauses

FUTURE	(a) After Kate **gets** to work today, she **is going to have / will have** a cup of coffee.	Example (a) expresses a specific activity in the future. The SIMPLE PRESENT is used in the time clause. *Be going to* or *will* is used in the main clause.
HABITUAL PRESENT	(b) After Kate **gets** to work (every day), she always **has** a cup of coffee.	Example (b) expresses habitual activities, so the SIMPLE PRESENT is used in both the time clause and the main clause.
FUTURE	(c) If it **rains** tomorrow, I **am going to / will wear** my raincoat to school.	Example (c) expresses a specific activity in the future. The SIMPLE PRESENT is used in the *if*-clause. *Be going to* or *will* is used in the main clause.
HABITUAL PRESENT	(d) If it **rains,** I **wear** my raincoat.	Example (d) expresses habitual activities, so the SIMPLE PRESENT is used in both the *if*-clause and the main clause.

❏ **Exercise 29. Looking at grammar.** (Chart 11-5)

Decide the meaning for each sentence: present habit or future activity.

1. Before I eat dinner, I set the table.   (present habit)   future activity

2. Before I eat dinner, I'm going to set the table.   present habit   future activity

3. When I play video games for too long,
   I get a headache.   present habit   future activity

4. If Jim takes the subway, he gets home quickly.   present habit   future activity

5. Before the movie starts, I'll turn off my cell phone.   present habit   future activity

6. When I go to bed, I turn off my phone.   present habit   future activity

❏ **Exercise 30. Looking at grammar.** (Chart 11-5)

Complete the sentences with the words in parentheses. Use **be going to** for the future.

1. When we (*go*) _____ to Quebec, we (*stay, usually*) _____

   _____ with my in-laws.

2. When I (*go*) _____ to Quebec next week, we (*stay*) _____

   _____ with my in-laws.

3. I (*have*) _____ some strong coffee before I (*go*) _____
to class today.

4. I (*have, usually*) _____ some strong coffee before I
(*go*) _____ to class.

5. I'm often tired in the evening after a long day at work. If I (*be*) _____ tired
in the evening, I (*stay, usually*) _____ home and (*go*)
_____ to bed early.

6. If I (*be*) _____ tired this evening, I (*stay*) _____
home and (*go*) _____ to bed early.

7. After I (*get*) _____ home in the evening, I (*sit, usually*) _____
_____ on the couch with my laptop and (*look at*)
_____ newspapers online.

8. After I (*get*) _____ home tonight, I (*sit*) _____ on the
couch with my laptop and (*look at*) _____ newspapers online.

9. Before the teacher (*walk*) _____ into the room every day, there (*be*)
_____ a lot of noise in the classroom.

10. People (*yawn, often*) _____ and (*stretch*) _____ when
they (*wake*) _____ up.

11. Simon (*close*) _____ all the windows in his apartment before he (*turn*)
_____ on the air-conditioning.

12. When I (*go*) _____ to Taiwan next month, I (*stay*) _____
_____ with my friend Mr. Chu. After I (*leave*) _____
Taiwan, I (*go*) _____ to Hong Kong.

13. Ms. Tan (*go*) _____ to Hong Kong often. When she (*be*) _____
there, she (*like*) _____ to take the ferry across the bay, but she (*take*)
_____ the subway under the bay if she (*be*) _____ in a hurry.

❑ **Exercise 31. Looking at grammar: small groups.** (Chart 11-5)
Work in small groups. Match each word or phrase in Column A with a phrase in Column B. Take turns making a sentence that expresses habitual activity for each situation. After you are finished, write a sentence for each one.

Column A

What does Steven do if he . . .

1. fails a test? _c_
2. is hungry? _____
3. is tired? _____
4. gets a mosquito bite? _____
5. oversleeps? _____
6. gets a sore throat? _____

Column B

a. takes a nap
b. skips breakfast
✓c. studies more
d. eats a piece of fruit
e. drinks tea with honey
f. tries not to scratch it

1. _____*If he fails a test, he studies more.*_____

2. _____

3. _____

4. _____

5. _____

6. _____

❑ **Exercise 32. Listening.** (Chart 11-5)

Listen to each sentence and choose the correct completion.

Example: You will hear: Before I go to bed every night,

You will choose: ⓐ I watch TV.   b. I'm going to watch TV.

1. a. I get a good night's sleep.   b. I'll get a good night's sleep.
2. a. I do my homework.   b. I'll do my homework.
3. a. I go shopping.   b. I'll go shopping.
4. a. I exercise.   b. I'll exercise.
5. a. I call my parents.   b. I'll call my parents.
6. a. I'm happy.   b. I'll be happy.
7. a. I know a lot of grammar.   b. I'll know a lot of grammar.

❑ **Exercise 33. Looking at grammar.** (Chart 11-5)
Complete the sentences with your own words.

1. Before I go home tonight, _____.

2. Before I go home, I usually _____.

3. I'm going to _____ tomorrow after I _____.

4. When I go to _____, I'm going to _____.

5. When I go to _____, I always _____.

6. If the weather _____ tomorrow, I _____.

7. If the weather _____ tomorrow, _____

   you going to _____?

8. I'll _____ if I _____.

9. After I _____ tonight, I _____.

10. Do you _____ after you _____?

❑ **Exercise 34. Warm-up.** (Chart 11-6)
Read the questions and answers. Which conversation asks, "What is your job"?

CONVERSATION 1. A: What do you do every day?   B: I deliver the mail.

CONVERSATION 2. A: What did you do yesterday?   B: I delivered the mail.

CONVERSATION 3. A: What do you do?   B: I'm a mail carrier.

11-6 Using *What* + a Form of *Do*

PRESENT		In (a) and (b):
(a) *What **do** you **do** every day?*	→ I *work* every day.	***What*** + a form of ***do*** is used to ask about activities.
(b) *What **are** you **doing** right now?*	→ *I'm studying English.*	
(c) *What **do** you **do**?*	→ *I'm a teacher.*	
PAST		In (c): *What do you do?* means "What kind of work do you do?" OR "What is your job?"
(d) *What **did** you **do** yesterday?*	→ I *went to school* yesterday.	
FUTURE		
(e) *What **are** you **going to do** tomorrow?*	→ *I'm going to go downtown* tomorrow.	
(f) *What **will** we **do** if it rains tomorrow?*	→ *We'll stay home* if it rains tomorrow.	

❑ **Exercise 35. Let's talk: class activity.** (Chart 11-6)
Your teacher will ask you questions. Answer them in complete sentences. Close your book for this activity.

Example:
TEACHER: What do you do when you get up in the morning?
STUDENT A: When I get up in the morning, I eat breakfast.
STUDENT B: I listen to music when I get up in the morning.

1. What do you do when you get up in the morning?
2. What are you going to do when you get up tomorrow morning?
3. What do you usually do before you eat breakfast?
4. What are you going to do after class today?
5. What are you going to do when you get home?
6. What do you usually do after you get home?
7. What do you like to do if the weather is nice?
8. What are you going to do if the weather is nice tomorrow?

❑ **Exercise 36. Looking at grammar.** (Chart 11-6)
Make questions for the given answer using a form of ***do***.

1. _____*What does she do?*_____ Nancy's an accountant.

2. _____ We're students.

3. _____ I'm a doctor.

4. _____ They're janitors.

an accountant

5. _____ He's a server at a restaurant.

a server

a plumber

6. _____ She's a plumber.

7. _____ You're a sales manager.

8. _____ William and I are taxi drivers.

☐ **Exercise 37. Let's talk: pairwork.** (Chart 11-6)
Work with a partner. Ask your partner questions. Use **What** + *a form of* **do** with the given
time expression. You can look at your book before you speak. When you speak, look at
your partner.

Example: yesterday
PARTNER A (*book open*):   What did you do yesterday?
PARTNER B (*book closed*):   I read a newspaper yesterday.

Change roles.

1. last night
2. every day
3. right now
4. tomorrow
5. yesterday afternoon
6. tomorrow morning
7. every morning

8. tomorrow evening
9. last Saturday
10. next Saturday
11. this morning
12. this afternoon
13. tonight
14. next week

☐ **Exercise 38. Looking at grammar.** (Chart 11-6)
Complete the sentences with the words in parentheses. Use **be going to** for the future.

1. A: What (*you, do*) ___*do you do*___ every Friday?

   B: I (*come*) ___*come*___ to class.

2. A: What (*you, do*) _____ last Friday?

   B: I (*come*) _____ to class.

3. A: What (*you, do*) _____ next Friday?

   B: I (*come*) _____ to class.

4. A: What (*you, do*) _____ yesterday evening?

   B: I (*chat*) _____ online with my friends.

5. A: What (*you, do*) _____ every evening?

   B: I (*chat*) _____ online with my friends.

6. A: What (*you, do*) _____ tomorrow evening?

   B: I (*chat*) _____ online with my friends.

7. A: What (*you, do*) _____ right now?

   B: I (*do*) _____ a grammar exercise.

8. A: What (*Marina, do*) _____ every morning?

   B: She (*go*) _____ to work.

9. A: What (*the students*) _____ right now?

   B: They (*work*) _____ on this exercise.

10. A: What (*they, do*) _____ in class tomorrow?

    B: They (*take*) _____ a test.

11. A: What (*Bakari, do*) _____ last night?

    B: He (*go*) _____ to a movie.

12. A: What (*the teacher, do*) _____ every day at the beginning of class?

    B: She (*put*) _____ her books on her desk, (*look*) _____ at the class, and (*say*) _____ "Good morning."

❏ **Exercise 39. Listening.** (Chapters 10 and 11)
Complete the conversations with the words you hear.

1. A: _____ late for the movie?

   B: No. The movie _____ at 7:30. We have plenty of time.

2. A: What _____ for dinner?

   B: Leftovers. Is that okay?

   A: Sure, but _____ probably _____ some rice to go with them.

3. A: _____ at Jon's wedding?

   B: Yes, but I _____ there until after it _____.
   I work until noon.

   A: Great. _____ you there.

4. A: What _____? We need to deposit this check, and
   the cash machine is broken. Our account is almost empty.

   B: No problem. _____ it with me to work. There's an ATM* next
   door.

❏ **Exercise 40. Looking at grammar.** (Chapter 11)
Choose the correct completion.

1. A: Are you going to go to the baseball game tomorrow afternoon?
   B: I don't know. I ____.

   a. will   b. am going to   c. maybe   d. might

2. A: Are Ruth and Simon going to be at the meeting?
   B: No, they're too busy. They ____ be there.

   a. don't   b. won't   c. will   d. may

3. A: Are you going to go to the store today?
   B: No. I went there ____ Friday.

   a. yesterday   b. next   c. last   d. ago

4. A: When are you going to go to the bank?
   B: I'll go there before I ____ to the post office tomorrow morning.

   a. will go   b. go   c. went   d. am going

5. A: Why is the teacher late today?
   B: I don't know. ____ he overslept.

   a. Maybe   b. Did   c. May   d. Was

---

*ATM = automatic teller machine (also called a cash machine); it allows customers to deposit or withdraw money from
their bank.

6. A: Do you like to go to New York City?

   B: Yes. When I'm in New York, I always _____ new things to do and places to see.

   a. found   b. find   c. will find   d. finds

7. A: Is Ricardo going to talk to us this afternoon about our plans for tomorrow?

   B: No. He'll _____ us this evening.

   a. calls   b. calling   c. call   d. called

8. A: _____ are you going to do after class today?

   B: I'm going to go home.

   a. When   b. Where   c. What   d. What time

9. A: Where _____ Ivonne live before she moved into her new apartment?

   B: She lived in a dormitory at the university.

   a. did   b. does   c. is   d. was

10. A: What time _____ Paulina and Yuri going to arrive?

    B: Six.

    a. is   b. do   c. will   d. are

❑ **Exercise 41. Looking at grammar: past, present, future.**
   (Chapters 3, 4, and 8 → 11)
Complete the sentences with the words in parentheses. Use any appropriate verb form.

1. A: I (*skip*) _____ class tomorrow.

   B: Why?

   A: Why not?

   B: That's not a very good reason.

2. A: How did you get here?

   B: I (*take*) _____ a plane. I (*fly*) _____ here from Bangkok.

3. A: How do you usually get to class?

   B: I (*walk, usually*) _____, but sometimes I (*take*)

   _____ the bus.

4. A: Where's my phone? It (*be, not*) _____ in my purse. Maybe I left it on the subway.

   B: Take it easy. Your phone (*be*) _____ right here.

5. A: Where's your homework?

   B: I (*lose*) _____ it.

   A: Oh?

   B: I (*forget*) _____ it.

   A: Oh?

   B: I (*give*) _____ it to Roberto to give to you, but he (*lose*)

     _____ it.

   A: Oh?

   B: Someone (*steal*) _____ it.

   A: Oh?

   B: Well, actually I (*have, not*) _____ enough time to finish it
     last night.

   A: I see.

6. A: (*you, stay*) _____ here during vacation next week?

   B: No. I (*take*) _____ a trip to Montreal. I (*visit*)

     _____ my cousins.

   A: How long (*you, be*) _____ away?

   B: About five days.

7. A: Is Carol here?

   B: No, she (*be, not*) _____. She (*leave*) _____ a few
     minutes ago.

   A: (*she, be*) _____ back soon?

   B: I think so.

   A: Where (*she, go*) _____?

   B: She (*go*) _____ to the drugstore.

❑ **Exercise 42. Check your knowledge.** (Chapter 11)
Correct the mistakes.

       is

1. If it ~~will be~~ cold tomorrow morning, my car won't start.

2. We maybe late for the concert tonight.

3. What time you are going to come tomorrow?

4. Amira will call us tonight when her plane will land.

5. Ellen may will be at the party.

6. When I'll see you tomorrow, I'll return your book to you.

7. I may don't be in class tomorrow.

8. Amin puts his books on his desk when he walked into his apartment.

9. I'll see my parents when I will return home for a visit next July.

10. What do you doing all day at work?

❏ **Exercise 43. Reading and writing. (Chapter 11)**
Part I. Read the writing sample. Look at new vocabulary with your teacher first.

snorkeling

penguins on an iceberg

Relaxation or Adventure?

I have an airline ticket in my pocket. It will take me anywhere in the world. Where will I go?

If I want a relaxing vacation, I may travel to Tahiti. Or if I want an adventure, I might travel to Antarctica. Both places have natural beauty. I want to travel to a place without many people or buildings.

If I go to Tahiti, I will sit on the beach in the sun. I will swim in the warm ocean. I might try windsurfing if I am not too scared. I love underwater swimming, so I will probably go snorkeling. But when I am snorkeling, I will stay away from sharks.

If I go to Antarctica, I will take all my warm clothes. There aren't any hotels, so I will probably take a tour boat to the South Pole. I definitely won't sit on a beach! When I am there, I want to see icebergs and penguins.

I'm excited about my trip. I just need to answer this question: What is more important to me right now: relaxation or adventure?

> *Do you know these words?*
>
> adventure
> windsurfing
> sharks

Part II. Now write your own story. Imagine someone gives you a plane ticket. You can travel anywhere in the world. Choose two places you would like to visit: one place for relaxation and one place for adventure. Use this model.

PARAGRAPH 1: Introduction
I have an airline ticket in my pocket. It will take me anywhere in the world. Where will I go?

PARAGRAPH 2: Name the two places. Choose a relaxing place and a place for adventure.
If I want a relaxing vacation, I may travel to ____. Or if I want an adventure, I might travel to ____. (Add one or two reasons.)

PARAGRAPH 3: Give details for the first place.
If I go to . . . .

PARAGRAPH 4: Give details for the second place.
If I go to . . . .

PARAGRAPH 5: Conclusion
I'm excited about my trip. I just need to answer this question: What is more important to me right now: relaxation or adventure?

Part III. Editing check: Work individually or change papers with a partner. Check (✓) for the following:

1. ____ indented paragraph

2. ____ capital letter at the beginning of each sentence

3. ____ period at the end of each sentence

4. ____ use of *will* or *be going to* for a future activity

5. ____ *might* or *may* + *base form of verb*

6. ____ *if* + *simple present tense* (for future meaning)

7. ____ correct spelling (use a dictionary or computer spell-check)

Chapter 12

Modals, Part 1: Expressing Ability

❏ **Exercise 1. Warm-up.** (Chart 12-1)
Which answers are true for you?

1. I can / can't sing well.

2. I can / can't stand on my head.

3. I can / can't sneeze with my eyes open.

12-1 Using *Can*

(a) I have some money. I **can buy** a book. (b) We have time and money. We **can go** to a movie. (c) Tom is strong. He **can lift** the heavy box.	***Can*** expresses *ability* and *possibility*.
(d) CORRECT: Yuko *can **speak*** English.	The base form of the main verb follows ***can***. In (d): *speak* is the main verb.
(e) INCORRECT: *Yuko can to speak English.*	A main verb following ***can*** is NOT preceded by ***to***. In (e): *to speak* is incorrect.
(f) INCORRECT: *Yuko can speaks English.*	A main verb following ***can*** does not have a final **-s**. In (f): *speaks* is incorrect.

(g) Alice **can not** come.
Alice **cannot** come.
Alice **can't** come.
	NEGATIVE
	    can + ***not*** = ***can not*** OR ***cannot***
	
	CONTRACTION
	    can + ***not*** = ***can't***

❏ **Exercise 2. Let's talk.** (Chart 12-1)
Work with a partner. Take turns making sentences from the given words. Use **can** or
can't.

Example: A bird \ sing
→ A bird can sing.

Example: A horse \ sing
→ A horse can't sing.

1. A bird \ fly
2. A cow \ fly
3. A child \ drive a car
4. An adult \ drive a car
5. A newborn baby \ walk
6. A fish \ breathe air

7. A deaf person \ hear
8. A blind person \ see
9. An elephant \ swim
10. An elephant \ climb trees
11. A cat \ climb trees
12. A boat \ float on water

❏ **Exercise 3. Let's talk: class activity.** (Chart 12-1)
Make sentences about yourself. Begin with **I can** or **I can't**.

Example: speak Chinese
Response: I can speak Chinese. OR
I can't speak Chinese.

1. whistle
2. ride a bicycle
3. touch my ear with my elbow
4. play the piano*
5. play the guitar
6. lift a refrigerator
7. fly a plane
8. fix a flat tire

9. swim
10. float on water
11. ski
12. do advanced math in my head
13. make a paper airplane
14. sew a button on a shirt
15. wiggle my ears
16. eat with chopsticks

---

* In expressions with *play*, **the** is usually used with musical instruments: *play the piano, play the guitar, play the violin*, etc.

❏ Exercise 4. Game: small groups. (Chart 12-1)

Work in small groups. Discuss each statement. Then circle *yes* or *no*. When you are finished, check your answers with your teacher.★ The group with the most correct answers wins.

1.	Some birds can't fly.	yes	no
2.	Elephants can jump.	yes	no
3.	Tigers can't swim.	yes	no
4.	An octopus can change colors.	yes	no
5.	Some fish can climb trees.	yes	no
6.	Horses can't sleep when they're standing up.	yes	no
7.	Turtles can't live more than 100 years.	yes	no
8.	All animals can see colors.	yes	no
9.	Whales can hold their breath underwater.	yes	no

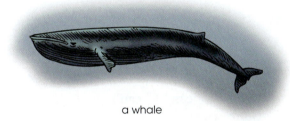

a whale

an octopus

❏ Exercise 5. Warm-up: listening. (Chart 12-2)

Listen to the sentences. Which statement (a. or b.) is true for you?

1. a. I can count to 100 in English.

   b. I can't count to 100 in English.

2. a. I can't ride a bike with no hands.

   b. I can ride a bike with no hands.

★*Teacher:* See *Let's Talk: Answers*, p. 503.

12-2 Pronunciation of *Can* and *Can't*

(a) Rick **can come** to the meeting.	**Can** is usually pronounced "kn" /kən/. It is unstressed.
(b) Mike **can't come** to the meeting.	**Can't** is usually pronounced "kant" /kænt/ with the same vowel sound as in the word *ant*. It is stressed. You will probably not hear the /t/.*

* Sometimes native speakers also have trouble hearing the difference between *can* and *can't*.

❏ **Exercise 6. Listening.** (Chart 12-2)

Listen to each sentence. Choose the word you hear.

Example: You will hear: We can understand you.
You will choose: (can) can't

Example: You will hear: We can't understand you.
You will choose: can (can't)

1.	can	can't	6.	can	can't
2.	can	can't	7.	can	can't
3.	can	can't	8.	can	can't
4.	can	can't	9.	can	can't
5.	can	can't	10.	can	can't

❏ **Exercise 7. Listening.** (Chart 12-2)

Read the help-wanted ad. Then listen to Matt talk about his job skills. Decide if Matt is a good person for the job. Explain your answer.

JOB OPENING AT SMALL INTERNATIONAL HOTEL

Looking for person with the following: good typing and word-processing skills, excellent knowledge of English, friendly manner on the phone. Needs to help guests with their suitcases and be available weekends.

QUESTIONS: Is Matt a good person for this job?   yes   no
Why or why not?

□ **Exercise 8. Warm-up.** (Chart 12-3)
Answer the questions.

1. Can you buy a hammer at a grocery store?
2. Where can you buy a hammer?

12-3 Using *Can:* Questions						
(QUESTION WORD) +	*CAN* +	SUBJECT +	MAIN VERB			ANSWER
(a)	**Can**	**you**	**speak**	Arabic?	→	**Yes, I can.**
					→	**No, I can't.**
(b)	**Can**	**Rosa**	**come**	to the party?	→	**Yes, she can.**
					→	**No, she can't.**
(c) **Where**	**can**	**I**	**buy**	a hammer?	→	**At a hardware store.**
(d) **When**	**can**	**you**	**help**	me?	→	**Tomorrow afternoon.**

□ **Exercise 9. Question practice.** (Chart 12-3)
Make yes/no questions. Give short answers.

1. A: _____*Can Daria speak English?*_____

   B: _____*Yes, she can.*_____ (Daria can speak English.)

2. A: _____*Can you speak French?*_____

   B: _____*No, I can't.*_____ (I can't speak French.)

3. A: _____

   B: _____ (Gabrielle can't fix her printer.)

4. A: _____

   B: _____ (I can whistle.)

5. A: _____

   B: _____ (Carmen can't ride a bike.)

6. A: _____

   B: _____ (Elephants can swim.)

7. A: _____

   B: _____ (The doctor can see you tomorrow.)

8. A: _____

   B: _____ (We can't have pets in the dorm.)

❑ **Exercise 10. Let's talk: pairwork.** (Chart 12-3)

Work with a partner. Take turns asking and answering questions.

　　Partner A: Ask a question. Begin with ***Can you . . . ?***

　　Partner B: Answer the question. Then ask ***How about you?*** and repeat the question.

Example: speak Arabic

PARTNER A: Can you speak Arabic?

PARTNER B: Yes, I can. OR No, I can't. How about you? Can you speak Arabic?

PARTNER A: Yes, I can. OR No, I can't. Your turn now.

PARTNER A	PARTNER B
1. ride a motorcycle	1. ride a horse
2. play the guitar	2. play the drums
3. float on water	3. whistle
4. touch your knee with your nose	4. touch your ear with your elbow
5. drive a stick-shift car	5. fix a flat tire
6. spell Mississippi	6. spell the teacher's last name

a stick shift

❑ **Exercise 11. Listening.** (Chart 12-3)

Listen to the conversations. Complete the sentences with the words you hear.

　1. A: Hello?

　　B: _____ speak to Mr. Hudson, please?

　　A: I'm sorry. _____ to the phone right now.

　　　_____ take a message? _____ return your call in about

　　a half-hour.

　　B: Yes. Please tell him Ron Myerson called.

2. A: _____ me lift this box?

   B: It looks very heavy. _____ to help you, but I think we need a
      third person.

   A: No, I'm pretty strong. I think _____ it together.

3. A: _____ the TV. _____ turn it up?

   B: _____ turn it up. I'm doing my homework.

   A: _____ your homework in another room?

   B: Oh, all right.

❑ **Exercise 12. Reading.** (Charts 12-1 → 12-3)
Read the paragraph. Complete the questions.

Color Blindness

   Some people can't see all the colors. They are color-blind. It doesn't mean they can't
see any colors. But they have trouble seeing the difference between certain colors. They
might confuse red and green or blue and purple. For example, people with red-green color
blindness can't see the difference between the red light and the green light on a traffic light.
But they can still drive safely because they can see the brightness of the lights. If the light
is red, for example, it will also be bright. Look at the picture below. People with red-green
color blindness can't see the number. Can you see the number?

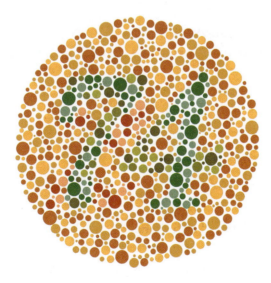

1. Color-blind people   can / can't   see all colors.

2. People who are color-blind   can / can't   drive.

3. If you can't see the number in the picture, you   are / aren't   color-blind.

❏ **Exercise 13. Warm-up.** (Chart 12-4)

Make sentences with some of the phrases from the box. Take turns completing the sentences with a partner.

Example:

PARTNER A: I (*can/can't*) fix a leaky faucet.

Do you know how to fix a leaky faucet?

PARTNER B: Yes, I do. OR No, I don't.

a leaky faucet

> change the oil in a car   read musical notes
> ✓ fix a leaky faucet   solve algebra problems
> make ice cream   write computer code for an app★

12-4 Using *Know How To*

(a) I **can** swim.	Both **can** and **know how to** express ability.
(b) I **know how to swim**.	**Know how to** expresses something a person learned to do.
(c) **Can** you cook?	
(d) **Do** you **know how to cook**?	

❏ **Exercise 14. Let's talk: pairwork.** (Chart 12-4)

Work with a partner. Take turns asking and answering questions.

Do you know how to . . .

1. cook?
2. dance?
3. play soccer?
4. replace a zipper?
5. get to the airport from here?
6. fix a computer hard drive?
7. write with both your left and right hands?
8. wiggle your nose?
9. knit?
10. make a YouTube video?

★ *app* = an application; a small, special program for a smartphone or tablet

Exercise 15. Speaking and writing: pairwork. (Chart 12-4)

Part I. Work with a partner. Make questions about the people in the chart. Use *know how to.*

ABILITY	JERRY	ALEXA	BILL AND TINA	YOU
1. change the oil in a car	no	yes	yes	
2. start a fire without matches	yes	yes	no	
3. type without looking at the keyboard	no	no	yes	

Part II. Write three questions and answers about the people in the chart.

1. _____ *Does Alexa know how to start a fire without matches? Yes, she does.* _____

2. _____

3. _____

□ **Exercise 16. Let's write: small groups.** (Chart 12-4)

Work in small groups. Complete the sentences together. Use a separate sheet of paper. Share some of your completions with the class.

1. Three-year-olds know how to _____.

2. Three-year-olds don't know how to _____.

3. Birds know how to _____.

4. Birds don't know how to _____.

5. We know how to _____.

6. We don't know how to _____.

7. (*name of a classmate*) knows how to _____.

8. Our teacher doesn't know how to _____.

9. Do you know how to _____?

□ **Exercise 17. Warm-up.** (Chart 12-4)

Choose the verb that is true for you.

Two years ago, I . . .

1. could / couldn't   speak English.

2. could / couldn't   drive a car.

3. could / couldn't   communicate with people from around the world.

12-5 Using *Could:* Past of *Can*

(a) Jake has a sore knee. He *can* walk, but he *can't* run.	*could* = the past form of *can*★
(b) Jake had a sore knee *last week*. He *could* walk, but he *couldn't* run.	NEGATIVE *could* + *not* = *couldn't*
(c) *Could you speak* English before you came here?	QUESTION *could* + *subject* + *main verb*

★Do not use the affirmative form of *could* for one completed action in the past.

> INCORRECT: *A week ago, Marc could pass his test.* One option is the simple past:
> CORRECT: *A week ago, Marc passed his test.* ***Be able to*** is also possible (see Chart 12-6).

❑ **Exercise 18. Let's talk: pairwork.** (Chart 12-5)

Work with a partner. Choose the answers that describe your childhood. Then tell your partner what you could and couldn't do when you were a child.

When I was a child, ...

1. I could stand on my head.   yes   no
2. I could sing in another language.   yes   no
3. I could tell time before the age of five.   yes   no
4. I could do cartwheels.   yes   no
5. I could read at the age of six.   yes   no
6. I could hold my breath underwater for one minute.   yes   no

a cartwheel

❑ **Exercise 19. Looking at grammar.** (Chart 12-5)

Complete the sentences by using *couldn't*. Use the expressions from the box or your own words.

call you	go to the movie
come to class	hear us
✓ finish my homework	light the candles
get into my car	wash his clothes
go swimming	watch TV

1. I _____couldn't finish my homework_____ last night because I was too tired.

2. I _____ yesterday because I lost your telephone number.

3. I _____ last night because my TV is broken.

4. Theo _____ because he didn't have any matches.

5. The teacher _____ yesterday because he was sick.

6. My grandmother _____ at the party last night because her hearing aid was broken.

7. Nat _____ because he didn't have any laundry soap.

8. We _____ yesterday because the water was too cold.

9. I _____ yesterday because I locked all the doors and left the keys inside.

10. I _____ last night because I had to study.

❑ **Exercise 20. Let's talk: pairwork.** (Chart 12-5)
Work with a partner. Take turns making sentences with *because*.

SITUATION: Mr. Kostis had a bad day yesterday. There are many things he wanted to do but couldn't. Tell what he couldn't do yesterday and give a reason.

Examples: eat breakfast \ get up late
→ Mr. Kostis couldn't eat breakfast because he got up late.

go downtown during the day \ have to work
→ Mr. Kostis couldn't go downtown during the day because he had to work.

1. eat lunch \ leave his wallet at home
2. finish his report \ have to go to a meeting
3. leave work at five \ have to finish his report
4. play tennis after work \ it \ be raining
5. enjoy dinner \ his wife \ be angry at him
6. watch his favorite TV show after dinner \ his TV \ not work
7. read quietly \ his children \ be very noisy
8. go to bed early \ his neighbors \ come to visit

❑ **Exercise 21. Let's talk: class activity.** (Chart 12-5)
Your teacher will make a statement. Give some of the negative results for the situations. Use **can't** or **couldn't**. Close your book for this activity.

Example:
TEACHER (*book open*): There was no heat in the classroom yesterday.
STUDENT (*book closed*): We couldn't stay warm.

1. I have only (*a small amount of money*) in my pocket / in my purse today.

2. Some people don't know how to use a computer.

3. Your parents had rules for you when you were a child.

4. This school has rules for students.

5. You didn't know much English last year.

6. You don't speak fluent English yet.

7. Millions of people in the world live in poverty.

❑ **Exercise 22. Check your knowledge.** (Charts 12-1 → 12-5)
Correct the mistakes.

1. Could you ~~to~~ drive a car when you were sixteen years old?

2. If your brother goes to the graduation party, he can meets my sister.

3. I couldn't opened the door because I didn't have a key.

4. Tyler know how to use sign language. He learned it when he was a child.

5. Please turn up the radio. I can't to hear it.

6. Where we can meet for our study group?

7. You cannot to change your class schedule. The deadline was last week.

8. Are you knowing how to fix a leaky faucet?

9. When Ernesto arrived at the airport last Tuesday, he can't found a parking space.

10. Excuse me. You can help me? I'm looking for a pair of work boots.

11. Mr. Lo was born in Hong Kong, but now he lives in Canada. He cannot understand spoken English before he moved to Canada, but now he speak and understand English very well.

Match each sentence on the left with its meaning on the right.

Column A	Column B
1. I can help you now.	a. I wasn't able to help you.
2. I'm sorry I couldn't help you last night.	b. I won't be able to help you.
3. I can't help you tomorrow.	c. I am able to help you.
4. I can help you next week.	d. I am not able to help you.
5. I can't help you now.	e. I will be able to help you.

12-6 Using *Be Able To*

PRESENT	(a) I *am able to touch* my toes. (b) I *can touch* my toes.	Examples (a) and (b) have basically the same meaning.
FUTURE	(c) I *will be able to go* shopping tomorrow. (d) I *can go* shopping tomorrow.	Examples (c) and (d) have basically the same meaning.
PAST	(e) I *wasn't able to finish* my homework last night. (f) I *couldn't finish* my homework last night.	Examples (e) and (f) have basically the same meaning.

❏ **Exercise 24. Looking at grammar.** (Chart 12-6).
On a separate sheet of paper, make sentences with the same meaning as the given sentences. Use *be able to*.

1. I can be here tomorrow at ten o'clock.
    → *I'll (I will) be able to be here tomorrow at ten o'clock.*
2. Two students couldn't finish the test.
    → *Two students weren't able to finish the test.*
3. Kalil is bilingual. He can speak two languages.
4. Nola can get her own apartment next year.
5. Can you touch your toes without bending your knees?
6. Alec couldn't describe the thief.
7. I couldn't sleep last night because my apartment was too hot.
8. My roommate can speak four languages. He's multilingual.
9. I'm sorry that I couldn't call you last night.
10. I'm sorry, but I can't come to your party next week.
11. We're going to drive to San Francisco for our vacation. Can we do it in one day?

Exercise 25. Reading and grammar. *(Chart 12-6)*
Part I. Read the story.

Maya's English Experience

Five years ago, Maya moved to Canada with her young children. They couldn't speak English. Her children started school and learned English very quickly. Maya didn't study English and could just say basic, common sentences. She only understood people who spoke very slowly and used simple language.

Maya felt very frustrated. She heard about an evening English program at a local community center. She enrolled and began to study. At first, she couldn't understand or say very much. But slowly she got better. She was excited when she went shopping and could have short conversations with the cashier. Her kids were also excited. They could talk to her in English.

Today Maya's English is pretty good. She can talk to friends and neighbors. She watches TV and can understand a lot of it. Maya and her kids speak to each other in both English and their native language. She can switch back and forth very easily. Maya encourages friends to take classes. She says, "Don't worry. Try it for a few months. You can do it!"

Part II. Underline all the verbs with *could, couldn't,* and *can.* Rewrite the sentences using a form of *be able to.*

1. _____

2. _____

3. _____

4. _____

5. _____

6. _____

7. _____

8. _____

9. _____

□ **Exercise 26. Listening.** (Charts 12-1 → 12-6)

Listen to the conversations. Complete the sentences with the words you hear.

1. A: _____ to talk to Adam last night?

   B: _____ reach him. I _____ again later today.

2. A: _____ pizza?

   B: Yes, I _____ it. What about you?

   A: No, but _____ me?

   B: Sure.

3. A: _____ the teacher?

   B: I _____ her in the beginning, but now I

   _____ most of her lectures.

   A: I still _____ her very well.

4. A: Professor Castro, when _____ correct our tests?

   B: I began last night, but I _____ finish.

   I _____ again tonight. I hope _____

   hand them back to you tomorrow.

5. A: Hello?

   B: Hi. This is Jan Quinn. I'm wondering if _____ get in to see
   Dr. Novack today or tomorrow.

   A: Well, she _____ you tomorrow morning at 11:00.

   _____ in then?

   B: Yes, _____. Please tell me where you are. I _____ the
   way to your office.

□ **Exercise 27. Warm-up.** (Chart 12-7)

Choose the correct response.

The weather is too warm.

   a. I want to spend the day outside.
   b. Let's turn on the air-conditioning.

12-7 Using *Very* and *Too* + Adjective

(a) The coffee is **very** *hot*, but I **can** *drink* it. (b) The coffee is **too** *hot*. I **can't** *drink* it. (c) The box is **very** *heavy*, but Tom **can** *lift* it. (d) The box is **too** *heavy*. Bob **can't** *lift* it.	**Very** and **too** come in front of adjectives; *heavy* and *hot* are adjectives. **Very** and **too** do NOT have the same meaning. In (c): *very heavy* = It is difficult but possible for Tom to lift the box. In (d): *too heavy* = It is impossible for Bob to lift the box.

Tom

Bob

(e) The coffee is **too** hot.
     NEGATIVE RESULT: I can't drink it.
 	
 (f) The weather is **too** cold.
     NEGATIVE RESULT: We can't go to the beach.
	In the speaker's mind, the use of **too** implies a negative result.

❏ **Exercise 28. Let's talk.** (Chart 12-7)
Make sentences for each picture. Use **very** or **too** and **can** or **can't** to describe the pictures.

Example: suitcase \ heavy \ lift
      → The suitcase is very heavy, but Mark can lift it.
      → The suitcase is too heavy. Benny can't lift it.

Mark

Benny

1. shoes \ tight \ wear

Marika

Mai

2. coat \ small \ wear

Bruno

Emily

3. soup \ hot \ eat

Salman

Ricardo

4. problem \ hard \ solve

Alan

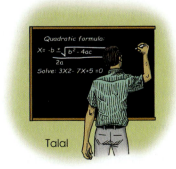

Talal

❏ **Exercise 29. Looking at grammar.** (Chart 12-7)
Complete the sentences with expressions from the box.

buy it	lift it
do his homework	reach the cookie jar
eat it	sleep
go camping	take a break

1. The soup is too hot. I can't _____

2. The diamond ring is too expensive. I can't _____

3. The weather is too cold. We can't _____

4. I am too busy. I can't _____

5. Samir is too tired. He can't _____

6. Peggy is too short. She can't _____

7. It's too noisy in the dorm at night. I can't _____

8. The couch is too heavy. I can't _____

❏ **Exercise 30. Looking at grammar.** (Chart 12-7)
Complete the sentences. Use *too* + adjectives from the box.

expensive	small	tired	windy
heavy	tall	uncomfortable	young

1. You can't lift a car. A car is _____

2. Jimmy is ten. He can't drive a car. He's _____

3. I can't sleep on an airplane. It's _____

4. I don't want to go fishing on the lake today. The weather is _____

5. Rachel doesn't want to play tennis this afternoon. She's _____

6. I can't buy a new car. A new car is _____

7. Patrick has gained weight. He can't wear his old shirt. It's _____

8. The basketball player can't stand up straight in the subway car. He's

_____

❏ **Exercise 31. Looking at grammar.** (Chart 12-7)
Complete the sentences. Use **too** or **very**.

1. The tea is ____*very*____ hot, but I can drink it.

2. The tea is ____*too*____ hot. I can't drink it.

3. I can't put my wallet in my pocket. My pocket is _____ small.

4. An elephant is _____ big. A mouse is _____ small.

5. I can't buy a boat because it's _____ expensive.

6. A sports car is _____ expensive, but Daniella can buy one if she wants to.

7. We went to the Swiss Alps for our vacation. The mountains are _____

beautiful.

8. I can't eat this food because it's _____ salty.

9. Larisa doesn't like her dorm room. She thinks it's _____ small.

10. I lost your jacket. I'm _____ sorry. I'll buy you a new one.

11. A: Do you like your math course?

    B: Yes. It's _____ difficult, but I enjoy it.

12. A: Do you like your math course?

    B: No. It's _____ difficult. I don't understand the problems.

13. A: Did you enjoy your dinner last night?

    B: Yes. The food was _____ good.

14. A: Are you going to buy that dress?

    B: No. It doesn't fit. It's _____ big.

15. A: My daughter wants to get married.

    B: What? But she can't! She's _____ young.

❏ **Exercise 32. Reading and listening.** (Chapter 12)

Part I. Read the story. Look at new vocabulary with your teacher first.

Memory Champions

Nelson Dellis is a memory champion. He can remember a lot of information. For example, he can look at a page of 500 numbers and say all of them. He can go through a deck of cards and say each number with its suit (diamonds, spades, hearts, and clubs) — in order.

> **Do you know these words?**
>
> champion
> a deck of cards
> suit (in a deck of cards)
> amazing
> train

Dellis won the 2011 U.S.A. Memory Championship. He was able to memorize 248 numbers in five minutes. He was also able to memorize a complete deck of cards in 63 seconds.

Memory champions can do amazing things. After they look at photos of 100 strangers, the memory champions can memorize the first and last names with the correct spelling in 15 minutes!

Dellis can't remember all this information naturally. He needs to study. He trains every day. One way he remembers names is to create pictures in his mind. For example, if Dellis wants to remember a person's last name, like "Hardy," he can imagine something "hard," like wood. Then he connects this picture to the person's face. Maybe he sees wood on top of the person's head. When he sees the face again, it will help him remember the name "Hardy."

Memory champions say they aren't special. They believe that with years of practice a person can develop a great memory.

Part II. Complete the sentences with ideas from the reading.

1. Nelson Dellis is a memory champion because he _____

2. In 2011, Dellis was able to memorize _____

3. When memory champions see photos of 100 strangers, they can _____

_____

4. Dellis can do amazing things with his memory, but he can't _____

_____

5. With a lot of training and practice, people _____

Part III. Complete the sentences with the words you hear.

1. Dellis _____ remember long rows of numbers.

2. Dellis _____ memorize a complete deck of cards.

3. In 2011, Dellis _____ win the U.S.A. Memory Championship.

4. Dellis _____ remember all this information naturally.

5. Memory champions _____ make pictures in their minds.

6. They say that with a lot of work a person _____ have a good memory.

❑ **Exercise 33. Check your knowledge.** (Chapter 12)
Correct the mistakes.

1. We ~~will~~ can go to the museum tomorrow afternoon.

2. Can you to memorize a deck of cards?

3. I saw a beautiful diamond necklace at a store yesterday, but I couldn't bought it.

4. The shirt is too small. I can wear it.

5. Sam Garder know how to count to 1,000 in English.

6. When I was on vacation, I can swim every day.

7. Honeybees not able to live in very cold climates.

8. Where we can go in the city for a good meal?

9. Hiroshi can reads in five languages.

10. I'm late. I'm too sorry. I didn't be able to find a parking spot.

☐ **Exercise 34. Writing.** (Chapter 12)

Part I. First, read the writing sample. Then think about a character (person, animal, or creature) from fiction. This character can do amazing things. Write a paragraph about this character. (If you can't think of a character, create your own and give it a name.)

Superman

Superman can do amazing things. He can fly very fast. He is able to jump over tall buildings. He has X-ray vision, so he can see through objects like buildings. He is very strong. He can bend steel, and he is able to lift cars and trains.

But there is one thing he can't do. He can't be around kryptonite. Kryptonite is a metal, and it makes Superman very weak. He isn't able to use his special powers. When Superman is away from kryptonite, he becomes strong again.

I admire Superman. He uses his powers in good ways. He fights for truth and justice. He catches criminals and rescues people in trouble. He is a hero.

Superhero

Include this information in your paragraph:

- Begin with this sentence: _____ *can do amazing things*.
- Give examples of things the character can do. Use *can* and *be able to*.
- Is there anything the character can't do? Give examples.
- Explain why he or she likes to do these things.
- Finish with this sentence: *I admire/don't admire* _____. Give reasons.

Part II. Editing check: Work individually or change papers with a partner. Check (✓) for the following:

1. _____ indented paragraph

2. _____ capital letter at the beginning of each sentence

3. _____ period at the end of each sentence

4. _____ no *to* with *can* or *can't*

5. _____ use of *too* for a negative result

6. _____ correct use of *is + able to* and *are + able to*

7. _____ correct spelling (use a dictionary or computer spell-check)

Chapter 13

Modals, Part 2: Advice, Necessity, Requests, Suggestions

❑ **Exercise 1. Warm-up.** (Chart 13-1)
Read about Ella's problem. Choose all the sentences that you agree with.

Ella bought a pair of shoes. After a week, the heel on one of her shoes broke. She was at work and didn't have another pair of shoes to wear. She had to miss a meeting with clients because she couldn't walk in a broken shoe.

She should . . .
1. take the shoes back to the store and get her money back.
2. take the shoes back to the store and get another pair of the same shoes.
3. fix the heel with glue.
4. write a letter to the store owner and ask for money because she missed a meeting.
5. never buy shoes with high heels again.
6. use social media to warn people about these shoes.

13-1 Using *Should*

(a) My clothes are dirty. I *should wash* them. (b) Tom is sleepy. He *should go* to bed. (c) You're sick. You *should see* a doctor.	*Should* means "This is a good idea. This is good advice."
(d) I You She He } *should go.* It We They	*Should* is followed by the base form of a verb. INCORRECT: *He should goes.* INCORRECT: *He should to go.*
(e) You *should not leave* your grammar book at home. You need it in class. (f) You *shouldn't leave* your grammar book at home.	NEGATIVE: *should not* CONTRACTION: *should + not = shouldn't*

Exercise 2. Looking at grammar. (Chart 13-1)
Complete the conversations. Begin each sentence with *You should*. Use the expressions from the box or your own words.

> call the credit card company   put on a bandaid
> call the manager   see a dentist
> drink tea with honey   sew it
> find an ATM   study harder
> ✓ go to the post office   take a nap

1. A: I want to mail a package.

   B: _____ *You should go to the post office.* _____

2. A: I'm sleepy.

   B: _____

3. A: I need to get some cash.

   B: _____

4. A: I have a toothache. I think I have a cavity.

   B: _____

5. A: I'm getting bad grades in all of my classes at school.

   B: _____

6. A: The toilet in my apartment doesn't work.

   B: _____

7. A: I lost my credit card.

   B: _____

8. A: My shirt has a hole under the arm.

   B: _____

9. I have a blister on my big toe. You should _____

10. My voice is hoarse. You should _____

Work in small groups. Make sentences with **should** and **shouldn't**. Share some of your answers with the class.

SITUATION 1: Dina has a headache from working at her computer too long.

Dina . . .

  a. see a doctor.
  b. take some medicine for her headache.
  c. lie down.
  d. go to the hospital emergency room.
  e. take a 15-minute break from the computer.

SITUATION 2: Nick stayed late after school to help his teacher. He missed the last bus and needs a ride home. It takes two hours to walk to his home, and it is a 15-minute ride by car.

Nick . . .

  a. call a taxi.
  b. hitchhike.
  c. ask his teacher for a ride.
  d. call a friend for a ride.
  e. walk.

SITUATION 3: Lydia's baby doesn't want to take a nap. He is crying.

Lydia . . .

  a. hold him.
  b. rock him.
  c. let him cry until he falls asleep.
  d. feed him.
  e. let him play.

SITUATION 4: The teacher is giving a final exam. One student keeps looking at a paper under his exam paper. It has the answers on it.

The teacher . . .

  a. take the paper away and give the student another chance.
  b. give the student a failing grade for the test.
  c. give the student a failing grade for the class.
  d. send the student to see the director of the school.

SITUATION 5: Marisa is 16 years old. A boy in her class wants her to go to dinner and a movie with him. This will be her first date.

Her parents . . .

  a. let her go if her older brother goes too.   d. let her go by herself.
  b. tell her to wait until she is older.   e. let her go to dinner only.
  c. go with her.

❑ **Exercise 4. Looking at grammar.** (Chart 13-1)
Complete the sentences with *should* or *shouldn't*.

1. Students _____*should*_____ come to class every day.

2. Students _____*shouldn't*_____ skip class.

3. We _____ waste our money on things we don't need.

4. It's raining. You _____ take your umbrella when you leave.

5. Timmy, you _____ pull the cat's tail!

6. People _____ hurt animals.

7. Your plane leaves at 8:00 A.M. You _____ get to the airport by 6:00.

8. Life is short. We _____ waste it.

9. You _____ smoke because it's bad for your health.

10. When you go to New York City, you _____ see a play on Broadway.

11. You _____ walk alone on city streets after dark. It's dangerous.

12. We _____ cross a street at an intersection. We _____ jaywalk.

❑ **Exercise 5. Let's talk: small groups.** (Chart 13-1)

Work in small groups. Each person presents a situation. The group gives advice by making a list of sentences using *should* and *shouldn't*.

SITUATION 1: English is not my native language. What advice can you give me about good ways to learn English?

SITUATION 2: I am a teenager. What advice can you give me about how to live a healthy lifestyle?

SITUATION 3: I am a newcomer. What advice can you give me about this school and this city?

SITUATION 4: I have a job interview tomorrow. What advice can you give me about going to a job interview?

SITUATION 5: I have a lot of trouble sleeping. I often wake up in the middle of the night and can't go back to sleep. What advice can you give me to help me sleep better?

❑ **Exercise 6. Listening.** (Chart 13-1)

Listen to each sentence and choose the verb you hear. After you check your answers, listen again. If you agree, circle *yes*. If you don't agree, circle *no*.

			DO YOU AGREE?	
1.	should	shouldn't	yes	no
2.	should	shouldn't	yes	no
3.	should	shouldn't	yes	no
4.	should	shouldn't	yes	no
5.	should	shouldn't	yes	no
6.	should	shouldn't	yes	no
7.	should	shouldn't	yes	no
8.	should	shouldn't	yes	no

❑ **Exercise 7. Warm-up.** (Chart 13-2)

Which two sentences have the same meaning?

1. I want to spell-check my writing.

2. I need to spell-check my writing.

3. I have to spell-check my writing.

4. I should spell-check my writing.

13-2 Using *Have* + Infinitive (*Have To / Has To / Had To*)

(a) People **need to eat** food. (b) People **have to eat** food. (c) Jack **needs to study** for his test. (d) Jack **has to study** for his test.	Examples (a) and (b) have basically the same meaning. Examples (c) and (d) have basically the same meaning. **Have** + *infinitive* has a special meaning: it expresses the same idea as **need**.
(e) I **had to study** last night.	PAST FORM: **had** + *infinitive*
(f) **Do** you **have to leave** now? (g) What time **does** Jim **have to leave**? (h) Why **did** they **have to leave** yesterday?	QUESTION FORM: **do**, **does**, or **did** is used in questions with **have to**.
(i) I **don't have to study** tonight. (j) The concert was free. We **didn't have to buy** tickets.	NEGATIVE FORM: **don't**, **doesn't**, or **didn't** is used with **have to**.

❏ **Exercise 8. Looking at grammar.** (Chart 13-3)
Rewrite the sentences using the correct form of **have to**.

1. I need to cash a check. _____I have to cash a check._____

2. Ellen needs to get a haircut. _____

3. The kids need to eat lunch. _____

4. The kids needed to eat lunch. _____

5. Jason needs to leave now. _____

6. Does Petra need to leave right now? _____

7. Why did you need to sell your car? _____

8. Malia doesn't need to work late. _____

9. The employees didn't need to work late. _____

10. The restaurant needed to close early. _____

❏ **Exercise 9. Let's talk: class activity.** (Chart 13-2)
Answer the questions your teacher asks you. Close your book for this activity.

1. What do you want to do today?
2. What do you have to do today?
3. What do you want to do tomorrow?
4. What do you have to do tomorrow?

5. What does a student need to do or have to do?

6. Who has to go shopping? Why?

7. Who has to go to the post office? Why?

8. Who has to go to the bank? Why?

9. Where do you have to go today? Why?

10. Where do you want to go tomorrow? Why?

11. What did you have to do yesterday? Why?

12. Did you have responsibilities at home when you were a child? What did you have to do?

13. If you're driving a car and the traffic light turns red, what do you have to do?

14. What do you have to do before you cross a busy street?

15. Do you have to learn English? Why?

16. Who has a job? What are some of the things you have to do when you're at work?

17. What kind of job did you have in the past? What did you have to do when you had that job?

❏ **Exercise 10. Let's talk: class activity.** (Chart 13-2)
Make sentences using *have to*/*has to* and *because*.

Example: go to the mall / buy some new shoes
STUDENT A: I have to go to the mall because I have to buy some new shoes.
   TEACHER: (*to Student B*) Why does (*Student A*) have to go to the mall?
STUDENT B: (*Student A*) has to go to the mall because he/she has to buy some new shoes.

1. go to the drugstore / buy some toothpaste

2. go to the grocery store / get some flour and sugar

3. go shopping / get a new coat

4. go to the post office / pick up a package

5. stay home tonight / study grammar

6. go to the hospital / visit a friend

7. go to the bank / cash a check

8. go downtown / go to the immigration office

9. go to the bookstore / buy a notebook

10. go to (*name of a store in the city*) / buy (*a particular thing at that store*)

❏ **Exercise 11. Looking at grammar.** (Chart 13-2)
Complete the sentences with the words in parentheses. Use a form of *have*/*has* + *infinitive*.

1. A: Franco can't join us for dinner tonight. (*he, work*) _____ *He has to work.* _____

   B: (*he, work*) _____ *Does he have to work* _____ tomorrow night too? If he doesn't, maybe we should postpone dinner until then.

2. A: Why (*you, go*) _____ to the library tonight?

   B: (*I, find*) _____ some information for my research paper.

3. A: Patricia's flight is at eight tonight. What time (*she, leave*) _____ _____ for the airport?

   B: Around five. (*she, be*) _____ there a little early to meet her group.

4. A: Why did you go to the bookstore after class yesterday?

   B: (*I, buy*) _____ some colored pencils.

   A: Oh? Why (*you, buy*) _____ colored pencils?

   B: I need them for some drawings I plan to do for my art class.

5. A: (*I, go*) _____ to the store.

   B: Why?

   A: Because (*I, get*) _____ some rice and fresh fruit.

6. A: Katie didn't come to the movie with us last night.

   B: Why?

   A: Because (*she, study*) _____ for a test.

7. A: What time (*you, be*) _____ at the dentist's office?

   B: Three. I have a three o'clock appointment.

8. A: (*Ted, find*) _____ a new apartment?

   B: Yes, he does. His old apartment is too small.

9. A: (*Miki, take, not*) _____ another English course. Her English is very good.

   B: (*you, take*) _____ another English course?

   A: Yes, I do. I need to study more English for my job.

10. A: Was Vince at home yesterday evening?

    B: No. (*he, stay*) _____ late at the office.

    A: Why?

    B: (*he, finish*) _____ a report for his boss.

Exercise 12. Listening. (Chart 13-2)

In spoken English, **have to** is often pronounced "hafta." **Has to** is often pronounced "hasta." Listen to each sentence and choose the correct verb.

Example: You will hear: We have to go now.
You will choose: (have to)   has to

1. have to	has to	6. have to	has to
2. have to	has to	7. have to	has to
3. have to	has to	8. have to	has to
4. have to	has to	9. have to	has to
5. have to	has to	10. have to	has to

◻ ### Exercise 13. Warm-up. (Chart 13-3)

Match each sentence to the correct meaning.

At the gym

1. Children under 12 must have an adult with them. ____

2. Children under 12 should have an adult with them. ____

3. Children under 12 have to have an adult with them. ____

a. It's a good idea.

b. There is no choice.

13-3 Using *Must, Have To / Has To,* and *Should*

MUST vs. HAVE TO

(a) People need food. People *have to eat* food. (b) People need food. People *must eat* food.	Examples (a) and (b) have basically the same meaning: *must eat = have to eat* **Have to** is more common in spoken English. **Must** is more common in written instructions and rules. Adults also use *must* with children. It is very strong.
(c) I You She He It We They } *must work*.	**Must** is followed by the base form of a verb. INCORRECT: He must works. INCORRECT: He must to work.

NEGATIVE: MUST vs. HAVE TO

(d) You *must not text* while you are driving. (e) You *don't have to go* to the movie with us if you don't want to.	**must not** = Don't do this! You don't have a choice.
	don't have to = It's not necessary; you have a choice.

MUST vs. SHOULD

MUST	SHOULD
Something is very important. Something is necessary. You do not have a choice.	Something is a good idea, but you have a choice.
(f) You *must take* an English course. You cannot graduate without it. (g) Johnny, look at me. You *must eat* your vegetables. You can't leave the table until you eat your vegetables.	(h) You *should take* an English course. It will help you. (i) Johnny, you *should eat* your vegetables. They're good for you. You'll grow up to be strong and healthy.

❑ **Exercise 14. Let's talk: small groups.** (Chart 13-3)
Work in small groups. Make two additional rules for each item.

1. Rules about driving/traffic:
   a. You must stop at a red light.
   b. You must not text and drive.

   c. _____

   d. _____

2. Rules on an airplane:
   a. You must fasten your seat belt during takeoff and landing.
   b. You must not smoke.

   c. _____

   d. _____

3. Rules a parent gives a young child:
   a. You must not run into the street.
   b. You must sit in a car seat in the car.

   c. _____

   d. _____

❏ **Exercise 15. Looking at grammar.** (Chart 13-3)
Complete the sentences. Use *must* and expressions from the box.

> apply in person   pay income tax
> ✓ have a driver's license   pay the first and last month's rent
> have a medical license   put on a jacket
> have a passport   take one tablet every six hours

1. According to the law,* a driver _____ *must have a driver's license.* _____

2. Mansour wants to get a job. According to the application, he _____

   _____ at 500 Broadway Avenue.

3. I want to travel abroad. According to the law, I _____

4. If you want to be a doctor, you _____

5. Davey! It's cold outside. You _____

6. Arthur's doctor gave him a prescription. According to the directions on

   the bottle, Arthur _____

7. I want to rent an apartment. According to the rental agreement, I

   _____

8. Pia has a job in Chicago. She earns a good salary. According to the law,

   she _____

_____

according to the law = the law says

Choose the correct completion.

1. If you want to keep your job, you ____ be late for work.

    a. must not   b. don't have to   c. doesn't have to

2. My office is near my apartment, so I can walk to work. I ____ take a bus. I take a bus only in bad weather.

    a. must not   b. don't have to   c. doesn't have to

3. Some schools require their students to wear uniforms to school, but my children's school doesn't require uniforms. They ____ wear uniforms to school.

    a. must not   b. don't have to   c. doesn't have to

4. Billy, it is very important to be careful with matches. You ____ play with matches.

    a. must not   b. don't have to   c. doesn't have to

5. Kevin is twenty-four, but he still lives with his parents. That saves him a lot of money. For example, he ____ pay rent or buy his own food.

    a. must not   b. don't have to   c. doesn't have to

6. Carly, the water in that river is polluted. You ____ play in it.

    a. must not   b. don't have to   c. doesn't have to

7. If you have a credit card, you ____ pay for things in cash. You can charge them.

    a. must not   b. don't have to   c. doesn't have to

8. Kyra is going to buy school supplies. She has a coupon for 20% off, so she ____ pay full price.

    a. must not   b. don't have to   c. doesn't have to

9. When an airplane is taking off, you have to be in your seat with your seat belt on. You ____ stand up and walk around when an airplane is taking off.

    a. must not   b. don't have to   c. doesn't have to

10. When Mrs. Wilson drives to the supermarket, she ____ park far away because she has a disabled person's parking permit for her car.

    a. must not   b. don't have to   c. doesn't have to

❑ **Exercise 17. Let's talk: small groups.** (Charts 13-1 → 13-3)
Work in small groups. Make sentences about your English class. Use **should** / **have to** / **don't have to** with the given phrases. Share a few of your answers with the class.

Example: Students . . . study.
Response: Students have to study.

Students . . .

1. come to class.
2. sit quietly.
3. take attendance.
4. bring a pencil and some paper to class.
5. listen carefully.
6. speak English in class.
7. stand up when the teacher enters the room.
8. knock on the door before entering the room.
9. raise their hands when they want to talk.
10. do their homework.
11. memorize vocabulary.
12. bring an English–English dictionary to class.
13. write homework answers in their books.

❑ **Exercise 18. Listening.** (Charts 13-1 and 13-3)
Listen to each pair of sentences. One sentence uses **should**, and the other uses **must**. Decide which sentence you agree with. Discuss your answers as a class.

Example: You will hear: a. People must learn how to use computers.
                                        b. People should learn how to use computers.

You will choose: *a OR b*

1. _____   4. _____   7. _____

2. _____   5. _____   8. _____

3. _____   6. _____   9. _____

❑ **Exercise 19. Warm-up.** (Chart 13-4)
Which two questions are more polite?

Child to parent

1. May I have a snack?
2. Can I have a snack?
3. Could I have a snack?

13-4 Polite Questions: *May I, Could I,* and *Can I*

(a) **May I borrow** your pen? (b) **Could I borrow** your pen? (c) **Can I borrow** your pen?	Examples (a), (b), and (c) have the same meaning: I want to borrow your pen. I am asking politely to borrow your pen. **Could** is more polite and formal than **can**. **May** is very polite and formal.
(d) *May I **please** borrow* your pen? (e) *Could I **please** borrow* your pen? (f) *Can I **please** borrow* your pen?	**Please** makes the request more polite.
TYPICAL RESPONSES (g) **Yes, of course.** (h) **Of course.** (i) **Certainly.** (j) **Sure.** (informal)* (k) **No problem.** (informal)	TYPICAL CONVERSATION A: *May I please borrow your pen?* B: **Yes, of course.** *Here it is.* A: *Thank you. / Thanks.*

*Informal English is typically used between friends and family members.

❏ **Exercise 20. Let's talk: pairwork.** (Chart 13-4)

Work with a partner. Look at the pictures. Write conversations. Use *May I, Can I,* or *Could I* and typical responses.

1

2

3

4

❑ **Exercise 21. Let's talk: pairwork.** (Chart 13-4)
Work with a partner. Ask and answer polite questions using *May I*, *Can I*, or *Could I*.

Example: Your partner has a pencil. You want to borrow it.
PARTNER A: May I (please) borrow your pencil?
PARTNER B: Sure. Here it is.
PARTNER A: Thank you. Your turn now.

PARTNER A	PARTNER B
1. Your partner has a calculator. You want to borrow it.	1. Your partner has some notebook paper. You forgot your notebook, and you need one piece of paper.
2. Your partner has an eraser. You want to use it for a minute.	2. Your partner has a pencil sharpener. You want to borrow it.
3. You are at your partner's home. You want to use the bathroom.	3. You are at your partner's home. You want a glass of water.
4. You are at a restaurant. Your partner is a server. You want to have a cup of coffee.	4. You are at a restaurant. Your partner is a server. You want to leave, and you need the check.★

❑ **Exercise 22. Warm-up.** (Chart 13-5)
Do the sentences have the same or a different meaning?

1. Could you hold the elevator for me?
2. Would you hold the elevator for me?

13-5 Polite Questions: *Could You* and *Would You*

(a) *Could you (please) open* the door? (b) *Would you (please) open* the door?	Examples (a) and (b) have the same meaning: I want you to open the door. I am asking you politely to open the door.
TYPICAL RESPONSES (c) *Yes, of course.* (d) *Certainly.* (e) *I'd be glad to.* (f) *I'd be happy to.* (g) *Sure.* (informal) (h) *No problem.* (informal)	A TYPICAL CONVERSATION A: *Could you please open the door?* B: *I'd be glad to.* A: *Thank you. / Thanks.*

★*the check* = the bill in a restaurant

❏ **Exercise 23. Let's talk: pairwork.** (Chart 13-5)
Work with a partner to complete the conversations. Use **Could you** or **Would you** and give typical responses. Then write them down and discuss them with the rest of the class.

1. A: Excuse me, sir. _____

   B: _____

   A: _____

2. A: _____

   B: Excuse me? I didn't understand you.

   A: _____

   B: _____

❏ **Exercise 24. Let's talk: pairwork.** (Chart 13-5)
Work with a partner. Make requests and give answers. Use **Could you** or **Would you**.

Example: You want your partner to open the window.
PARTNER A: Could you (please) open the window?
PARTNER B: Sure.
PARTNER A: Thank you.

You want your partner to . . .

1. close the door.
2. turn on the light.
3. turn off the light.
4. pass you the salt and pepper.

5. hand you that book.
6. translate a word for you.
7. tell you the time.
8. hold your books for a minute.

❏ **Exercise 25. Let's talk: pairwork.** (Chart 13-5)

Work with a partner. Ask and answer polite questions that fit each situation. Share your conversations with the rest of the class.

Example: A professor's office: Partner A is a student. Partner B is the professor.
PARTNER A: (*knocks on door*) May I come in?
PARTNER B: Certainly. Come in. How are you today?
PARTNER A: Fine, thanks. Could I talk to you for a few minutes? I have some questions about the last assignment.
PARTNER B: Of course. Have a seat.
PARTNER A: Thank you.

1. A restaurant: Partner A is a customer. Partner B is a server.
2. A classroom: Partner A is a teacher. Partner B is a student.
3. A kitchen: Partner A is a parent. Partner B is a teenager.
4. A clothing store: Partner A is a customer. Partner B is a salesperson.
5. An apartment: Partner A and B are roommates.
6. A car: Partner A is a passenger. Partner B is the driver.
7. An office: Partner A is a manager. Partner B is an employee.
8. A house: Partner B answers the phone. Partner A wants to talk to (*someone*).

❏ **Exercise 26. Warm-up.** (Chart 13-6)

What do you think is a good suggestion for each situation? Use **Run!** or **Don't run!** Discuss your answers with the class.

a bear

a cougar

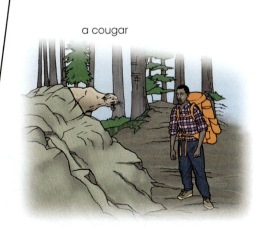

13-6 Imperative Sentences

(a) A: **Close the door**, Jimmy. It's cold outside. B: Okay, Mom.	In (a): **Close the door** is an IMPERATIVE SENTENCE. The sentence means "Jimmy, I want you to close the door. I am telling you to close the door."
(b) **Sit** down. (c) **Be** careful!	An imperative sentence uses the base form of a verb (*close, sit, be, etc.*). The subject is **you**. Sit down. = (You) sit down.
(d) **Don't open** the window. (e) **Don't be** late.	NEGATIVE IMPERATIVE **don't** + *the base form of a verb*
(f) ORDERS: **Stop**, thief! (g) DIRECTIONS: **Open** your books to page 24. (h) ADVICE: **Don't worry.** (i) REQUESTS: **Please close** the door.	Imperative sentences give orders, commands, directions, and advice. With the addition of **please**, as in (i), imperatives sound more polite.

❏ **Exercise 27. Let's talk.** (Chart 13-6)
Write the correct command for each picture.

> Don't let go! Hurry up! March! Relax. Wait for me!

1. _____   2. _____   3. _____

4. _____   5. _____

Exercise 28. Looking at grammar. (Chart 13-6)

<u>Underline</u> the imperative verbs in the conversations.

1. TOM: What's the matter?

   JIM: I have the hiccups.

   TOM: Hold your breath.

   BOB: Drink some water.

   JOE: Breathe into a paper bag.

   KEN: Eat a piece of bread.

   JIM: It's okay. My hiccups are gone.

2. ANYA: I need to leave now.

   IVAN: Wait for me.

   ANYA: Don't forget your keys.

   IVAN: I have them.

3. ANDY: Bye, Mom. I'm going over to Billy's house.

   MOM: Wait a minute. Did you clean up your room?

   ANDY: I'll do it later.

   MOM: No. Do it now, before you leave.

   ANDY: What do I have to do?

   MOM: Hang up your clothes. Make your bed. Put your books back on the shelf. Empty the wastepaper basket. Okay?

   ANDY: Okay.

❑ ### **Exercise 29. Looking at grammar.** (Chart 13-6)

Look at the pictures. Write an imperative sentence for each one.

1. _____   2. _____

3. _____   4. _____

❏ **Exercise 30. Reading and writing.** (Chart 13-6)

Part I. Read the conversation. Look at new vocabulary with your teacher first.

QUESTION: How do I get to the post office from here?

DIRECTIONS: Walk two blocks to 16th Avenue. Then turn right on Forest Street. Go two more blocks to Market Street and turn left at the light. The post office is halfway down the street on the right-hand side.

Do you know these words?

block
turn right/left
halfway
right-hand

Part II. Complete this question: How do I get to _____ from here? Then write directions. Use four or more imperative verbs. Here is some vocabulary you may want to use.

walk	right-hand side	up the street
turn right	left-hand side	down the street
go (to)	cross	in the middle of the street
turn left	crosswalk	at the light

❏ **Exercise 31. Let's talk: class activity.** (Chart 13-6)

Listen to your teacher's questions. Make some imperative sentences for these situations. Close your book for this activity.

Example:

TEACHER: Your friend has a headache. What are some typical suggestions?

STUDENT A: Take an aspirin.

STUDENT B: Lie down and close your eyes for a little while.

STUDENT C: Put a cold cloth on your forehead.

STUDENT D: Don't read for a while.

STUDENT E: Take a hot bath and relax.

             Etc.

1. You are the teacher of this class. You are assigning homework for tomorrow. What are some typical imperative sentences for this situation?

2. Your friend is coughing and sneezing. What are some typical imperative sentences for this situation?

3. Your eight-year-old son/daughter is walking out the door to go to school. What are some typical imperative sentences for this situation?

4. Your friend is going to cook rice for the first time this evening. Tell him/her how to cook rice.

5. Your friend wants to win a scholarship to a university. Tell him/her what to do and what not to do.

6. A friend from another country is going to visit your country for the first time next month. Tell him/her what to do and what to see as a tourist in your country.

❏ **Exercise 32. Warm-up.** (Chart 13-7)
Complete each sentence with all the possible verbs from the box.

can	has	is able	is going	may

1. Nate _____ to come the meeting.

2. Petra _____ come to the meeting.

13-7 Modal Auxiliaries

(a) Anita	*can* *could* *may* *might* *must* *should* *will* } go to class.	An auxiliary is a helping verb. It comes in front of the base form of a main verb. The following helping verbs are called "modal auxiliaries": *can*, *could*, *may*, *might*, *must*, *should*, *will*, *would*.
(b) Anita	*is able to* *is going to* *has to* } go to class.	Expressions that are similar to modal auxiliaries are *be able to*, *be going to*, *have to*.

❏ **Exercise 33. Looking at grammar.** (Chart 13-7)
Add *to* where necessary. If *to* is not necessary, write **Ø**.

1. My sister can _____Ø_____ play the guitar very well.

2. We have _____to_____ pay our rent on the first of the month.

3. Could you please _____ open the window? Thanks.

4. I wasn't able _____ visit my friends yesterday because I was busy.

5. You shouldn't _____ drink twenty cups of coffee a day.

6. Will you _____ be at the meeting tomorrow?

7. Does everyone have _____ be at the meeting?

8. You must not _____ miss the meeting. It's important.

9. Vanessa might not _____ be there tomorrow.

10. May I _____ use your phone?

11. We couldn't _____ go to the concert last night because we didn't have tickets.

12. Can you _____ play a musical instrument?

13. What time is the plane going _____ arrive?

14. It may _____ be too cold for us to go swimming tomorrow.

13-8 Summary Chart: Modal Auxiliaries and Similar Expressions

AUXILIARY*	MEANING	EXAMPLE
(a) *can*	ability	I *can* sing.
	polite question	*Can* you please help me?
(b) *could*	past ability	I *couldn't* go to class yesterday.
	polite question	*Could* you please help me?
(c) *may*	possibility	It *may* rain tomorrow.
	polite question	*May* I help you?
(d) *might*	possibility	It *might* rain tomorrow.
(e) *must*	necessity	You *must* have a passport.
(f) *should*	advisability	You *should* see a doctor.
(g) *will*	future event	My sister *will* meet us at the airport.
(h) *would*	polite question	*Would* you please open the door?
(i) *be able to*	ability	I *wasn't able to* attend the meeting.
(j) *be going to*	future event	Tina *is going to* meet us at the airport.
(k) *have to/has to*	necessity	I *have to* study tonight.
(l) *had to*	past necessity	I *had to* study last night too.

*See the following charts for more information: *can*, Chart 12-1, p. 361, and Chart 12-3, p. 365; *could*, Chart 12-5, p. 370; *may* and *might*, Chart 11-1, p. 334; *must*, Chart 13-3, p. 392; *should*, Chart 13-1, p. 383; *will*, Chart 10-6, p. 319, Chart 10-7, p. 321, and Chart 11-1, p. 334; *would*, Chart 13-5, p. 397; *be able to*, Chart 12-6, p. 373; *be going to*, Chart 10-1, p. 303; *have/has/had to*, Chart 13-2, p. 388.

❑ **Exercise 34. Let's talk: small groups.** (Chart 13-8)
Work in small groups. Each person in the group should give a different response. Share a few of your answers with the class.

Example: Name something you *had to* do yesterday.
STUDENT A: I had to go to class.
STUDENT B: I had to go to the post office to buy some stamps.
STUDENT C: I had to study for a test.

1. Name something you *can* do.

2. Name something you *couldn't* do yesterday.

3. Name something you *may* do tomorrow.

4. Name something you *might* do tomorrow.

5. Name something you *must* do this week.

6. Name something you *have to* do today.

7. Name something you *don't have to* do today.

8. Name something you *should* do this evening.

9. Name something you *will* do this evening.

10. Name something you *are going to* do this week.

11. Name something you *weren't able to* do when you were a child.

12. Name something you *had to* do when you were a child.

13. You want to borrow something from a classmate. Ask a polite question with *could*.

14. You want a classmate to do something for you. Ask a polite question with *would*.

15. A classmate has something that you want. Ask a polite question with *may*.

16. Name something that *may* happen in the world in the next ten years.

17. Name something that (probably) *won't* happen in the world in the next ten years.

18. Name some things that this school *should* do to make it a better place for students.

❑ **Exercise 35. Looking at grammar.** (Chart 13-8)
Choose the correct completion.

1. Doug _____ every day.
   a. shaves   b. is shaving   c. has to shaves

2. _____ to class every day?
   a. Are you go   b. Do you have to go   c. You going

3. Matsu _____ to be here tomorrow.
   a. might   b. is going   c. must

4. Carl _____ be in class yesterday.
   a. didn't   b. wasn't   c. couldn't

5. Fatima _____ to her sister on the phone yesterday.
    a. spoke   b. can speak   c. speaks

6. I _____ my rent last month.
    a. might pay   b. will pay   c. paid

7. I want to go to a movie tonight, but I _____ home and study.
    a. should stay   b. stayed   c. stay

8. We _____ downtown tomorrow.
    a. going   b. might go   c. will can go

9. _____ you like some hot coffee now?
    a. Will   b. Would   c. Do

❏ **Exercise 36. Listening.** (Chart 13-8)

Listen to each sentence. Choose the sentence that is closest in meaning.

Example: You will hear: It might snow tomorrow.
           You will choose: a. It will snow.   (b.) It may snow.   c. It must snow.

1. a. Tom should work.
   b. Tom must work.
   c. Tom might work.

2. a. Becky can swim.
   b. Becky may swim.
   c. Becky will swim.

3. a. The teacher should correct papers.
   b. The teacher had to correct papers.
   c. The teacher wanted to correct papers.

4. a. You may study for the test.
   b. You must study for the test.
   c. You should study for the test.

5. a. We should go to a movie.
   b. It's possible we will go to a movie.
   c. We have to go to a movie.

6. a. We couldn't help.
   b. We didn't need to help.
   c. We weren't able to help.

7. a. I didn't want to go to school.
   b. I didn't have to go to school.
   c. I wasn't able to go to school.

Part I. Read the article. Look at new vocabulary with your teacher first.

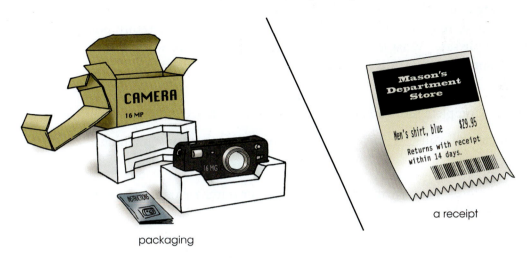

packaging

a receipt

Returning an Item to a Store

Many stores have a return policy* for items you buy.
Generally, you must have a receipt for a return. Some stores
may have your purchase on their computer, but most require a
receipt.

> **Do you know these words?**
>
> item
> purchase
> exception
> exchange
> unpleasant

In general, clothes must still have the tags. Stores don't
want you to wear something and then return it. Usually, you
can wear shoes, but you have to stay on carpets and not walk
outside in them. The soles of the shoes should look like new. It is also important to keep
the box and other packaging. Stores would like to resell the item, so they want to have the
original packaging.

There is usually a time limit for returns. Some stores might give you two weeks, while
others may give you 90 days. A few stores have no time limit because they want you to be
completely satisfied.

If you buy electronics, like a computer or a TV, there is often a restocking fee. This is
a charge to put the item back on the shelf. Often the fee is 15 percent of the cost or more.
Here's an example. John bought a camera, but he couldn't understand how to use it. He
decided to return it. The company returned his money but kept 15 percent of the camera
cost. There is an exception. If an item is defective (damaged or broken), the company will
probably return all your money. Generally, a DVD or CD is not returnable if you open it.
Be sure you are going to keep it before you open the packaging.

---

* *return policy* = rules a store has for returning an item

Items on sale usually have this policy: "All sales final." This means there are no returns on sale items. Sometimes a store might let you exchange the item for something else.

Every store is different, so it is important to ask about the return policy before you buy. Simply say, "What is your return policy for ____?" You may save yourself some unpleasant surprises if you get all the information before you buy.

Part II. Complete the sentences with the correct verb according to the article.

1. In general, you ____ have a receipt if you want to return something.
   a. might   b. must

2. The store ____ have information about your purchase on its computer.
   a. might   b. will

3. If you want to return shoes, you ____ wear them outside.
   a. don't have to   b. must not

4. Generally, you ____ keep the original packaging if you want to return an item.
   a. must   b. may

5. A store ____ give you two weeks to return an item.
   a. must   b. may

6. If you buy an item and it is broken, you ____ return it.
   a. can   b. can't

7. At most stores, you ____ return sale items.
   a. can   b. can't

8. You ____ ask the salesperson about the store's return policy.
   a. should   b. will

❏ **Exercise 38. Warm-up.** (Chart 13-9)
Imagine you are Speaker B. What answers do you like?

A: It's a beautiful day.

B: a. Let's watch TV.

   b. Let's go to the beach.

   c. Let's go to the park.

   d. Let's go hiking.

   e. Let's play video games.

13-9 Using *Let's*

(a) A: What should we do tonight? B: **Let's go to a movie.** A: Okay. (b) A: I'm tired. B: I'm tired too. **Let's take a break.** A: That's a good idea!	*Let's (do something)* = I have a suggestion for you and me. *Let's* = Let us In (a): *Let's go to a movie.* = I think we should go to a movie. Do you want to go to a movie?

❏ **Exercise 39. Looking at grammar.** (Chart 13-9)
Complete the conversations with *let's*. Use the words from the box or your own words.

eat get a cup of coffee go dancing go to Florida go to a movie	go to a seafood restaurant go swimming ✓ leave at six-thirty just stay home and relax walk

1. A: What time should we leave for the airport?

   B: _____Let's leave at six-thirty._____

   A: Okay.

2. A: Where should we go for our vacation?

   B: _____

   A: That's a good idea.

3. A: Where do you want to go for dinner tonight?

   B: _____

4. A: The weather is beautiful today. _____

   B: Okay. Great!

5. A: I'm bored. _____

   B: I can't. I have to study.

6. A: Should we take the bus downtown or walk downtown?

   B: It's a nice day. _____

7. A: Dinner's ready. The food's on the table.

   B: Great! _____ . I'm starving.

8. A: Where should we go Saturday night?

   B: _____

   A: Wonderful idea!

9. A: We have an hour between classes. _____

   B: Okay. That sounds good.

❑ **Exercise 40. Let's talk: pairwork.** (Chart 13-9)
Work with a partner. Take turns making suggestions with *let's*. Give two suggestions for each situation.

Example: It's a beautiful day today. What should we do?
PARTNER A: It's a beautiful day today. What should we do?
PARTNER B: Let's go to Woodland Park Zoo.
PARTNER A: That's a possibility. Or, let's go to the beach.

1. I don't have to work tonight. What should we do?
2. Next Monday's a holiday and there's no school. We should do something fun.
3. I don't know anyone at this party. I want to leave.
4. What time should we leave for the airport tomorrow? There will be a lot of traffic.
5. It's your birthday next week. What would you like to do?
6. Parent to child: I have a little free time right now. I can spend it with you.

❑ **Exercise 41. Check your knowledge.** (Chapters 12 and 13)
Correct the mistakes.

1. Would you please ~~to~~ help me?

2. I will can go to the meeting tomorrow.

3. My brother wasn't able calling me last night.

4. Tariq should calls us.

5. I have to went to the store yesterday.

6. Susie! You must not to hit your brother!

7. May you please hand me that book?

8. Alessandra couldn't answered my question.

9. Shelley can't goes to the concert tomorrow.

10. Let's going to a movie tonight.

11. Don't to interrupt. It's not polite.

12. Can you to stand on your head?

13. I saw a beautiful dress at a store yesterday, but I couldn't bought it.

14. Closing the door, please. Thank you.

15. May I please to borrow your dictionary? Thank you.

☐ **Exercise 42. Reading and writing.** (Chapter 13)

Part I. Read the passage about Manhattan.   Look at new vocabulary with your teacher.

A Great Place to Visit

capital letter

I grew up in Manhattan.* Manhattan is a very exciting part of New York City. You should go there because there are so many interesting sights to see.

> Do you know these words?
>
> incredible
> landmark

First, the museums are amazing. You can find art, natural science, and history museums. My favorite museum is on Ellis Island. Ellis Island was the entry point for immigrants from 1892 to 1954, and you can learn a lot about history. My family came through Ellis Island, and I was able to find my grandparents' names.

Many tall buildings have incredible views of the city. You can go to the top of the Empire State Building, Rockefeller Center, or even the Statue of Liberty. Take your camera because you will want to get great photos. The most popular places have long lines, so you should check wait times before you go. Sometimes you have to make reservations.

Statue of Liberty

---

* See Appendix Chart A5-1, p. 487 for capitalization rules for place names.

A good way to learn about the city is to take a boat tour. Manhattan is an island, and you can see many famous landmarks from the water. A tour guide can tell you a lot about the history of the sites and the different neighborhoods. It's also fun to ride under the famous bridges, like the Brooklyn Bridge.

Central Park is very beautiful and relaxing. It's a wonderful place for walking, running, biking, boating, or just people-watching. Sometimes there are concerts in the park. Millions of people visit the park every year, but it's very large, so it doesn't feel crowded.

There is something else you should know. Manhattan is very expensive. Make sure you have enough money and be careful when you are walking around town. Keep your money in a safe place and stay away from dangerous places. Your hotel can tell you about places you shouldn't visit.

If you go to Manhattan, you will have special memories. Don't forget to send me pictures!

Part II. Write a paragraph about your hometown or a city you like. Imagine you are talking to someone who wants to visit your hometown (or choose another city). First, answer these questions:

- Why is your hometown (or other city) a good place for me to visit?
- What should I do when I'm there?
- Where should I go?
- What should I see?
- Are there places I shouldn't visit?

Begin this way:

I grew up in _____. It is a very exciting/beautiful/interesting place. You should go there because there are so many wonderful sights to see. OR

One of my favorite places to visit is _____. It is a very exciting/beautiful/interesting city, and there are many wonderful sights to see.

Part III. Editing check: Work individually or change papers with a partner. Check (✓) for the following:

1. ____ indented paragraph

2. ____ capital letter at the beginning of each sentence

3. ____ capital letter for cities and place names (See Appendix Chart A5-1, p. 487.)

4. ____ period at the end of each sentence

5. ____ use of some modal verbs

6. ____ correct spelling (use a dictionary or computer spell-check)

Chapter 14
Nouns and Modifiers

☐ **Exercise 1. Warm-up.** (Chart 14-1)
Match the sentences to the pictures. Are the words in red used as nouns or adjectives?

1. an old computer
2. a computer mouse
3. a computer keyboard

Picture A

Picture B

Picture C

14-1	**Modifying Nouns with Adjectives and Nouns**

ADJECTIVE + NOUN (a) I bought an **expensive** *book*. (b) I bought **expensive** *books*.	Adjectives can modify nouns, as in (a) and (b). See Chart 6-3, p. 164, for a list of common adjectives. NOTE: Adjectives do not have plural forms. *INCORRECT: expensives books*
NOUN + NOUN (c) I bought a *grammar* **book**. (d) I bought *grammar* **books**.	Nouns can modify other nouns. In (c) and (d): *grammar* is a noun that is used as an adjective to modify another noun (*book/books*).
NOUN + NOUN (e) He works at a *shoe* **store**. *INCORRECT: He works at a shoes store.*	A noun that is used as an adjective is usually in the singular form. In (e): the store sells shoes, but it is called a *shoe* (singular form) *store*.
ADJECTIVE + NOUN + NOUN (f) I bought an **expensive** *grammar* **book**. *INCORRECT: I bought a grammar expensive book.*	Both an adjective and a noun can modify a noun, as in (f); the adjective comes first, the noun second.

❏ **Exercise 2. Looking at grammar.** (Chart 14-1)

Underline each adjective and draw an arrow to the noun it modifies.

1. I drank some hot tea.

2. My grandmother is a smart woman.

3. English is not my native language.

4. The busy waitress poured coffee into the empty cup.

5. A young man carried the heavy suitcase for his pregnant wife.

6. I slept in an uncomfortable bed at an old hotel.

❏ **Exercise 3. Looking at grammar.** (Chart 14-1)

Underline each noun used as an adjective and draw an arrow to the noun it modifies.

1. We sat at the kitchen table.

2. Have you paid the phone bill yet?

3. We met Steve at the train station.

4. Vegetable soup is nutritious.

5. The movie theater is next to the furniture store.

6. The waiter handed us a lunch menu.

7. The traffic light was red, so we stopped.

8. Ms. Bell gave me her business card.

❏ **Exercise 4. Listening.** (Chart 14-1)

Listen to the sentences. Decide if the given word is used as a noun or adjective.

Example: You will hear: This **grammar** book has a lot of information.
You will choose: NOUN   (ADJ)

1. kitchen	NOUN	ADJ	6. car	NOUN	ADJ
2. kitchen	NOUN	ADJ	7. car	NOUN	ADJ
3. apartment	NOUN	ADJ	8. chicken	NOUN	ADJ
4. apartment	NOUN	ADJ	9. chicken	NOUN	ADJ
5. music	NOUN	ADJ	10. grammar	NOUN	ADJ

Exercise 5. Let's talk: small groups. (Chart 14-1)

Work in small groups. Which noun in the box can be used with all three of the nouns used as modifiers? For example, in the first sentence, the completion can be *a university education, a high school education,* or *a college education.*

class	number	race	store
✓ education	official	room	tickets
keys	program	soup	trip

1. Regina has a { university / high school / college } _____*education.*_____

2. We went to a { furniture / shoe / clothing } _____

3. I took a { history / math / science } _____

4. We watched a { horse / car / foot } _____

5. I talked to a { government / city / school } _____

6. Mom made some { vegetable / bean / chicken } _____

7. He told me about a { radio / computer / TV } _____

8. We took a/an { boat / bus / airplane } _____

9. We visited Meg in her { hospital / hotel / dorm } _____

10. We bought some { theater / concert / airplane } _____

11. I couldn't find my $\left\{\begin{array}{l}\text{car}\\\text{house}\\\text{locker}\end{array}\right\}$ _____

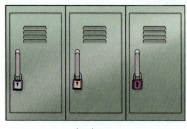

lockers

license plate

12. What is your $\left\{\begin{array}{l}\text{phone}\\\text{apartment}\\\text{license plate}\end{array}\right\}$ _____

❑ **Exercise 6. Looking at grammar.** (Chart 14-1)

Complete the sentences. Use the information in the first part of the sentence. Use a noun that modifies another noun in the completion.

1. Vases for flowers are called ____*flower vases*_____ .

2. A cup for coffee is called a ____*coffee cup*_____ .

3. An article in a newspaper is called a _____ .

4. Rooms in hotels are called _____ .

5. A worker in an office is called an _____ .

6. A tag that gives the price of something is called a _____ .

7. Seats on airplanes are called _____ .

8. A bench in a park is called a _____ .

9. Soup that is made of beans is called _____ .

10. A house that is made of bricks is called a _____ .

Exercise 7. Looking at grammar. (Chart 14-1)
Each item lists two nouns and one adjective. Write them in the correct order.

1. homework
   long
   assignment

   The teacher gave us a _____*long homework assignment*_____ .

2. show
   good
   TV

   I watched a _____ .

3. road
   mountain
   dangerous

   We drove on a _____ .

4. car
   bad
   accident

   Sofia was in a _____ .

5. article
   magazine
   interesting

   I read an _____ .

6. delicious
   vegetable
   soup

   Mrs. Montero made some _____ .

7. card
   funny
   birthday

   My sister gave me a _____ .

8. narrow
   seats
   airplane

   People don't like to sit in _____ .

❑ **Exercise 8. Warm-up.** (Chart 14-2)

Answer the questions. Then complete the description.

1. Is it large?   yes   no

2. Is it expensive?   yes   no

3. What is the stone? _____

Now describe it: a _____ _____ _____ ring.
                        a. size   b. cost   c. material

14-2 Word Order of Adjectives

(a) a *large red* car INCORRECT: *a red large car*	In (a): two adjectives (*large* and *red*) modify a noun (*car*). Adjectives follow a particular order. In (a): an adjective describing SIZE (*large*) comes before an adjective describing COLOR (*red*).
(b) a *beautiful young* woman (c) a *beautiful red* car (d) a *beautiful Greek* island	The adjective *beautiful* expresses an opinion. Opinion adjectives usually come before all other adjectives. In (b): opinion precedes age. In (c): opinion precedes color. In (d): opinion precedes nationality.

(e) **OPINION ADJECTIVES**
 	
    dangerous   favorite   important
    difficult   good   interesting
    dirty   happy   strong
    expensive honest   wonderful
	There are many opinion adjectives. The words in (e) are examples of common opinion adjectives.

USUAL WORD ORDER OF ADJECTIVES

(1) **OPINION**	(2) **SIZE**	(3) **AGE**	(4) **COLOR**	(5) **NATIONALITY***	(6) **MATERIAL**
beautiful	large	young	red	Greek	metal
delicious	tall	old	blue	Chinese	glass
kind	little	middle-aged	black	Mexican	plastic

(f) some *delicious Mexican* food (g) a *small glass* vase (h) a *kind old Chinese* man	A noun is usually modified by only one or two adjectives, although sometimes there are three.
(i) RARE a *beautiful small old brown Greek metal* coin	It is very rare to find a long list of adjectives in front of a noun.

* NOTE: Adjectives that describe nationality are capitalized: *Korean, Venezuelan, Saudi Arabian,* etc.

❏ **Exercise 9. Looking at grammar.** (Chart 14-2)
Describe each picture. Use two or three adjectives for each noun. Answers may vary.

Example:

OPINION	SIZE	AGE	COLOR	NATIONALITY	MATERIAL	NOUN
expensive	Ø	Ø	gray	Ø	wool	suit

1.

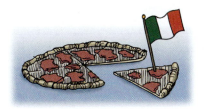

OPINION	SIZE	AGE	COLOR	NATIONALITY	MATERIAL	NOUN

2.

OPINION	SIZE	AGE	COLOR	NATIONALITY	MATERIAL	NOUN

3

OPINION	SIZE	AGE	COLOR	NATIONALITY	MATERIAL	NOUN

4

OPINION	SIZE	AGE	COLOR	NATIONALITY	MATERIAL	NOUN

5

OPINION	SIZE	AGE	COLOR	NATIONALITY	MATERIAL	NOUN

❑ **Exercise 10. Looking at grammar.** (Chart 14-2)
Complete each sentence with a word from the box.

Asian	✓cotton	designer
brick	important	soft
Canadian	glass	unhappy

1. Marcos is wearing a white _____*cotton*_____ shirt.

2. Hong Kong is an important _____ city.

3. Luke likes to wear expensive _____ suits.

4. Misha was a/an _____ little boy when he broke his favorite toy.

5. Teresa has a/an _____ wool blanket on her bed.

6. Our dorm is a tall red _____ building.

7. The laptop computer is a/an _____ modern invention.

8. I keep leftover food in round _____ containers.

9. Ice hockey is a popular _____ sport.

❑ **Exercise 11. Looking at grammar.** (Chart 14-2)
Put the given words in the correct order.

1. red   a _____*big red*_____ tomato
   big

2. delicious   some _____ food
   Thai

3. red   some _____ tomatoes
   small

4. old   some _____ cows
   big
   brown

5. narrow   a _____ road
   dirt

6. young   a _____ woman
   serious

7. long   _____ hair
   black
   beautiful

8. Chinese   a/an _____ work of art
   famous
   old

9. leather   a _____ belt
   brown
   thin

10. wonderful a/an _____ story
    old
    Native American

❑ **Exercise 12. Looking at grammar.** (Chart 14-2)
   Add adjectives or nouns used as adjectives to complete the sentences. Share some of your
   answers with the class.

   1. We had some hot _____ food.

   2. My dog, Buddy, is a/an _____ old dog.

   3. We bought a blue _____ blanket.

   4. Alison has _____ gold earrings.

   5. Jeremy has short _____ hair.

   6. Mr. Yu is a/an _____ young man.

   7. Omar lives in a large _____ brick house.

   8. I bought a big _____ suitcase.

   9. Sally picked a/an _____ red flower.

   10. Charlie wore an old _____ shirt to the picnic.

❏ **Exercise 13. Looking at grammar.** (Charts 14-1 and 14-2)
Choose the correct completion.

1. Mr. Lane wore ____.
   a. a cotton shirt old   b. an old cotton shirt

2. She put some honey in a ____.
   a. blue glass jar   b. glass blue jar

3. The Great Wall is a ____.
   a. famous Chinese landmark   b. Chinese landmark famous

4. Len is a/an ____.
   a. man young honest   b. honest young man

5. Pizza is my ____.
   a. favorite food Italian   b. favorite Italian food

6. Vincent usually wears ____.
   a. brown old comfortable leather shoes   b. comfortable old brown leather shoes

7. I used a ____ to mail a gift to my sister.
   a. brown cardboard box   b. box brown cardboard

8. Ilya is a ____.
   a. handsome middle-aged man   b. middle-aged handsome man

❏ **Exercise 14. Let's talk: pairwork.** (Charts 14-1 and 14-2)
Work with a partner. Take turns giving a prompt and completing it with a noun.
Note: Don't let your intonation drop when you give the prompt.

Example: a dark . . .
PARTNER A: a dark . . .
PARTNER B: night (room, building, day, cloud, etc.)

1. a kitchen . . .

2. a busy . . .

3. a public . . .

4. a true . . .

5. some expensive . . .

Change roles.

6. a birthday . . .

7. a computer . . .

8. a baby . . .

9. a soft . . .

10. an easy . . .

Change roles.
11. a telephone . . .

12. a fast . . .

13. some comfortable . . .

14. a foreign . . .

15. a famous Italian . . .

Change roles.
16. an interesting old . . .

17. an airplane . . .

18. a dangerous . . .

19. a beautiful Korean . . .

20. some delicious Mexican . . .

Change roles.
21. a government . . .
22. some hot . . .
23. a flower . . .
24. a bright . . .
25. some small round . . .

Change roles.
26. a bus . . .
27. a history . . .
28. an icy cold . . .
29. a hospital . . .
30. a movie . . .

 Exercise 15. Listening. (Charts 14-1 and 14-2)

Listen to each sentence. Choose the best completion(s). There may be more than one answer.

Example: You will hear: We watched an interesting TV . . .
You will choose: a. store. (b.) movie. (c.) show.

1. a. card.   b. cake.   c. party.

2. a. friend.   b. bus.   c. keys.

3. a. jeans.   b. shoes.   c. flowers.

4. a. test.   b. classroom.   c. eraser.

5. a. room.   b. games.   c. desk.

6. a. mail.   b. article.   c. story.

Exercise 16. Game. (Charts 14-1 and 14-2)

Work in teams. Your teacher will put 10–15 objects on a tray. You will have one minute to look at the tray. Then your teacher will take it away. Write down all the objects on the tray. Add adjectives to describe the objects. You will get one point for each object and one point for each adjective you use. The team with the most points wins.

Exercise 17. Warm-up. (Chart 14-3)

Complete the sentences with words from the box. Give your opinion.

good	bad	sweet	sour

1. Lemons are _____.

2. Chocolate tastes _____.

3. Flowers smell _____.

14-3 Linking Verbs + Adjectives

	BE + ADJECTIVE	Adjectives can follow **be**, as in (a). The adjective describes the subject of the sentence. See Chart 1-7, p. 16.
(a)	The flowers **were** **beautiful**.	

	LINKING VERB + ADJECTIVE	Adjectives can follow a few other verbs. These verbs are called "linking verbs." The adjective describes the subject of the sentence. Common linking verbs are *look, smell, feel, taste,* and *sound.*
(b)	The flowers **looked** **beautiful**.	
(c)	The flowers **smelled** **good**.	
(d)	I **feel** **good**.	
(e)	Candy **tastes** **sweet**.	
(f)	That book **sounds** **interesting**.	

❏ **Exercise 18. Let's talk: pairwork.** (Chart 14-3)
Work with a partner. Take turns completing the sentences with linking verbs.

Part I. Make three sentences to tell your partner how you feel today. Begin each sentence with ***I feel . . . .*** Take turns using these words.

1. good	4. lazy	7. terrific	10. calm
2. fine	5. nervous	8. sleepy	11. sick
3. terrible	6. happy	9. tired	12. old

Part II. Take turns naming things that you can taste and smell.

13. taste good	17. taste sour
14. taste terrible	18. smell good
15. taste delicious	19. smell bad
16. taste sweet	20. smell wonderful

Part III. Take turns naming things that are . . .

21. clean.	23. new.	25. expensive.	27. uncomfortable.
22. dirty.	24. old.	26. comfortable.	28. messy.

❏ **Exercise 19. Let's talk.** (Chart 14-3)
Work in groups or as a class. Take turns showing and describing emotions.
  Student A: Choose one of the emotions listed below. Show that emotion with an expression on your face or with actions. Don't say the emotion you are trying to show.
  Student B: Describe how Student A looks. Use the linking verb ***look*** and an adjective.

1. angry	3. happy	5. busy	7. surprised
2. sad/unhappy	4. tired/sleepy	6. comfortable	8. nervous

Exercise 20. Looking at grammar. (Chart 14-3)

Use any possible completions for these sentences. Use the adjectives from the box or your own adjectives.

easy	delicious	terrible / awful
good / terrific / wonderful / great	interesting	tired / sleepy

1. Gabriela told me about a new book. I want to read it. It sounds _____*interesting /*_____

   _____*good / terrific / etc.*_____

2. Karen learned how to make paper flowers. She told me how to do it. It sounds

   _____.

3. There's a new comedy on TV tonight. I read a review of it and would like to watch it.

   It sounds _____.

4. Professor Wilson is going to lecture on Internet security tomorrow evening. I think I'll

   go. It sounds _____.

5. Chris explained how to fix a flat tire. I think I can do it. It sounds _____.

6. Marcia didn't finish her dinner because it didn't taste _____.

7. I put too much salt in the soup. Sorry, it tastes _____.

8. Amy didn't get any sleep last night because she studied all night for a final exam.

   Today she looks _____.

9. Yum! This dessert tastes _____. What is it?

10. A: What's the matter? Do you feel okay?

    B: No. I feel _____. I think I'm getting a cold.

11. A: Do you like my new dress, darling?

    B: You look _____, honey.

12. A: Pyew!* Something smells _____! Do you smell it too?

    B: I sure do. It's the garbage in the alley.

---

* *Pyew* is sometimes said "p.u." Both *Pyew* and *p.u.* mean that something smells very bad.

□ **Exercise 21. Let's talk.** (Chart 14-3)

Work in pairs or small groups. Your teacher will choose a noun and give you a time limit (e.g., one minute, three minutes, etc.). Think of as many adjectives or nouns used as adjectives as you can that describe the given nouns. Make a list. Then your teacher will choose another noun.

Example: car
Response: big, little, fast, slow, comfortable, small, large, old, new, used, noisy, quiet, foreign, electric, antique, police, etc.

1. weather
2. animal
3. food
4. movie
5. country
6. person
7. river
8. student

□ **Exercise 22. Warm-up.** (Chart 14-4)

Complete the sentences with the correct form of the word in red.

Example: Professor Hakim is a slow speaker. Professor Hakim speaks slowly.

Example: Martha is a careful writer. Martha writes carefully.

1. Pierre is a fluent Spanish speaker. He speaks Spanish _____.

2. Suzanne is a quick learner. She learns _____.

14-4 Adjectives and Adverbs

	ADJECTIVE	ADVERB	
(a) Ann is a *careful* driver. (adjective) (b) Ann drives *carefully*. (adverb)	**careful** **slow** **quick** **easy**	**carefully** **slowly** **quickly** **easily**	An ADJECTIVE describes a noun. In (a): *careful* describes *driver*. An ADVERB describes the action of a verb. In (b): *carefully* describes *drives*. Most adverbs are formed by adding *-ly* to an adjective.
(c) John is a *fast* driver. (adjective) (d) John drives *fast*. (adverb)	**fast** **hard** **early** **late**	**fast** **hard** **early** **late**	The adjective form and the adverb form are the same for *fast*, *hard*, *early*, and *late*.
(e) Linda is a *good* writer. (adjective) (f) Linda writes *well*. (adverb)	**good**	**well**	*Well* is the adverb form of *good*.*

* *Well* can also be used as an adjective to mean "not sick." *Paul was sick last week, but now he's well.*

❑ **Exercise 23. Looking at grammar.** (Chart 14-4)
Choose the correct completion.

1. My hometown is small and   quiet / quietly.

2. Mr. Callis whispered. He spoke   quiet / quietly.

3. Anna pronounces every word   careful / carefully.

4. Samuel is a   careful / carefully   writer.

5. We like to go boating in   clear / clearly   weather.

6. Nathan has poor eyesight. He can't see   clear / clearly   without his glasses.

7. Boris makes a lot of mistakes when he writes. He's a   careless / carelessly   writer.

8. Boris writes   careless / carelessly.

9. The teacher asked an   easy / easily   question.

10. I answered the teacher's question   easy / easily.

11. Fernando is kind, generous, and thoughtful. He is a   good / well   person.

12. Diana and I went to high school together. I know her   good / well.

❑ **Exercise 24. Looking at grammar.** (Chart 14-4)
Part I. Write adverb forms.

ADJECTIVE	ADVERB		ADJECTIVE	ADVERB
1. fast	_____		5. beautiful	_____
2. late	_____		6. fluent	_____
3. good	_____		7. hard	_____
4. easy	_____		8. early	_____

Part II. Write the correct adjective or adverb form. Use words from *Part I.*

1. Did you have a _____*good*_____ sleep? Did you sleep _____?

2. The teacher speaks too _____. The students want her to slow down.

3. It rained _____ yesterday.

4. I forgot about my telephone bill. I paid it _____.

5. Do you want to be a _____ speaker of English?

6. Vincent lifted the heavy box _____. He's very strong.

7. Nadia speaks French _____. She has no accent.

8. Thank you! The flowers look _____.

❑ **Exercise 25. Looking at grammar.** (Chart 14-4)
Complete each sentence with the correct form (adjective or adverb) of the given words.

1. careful   Do you drive _____*carefully*_____?

2. correct   Shari gave the _____ answer to the question.

3. correct   She answered the question _____.

4. fast   Justin is a _____ reader.

5. quick   Justin reads _____.

6. fast   Justin reads _____.

7. neat   Barbara has _____ handwriting. It is easy to read what she writes.

8. neat   Barbara writes _____.

9. hard   I study _____.

10. hard   The students took a _____ test.

11. honest   Roberto answered the question _____.

12. slow   Valery and Fumiko walked through the park _____.

13. quick   We were in a hurry, so we ate lunch _____.

14. careless   I made some _____ mistakes in my last composition.

15. early   Last night, we had dinner _____ because we had to
               leave for a meeting at 6:00.

16. early   We had an _____ dinner last night.

17. loud   I speak _____ when I talk to my grandfather
               because he has trouble hearing.

18. slow, clear Nina speaks English _____ and _____.

❑ **Exercise 26. Reading, grammar, and speaking.** (Charts 14-3 and 14-4)
Read the story. Put one line under each adjective. Put two lines under each adverb. Then
answer the questions in small groups.

Elvis Presley

Elvis Presley is very <u>important</u> to <u>popular</u> music. He
has a special title: the King of Rock and Roll. But when he
came on stage in the 1950s, he wasn't popular with many
parents. His style of dancing shocked them. They thought he
jumped around the stage too excitedly and danced wildly. His
music was a combination of country music and rhythm and

Do you know these words?

popular
shock
wild
combination
scream
appear
huge

blues. To many parents, he sang too loudly. They believed his music was bad for children. But audiences loved him and screamed for more. He kept making music, and he appeared on TV and in movies. Soon Elvis was a huge star.

1. Who is a popular singer right now?
2. Describe his/her type of music. Use several adjectives.
3. Why is he/she popular?

❑ **Exercise 27. Warm-up.** (Chart 14-5)
Which statement best describes the picture?

1. Some of the flowers are red.
2. All of the flowers are red.
3. Most of the flowers are red.

14-5 Expressions of Quantity: *All Of, Most Of, Some Of, Almost All Of*

(a) Rita ate **all of** *the food* on her plate. (b) Mike ate **most of** *his food*. (c) Susie ate **some of** *her food*.	**All of**, **most of**, and **some of** express quantities. *all of* = 100% *most of* = a large part but not all *some of* = a small or medium part NOTE: These expressions require a determiner (*the*, *his*, *her*, etc.). INCORRECT: *Most of food*
(d) Matt ate **almost all of** *his food*. INCORRECT: *Matt ate almost of his food*.	*all of* = 100% *almost all of* = close to 100% **Almost** is used with **all**, as in (d). **All** cannot be omitted.

□ **Exercise 28. Looking at grammar.** (Chart 14-5)
Complete each sentence with (*almost*) *all of*, *most of*, or *some of*.

1. 2, 4, 6, 8: _____*All of*_____ these numbers are even.

2. 1, 3, 5, 7: _____ these numbers are odd.

3. 1, 3, 4, 6, 7, 9: _____ these numbers are odd.

4. 1, 3, 4, 6, 7, 8: _____ these numbers are odd.

5. 1, 3, 4, 5, 7, 9: _____ these numbers are odd.

6. _____ the birds in Picture A are flying.

7. _____ the birds in Picture B are flying.

8. _____ the birds in Picture C are flying.

9. _____ the birds in Picture D are flying.

Picture A

Picture B

Picture C

Picture D

10. _____ the students in this class have dark hair.

11. _____ the students in this class are using pens rather than pencils to do this exercise.

12. _____ the students in this class wear glasses.

13. _____ the students in this class can speak English.

□ **Exercise 29. Warm-up.** (Chart 14-6)
Look at the phrases in red. <u>Underline</u> the noun and the quantity word. Decide which word the verb agrees with.

   1. All of the money is in my wallet.

   2. All of the coins are on the kitchen counter.

14-6 Expressions of Quantity: Subject–Verb Agreement

(a) *All of my* **work is** finished. (b) *All of my* **friends are** kind. (c) *Some of my* **homework is** finished. (d) *Some of my* **friends are** coming to my birthday party.	In (a): *all of* + **singular** noun + **singular** verb In (b): *all of* + **plural** noun + **plural** verb In (c): *some of* + **singular** noun + **singular** verb In (d): *some of* + **plural** noun + **plural** verb
	When a subject includes an expression of quantity, the verb agrees with the noun that immediately follows **of**.

COMMON EXPRESSIONS OF QUANTITY

all of	a lot of	most of
almost all of	half of	some of

□ **Exercise 30. Looking at grammar.** (Chart 14-6)
Choose the correct completion.

   1. All of that money _____*is*_____ mine.
                     is/are

   2. All of the windows _____ open.
                        is/are

   3. We saw one movie. Some of the movie _____ interesting.
                                      was/were

   4. We saw five movies. Some of the movies _____ interesting.
                                      was/were

   5. A lot of those words _____ new to me.
                          is/are

   6. A lot of that vocabulary _____ new to me.
                            is/are

7. Half of the glasses _____ empty, and half of the glasses _____ full.
   is/are   is/are

8. Half of the glass _____ empty.
   is/are

Pessimist   Optimist

9. Almost all of the air in the city _____ polluted.
   is/are

10. Almost all of the rivers in this area _____ polluted.
    is/are

11. Most of the students _____ to class on time.
    comes/come

12. Most of our mail _____ in the morning.
    comes/come

❏ **Exercise 31. Listening.** (Charts 14-5 and 14-6)
Listen to each sentence. Circle the percentage that means the same as the quantity you hear.

Example: You will hear: Half of the coffee was gone.
         You will choose: 100% ⟨50%⟩ 10%

1. 100%   80%   10%
2. 100%   30%   0%
3. 90%   100%   10%
4. 10%   20%   70%
5. 25%   50%   85%

❑ **Exercise 32. Let's talk: class activity.** (Charts 14-5 and 14-6)
Your teacher will ask you questions. Answer each question using a complete sentence and an expression of quantity (*all of, most of, some of, a lot of, three of,* etc.). If the answer is zero, use *none of*. Close your book for this activity.

Example:
TEACHER: How many of the people in this room are wearing shoes?
STUDENT A: All of the people in this room are wearing shoes.
TEACHER: How many of us are wearing blue jeans?
STUDENT B: Some of us are wearing blue jeans.

1. How many of the people in this room have (short) hair?
2. How many of the students in this class have red grammar books?
3. How many of us are sitting down?
4. How many of your classmates are from (*name of a country*)?
5. How many of the people in this room can speak Chinese?
6. How many of the women in this room are wearing earrings? How many of the men?
7. What are some of your favorite TV programs?
8. How many of the people in this city are friendly?
9. How many of the married women in your country work outside the home?

❑ **Exercise 33. Looking at grammar.** (Charts 14-5 and 14-6)
Choose the correct sentence in each group.

1. a. Some of furniture is old.
   b. Some of the furniture are old.
   c. Some of the furniture is old.

2. a. Some of the coins are valuable.
   b. Some of coins are valuable.
   c. Some of the coin are valuable.

3. a. All of people look happy.
   b. All of the people looks happy.
   c. All of the people look happy.

4. a. Almost all of the students are absent.
   b. Almost all of students are absent.
   c. Almost all of the students is absent.

5. a. Half of homework is due.
   b. Half of the homework is due.
   c. Half of the homework are due.

6. a. Half of the assignments is due.
   b. Half of assignments are due.
   c. Half of the assignments are due.

7. a. Most of the apartments is empty.
   b. Most of the apartments are empty.
   c. Most of apartments are empty.

❑ **Exercise 34. Warm-up.** (Chart 14-7)
Complete the sentences with words that make sense. Are the verbs (in red) singular or plural?

1. After a rain shower, every street is _____.

2. During a snowstorm, everything looks _____.

3. In the summer, everybody likes _____.

14-7 Using *Every, Everyone, Everybody, Everything*

(a) ***Every student has*** a book.
(b) ***All of the students* have** books.
 	
    INCORRECT: *Every of the students has a book.*
    INCORRECT: *Every students have books.*
	Examples (a) and (b) have essentially the same meaning. Note the following pattern:
	In (a): **every** + **singular** noun + **singular** verb

	Every is not immediately followed by **of**. **Every** is immediately followed by a **singular** noun, as in (a), NOT a plural noun.
(c) ***Everyone has*** a book. (d) ***Everybody has*** a book.	Examples (c) and (d) have the same meaning. ***Everyone*** and ***everybody*** are followed by a **singular** verb. Example (c) is more common in writing. Example (d) is more common in speaking.*
(e) I looked at ***everything*** in the museum. (f) ***Everything is*** okay.	In (e): ***everything*** = each thing In (f): ***Everything*** is followed by a **singular** verb.

* In general, indefinite pronouns with *one* are more common in writing. Indefinite pronouns with *body* are more common in speaking.

❏ **Exercise 35. Looking at grammar.** (Chart 14-7)
Choose the correct completion.

1. All of the _____*books*_____ on this desk _____*are*_____ mine.
                book / books   is / are

2. Every _____ on this desk _____ mine.
               book / books   is / are

3. All of the _____ _____ here today.
                 student / students   is / are

4. Every _____ _____ here today.
               student / students   is / are

5. Every _____ at my college _____ tests regularly.
               teacher / teachers   gives / give

6. All of the _____ at my college _____ a lot of tests.
                  teacher / teachers   gives / give

7. Every _____ in the world _____ bedtime stories.
               child / children   likes / like

8. All of the _____ in the world _____ that story.
                 child / children   knows / know

9. All of the _____ in this class _____ studying English.
  person / people   is / are

10. Everyone in this class _____ to learn English.
                             wants / want

11. _____ all of the _____ in this class speak English well?
   Does / Do   student / students

12. _____ every _____ in the world like to listen to music?
   Does / Do   person / people

13. _____ all of the _____ in the world like to dance?
   Does / Do   person / people

14. Every _____ in Sweden _____ a good transportation system.
        city / cities   has / have

15. _____ everybody in the world have enough to eat?
   Does / Do

❑ **Exercise 36. Warm-up.** (Chart 14-8)
Read the conversation. Can you figure out the answer to the mystery?

A mystery

A: Here's a puzzle. See if you can solve it.

B: Okay.

A: Victor was standing in his kitchen and looking out the window. It was night. He knew that someone was in the house. He knew that somebody was coming up behind him. How did he know?

B: Did he hear anyone?

A: No, he didn't hear anybody.

B: Did he see someone behind him?

A: Well, he never turned around.

B: I know! He smelled someone!

A: No, sorry.

B: Did his dog bark?

A: Victor doesn't have a dog.

B: I have no idea.

14-8 Indefinite Pronouns: *Something, Someone, Somebody, Anything, Anyone, Anybody*

AFFIRMATIVE STATEMENT	(a) Mari bought *something*. (b) Mari saw *someone*. (c) Mari saw *somebody*.	In affirmative sentences, a form of **some** is used: **something**, **someone**, or **somebody**. **Someone** and **somebody** have the same meaning. **Somebody** is more common in speaking.
NEGATIVE STATEMENT	(d) Joe didn't buy *anything*. (e) Joe didn't see *anyone*. (f) Joe didn't see *anybody*.	In negative sentences, a form of **any** is used: **anything**, **anyone**, or **anybody**. **Anyone** and **anybody** have the same meaning. **Anybody** is more common in speaking.

QUESTION	(g) Did Sam buy *something*?
	(h) Did Sam buy *anything*?
	(i) Did Sam see *someone*?
	(j) Did Sam see *anyone*?
	(k) Did Sam see *somebody*?
	(l) Did Sam see *anybody*?
		In questions, a form of **some** or **any** is used:
		    something/anything,
		    someone/anyone, OR
		    somebody/anybody.

❏ **Exercise 37. Looking at grammar.** (Chart 14-8)

Choose the correct completions. Sometimes both answers are correct.

1. A: Who are you going to work with on the project?
   B: I'm not going to work with _____.
      (a.) anyone   (b.) anybody

2. A: What do you need from the store?
   B: I don't need _____.
      a. someone   b. anything

3. A: Did Thomas talk to _____ at the party?
   B: No, he was really quiet.
      a. somebody   b. someone

4. A: Do you have _____ for me?
   B: Yes, you need to sign these papers.
      a. anything   b. anybody

5. A: You dropped _____.
   B: Oh, my keys. Thanks!
      a. anything   b. something

6. A: _____ called, but I don't remember who or why.
   B: You need to write messages down!
        a. Somebody   b. Anyone

7. A: I have _____ for you: a dozen roses.
   B: For me? Why?
   A: It's our anniversary. Did you forget?
        a. something   b. someone

8. A: Listen! Someone's outside.
   B: I don't see _____.
        a. anyone   b. anybody

❏ **Exercise 38. Looking at grammar.** (Chart 14-8)
Complete the sentences. Use *something, someone, somebody, anything*, or *anyone, anybody*.

1. I have _____*something*_____ in my pocket.

2. Do you have _____ in your pocket?

3. Ryan doesn't have _____ in his pocket.

4. I bought _____ when I went shopping yesterday.

5. Bianca didn't buy _____ when she went shopping.

6. Did you buy _____ when you went shopping?

7. My roommate is talking to _____ on the phone.

8. Kyoko didn't tell _____ her secret.

9. I didn't meet _____ last night.

10. I talked to _____ at the electric company about my bill.

11. Did you talk to _____ about your problem?

12. Carla gave me _____ for my birthday.

13. Frank didn't give me _____ for my birthday.

14. Did Frank give you _____ for your birthday?

15. My brother is sitting at his desk. He's writing an email to _____.

16. The hall is empty. I don't see _____.

17. A: Listen. Do you hear a noise?

    B: No, I don't. I don't hear _____.

18. A: Did you talk to Jim on the phone last night?

    B: No. I didn't talk to _____.

19. A: Where's your bike?

    B: _____ stole it.

20. A: What did you do last weekend?

    B: I didn't do _____. I stayed home.

21. A: Does _____ have some change? I don't have enough for the
    vending machine. I want to get _____ to eat.

    B: Here.

    A: Thanks. I'll pay you back later.

a vending machine

❑ **Exercise 39. Looking at grammar.** (Chart 14-8)
Your teacher will ask you questions. Answer in complete sentences. Use *anything*,
anyone, or *anybody*. Close your book for this activity.

1. Close your eyes. Who do you see?

2. Cover your ears. Who do you hear?

3. Close your eyes. What do you see?

4. Cover your ears. What do you hear?

5. You have no money. What are you going to buy at the store?

6. A little boy is holding a candy bar behind his back. His mother asks, "What do you
   have?" He doesn't want to tell the truth. What does he say?

7. A little girl hits her baby sister, and the baby starts crying. Her mother asks, "What
   did you do?" She doesn't want to tell the truth. What does she say?

☐ **Exercise 40. Listening.** (Charts 14-5 → 14-8)

Listen to each sentence and choose *yes* or *no*.

Example: You will hear: Someone is wearing sunglasses.
You will choose: (yes)   no

1. yes	no	3. yes	no	5. yes	no
2. yes	no	4. yes	no	6. yes	no

☐ **Exercise 41. Looking at grammar.** (Chapter 14)

Choose the correct completion.

1. The teacher gave a test paper to every ____ in the class.
   a. student
   b. students
   c. of student
   d. of students

2. Ariana is a ____ woman.
   a. beautiful Mexican young
   b. beautiful young Mexican
   c. Mexican beautiful young
   d. young beautiful Mexican

3. ____ the students in our class have dark hair.
   a. All most of
   b. Almost of
   c. Almost
   d. Almost all of

4. I had some ____ soup for lunch.
   a. vegetable good
   b. good vegetables
   c. good vegetable
   d. vegetables good

5. The flowers ____.
   a. looked beautiful
   b. looked beautifully
   c. beautiful look
   d. beautifully look

6. ____ have jobs after school.
   a. A lots of students
   b. A lot students
   c. A lot of students
   d. A lot student

7. I didn't talk to ____.
   a. something
   b. anyone
   c. anything
   d. somebody

❑ **Exercise 42. Let's talk.** (Chapter 14)

Work in pairs or small groups. Read the facts about eight friends.

Facts:

- Jack, Jim, Jake, John, Jill, Julie, Joan, and Jan are all friends.
- Two of them are secretly engaged.
- They met five months ago.
- They are going to get married next year.

Who is engaged? Read the clues to find out. (Be careful! Some of the clues are only additional information. They will not help you find the answer.)

Fill in the chart as you work through the clues to solve the puzzle.

Engaged	Jack	Jim	Jake	John	Jill	Julie	Joan	Jan
yes								
no						X		

Clues:

1. For Julie's wedding next month, she is going to wear her mother's long white wedding dress. Her mother wore it 30 years ago.

   → *Julie's wedding is next month. The engaged couple is getting married next year, so it's not Julie.*

2. Joan's husband is working in another city right now. They hope to see each other soon.

3. Jill and Jack love each other. They met at Jill's sister's wedding.

4. Jill's sister got married a year ago.

5. Jim is the only computer science student in the group.

6. Joan is a computer science teacher. She began teaching two years ago.

7. Jan's boyfriend is a medical student.

8. All of the friends think Julie is very funny.

9. John loves Jan, but she doesn't love him. He's a friend to her, not a boyfriend.

❑ **Exercise 43. Check your knowledge.** (Chapter 14)

Correct the mistakes.

          wants   *happy*
1. Everybody ~~want~~ to be ~~happily~~.

2. I didn't see nobody at the mall.

3. At the library, you need to do your work quiet.

4. I walk in the park every days.

5. Mr. Spencer teaches English very good.

6. The answer looks clearly. Thank you for explaining it.

7. Every grammar test have a lot of difficult questions.

8. I work hard every days.

9. We saw a pretty flowers garden in the park.

10. Galina drives a blue small car.

11. Every of students in the class have a grammar book.

12. The work will take a long time. We can't finish every things today.

13. Everybody in the world want peace.

□ **Exercise 44. Reading and writing.** (Chapter 14)
Part I. Read the passage.

Ways to Create Happiness

Can money buy happiness? Some psychologists try to answer this question. They do "happiness research." One answer they found is that we can create happiness with memories. We can "buy" memories, and we don't need to spend a lot of money. They believe that simple things in life can create a lot of wonderful memories. Here are some suggestions they give.

- Take someone in your family to a sports event, such as a soccer match or a baseball game.
- Go camping with family or friends.
- Celebrate something important like graduation.
- Have a meal at a restaurant with family and friends.

It's also important to do something to save these special memories. One way is with photos, postcards, or souvenirs. When you see these items later, they will remind you of the fun times you had.

Part II. Write one or more paragraphs about a way you can create special memories with someone. Answer these questions in your paragraph(s). (See the writing sample on the next page.)

1. Who is the person (or people)?

2. What do you like to do together and why?

3. How do you remember your time with this person?

Two Simple Ways I Create Special Memories

I like to spend time with my parents. They are elderly, and they don't drive anymore. We do a few simple things together.

I sometimes go with them for walks. They live in the city, and we like to take walks in the park. I tell them about my week and my plans. They like to hear about my life. We walk for about an hour and enjoy the easy exercise.

I also like to have meals with my parents. Sometimes we go out to a local restaurant. Other times I bring them food from a favorite restaurant or deli.* I buy a nice lunch or dinner, and we eat it at their apartment. Sometimes there is a sports show on TV. We talk about the show while we are eating our meal. We have good memories of our time together.

Part III. Editing check: Work individually or change papers with a partner. Check (✓) for the following:

1. _____ indented paragraph

2. _____ capital letter at the beginning of each sentence

3. _____ period at the end of each sentence

4. _____ use of adjectives and adverbs

5. _____ correct word order for adjectives and adverbs

6. _____ correct spelling (use a dictionary or computer spell-check)

---

*deli = delicatessen: a store that sells meats and cheeses, and also makes sandwiches, salads, and soups

Chapter 15
Making Comparisons

❑ **Exercise 1. Warm-up.** (Chart 15-1)
Check (✓) the true sentences.

1. _____ Josh is taller than Lisa.

2. _____ Lisa is taller than Josh.

3. _____ Josh is older than Lisa.

Lisa   Josh

15-1 The Comparative: Using *-er* and *More*

Mary is 25 years old.
John is 20 years old.

(a) Mary is *older than* John.
(b) Health is *more important than* money.

INCORRECT: Mary is more old than John.
INCORRECT: Health is importanter than money.

When we use adjectives (e.g., *old, important*) to compare two people or two things, the adjectives have special forms.
In (a): We add *-er* to an adjective, OR
In (b): We use *more* in front of an adjective.
The use of *-er* or *more* is called the COMPARATIVE FORM.

Notice in the examples: *than* follows the comparative form (*older than, more important than*).

	ADJECTIVE	COMPARATIVE	
ADJECTIVES WITH ONE SYLLABLE	**big** **cheap** **old**	**bigger** **cheaper** **older**	Add *-er* to one-syllable adjectives.
			Spelling note: If an adjective ends in one vowel and one consonant, double the consonant: *big–bigger, fat–fatter, hot–hotter, thin–thinner.*
ADJECTIVES THAT END IN -Y	**funny** **pretty**	**funnier** **prettier**	If an adjective ends in *-y*, change the *-y* to *-i* and add *-er.*
ADJECTIVES WITH TWO OR MORE SYLLABLES	**famous** **important** **interesting**	**more famous** **more important** **more interesting**	Use *more* in front of adjectives that have two or more syllables (except adjectives that end in *-y*).
IRREGULAR COMPARATIVE FORMS	**good** **bad** **far**	**better** **worse** **farther/further**	The comparative forms of *good, bad,* and *far* are irregular.

❏ **Exercise 2. Looking at grammar.** (Chart 15-1)

Write the comparative form for these adjectives.

1. old _____ *older than* _____

2. small _____

3. big _____

4. important _____

5. easy _____

6. difficult _____

7. long _____

8. heavy _____

9. expensive _____

10. sweet _____

11. hot _____

12. good _____

13. bad _____

14. far _____

❏ **Exercise 3. Looking at grammar.** (Chart 15-1)

Complete the sentences. Use the comparative form of the given words.

1. comfortable   A mattress is _____ *more comfortable than* _____ a floor.

2. deep   The Pacific Ocean is _____ the Mediterranean Sea.

3. important   Love is _____ money.

4. lazy   I'm _____ my roommate.

5. tall   My brother is _____ I am.*

6. heavy   Iron is _____ wood.

_____

*Formal written English: *My brother is taller than I (am).*
Informal spoken English: *My brother is taller than me.*

7. difficult   My physics course is _____

my math course.

8. hot   Thailand is a _____ country _____ Korea.

9. thin   A giraffe's neck is _____ an elephant's neck.

10. warm   It's _____ today _____ yesterday.

11. good   Natasha's English is _____ her husband's.

12. long   The Nile River is _____ the Mississippi.

13. intelligent   A dog is _____ a chicken.

14. short   My little finger is _____ my middle finger.

15. bad   The weather yesterday was _____ it is today.

16. far   Your apartment is _____ from school

_____ mine.

17. strong   A horse is _____ a person.

18. curly   Jake's hair is _____ mine.

19. nervous   The groom was _____ at the wedding

_____ the bride.

20. happy   The bride looked _____ the groom.

21. uncomfortable   The groom looked _____

the bride.

❏ **Exercise 4. Let's talk: pairwork.** (Chart 15-1)
Work with a partner. Use the adjective in parentheses to compare each pair of items. Use *more* or *-er*.

Example: a mouse, an elephant (small)
→ A mouse is smaller than an elephant.

PARTNER A	PARTNER B
1. a bus, car (big)	1. this book, that one (good)
2. my old shoes, my new shoes (comfortable)	2. my hair, her hair (curly)
3. your hair, my hair (dark)	3. her hair, his hair (straight)
4. my arm, your arm (long)	4. the weather here, the weather in my hometown (bad)
5. biology, chemistry (interesting)	5. this chapter, Chapter 10 (easy)
6. I, my friend (happy)	6. Japanese grammar, English grammar (difficult)

❏ **Exercise 5. Let's talk: class activity.** (Chart 15-1)
Your teacher will put several different books in a central place. Compare one to another using the given adjectives.

Example: big
Response: This book is bigger than that book/that one.

1. large	5. difficult	9. expensive
2. interesting	6. easy	10. cheap
3. small	7. good	11. thick
4. heavy	8. bad	12. important

❏ **Exercise 6. Listening.** (Chart 15-1)
Listen to each sentence. Choose the adjective you hear.

Example: You will hear: Sky Airlines is cheaper than World Airlines.
You will choose: cheap   (cheaper)

1. cold	colder		7. safe	safer	
2. cold	colder		8. safe	safer	
3. cold	colder		9. safe	safer	
4. happy	happier		10. fresh	fresher	
5. happy	happier		11. funny	funnier	
6. happy	happier		12. funny	funnier	

❏ **Exercise 7. Looking at grammar.** (Chart 15-1)
Complete the sentences. Use the comparative form of the words from the box or your own words.

big	cold	expensive	hot	large
bright	comfortable	fast	important	sweet
cheap	easy	high	intelligent	warm

1. A bear is ___*bigger than / larger than*___ a mouse.

2. A lemon is sour. An orange is _____ a lemon.

3. The weather today is _____ it was yesterday.

4. When Mrs. Vallero's feet hurt, she wears tennis shoes. Tennis shoes are

_____ high heels.

a tennis shoe

a high heel

5. I can afford a radio but not a TV. A radio is _____

_____ a TV.

6. An airplane moves quickly. An airplane is _____ a car.

7. A person can think logically. A person is _____

an animal.

8. Hills are low. Mountains are _____ hills.

9. The sun gives off a lot of light. The sun is _____ the moon.

10. A motorcycle costs a lot of money. A motorcycle is _____

_____ a bike.

11. Arithmetic isn't difficult. Arithmetic is _____ algebra.

12. Good health is _____ money.

❑ **Exercise 8. Let's talk.** (Chart 15-1)
Work in pairs, in groups, or as a class. Make comparisons.

Example: feathers to rocks
→ *Feathers are lighter than rocks.* OR
Rocks are heavier than feathers.

1. an orange to a lemon
2. a lake to an ocean
3. good health to money
4. an airplane to a car
5. a person to an animal
6. the sun to the moon
7. dust to sand
8. arithmetic to algebra
9. bedroom slippers to high heels
10. a giraffe to a person
11. your little finger to your ring finger
12. your ring finger to your thumb
13. love to money
14. a picture from a camera and a picture from a smartphone
15. emailing to texting
16. the weather today to the weather yesterday

❑ **Exercise 9. Let's talk: small groups.** (Chart 15-1)
Work in small groups. Agree or disagree with the statements. Discuss your answers.

In general,

1. women are stronger than men (physically).	yes	no
2. women are stronger than men (emotionally).	yes	no
3. girls are better students than boys.	yes	no
4. strict parents raise better children than lenient* parents.	yes	no
5. relaxed teachers are better than serious teachers.	yes	no
6. cats make better pets than dogs.	yes	no
7. understanding English is harder than speaking it.	yes	no
8. writing English is easier than reading it.	yes	no

---

lenient = not strict; not so many rules

❑ **Exercise 10. Let's talk: pairwork.** (Chart 15-1)
Work in pairs. Make comparisons.
    Partner A: Ask your partner a question. Your book is open.
    Partner B: Answer in a complete sentence. Your book is closed.

Example: Name something that is sweeter than an apple.
PARTNER A: What's sweeter than an apple?
PARTNER B: Candy is sweeter than an apple.

1. Name a country that is larger than Mexico.
2. Name a planet that is closer to the sun than the Earth.
3. Name someone who is younger than I am or you are.
4. Name an animal that is more dangerous than a wild dog.
5. Name a bird that is larger than a chicken.
6. Name something that is more expensive than a Mercedes car.
7. Name a sport that is more popular internationally than baseball.
8. Name someone who is more famous than me.

Change roles.
9. Name someone who is taller than you.
10. Name something that is more interesting than basic arithmetic.
11. Name an ocean that is smaller than the Pacific Ocean.
12. Name a place that is farther away from school than your home is.
13. Name an animal that is stronger than a sheep.
14. Name a sport that, in your opinion, is more exciting than golf.
15. Name a place that is colder than this city.
16. Name a place that is more beautiful than this city.

❑ **Exercise 11. Warm-up.** (Chart 15-2)
Which statements do you agree with?

1. Rome is the prettiest city in the world.	yes	no
2. Tokyo is the most expensive city in the world.	yes	no
3. New York is the most exciting city in the world.	yes	no

15-2 The Superlative: Using -est and Most

(a)	COMPARATIVE	The comparative (**-er/more**) compares two things or people.
	My thumb is **shorter than** my index finger.	
(b)	SUPERLATIVE	The superlative (**-est/most**) compares three or more things or people.
	My hand has five fingers. My thumb is **the shortest** (finger) of all.	

	ADJECTIVE	COMPARATIVE	SUPERLATIVE
ADJECTIVES WITH ONE SYLLABLE	**old** **big***	**older** (than) **bigger** (than)	**the oldest** (of all) **the biggest** (of all)
ADJECTIVES THAT END IN -Y	**pretty** **easy**	**prettier** (than) **easier** (than)	**the prettiest** (of all) **the easiest** (of all)
ADJECTIVES WITH TWO OR MORE SYLLABLES	**expensive** **important**	**more expensive** (than) **more important** (than)	**the most expensive** (of all) **the most important** (of all)
IRREGULAR FORMS	**good** **bad** **far**	**better** (than) **worse** (than) **farther/further** (than)	**the best** (of all) **the worst** (of all) **the farthest/furthest** (of all)

* Spelling note: If an adjective ends in one vowel and one consonant, double the consonant to form the superlative: *big-biggest, fat-fattest, hot-hottest, thin-thinnest.*

❑ **Exercise 12. Looking at grammar.** (Charts 15-1 and 15-2)
Write the comparative and superlative forms of the given adjectives.

	COMPARATIVE	SUPERLATIVE
1. long	*longer than*	*the longest*
2. small		
3. heavy		
4. comfortable		
5. hard		
6. difficult		
7. easy		
8. good		
9. hot		
10. cheap		

11. interesting _____ _____

12. pretty _____ _____

13. far _____ _____

14. strong _____ _____

15. bad _____ _____

❏ **Exercise 13. Looking at grammar.** (Charts 15-1 and 15-2)
Complete the sentences. Use the comparative or superlative form of the given adjectives.

1. large   _____*The largest*_____ city in Canada is Toronto.

2. long   The Nile is _____ river in the world.

3. interesting   I'm taking four classes. My history class is _____

    _____ of all.

4. high   Mt. McKinley in Alaska is _____ mountain in
   North America.

5. tall   The Sears Tower is _____ building in Chicago.

6. big   Lake Superior is _____ lake in North America.

7. short   February is _____ month of the year.

8. fast   The _____ way to travel is by airplane.

9. far   Neptune is _____ planet from the sun.

10. beautiful   In my opinion, Montreal and Vancouver are _____

    _____ cities in Canada.

11. famous   The Gateway Arch is _____
   landmark in St. Louis, Missouri.

12. good   In my opinion, Café Fresh has _____ food in the city.

13. large   Asia is _____ continent in the world.

14. comfortable   Theo is sitting in _____ chair in the room.

15. good   When you feel sad, laughter is _____ medicine.

16. small   Australia is _____ continent in the world.

17. expensive   Gina ordered _____ food on the menu for dinner last night.

18. easy   Taking a taxi is _____ way to get to the airport.

19. important   I think good health is _____ thing in life.

20. bad   In my opinion, Harry's Steak House is _____ restaurant in the city.

❏ **Exercise 14. Listening.** (Charts 15-1 and 15-2)

 Look at the people in the picture and listen to each sentence. Choose the correct answer.

Example: You will hear: Selena is the youngest.
       You will choose: yes (no)

Selena
(18 years old)

Alberto
(60 years old)

Rudy
(15 years old)

1. yes	no	6. yes	no
2. yes	no	7. yes	no
3. yes	no	8. yes	no
4. yes	no	9. yes	no
5. yes	no	10. yes	no

❑ **Exercise 15. Looking at grammar.** (Charts 15-1 and 15-2)

Work in small groups or as a class. Make comparisons about each group of pictures.

A. COMPARE THE SIZES OF THE THREE BALLS.

1. The golf ball is _____*smaller than*_____ the baseball.

2. The soccer ball is _____*larger than*_____ the baseball.

3. The soccer ball is _____*the largest*_____ of all.

B. COMPARE THE AGES OF THE THREE CHILDREN.

Tommy	Lin	Emma
(1 year old)	(6 years old)	(8 years old)

4. Emma is _____ Lin.

5. Lin is _____ Tommy.

6. Tommy is _____ Lin and Emma.

7. Emma is _____ of all.

C. COMPARE THE HEIGHTS OF THE THREE WOMEN.

Sachi   Karen   Alice

8. _____ is the tallest.

9. _____ is the shortest.

10. _____ is taller than _____ but shorter than

_____.

D. COMPARE THE STRENGTH OF THE THREE MEN.

Brad   Keith   Lars

11. _____

12. _____

13. _____

14. _____

E. COMPARE THE PRICES OF THE THREE VEHICLES.

15. _____

16. _____

17. _____

18. _____

F. COMPARE THE GRADES OF THE THREE TEST PAPERS.

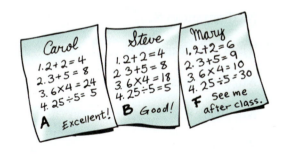

19. _____

20. _____

21. _____

22. _____

G. COMPARE HOW INTERESTING (TO YOU) THE THREE BOOKS LOOK.

23. _____

24. _____

25. _____

26. _____

❏ **Exercise 16. Looking at grammar.** (Charts 15-1 and 15-2)
Complete the sentences. Use the correct form (comparative or superlative) of the given adjectives.

1. long   The Yangtze River is _____ the Mississippi River.

2. long   The Nile is _____ river in the world.

3. large   The Caribbean Sea is _____ the
               Mediterranean Sea.

4. large   The Caribbean Sea is _____ sea in the world.

5. high   Mt. Everest is _____ mountain in the world.

6. high   Mt. Everest is _____ Mt. McKinley.

7. big   Africa is _____ North America.

8. small   Europe is _____ South America.

9. large   Asia is _____ continent in the world.

10. big   Canada is _____ the United States in area.

11. large   Indonesia is _____ Japan in population.

12. good   Fruit is _____ for your health _____ candy.

13. good   The student cafeteria has _____ roast beef
               sandwiches in the city.

14. comfortable   I have a pair of boots, a pair of sandals, and a pair of running shoes.

The sandals are _____

the boots, but the running shoes are _____

_____ of all.

15. easy   This exercise is _____ the next one.

16. bad   A: Which is _____: a backache or a toothache?

B: I think a toothache is much _____

a backache.

❏ **Exercise 17. Listening.** (Charts 15-1 and 15-2)

Listen to the sentences about shopping in a clothing store. Write the words you hear.

1. The blue dress ____*is more expensive than*____ the red one.

2. Well, I think the red one looks _____.

3. Is it too _____, or does it look okay?

4. It's _____ of all the dresses you tried on.

5. I'm not going to buy the brown shoes. They're too _____.

6. This hat is too small. I need a _____ size.

7. Here, this is _____ size they have.

8. I need a belt, but that one is _____ my old one.

9. Is this belt _____ enough?

10. It's perfect. And it's _____ of all of them.

❏ **Exercise 18. Warm-up.** (Chart 15-3)

Complete the sentences with your own words.

1. One of my favorite foods is _____.

2. One of the best movies in theaters right now is _____.

3. One of the hardest classes for me is _____.

4. One of the most interesting cities to visit is _____.

15-3 Using *One Of* + Superlative + Plural Noun

(a) The Amazon is **one of the longest rivers** in the world.
 	
   INCORRECT: *The Amazon is one of the longest river
        in the world.*
 	
   INCORRECT: *The Amazon is one of longest rivers
        in the world.*
 	
(b) A Rolls Royce is **one of the most expensive cars**
    in the world.
 	
(c) Alice is **one of the most intelligent people** in our class.
	The superlative often follows **one of**.
	Notice the pattern:
	   one of + superlative + plural noun

❑ **Exercise 19. Looking at grammar.** (Chart 15-3)
Use the given phrases to make sentences. Use **one of** + *superlative* + *plural noun.*

1. a high mountain in the world
   → *Mt. McKinley is one of the highest mountains in the world.*

2. a pretty park in (*the world*)
   → *Monsanto Forest Park in Lisbon is one of the prettiest parks in the world.*

3. a tall person in our class
   → *Talal is one of the tallest people* in our class.*

4. a big city in the world

5. a beautiful place in the world

6. a long river in the world

7. a good restaurant in (*this city*)

8. a famous landmark in the world

9. an important event in the history of the world

❑ **Exercise 20. Let's talk: class interview.** (Chart 15-3)
Walk around the room. Ask and answer questions using **one of** + *superlative* + *plural noun.*
Ask two students each question. Write their first names and their answers. Then ask two
different students the next question. Share some of their answers with the class.

Example: a big city in Canada
QUESTION: What is one of the biggest cities in Canada?
STUDENT A: Toronto is one of the biggest cities in Canada.
STUDENT B: Vancouver is one of the biggest cities in Canada.

---

* *People* is usually used instead of *persons* in the plural.

	NAME	ANSWER	NAME	ANSWER
1. a big city in Asia				
2. a large state in the United States				
3. a beautiful city in the world				
4. a tall person in our class				
5. a good place to visit in the world				
6. a famous person in the world				
7. an important thing in life				
8. a bad restaurant in (*this city*)				
9. a famous landmark in (*name of a country*)				
10. a tall building in (*name of a city*)				
11. a dangerous sport in the world				
12. a serious problem in the world				

Work in small groups or as a class. Answer these questions.

1. How many brothers and sisters do you have? Are you the oldest?
2. Who is one of the most famous movie stars in the world?
3. In your opinion, what is the scariest animal in the world?
4. In your opinion, what is one of the most frightening natural events (earthquake, cyclone, volcano, tsunami, etc.)?
5. What is one of the most important inventions in the modern world?
6. What is one of the worst experiences of your life?
7. What are the best things in life?
8. What was the happiest day of your life — or one of the happiest days of your life?
9. Who are the most important people in your life today?

❏ **Exercise 22. Let's talk: small groups.** (Charts 15-1 → 15-3)

First, take the entire quiz by yourself. Circle the letters of the correct answers. If you don't know an answer, guess. Second, form small groups to discuss your answers. You can figure out the correct answers by looking at the *Table of Statistics* on p. 465.

Part I.

1. What is the longest river in the world?
    a. the Yangtze
    b. the Amazon
    c. the Nile
    d. the Mississippi

2. Is the Amazon River longer than the Mississippi River?
    a. yes
    b. no

3. Is the Yangtze River longer than the Mississippi River?
    a. yes
    b. no

4. Which two rivers are almost the same length?
    a. the Nile and the Amazon
    b. the Amazon and the Yangtze
    c. the Nile and the Mississippi
    d. the Mississippi and the Amazon

Part II.

5. What is the largest sea in the world?

    a. the Mediterranean Sea

    b. the South China Sea

    c. the Caribbean Sea

6. Is the South China Sea the smallest of the three seas listed above?

    a. yes

    b. no

Part III.

7. What is the deepest ocean in the world?

    a. the Atlantic Ocean

    b. the Indian Ocean

    c. the Pacific Ocean

8. Is the Indian Ocean larger than the Atlantic Ocean?

    a. yes

    b. no

Part IV.

9. Below is a list of the continents in the world. List them in order according to size, from the largest to the smallest.

> Africa
> ✓ Antarctica
> Asia
> Australia
> Europe
> North America
> South America

    (1) _____ (the largest)

    (2) _____

    (3) _____

    (4) ____*Antarctica*_____

    (5) _____

    (6) _____

    (7) _____ (the smallest)

Part V.

10. Which of the following cities has the largest population in the world?
    a. New York City, U.S.A.
    b. Seoul, South Korea
    c. Tokyo, Japan
    d. Mexico City, Mexico

11. Is the population of Sao Paulo, Brazil, larger than the population of New York City, U.S.A.?
    a. yes
    b. no

12. Is the population of Sao Paulo, Brazil, larger than the population of Seoul, South Korea?
    a. yes
    b. no

13. What is the largest city in North America?
    a. Mexico City
    b. New York City

Part VI.

14. Which of the following countries has the largest area in the world?
    a. Canada
    b. China
    c. the United States
    d. Brazil

15. Which of the following two countries is larger in area?
    a. Canada
    b. Brazil

16. Which of the following countries has the largest population in the world?
    a. India
    b. Indonesia
    c. the United States
    d. China

17. Which of the following two countries has the larger population?
    a. India
    b. Indonesia

18. Which of the following two countries has the larger population?
    a. the United States
    b. Brazil

19. Which of the following two countries has the smaller population?
    a. Egypt
    b. Japan

TABLE OF STATISTICS

PART I.

RIVER	LENGTH
the Amazon River	4,000 miles
the Mississippi River	2,350 miles
the Nile River	4,160 miles
the Yangtze River	3,900 miles

PART II.

SEA	SIZE
the Caribbean Sea	970,000 square miles
the Mediterranean Sea	969,000 square miles
the South China Sea	895,000 square miles

PART III.

OCEAN	SIZE	AVERAGE DEPTH
Atlantic Ocean	31,820,000 square miles	12,100 feet
Indian Ocean	29,000,000 square miles	12,750 feet
Pacific Ocean	64,000,000 square miles	13,000 feet

PART IV.

CONTINENT	SIZE
Africa	12,000,000 square miles
Antarctica	7,000,000 square miles
Asia	17,129,000 square miles
Australia	3,000,000 square miles
Europe	3,837,000 square miles
North America	9,355,000 square miles
South America	6,886,000 square miles

PART V.

CITY	POPULATION*
Mexico City, Mexico	20 million
New York, U.S.A.	21 million
Sao Paulo, Brazil	20 million
Seoul, South Korea	23 million
Tokyo, Japan	37 million

PART VI.

COUNTRY	AREA	POPULATION
Brazil	3,265,059 sq mi	206 million
Canada	3,612,187 sq mi	34 million
China	3,600,927 sq mi	1,343 million*
Egypt	384,000 sq mi	84 million
India	1,147,949 sq mi	1,205 million
Indonesia	767,777 sq mi	248 million
Japan	146,000 sq mi	127 million
the United States	3,539,224 sq mi	314 million

*Approximate population; *1,343 million* is said as "one billion, three hundred forty-three million."

Read the story and <u>underline</u> the comparisons. Then answer the question. Give several reasons for your answer. Look at new vocabulary with your teacher first.

a basic phone

a smart phone

Which Phone?

Jon needs to buy a cell phone. He is trying to decide if he should get a basic phone or a smart phone. His teenage children want him to get a smart phone. They say it is <u>more useful than</u> a basic phone.

> **Do you know these words?**
>
> social media
> Wi-Fi access
> surf the Internet
> eyesight
> QWERTY keyboard
> cool-looking

With a smart phone, Jon can use the Internet to get news and weather, play games, use social media, shop, etc. With a basic phone, Jon can just send voice and text messages and take pictures.

Jon sometimes travels. Right now he uses the Internet on his computer when he has Wi-Fi access. With a smart phone, Jon can always get on the Internet. But he doesn't really like to surf the Internet on a phone screen because his eyesight isn't very good.

John wants to be able to send text messages to his wife and kids. Texting on a smart phone is easier than on a basic phone because a smart phone has a QWERTY keyboard.

Jon doesn't like to spend money. A basic phone is cheaper than a smart phone. Also, the service plan for a basic phone is cheaper.

Jon's kids keep telling him a smart phone is more convenient and modern. They say one of the best things about a smart phone is that it is "cool-looking." Jon doesn't care about that, but in general, he likes to make his children happy.

QUESTION: Which type of phone do you think Jon should buy and why?

❏ **Exercise 24. Warm-up.** (Chart 15-4)

Answer the questions.

1. Who speaks English more fluently: you or your teacher?
2. Who speaks your language more slowly: you or someone in your family?
3. Who gets to school earlier: you or a classmate?

15-4 Making Comparisons with Adverbs

	COMPARATIVE	SUPERLATIVE	
(a) Kim speaks *more fluently than* Ali (does). (b) Anna speaks *the most fluently of all*.	**more fluently** **more slowly** **more quickly**	**the most fluently** **the most slowly** **the most quickly**	Use **more** and **most** with adverbs that end in **-ly**.*
(c) Mike worked *harder than* Sam (did). (d) Sue worked *the hardest of all*.	**harder** **faster** **earlier** **later**	**the hardest** **the fastest** **the earliest** **the latest**	Use **-er** and **-est** with irregular adverbs: *hard, fast, early, late.*
(e) Rosa writes *better than* I do. (f) Kim writes *the best of all*.	**better**	**the best**	**Better** and **best** are forms of the adverb *well.*

*Exception: *early–earlier–the earliest*

❏ **Exercise 25. Looking at grammar.** (Chart 15-4)
Complete the sentences with the correct form (comparative or superlative) of the given adverbs.

1. late   Diana got home ___*later than*___ Claire (did).

2. quickly   I finished my work _____ Jamal (did).

3. beautifully   Zara sings _____ Lila (does).

4. beautifully   Arianna sings _____ of all.

5. hard   My sister works _____ I (do).

6. hard   My brother works _____ of all.

7. carefully   My husband drives _____ I (do).

8. early   We arrived at the party _____ the Smiths (did).

9. early   The Wilsons arrived at the party _____ of all.

10. well   You can write _____ I (can).

11. well   Pavel can write _____ of all.

12. clearly   Larisa pronounces her words _____

               Katerina (does).

13. fluently   Ava speaks Spanish _____ I (do).

14. fluently   Ian speaks Spanish _____ of all.

❏ **Exercise 26. Looking at grammar.** (Chart 15-1 → 15-4)
Use the correct form (adjective or adverb, comparative or superlative) of the given words.

1. careful   Molly drives _____*more carefully than her*_____ brother does.

2. beautiful   A tiger is _____ a goat.

3. neat   Yukio's apartment is _____ mine.

4. neat   Henry's apartment is _____ of all.

5. neat   You write _____ I do.

6. neat   Lauren writes _____ of all.

7. clear   This author explains her ideas _____ that author.

8. good   I like rock music _____ classical music.

9. good   My husband can sing _____ I can.

10. good   My daughter can sing _____ of all.

11. late   David usually goes to bed _____ his roommate.

12. clear   Helen pronounces her words _____

    of all the students in the class.

13. sharp   A razor is usually _____ a kitchen knife.

14. artistic   My son is _____ my daughter.

15. slow   I eat _____ my husband does.

16. long   Serena has the _____ hair of all the kids in her class.

❏ **Exercise 27. Listening.** (Charts 15-1 → 15-4)
Listen to each sentence. Write the words you hear.

1. I work _____*faster than*_____ Alec does.

2. Toshi finished his work _____ of all.

3. Mimi studies _____ Fred.

4. Jean studies _____ of all.

5. Is a motorcycle _____ a bike?

6. Kalil speaks _____ Haruko does.

7. A turtle moves _____ a cat does.

8. This suitcase is _____ that one.

9. My glasses are _____ my contact lenses.

10. I can see _____ with my glasses.

❑ **Exercise 28. Warm-up.** (Chart 15-5)
Agree or disagree with these statements about sports.

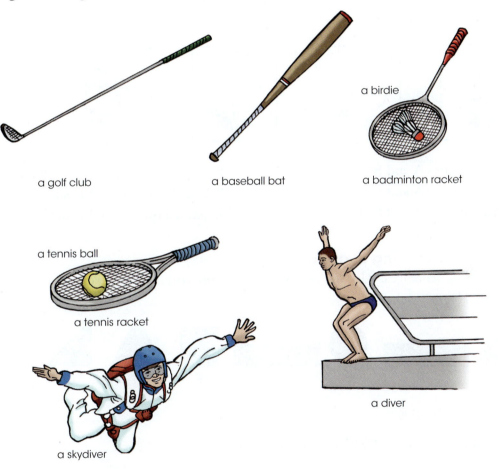

a golf club

a baseball bat

a birdie

a badminton racket

a tennis ball

a tennis racket

a skydiver

a diver

1. Golf is similar to baseball.	yes	no
2. Badminton and tennis are the same.	yes	no
3. Diving is very different from skydiving.	yes	no

15-5 Comparisons: Using *The Same (As)*, *Similar (To)*, and *Different (From)*

THE SAME (AS)	SIMILAR (TO)	DIFFERENT (FROM)
 A B	 C D	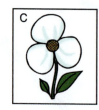  E F
A and B are *the same*. A is *the same as* B.	C and D are *similar*. C is *similar to* D.	E and F are *different*. E is *different from* F.

❏ **Exercise 29. Let's talk: class activity.** (Chart 15-5)
Answer the questions.

1. Are Pictures A and B the same?
2. Are Pictures A and C the same?
3. Are Pictures A and C similar?

4. Are Pictures A and C different?
5. Are Pictures C and D similar?
6. Are Pictures C and D different?

❏ **Exercise 30. Looking at grammar.** (Chart 15-5)
Complete the sentences. Use *the same* (*as*), *similar* (*to*), and *different* (*from*) in your completions.

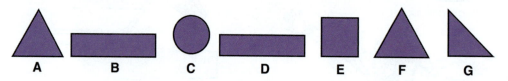

1. A _____ *is the same as* _____ F.

2. D and E _____ *are similar** OR *are different* _____.

3. C _____ D.

---
*Similar gives the idea that two things are the same in some ways (e.g., both D and E have four edges) but different in other ways (e.g., D is a rectangle, and E is a square).

4. B _____ D.

5. B and D _____ .

6. C and D _____ .

7. A and F _____ .

8. F and G _____ .

9. F _____ G.

10. G _____ A and F but _____ C.

❏ **Exercise 31. Listening.** (Chart 15-5)

 Listen to the comparisons of Pictures A through G in Exercise 30. Are these comparisons correct?

Example: You will hear: A and F are the same.
You will choose: (yes)   no

1. yes	no		4. yes	no		6. yes	no
2. yes	no		5. yes	no		7. yes	no
3. yes	no						

❏ **Exercise 32. Let's talk: class activity.** (Chart 15-5)

Answer the questions.

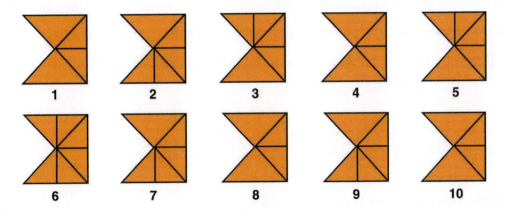

1. Which figures have the same design?

2. Is there at least one figure that is different from all the rest?

Just for fun:

3. How many triangles are there in figure 1? (*Answer: Seven.*)

4. How many triangles are there in figure 2?

5. How many triangles are there in figure 6?

Your teacher will ask you questions. Practice using *the same* (*as*), *similar* (*to*), and *different* (*from*). Close your book for this activity.

Example: Look at (. . .)'s clothes and (. . .)'s clothes. What is different about them?
Response: Their shoes are different. (. . .) is wearing running shoes, and (. . .) is wearing sandals.

1. Look around the room. Name things that are the same.

2. Look around the room. Name things that are similar but not the same.

3. Find two pens that are the same length. Find two pieces of paper that are the same size. Find two notebooks that are different sizes.

4. Find two people in the class who are wearing (earrings). Are their (earrings) the same, similar, or different?

5. Who in the class has a (notebook, briefcase, backpack) that is similar to yours? Does anyone have a (notebook, briefcase, backpack) that is the same as yours?

6. Do any of the people in this room have the same hairstyle? Name two people who have similar hairstyles.

7. Whose shirt is the same color as yours today? Name some things in this room that are the same color. Name things that are similar colors.

8. Do any of the people in this room come from the same country? Who? Name two people who come from different countries.

9. Name an animal that is similar to a tiger. Name a bird that is similar to a duck.

10. Are Egypt and Italy on the same continent? Egypt and Algeria? Thailand and South Korea? Mexico and Brazil?

❏ **Exercise 34. Warm-up.** (Chart 15-6)
Which statements do you agree with?

1. a. White chocolate and dark chocolate are alike.

   b. White chocolate is not like dark chocolate.

2. a. Broccoli and cauliflower are alike.

   b. Broccoli is not like cauliflower.

3. a. Towels are like sheets.

   b. Towels and sheets aren't alike.

15-6 Comparisons: Using *Like* and *Alike*

You have a pen with blue ink.
I have a pen with blue ink.
 	
(a) Your pen *is like* my pen.
(b) Your pen and my pen *are alike*.
(c) Our pens *are alike*.
	like = similar to
	alike = similar
	
	Like and **alike** have the same meaning, but the sentence patterns are different.
	    this + **be** + **like** + that
	    this and that + **be** + **alike**

❑ **Exercise 35. Let's talk: pairwork.** (Chart 15-6)

Work with a partner. Take turns making sentences with *like.* Check (✓) the things in Column B that compare with the items in Column A. Discuss the ways in which the two things you are comparing are similar.

Example: a pencil, a bus

Column A	Column B
1. a pencil 2. a bus	a glass a human hand ✓ a pen a lemon ✓ a taxi

PARTNER A: A pencil is like a pen in some ways. You can write with both of them. Your turn now.

PARTNER B: A bus is like a taxi. You can ride in both of them. Your turn now. Etc.

Column A	Column B
1. a bush	a glass
2. a cup	a human hand
3. a hill	a lemon
4. honey	a chair
5. a monkey's hand	a mountain
6. an orange	an ocean
7. an alley	a street
8. a sea	sugar
9. a couch	a bird
10. a jacket	a suit coat
11. a butterfly	a tree

❏ **Exercise 36. Looking at grammar.** (Chart 15-6)
Complete the sentences with *like* and *alike*.

1. You and I have similar books. In other words, your book is _____*like*_____ mine.

   Our books are _____*alike*_____ .

2. Mr. Wong and I have similar coats. In other words, Mr. Wong's coat is

   _____ mine. Our coats are _____ .

3. Tess and Matt have similar cars. In other words, their cars are _____ .

4. You and I have similar hats. In other words, your hat is _____ mine.

5. A town is _____ a city in some ways.

6. A foot and a hand are _____ in some ways but different in other ways.

7. A dormitory and an apartment building are _____ in many ways.

8. A motorcycle is _____ a bike in some ways.

❏ **Exercise 37. Looking at grammar.** (Charts 15-5 and 15-6)
Choose <u>all</u> the completions that are grammatically correct and make sense.

1. French and Spanish are _____.
   a. different from
   b. like
   c. alike
   d. the same
   e. similar

2. French is _____ Spanish.
   a. different from
   b. similar
   c. alike
   d. the same as
   e. similar to

3. Coffee tastes _____ lemonade.
   a. different
   b. similar to
   c. the same as
   d. different from
   e. like

4. Fog and smog sometimes look _____.
   a. similar to
   b. similar
   c. like
   d. different from
   e. alike

❏ **Exercise 38. Warm-up.** (Chart 15-7)
Complete the sentences. Give your opinion.

1. The weather in _____ is often cold and wet, but the weather in
   (*name of a country*)

   _____ is often warm and clear.
   (*name of a country*)

2. _____ is a great place for a vacation, but _____ is
   (name of a city)   *(name of a city)*

   a boring place to visit.

15-7 Using *But*

(a) John is rich, ***but*** Mary is poor.	***But*** gives the idea that "This is the opposite of that."
(b) The weather was cold, ***but*** we were warm inside our house.	A comma comes before ***but*** as in (b), when it introduces a main clause.

❏ **Exercise 39. Looking at grammar.** (Chart 15-7)

Complete the sentences with adjectives.

1. An orange is sweet, but a lemon is _____*sour*_____.

2. The coffee in this cup is hot, but the coffee in that cup is _____.

3. These dishes are clean, but those dishes are _____.

4. This suitcase is heavy, but that suitcase is _____.

5. My hair is light, but my brother's hair is _____.

6. These shoes are uncomfortable, but those shoes are _____.

7. This street is narrow, but that street is _____.

8. This exercise is easy, but that exercise is _____.

9. A chicken is stupid, but a human being is _____.

10. This answer is right, but that answer is _____.

11. This towel is dry, but that towel is _____.

12. This cup is full, but that cup is _____.

13. Those dishcloths are dirty, but these dishcloths are _____.

14. A pillow is soft, but a rock is _____.

🎧 Listen to each sentence and write an adjective with the opposite meaning.

Example: You will hear: This exercise is easy, but that exercise is . . .

You will write: _____*hard*_____.

1. _____.
2. _____.
3. _____.
4. _____.

5. _____.
6. _____.
7. _____.
8. _____.

❏ **Exercise 41. Warm-up.** (Chart 15-8)

Are any of these sentences true for you? What do you notice about the verbs in red?

1. I don't study a lot, but my friends do.	T	F
2. I can't fly an airplane, but someone in my family can.	T	F
3. I like rock music, but some of my friends don't.	T	F
4. I will be here next year, but some of my friends won't.	T	F
5. I didn't drive to school today, but my teacher did.	T	F
6. I grew up with a pet, but my parents didn't.	T	F

15-8 Using Verbs after *But*

AFFIRMATIVE VERB	+	*BUT*	+	NEGATIVE VERB	
(a) John *is* rich,		*but*		Mary *isn't*.	Often the verb phrase following *but* is shortened, as in the examples.
(b) Balls *are* round,		*but*		boxes *aren't*.	
(c) I *was* in class,		*but*		Po *wasn't*.	
(d) Sue *studies* hard,		*but*		Sam *doesn't*.	
(e) We *like* movies,		*but*		they *don't*.	
(f) Alex *came*,		*but*		Maria *didn't*.	
(g) People *can* talk,		*but*		animals *can't*.	
(h) Olga *will* be there,		*but*		Ivan *won't*.	

NEGATIVE VERB	+	*BUT*	+	AFFIRMATIVE VERB
(i) Mary *isn't* rich,		*but*		John *is*.
(j) Boxes *aren't* round,		*but*		balls *are*.
(k) Po *wasn't* in class,		*but*		I *was*.
(l) Sam *doesn't* study,		*but*		Sue *does*.
(m) They *don't* like cats,		*but*		we *do*.
(n) Maria *didn't* come,		*but*		Alex *did*.
(o) Animals *can't* talk,		*but*		people *can*.
(p) Ivan *won't* be there,		*but*		Olga *will*.

Complete each sentence with an appropriate verb, affirmative or negative.

1. Lana is at home, but her husband _____*isn't*_____.

2. Hiroki isn't at home, but his wife _____.

3. Beds are comfortable, but park benches _____.

4. I wasn't at home last night, but my roommate _____.

5. Fran was in class yesterday, but Irena and Maggie _____.

6. I don't want to go to the movie, but my friends _____.

7. Tariq can speak French, but I _____.

8. Leah will be at the meeting, but Evelyn _____.

9. This shirt is clean, but that one _____.

10. These shoes aren't comfortable, but those shoes _____.

11. Ethan doesn't write clearly, but Andrew _____.

12. I ate breakfast this morning, but my roommate _____.

13. Carol has a car, but Jerry _____.

14. Jerry doesn't have a car, but Carol _____.

15. Ron was at the party, but his wife _____.

16. Ron went to the party, but his wife _____.

17. Boris can't speak Spanish, but his wife _____.

18. I won't be at home tonight, but Mia _____.

19. Liam will be in class tomorrow, but Tyler _____.

20. Olivia won't be here tomorrow, but Renata _____.

21. The hotel wasn't expensive, but the plane tickets _____.

22. Evan is going to graduate on time, but his twin bother _____.

23. Gabrielle doesn't know how to drive yet, but her friends _____.

24. I have to work late tonight, but my co-workers _____.

❏   **Exercise 43. Listening.** (Chart 15-8)

Listen to the sentences. Complete each sentence with an appropriate verb, affirmative or negative.

Example: You will hear: The students wanted to play a vocabulary game, but their
teacher . . .

You will write: _____ *didn't* _____ .

1. _____ .   6. _____ .

2. _____ .   7. _____ .

3. _____ .   8. _____ .

4. _____ .   9. _____ .

5. _____ .   10. _____ .

❏   **Exercise 44. Let's talk: class activity.** (Chart 15-8)

Your teacher will ask you questions. Answer them using **but**. Close your book for this activity.

Example: Who in the class was at home last night? Who wasn't at home last night?
TEACHER: Who was at home last night?
STUDENT A: I was.
TEACHER: Who wasn't at home last night?
STUDENT B: I wasn't at home last night.
TEACHER: (*to Student C*) Summarize, using *but*.
STUDENT C: (*Student A*) was at home last night, but (*Student B*) wasn't.

1. Who wears glasses? Who doesn't wear glasses?

2. Who is married? Who isn't married?

3. Who didn't watch TV last night? Who watched TV last night?

4. Who will be in class tomorrow? Who won't be in class tomorrow?

5. Who has a pet? Who doesn't have a pet?

6. Who studied last night? Who didn't study last night?

7. Who can play (*a musical instrument*)? Who can't play (*that musical instrument*)?

8. Who is hungry right now? Who isn't hungry right now?

9. Who lives in an apartment? Who doesn't live in an apartment?

10. Who doesn't drink coffee? Who drinks coffee?

11. Who won't be at home tonight? Who will be at home tonight?

12. Who was in class yesterday? Who wasn't in class yesterday?

13. Who can't speak (*a language*)? Who can speak (*a language*)?

14. Who didn't stay home last night? Who stayed home last night?

15. Who has _____? Who doesn't have _____?

❏ **Exercise 45. Let's talk: pairwork.** (Chart 15-8)

Work with a partner. Picture A and Picture B are not the same. There are many differences between them. Can you find all of the differences? Take turns pointing out the differences.

Example:

PARTNER A: The woman is sitting in Picture A, but she's lying down in Picture B.
Your turn now.

PARTNER B: There's a small fish in Picture A but a large fish in Picture B.
Your turn now.
Etc.

Picture A

Picture B

Exercise 46. Let's talk: pairwork. (Chapter 15)
Work with a partner.
   Partner A: Ask Partner B questions. Your book is open.
   Partner B: Answer in complete sentences. Your book is closed.

1. What's the longest river in the world?★

2. What's the biggest continent? What's the second biggest continent?

3. What country has the largest population?

4. Is a square the same as a rectangle?

5. Name a country that is farther south than Mexico.

6. Name an animal that is similar to a horse.

7. Name a place that is noisier than a library.

8. Is a dormitory like an apartment building? How are they different/similar?

9. Is (. . .)'s grammar book different from yours?

10. What is one of the most famous landmarks in the world?

Change roles.

11. Is the population of Seoul, South Korea, larger or smaller than the population of São Paulo, Brazil?

12. Is the Atlantic Ocean deeper than the Indian Ocean?

13. What's the smallest continent in the world?

14. Name two students in this class who speak the same native language. Do they come from the same country?

15. Look at all the desks in the classroom. Are they different? How?

16. Is a lake like a river? How are they different? How are they similar?

17. Name an insect that is smaller than a bee.

18. Name a city that is farther north than Rome, Italy.

19. What is the most popular sport in your country?

20. What is one of the most important inventions in the modern world? Why is it more important than (*name of another invention*)?

❏ **Exercise 47. Looking at grammar.** (Chapter 15)
Choose the correct completion.

1. A lion is _____ a tiger.
   a. similar   b. similar with   c. similar from   d. similar to

2. Lions and tigers are _____.
   a. the same   b. similar   c. similar to   d. the same as

3. Good health is one of _____ in a person's life.
   a. best thing   c. the best things
   b. the best thing   d. best things

★If you need to, look at the *Table of Statistics* on p. 465.

4. There were many chairs in the room. I sat in _____ chair.
    a. the comfortablest
    b. the most comfortable
    c. most comfortable
    d. more comfortable

5. Jane's story was _____ Jack's story.
    a. funnier than
    b. funny than
    c. more funnier than
    d. more funny

6. My last name is _____ my cousin's.
    a. same
    b. same as
    c. same as
    d. the same as

7. I live _____ away from school than you do.
    a. far   b. farther   c. more far   d. farthest

8. Emir speaks _____ than Hamid.
    a. more clearly
    b. clearlier
    c. more clear
    d. more clearer

9. Roger works hard every day, but his brother _____.
    a. is   b. isn't   c. does   d. doesn't

❏ **Exercise 48. Check your knowledge. (Chapter 15)**
Correct the mistakes.

              harder
1. English is ~~hard, more~~ than my language.

2. A monkey is intelligenter than a cow.

3. My grade on the test was worst from yours. You got a more better grade.

4. Soccer is one of most popular sport in the world.

5. Felix speaks English more fluent than Ernesto.

6. Girls and boys are differents. Girls are different to boys.

7. A rectangle and a square similar.

8. Nola's coat is similar with mine.

9. Victor's coat is same mine.

10. Nicolas and Malena aren't a same height. Nicolas is more tall than Malena.

11. Professor Wilson teaches full-time, but her husband isn't.

12. Your pen, my pen they alike.

13. My cousin is the same age with my brother.

14. What is most pretty place in the world?

15. For me, chemistry most difficult than biology.

❏ **Exercise 49. Reading and writing.** (Chapter 15)

Part I. Read the story.

My Best Friend

My best friend is Jacob. We have an interesting friendship because we are similar and different in several ways.

We like to study, and we are both smart but in different subjects. His math scores are higher than mine, but my language and history grades are better than his.

Physically we are not alike. Jacob is medium height and very athletic. He is stronger than me, and he can run faster than me. I am tall, and I can't lift heavy weights because it hurts my back. I'm also a slower runner than Jacob.

We like to go to sports events together. One of our favorite sports is baseball. We can talk about baseball for hours.

Jacob is quiet, and I am more talkative. Sometimes Jacob says I talk too much, but he laughs when he says it. He is a better listener than me, so people say we make a good pair.

We enjoy our time together. We think this is because we're not the same and we're not really different.

Part II. Write one or more paragraph(s) about you and a friend. Write about your similarities and differences. The box contains comparison words you may want to use in your paragraph.

WORDS USED IN COMPARISONS		
alike	-er/more	similar (to)
but	-est/most	the same (as)
different (from)	like	

Part III. Editing check: Work individually or change papers with a partner. Check (✓) for the following:

1. _____ indented paragraph

2. _____ capital letter at the beginning of each sentence

3. _____ period at the end of each sentence

4. _____ use of *-er/more* for comparing two things

5. _____ use of *the -est/most* for comparing three or more things

6. _____ correct use of *like/alike, similar (to), the same (as), different (from)*

7. _____ correct spelling (use a dictionary or computer spell-check)

Appendix 1
English Handwriting

English Handwriting	
PRINTING	CURSIVE

PRINTING

Aa	Jj	Ss
Bb	Kk	Tt
Cc	Ll	Uu
Dd	Mm	Vv
Ee	Nn	Ww
Ff	Oo	Xx
Gg	Pp	Yy
Hh	Qq	Zz
Ii	Rr	

CURSIVE

Aa	Jj	Ss
Bb	Kk	Tt
Cc	Ll	Uu
Dd	Mm	Vv
Ee	Nn	Ww
Ff	Oo	Xx
Gg	Pp	Yy
Hh	Qq	Zz
Ii	Rr	

Vowels = *a, e, i, o, u*
Consonants = *b, c, d, f, g, h, j, k, l, m, n, p, q, r, s, t, v, w, x, y, z*★

★The letter *z* is pronounced "zee" in American English and "zed" in British English.

Appendix 2
Numbers

CARDINAL NUMBERS

1	one
2	two
3	three
4	four
5	five
6	six
7	seven
8	eight
9	nine
10	ten
11	eleven
12	twelve
13	thirteen
14	fourteen
15	fifteen
16	sixteen
17	seventeen
18	eighteen
19	nineteen
20	twenty
21	twenty-one
22	twenty-two
23	twenty-three
24	twenty-four
25	twenty-five
26	twenty-six
27	twenty-seven
28	twenty-eight
29	twenty-nine
30	thirty
40	forty
50	fifty
60	sixty
70	seventy
80	eighty
90	ninety
100	one hundred
200	two hundred
1,000	one thousand
10,000	ten thousand
100,000	one hundred thousand
1,000,000	one million

ORDINAL NUMBERS

1st	first
2nd	second
3rd	third
4th	fourth
5th	fifth
6th	sixth
7th	seventh
8th	eighth
9th	ninth
10th	tenth
11th	eleventh
12th	twelfth
13th	thirteenth
14th	fourteenth
15th	fifteenth
16th	sixteenth
17th	seventeenth
18th	eighteenth
19th	nineteenth
20th	twentieth
21st	twenty-first
22nd	twenty-second
23rd	twenty-third
24th	twenty-fourth
25th	twenty-fifth
26th	twenty-sixth
27th	twenty-seventh
28th	twenty-eighth
29th	twenty-ninth
30th	thirtieth
40th	fortieth
50th	fiftieth
60th	sixtieth
70th	seventieth
80th	eightieth
90th	ninetieth
100th	one hundredth
200th	two hundredth
1,000th	one thousandth
10,000th	ten thousandth
100,000th	one hundred thousandth
1,000,000th	one millionth

Appendix 3
Ways of Saying Time

9:00   It's nine o'clock.
       It's nine.

9:05   It's nine-oh-five.
       It's five (minutes) after nine.
       It's five (minutes) past nine.

9:10   It's nine-ten.
       It's ten (minutes) after nine.
       It's ten (minutes) past nine.

9:15   It's nine-fifteen.
       It's a quarter after nine.
       It's a quarter past nine.

9:30   It's nine-thirty.
       It's half past nine.

9:45   It's nine-forty-five.
       It's a quarter to ten.
       It's a quarter of ten.

9:50   It's nine-fifty.
       It's ten (minutes) to ten.
       It's ten (minutes) of ten.

12:00 It's noon.
       It's midnight.

A.M. = morning: It's nine A.M.
P.M. = afternoon/evening/night: It's nine P.M.

Appendix 4

Days/Months/Seasons

DAYS	ABBREVIATION	MONTHS	ABBREVIATION	SEASONS*
Monday	Mon.	January	Jan.	winter
Tuesday	Tues.	February	Feb.	spring
Wednesday	Wed.	March	Mar.	summer
Thursday	Thurs.	April	Apr.	fall or autumn
Friday	Fri.	May	May	
Saturday	Sat.	June	Jun.	
Sunday	Sun.	July	Jul.	
		August	Aug.	
		September	Sept.	
		October	Oct.	
		November	Nov.	
		December	Dec.	

*Seasons of the year are only capitalized when they begin a sentence.

WRITING DATES:

Month/Day/Year

10/31/41	=	October 31, 1941
4/15/98	=	April 15, 1998
7/4/1906	=	July 4, 1906
7/4/07	=	July 4, 2007

SAYING DATES:

Usual Written Form	Usual Spoken Form
January 1	January first / the first of January
March 2	March second / the second of March
May 3	May third / the third of May
June 4	June fourth / the fourth of June
August 5	August fifth / the fifth of August
October 10	October tenth / the tenth of October
November 27	November twenty-seventh / the twenty-seventh of November

Appendix 5
Supplementary Charts

A5-1 Basic Capitalization Rules

	Use a capital letter for:
(a) Joan and **I** are friends.	the pronoun "I"
(b) **They** are late.	the first word of a sentence
(c) **S**am **B**ond and **T**om **A**dams are here.	names of people
(d) **M**rs. **P**eterson **P**rofessor **J**ones **D**r. **C**osta	titles of people*
(e) **M**onday, **T**uesday, **W**ednesday	the days of the week
(f) **A**pril, **M**ay, **J**une	the months of the year
(g) **N**ew **Y**ear's **D**ay	holidays
(h) **L**os **A**ngeles **F**lorida, **O**ntario **G**ermany **L**ake **B**aikal **A**mazon **R**iver **P**acific **O**cean **M**ount **E**verest **B**roadway, **F**ifth **A**venue	names of places: cities, states and provinces, countries, lakes, rivers, oceans, mountains, streets
(i) **G**erman, **C**hinese, **S**wedish	languages and nationalities
(j) **P**irates of the **C**aribbean **R**omeo and **J**uliet	the first word of a title, for example, in a book or movie. Capitalize the other words, but not: articles (***the, a, an***), short prepositions (***with, in, at***, etc.), and these words: ***and, but, or***.
(k) **B**uddhism, **C**hristianity, **H**induism, **I**slam, **J**udaism	religions

* *Mrs.* = woman: married   *Miss* = woman: unmarried
  Ms. = woman: married or unmarried   *Mr.* = man: married or unmarried

A5-2 Voiceless and Voiced Sounds for *-s* Endings on Verbs

Voiceless	Voiced	
(a) /p/ slee**p** /t/ wri**t**e /f/ lau**gh**	(b) /b/ ru**b** /d/ ri**d**e /v/ dri**v**e "I can feel my voice box. It vibrates."	Some sounds are "voiceless." You don't use your voice box. You push air through your teeth and lips. For example, the sound /p/ comes from air through your lips. The final sounds in (a) are voiceless. Common voiceless sounds are **f, k, p, t, sh, ch,** and voiceless **th**.
		Some sounds are "voiced." You use your voice box to make voiced sounds. For example, the sound /b/ comes from your voice box. The final sounds in (b) are voiced. Common voiced sounds are **b, d, g, j, l, m, n, r, v,** and voiced **th**.
(c) sleep**s** = sleep/s/ write**s** = write/s/ laugh**s** = laugh/s/	(d) rub**s** = rub/z/ ride**s** = ride/z/ drive**s** = drive/z/	Final **-s** is pronounced /s/ after voiceless sounds, as in (c). Final **-s** is pronounced /z/ after voiced sounds, as in (d).

A5-3 Final *-ed* Pronunciation for Simple Past Verbs

Final **-ed** has three pronunciations: /t/, /d/, and /əd/.

End of Verb	Base Form	Simple Past	Pronunciation	
VOICELESS	(a) help laugh wash	helped laughed washed	*help/t/* *laugh/t/* *wash/t/*	Final **-ed** is pronounced /t/ if a verb ends in a voiceless sound, as in (a).
VOICED	(b) rub live smile	rubbed lived smiled	*rub/d/* *live/d/* *smile/d/*	Final **-ed** is pronounced /d/ if a verb ends in a voiced sound, as in (b).
-d OR **-t**	(c) need want	needed wanted	*need/əd/* *want/əd/*	Final **-ed** is pronounced /əd/ if a verb ends in the letters **d** or **t**, as in (c).

Listening Script

NOTE: You may want to pause the audio after each item or in longer passages so that there is enough time to complete each task.

Chapter 1: Using *Be*

Exercise 20, p. 11.

A: Hi. My name is Mrs. Smith. I'm the substitute teacher.
B: Hi. I'm Franco.
C: Hi. I'm Lisa. We're in your class.
A: It's nice to meet you.
B: We're glad to meet you too.

Exercise 24, p. 12.

A: Hello. I'm Mrs. Brown. I'm the substitute teacher.
B: Hi. I'm Paulo, and this is Marie. We're in your class.
A: It's nice to meet you.
B: We're happy to meet you too.
A: It's time for class. Please take a seat.

Exercise 28, p. 14.

1. Andrew isn't a child.
2. Isabelle is an aunt.
3. Marie is a mom.
4. David isn't a dad.
5. Billy and Janey are brother and sister.
6. Marie and Andrew are adults.
7. Billy and Janey aren't parents.
8. David and Andrew aren't daughters.

Exercise 41, p. 23.

The First Day of Class

Paulo is a student from Brazil. Marie is a student from France. They're in the classroom. Today is an exciting day. It's the first day of school, but they aren't nervous. They're happy to be here. Mrs. Brown is the teacher. She isn't in the classroom right now. She's late today.

Exercise 44, p. 25.

1. Grammar's easy.
2. My name's Josh.

3. My books're on the table.
4. My brother's 21 years old.
5. The weather's cold today.
6. The windows're open.
7. My money's in my wallet.
8. Mr. Smith's a teacher.
9. My parents're at work now.
10. The food's good.
11. Tom's sick today.
12. My roommates're from Chicago.
13. My sister's a student in high school.

Chapter 2: Using *Be* and *Have*

Exercise 4, p. 29.

A: Elena's absent today.
B: Is she sick?
A: No.
B: Is her husband sick?
A: No.
B: Are her children sick?
A: No.
B: Is she homesick?
A: No.
B: So? What's the matter?
A: Her turtle is sick!
B: Are you serious? That's crazy!

Exercise 25, p. 43.

Anna's clothes

1. Her boots have zippers.
2. She has a raincoat.
3. Her raincoat has buttons.
4. They are small.
5. Her sweater has long sleeves.
6. She has earrings on her ears.
7. They are silver.
8. She has on jeans.
9. Her jeans have pockets.

Exercise 36, p. 52.

In the kitchen

1. That is my coffee cup.
2. This is your dessert.
3. Those are our plates.
4. Those sponges are wet.
5. These dishcloths are dry.
6. That frying pan is dirty.
7. This frying pan is clean.
8. That salt shaker is empty.

Chapter 3: Using the Simple Present

Exercise 4, p. 61.

1. I wake up early every day.
2. My brother wakes up late.
3. He gets up at 11:00.
4. I go to school at 8:00.
5. My mother does exercises every morning.
6. My little sister watches TV in the morning.
7. I take the bus to school.
8. My brother takes the bus to school.
9. My friends take the bus too.
10. We talk about our day.

Exercise 15, p. 66.

1. eat
2. eats
3. push
4. pushes
5. sleeps
6. fixes

Exercise 17, p. 68.

1. Mrs. Miller teaches English on Saturdays.
2. Mr. and Mrs. Hanson teach English in the evenings.
3. Chang fixes cars.
4. His son fixes cars too.
5. Carlos and Chris watch DVDs on weekends.
6. Their daughter watches TV shows on her computer.
7. I brush my hair every morning.
8. Jimmy seldom brushes his hair.
9. The Nelsons wash their car every weekend.
10. Jada rarely washes her car.

Exercise 24, p. 71.

Marco is a student. He has an unusual schedule. All of his classes are at night. His first class is at 6:00 P.M. every day. He takes a break from 7:30 to 8:00. Then he has classes from 8:00 to 10:00.

He leaves school and goes home at 10:00. After he has dinner, he watches TV. Then he does his homework from midnight to 3:00 or 4:00 in the morning.

Marco has his own computer at home. When he finishes his homework, he usually goes on the Internet.

He often stays at his computer until the sun comes up. Then he does a few exercises, has breakfast, and goes to bed. He sleeps all day. Marco thinks his schedule is great, but his friends think it is strange.

Chapter 4: Using the Present Progressive

Exercise 7, p. 99.

1. Tony is sitting in the cafeteria.
2. He is sitting alone.
3. He is wearing a hat.
4. He is eating lunch.
5. He is reading his grammar book.
6. He is holding a cup.
7. He is studying hard.
8. He is smiling.
9. He is listening to the radio.
10. He is waving to his friends.

Exercise 24, p. 111.

1. I write in my grammar book . . .
2. I am writing in my grammar book . . .
3. It is raining outside . . .
4. It doesn't rain . . .
5. My cell phone rings . . .
6. My cell phone isn't ringing . . .
7. My friends and I listen to music in the car . . .
8. We're not listening to music . . .

Exercise 28, p. 114.

A: What are you doing? Are you working on your English paper?
B: No, I'm not. I'm writing an email to my sister.
A: Do you write to her often?
B: Yes, but I don't write a lot of emails to anyone else.
A: Does she write to you often?
B: No, but she texts me a lot.

Chapter 5: Talking About the Present

Exercise 6, p. 129.

1. I have class in the morning. I was born in July. I was born in 1990. Who am I?
2. My birthday is in June. I was born on June 24th. I have class every day at 1:00 o'clock. Who am I?
3. I was born in 1997. My birthday is July 7th. I go to class at night. Who am I?
4. I have class at 7:00 o'clock. I go to class in the morning. I was born in 1992. Who am I?

Exercise 16, p. 134.

1. There're ten students in the classroom.
2. There's a new teacher today.
3. There're two new math teachers this year.
4. There's a piece of gum on the floor.
5. There's some information on the bulletin board.
6. There're some spelling mistakes on this paper.
7. There's a grammar mistake in this sentence.
8. There're two writing assignments for tonight.

Exercise 32, p. 145.

1. There are trees behind the train.
2. A bird is under the picnic table.
3. There are butterflies near the flowers.
4. There is a knife on top of the table.
5. There is a fishing pole on the boat.
6. A boat is under the water.
7. The bridge is below the water.
8. There are clouds above the mountains.
9. There are flowers beside the river.
10. There are flowers next to the river.
11. A guitar is in back of the table.
12. Two bikes are under the tree.
13. A fish is in the water.
14. The table is between the tree and the river.
15. The boots are far from the picnic bench.

Exercise 41, p. 151.

1. I'd like a hamburger for dinner.
2. We like to eat at fast-food restaurants.
3. Bob'd like to go to the gym now.
4. He likes to exercise after work.
5. The teacher'd like to speak with you.
6. The teacher likes your work.
7. We like to ride our bikes on weekends.
8. We'd like to ride in a race.
9. Bill and Kay like jazz music.
10. They'd like to go to a concert next week.

Chapter 6: Nouns and Pronouns

Exercise 18, p. 168.

1. Renata knows Oscar. She knows him very well.
2. Where does Shelley live? Do you have her address?
3. There's Vince. Let's go talk to him.
4. There are Dave and Lois. Let's go talk to them.
5. I'm looking online for JoAnne's phone number. What's her last name again?
6. I need to see our airline tickets. Do you have them?

Exercise 19, p. 169.

1. A: Mika and I are going downtown this afternoon. Do you want to come with us?
   B: I don't think so, but thanks anyway. Chris and I are going to the library. We need to study for our test.

2. A: Hi, Abby. How do you like your new apartment?
   B: It's great. I have a new roommate too. She's very nice.
   A: What's her name?
   B: Rita Lopez. Do you know her?
   A: No, but I know her brother. He's in my math class.

3. A: Do you see Mike and George very much?
   B: Yes, I see them often. We play video games at my house.
   A: Who usually wins?
   B: Mike. We never beat him!

Exercise 22, p. 172.

1. toys
2. table
3. face
4. hats
5. offices
6. boxes
7. package
8. chairs
9. edge
10. tops

Exercise 23, p. 173.

1. The desks in the classroom are new.
2. I like to visit new places.
3. Luke wants a sandwich for lunch.
4. The teacher is correcting sentences with a red pen.
5. This apple is delicious.
6. The students are finishing a writing exercise in class.
7. I need two pieces of paper.
8. Roses are beautiful flowers.
9. Your rose bush is beautiful.
10. The college has many scholarships for students.

Exercise 40, p. 184.

1. Mack's parents live in Singapore.
2. Mack has two brothers and one sister.
3. My teacher's apartment is near mine.
4. My teacher is very funny.
5. What is your friend saying?
6. My friend's birthday is today.
7. The store manager's name is Dean.
8. My cousin studies engineering.

Exercise 45, p. 186.

1. Who's that?
2. Whose glasses are on the floor?
3. Who's coming?
4. Who's next?
5. Whose homework is this?
6. Whose car is outside?
7. Who's ready to begin?
8. Whose turn is it?
9. Whose work is ready?
10. Who's absent?

Chapter 7: Count and Noncount Nouns

Exercise 10, p. 197.
1. I live in an apartment.
2. It's a small apartment.
3. My biology class lasts an hour.
4. It's an interesting class.
5. We have a fun teacher.
6. My mother has an office downtown.
7. It's an insurance office.
8. My father is a nurse.
9. He works at a hospital.
10. He has a busy job.

Exercise 43, p. 216.
1. Vegetables have vitamins.
2. Cats make nice pets.
3. The teacher is absent.
4. I love bananas.
5. Cars are expensive.
6. I need the keys to the car.
7. Are the computers in your office working?
8. Let's take a walk in the park.

Exercise 45, p. 217.
1. A: Do you have a pen?
   B: There's one on the counter in the kitchen.

2. A: Where are the keys to the car?
   B: I'm not sure. You can use mine.

3. A: Shh. I hear a noise.
   B: It's just a bird outside, probably a woodpecker. Don't worry.

4. A: Henry Jackson teaches at the university.
   B: I know. He's an English professor.
   A: He's also the head of the department.

5. A: Hurry! We're late.
   B: No, we're not. It's five o'clock, and we have an hour.
   A: No, we don't. It's six! Look at the clock.
   B: Oops. I need a new battery for my watch.

Chapter 8: Expressing Past Time, Part 1

Exercise 8, p. 227.
1. I wasn't at home last night.
2. I was at the library.
3. Our teacher was sick yesterday.
4. He wasn't at school.
5. There was a substitute teacher.
6. She was friendly and funny.
7. Many students were absent.
8. They weren't at school for several days.
9. My friends and I were nervous on the first day of school.
10. You weren't nervous.

Exercise 19, p. 234.
A soccer coach
1. Jeremy works as a soccer coach.
2. His team plays many games.
3. His team played in a tournament.
4. Yesterday, they scored five goals.
5. Jeremy helped the players a lot.
6. They learned about the other team.
7. They watched movies of the other team.
8. The players like Jeremy.
9. All year, they worked very hard.
10. Every practice, each player works very hard.

Exercise 25, p. 238.
Part I.
1. What day was it two days ago?
2. What day was it five days ago?
3. What day was it yesterday?
4. What month was it last month?
5. What year was it ten years ago?
6. What year was it last year?
7. What year was it one year ago?

Part II.
1. What time was it one hour ago?
2. What time was it five minutes ago?
3. What time was it one minute ago?

Exercise 30, p. 242.
1. I ate . . .
2. We sat . . .
3. They came . . .
4. She had . . .
5. He got . . .
6. I stood . . .

Exercise 40, p. 248.
1. Did we do well on the test?
2. Did you finish the assignment?
3. Did it make sense?
4. Did I answer your question?
5. Did they need more help?
6. Did he understand the homework?
7. Did she explain the project?
8. Did they complete the project?
9. Did you do well?
10. Did she pass the class?

Exercise 42, p. 249.

Part I.

1. Did you see the news this morning?

2. A: Jim called.
   B: Did he leave a message?

3. A: Julia called.
   B: Did she leave a message?

4. Did it rain yesterday?

5. A: The kids are watching TV.
   B: Did they finish their homework?

6. My keys aren't here. Did I leave them in the car?

Part II.

1. Did you finish the homework assignment?
2. Did it take a long time?
3. Did you hear my question?
4. Did they hear my question?
5. Did I speak loud enough?
6. Did he understand the information?
7. Did she understand the information?
8. Did you want more help?
9. Did I explain it okay?
10. Did he do a good job?

Exercise 48, p. 253.

1. She caught . . .
2. They drove . . .
3. We read . . .
4. I rode . . .
5. He bought . . .
6. We ran . . .

Exercise 54, p. 257.

A doctor's appointment

I woke up with a headache this morning. I took some medicine and went back to bed. I slept all day. The phone rang. I heard it, but I was very tired. I didn't answer it. I listened to the answering machine. It was the doctor's office. The nurse said I missed my appointment. Now my headache is really bad!

Exercise 59, p. 260.

A wedding ring

My mother called me early this morning. She had wonderful news for me. She had my wedding ring. I lost it last year during a party at her house. She told me she was outside in her vegetable garden with her dog. The dog found my ring under some vegetables. My mom said she immediately put it on her finger and wore it. She didn't want to lose it. I was so happy. I hung up the phone and began to laugh and cry at the same time.

Chapter **9**: Expressing Past Time, Part 2

Exercise 5, p. 267.

1. Where did Sabrina go?
2. Why did Sabrina go there?
3. Where did Isabel go?
4. When did Isabel get there?
5. Why did Isabel go there?
6. Where did Marco go?
7. When did Marco get there?
8. Where did Bill go?
9. What time did Bill get there?

Exercise 7, p. 268.

1. Why did you leave early?
2. Why didn't she help us?
3. Why didn't they believe him?
4. Why did he do that?
5. Why didn't we know about the problem?
6. Why did we come here?
7. Why did I say that?
8. Why didn't I say that?

Exercise 13, p. 271.

1. When did he arrive?
2. Why did you leave?
3. What did she want?
4. Where did you study?
5. What did he say?
6. When did they move?
7. Where did they move to?

Exercise 19, p. 276.

1. When did you leave?
2. Where did Sally meet her husband?
3. What did you need?
4. Where was the party?
5. Why did you move here?
6. Who came late?
7. Why didn't you help?

Exercise 24, p. 279.

1. The student didn't understand . . .
2. The woman spent . . .
3. Did you cut . . .
4. The car hit . . .
5. The man forgot . . .

Exercise 28, p. 281.

1. A tree fell . . .
2. The girls won . . .

3. The teacher drew . . .
4. I felt . . .
5. My brother threw . . .

Exercise 32, p. 283.

1. Mrs. Brown fed . . .
2. Mr. and Mrs. James built . . .
3. The dog bit . . .
4. The children hid . . .
5. The teacher held . . .

Exercise 51, p. 296.

Part III.

1. Steve Jobs was born in 1955.
2. While he was growing up in Palo Alto, California, he became interested in computers.
3. Jobs and Wozniak built their first computer together.
4. After Jobs graduated from high school, he went to Reed College.
5. He wasn't there very long, but he stayed in the area.
6. He learned a lot about calligraphy, and it helped him with the design of his products.
7. In 1985, Apple fired him, so he started NeXT Computer, Incorporated.
8. While he was working at NeXT, he met Laurene Powell, and they got married.
9. Under Jobs, Apple became very successful.
10. Unfortunately, while Jobs was working at Apple, he got cancer.
11. Medical treatments didn't cure him, and Jobs died in 2011.

Chapter 10: Expressing Future Time, Part 1

Exercise 9, p. 308.

1. Look. The doctor is coming.
2. The doctor is coming soon.
3. Oh, no. It's raining.
4. We are leaving early in the morning.
5. Run! The bus is coming.
6. Shh. Class is beginning.
7. We're going to a movie this afternoon.
8. My parents are coming over tonight.

Exercise 11, p. 308.

1. I am leaving soon.
2. Our class starts at nine.
3. Silvia is coming to the meeting tomorrow.
4. The doctor is going to call you.
5. Are you going to study tonight?
6. We are having dinner at a restaurant tomorrow.
7. We aren't going to the concert tonight.
8. Evan always eats a snack at midnight.
9. Who is going to help me?

Exercise 18, p. 312.

1. Maggie is going to the office . . .
2. My boss left . . .
3. The Carlsons got married . . .
4. The store is going to open . . .
5. The movie started . . .
6. We took a vacation . . .
7. Janet is going to graduate . . .
8. I'm going to buy a car . . .
9. There was a meeting at school . . .

Exercise 25, p. 316.

1. Jean is going to leave in a couple of days.
2. Lena is going to leave in a few weeks.
3. We sold our house a couple of years ago.
4. The phone rang a few minutes ago.
5. Marc is going to be here in a few minutes.

Exercise 31, p. 319.

1. They are going to finish this Thursday.
2. They talked about the project this morning.
3. It is going to rain this week.
4. It rained a lot this month.
5. It's raining really hard this week.
6. I am going to graduate from college this year.
7. Suzanne is doing her homework in the library.
8. The professor spoke for two hours this morning.
9. She's going to give us a test this week.
10. We had a lot of homework today.

Exercise 35, p. 320.

Part I.

1. a. The doctor will see you in a few minutes. OR
   b. The doctor'll see you in a few minutes.

2. a. Mom will be home late. OR
   b. Mom'll be home late.

3. a. Bob will pick us up. OR
   b. Bob'll pick us up.

Part II.

1. The nurse'll give you some medicine.
2. Your headache'll go away quickly.
3. The weather will be nice tomorrow.
4. Sorry, dinner'll be late tonight.
5. The bus will be here in a few minutes.
6. Dad'll help you with your homework later.
7. The students will need more time for review.

Exercise 39, p. 323.

1. Where will you go?
2. When will you go there?
3. Why will you go there?
4. Who will go with you?
5. What will you do there?

Exercise 40, p. 324.

1. Will Samantha study more?
2. Will Samantha go to more parties on weekends?
3. Will Samantha begin smoking?
4. Will Samantha exercise with her grandmother?
5. Will Samantha graduate from a university next year?
6. Will Samantha go on a diet?
7. Will Samantha exercise only two times a week?
8. Will Samantha spend more time with her grandmother?

Exercise 41, p. 324.

1. I want a new car.
2. A new car won't be cheap.
3. You won't get much help from your parents.
4. My parents want me to get married.
5. They want grandchildren.
6. I won't get married for a long time.
7. I want a good education.
8. You won't believe the news!

Exercise 43, p. 326.

A restaurant meal

1. Bert doesn't like meat, eggs, or fish.
2. He's a vegetarian. He doesn't eat meat. He didn't eat it as a child either.
3. His wife, Beth, doesn't eat meat, but she isn't a vegetarian.
4. She doesn't enjoy the taste of meat.
5. They are going to try a new restaurant tomorrow.
6. It opened last month, and online reviews say it is excellent.
7. Bert will probably have a dish with lots of vegetables.
8. Beth won't have vegetables for a main dish. She'll probably ask for some type of fish.
9. Are they going to enjoy themselves?
10. Will they go back to this restaurant?

Exercise 49, p. 330.

Jack and the Beanstalk

NARRATOR: Once upon a time there was a boy named Jack. He lived with his mother in a small village.
MOTHER: We are very poor. We have no money. Our cow has no milk.
JACK: What are we going to do?
MOTHER: You'll go to the market and sell the cow.
NARRATOR: Jack left his home and met an old man on the road.
OLD MAN: I will buy your cow. I will pay you with beans. Here, these are magic beans.
NARRATOR: Jack took the beans home to his mother.
MOTHER: You stupid boy. We have nothing now. We are going to die.
NARRATOR: She threw the beans out the window. The next morning, Jack woke up and saw a huge beanstalk outside his window. It went into the clouds. He decided to climb it. At the top, he saw a castle. Inside the castle, there lived a giant and his wife. He went into the castle.
WIFE: What are you doing? My husband likes to eat boys for breakfast. You need to hide or he will eat you.
JACK: I'm so scared. Please help me.
WIFE: Here, climb inside the oven. After breakfast, my husband will fall asleep.
GIANT: Fee-Fi-Fo-Fum,
I smell the blood of an Englishman.
If he's alive or if he's dead,
I'll use his bones to make my bread.
Hmm. I smell a boy. Wife, are you going to feed me a boy for breakfast?
WIFE: No, I think the smell is the boy from last week. Here's your breakfast.
NARRATOR: The giant ate, counted his gold coins, and soon fell asleep. Jack got out of the oven, took a few gold coins, climbed down the beanstalk, and ran to his mother.
MOTHER: Oh, Jack. You saved us. Now we have money for food. But you are not going to go back to the castle. The giant will eat you.
NARRATOR: But Jack wanted more money. Soon he climbed the beanstalk. Again the giant's wife hid Jack in the oven. The giant had a hen. It laid golden eggs. After the giant fell asleep, Jack stole the hen.
MOTHER: What will we do with a hen? Why didn't you bring more gold coins? Jack, you have no sense.
JACK: Wait, mother. The hen is going to lay a golden egg. Watch.
NARRATOR: The hen laid a golden egg.
MOTHER: Oh, you wonderful boy! We will be rich.

NARRATOR: But Jack wanted more from the giant, so he went up the beanstalk one more time. This time, a golden harp was playing. It made beautiful music. Soon the giant went to sleep, and Jack took the harp. The giant heard a noise and woke up.

GIANT: I will catch you and eat you alive.

NARRATOR: The giant ran after Jack. Jack climbed down the beanstalk. The giant followed. Jack took an axe and chopped down the stalk. The giant fell.

GIANT: Ahhhhhhhhhh!

JACK: The giant is dead.

MOTHER: Now we are safe. The harp will give us beautiful music. My sadness will go away. Our lives will be happy. You saved us!

NARRATOR: And they lived happily ever after.

Chapter 11: Expressing Future Time, Part 2

Exercise 10, p. 339.

1. We may be late for class tomorrow.
2. Your birthday present may come early.
3. Maybe you'll get a package in the mail tomorrow.
4. I may go to bed early tonight.
5. Maybe I'll go shopping tomorrow.
6. Maybe you will get married next year.
7. The weather may be sunny tomorrow.
8. Maybe it will rain tomorrow.

Exercise 13, p. 341.

1. There may be a change in our plans.
2. The weather report says it'll rain tomorrow.
3. We might finish this grammar book soon.
4. Henry may get good news tomorrow.
5. The class'll start on time.

Exercise 26, p. 347.

1. What are you going to do if the weather is nice after class tomorrow?
2. What are you going to do if your teacher cancels class tomorrow?
3. What are you going to do if your teacher begins talking too fast?
4. What are you going to do if you're sick tomorrow?

Exercise 32, p. 351.

1. If I go to bed early tonight,
2. After I get home from school every day,
3. If class finishes early today,
4. Before I eat breakfast every day,
5. After I finish breakfast today,
6. If I get all the answers in this exercise correct,
7. When I finish this grammar book,

Exercise 39, p. 356.

1. A: Are we going to be late for the movie?
   B: No. The movie starts at 7:30. We have plenty of time.

2. A: What are we going to have for dinner?
   B: Leftovers. Is that okay?
   A: Sure, but I'll probably make some rice to go with them.

3. A: Are you going to be at Jon's wedding?
   B: Yes, but I won't get there until after it begins. I work until noon.
   A: Great. I'll see you there.

4. A: What are we going to do? We need to deposit this check, and the cash machine is broken. Our account is almost empty.
   B: No problem. I'll take it with me to work. There's an ATM next door.

Chapter 12: Modals, Part 1: Expressing Ability

Exercise 5, p. 363.

1. a. I can count to 100 in English.
   b. I can't count to 100 in English.

2. a. I can't ride a bike with no hands.
   b. I can ride a bike with no hands.

Exercise 6, p. 364.

1. Some students can't finish the test.
2. The teacher can give you extra help.
3. I can't hear you.
4. You can do it.
5. Don can't work today.
6. The doctor can't see you today.
7. Professor Clark can meet with you tomorrow.
8. I can't find my glasses.
9. The kids can't wait for the party!
10. We can stop now.

Exercise 7, p. 364.

In my last job, I was an office assistant. I have good computer skills. I can do word-processing, and I can type quickly. I like talking to people and can answer the phone with a friendly voice. I also like languages. I can speak French and Chinese. I also studied English. I can read it, but I can't speak it well. I hurt my back a few years ago. I can't carry suitcases. I can work both Saturdays and Sundays.

Exercise 11, p. 366.

1. A: *(phone rings)* Hello?
   B: Can I speak to Mr. Hudson, please?
   A: I'm sorry. He can't come to the phone right now. Can I take a message? He can return your call in about a half-hour.
   B: Yes. Please tell him Ron Myerson called.

2. A: Can you help me lift this box?
   B: It looks very heavy. I can try to help you, but I think we need a third person.
   A: No, I'm pretty strong. I think we can do it together.

3. A: I can't hear the TV. Can you turn it up?
   B: I can't turn it up. I'm doing my homework.
   A: Can you do your homework in another room?
   B: Oh, all right.

Exercise 26, p. 375.

1. A: Were you able to talk to Adam last night?
   B: I couldn't reach him. I can try again later today.

2. A: Do you know how to make pizza?
   B: Yes, I can make it. What about you?
   A: No, but can you teach me?
   B: Sure.

3. A: Are you able to understand the teacher?
   B: I couldn't understand her in the beginning, but now I can understand most of her lectures.
   A: I still can't understand her very well.

4. A: Professor Castro, when will you be able to correct our tests?
   B: I began last night, but I wasn't able to finish. I'll try again tonight. I hope I will be able to hand them back to you tomorrow.

5. A: *(phone rings)* Hello?
   B: Hi. This is Jan Quinn. I'm wondering if I can get in to see Dr. Novack today or tomorrow.
   A: Well, she can see you tomorrow morning at 11:00. Can you come in then?
   B: Yes, I can. Please tell me where you are. I don't know the way to your office.

Exercise 32, p. 380.

Part III.

1. Dellis can remember long rows of numbers.
2. Dellis is able to memorize a complete deck of cards.
3. In 2011, Dellis was able to win the U.S.A. Memory Championship.

4. Dellis can't remember all this information naturally.
5. Memory champions are able to make pictures in their minds.
6. They say that with a lot of work a person can have a good memory.

Chapter 13: Modals, Part 2: Advice, Necessity, Requests, Suggestions

Exercise 6, p. 387.

1. People should exercise four or five times a week.
2. People should eat a lot of candy.
3. People shouldn't steal money.
4. People should keep some money in a bank.
5. Students should study every day.
6. Students shouldn't study on weekends.
7. English students should speak English in class.
8. English teachers shouldn't translate for their students.

Exercise 12, p. 391.

1. I have to leave early today.
2. You have to come with me.
3. Where does your friend have to go?
4. She has to go to the dentist.
5. My teachers have to correct a lot of homework.
6. Why do they have to give so much work?
7. Our school has to hire a new teacher.
8. My dad has to have surgery.
9. My mom and I have to take him to the hospital tomorrow.
10. He has to stay there for two days.

Exercise 18, p. 395.

1. a. People must eat.
   b. People should eat.

2. a. People should keep their homes clean.
   b. People must keep their homes clean.

3. a. People should stop their cars for a police siren.
   b. People must stop their cars for a police siren.

4. a. People must wear coats in cool weather.
   b. People should wear coats in cool weather.

5. a. People should pay taxes to their government.
   b. People must pay taxes to their government.

6. a. People must drive the speed limit.
   b. People should drive the speed limit.

7. a. People should wear seat belts when they're in a car.
   b. People must wear seat belts when they're in a car.

8. a. People must be polite to one another.
   b. People should be polite to one another.

9. a. People must wear clothes outdoors.
   b. People should wear clothes outdoors.

Exercise 36, p. 406.
1. Tom has to work.
2. Becky knows how to swim.
3. The teacher needed to correct papers.
4. It's a good idea to study for the test tomorrow.
5. We may go to a movie tonight.
6. We didn't have to help.
7. I couldn't go to school yesterday.

Chapter 14: Nouns and Modifiers

Exercise 4, p. 414.
1. Your phone is on the kitchen counter.
2. Your phone is in the kitchen.
3. I'm moving to a new apartment next month.
4. The apartment building has a swimming pool.
5. How do you like your music class?
6. Where are the keys to the car?
7. I'm always losing my car keys.
8. Let's have some chicken soup.
9. The soup is good, but where's the chicken?
10. The grammar in this book is clear.

Exercise 15, p. 424.
1. That was a delicious birthday . . .
2. Here are the car . . .
3. I need to buy some comfortable . . .
4. The teacher gave the class an easy . . .
5. The little boy is playing computer . . .
6. I'd like to read the newspaper . . .

Exercise 31, p. 434.
1. All of the coffee is gone.
2. Some of the coffee is gone.
3. Almost all of the coffee is gone.
4. A lot of the coffee is gone.
5. Most of the coffee is gone.

Exercise 40, p. 441.
1. Most of the people are happy.
2. All of them are smiling.
3. Someone is unhappy.
4. Everyone has a hat.
5. Somebody has sunglasses.
6. Almost all of them look happy.

Chapter 15: Making Comparisons

Exercise 6, p. 448.
1. It's getting cold outside.
2. The weather today is colder than yesterday.
3. I am always colder than you.
4. Our teacher is happier this week than last week.
5. Professor Frank is happy every day.
6. Are you happy today?
7. Is a big car safer than a small car?
8. I want to drive a safe car.
9. I need to get a safer car.
10. The coffee is fresh and tastes delicious.
11. Amy told a very funny story in class yesterday.
12. Amy and Sami both told stories. Sami's story was funnier than Amy's story.

Exercise 14, p. 454.
1. Rudy is older than Alberto.
2. Selena looks happier than Rudy.
3. Alberto is the tallest of all.
4. Selena is younger than Alberto.
5. Rudy looks the most serious.
6. Alberto is shorter than Rudy.
7. Alberto looks happier than Rudy.
8. Rudy is the youngest.
9. Selena is shorter than Alberto.
10. Alberto looks more serious than Selena.

Exercise 17, p. 459.
1. The blue dress is more expensive than the red one.
2. Well, I think the red one looks prettier.
3. Is it too short, or does it look okay?
4. It's the nicest of all the dresses you tried on.
5. I'm not going to buy the brown shoes. They're too small.
6. This hat is too small. I need a bigger size.
7. Here, this is the biggest size they have.
8. I need a belt, but that one is shorter than my old one.
9. Is this belt long enough?
10. It's perfect. And it's the cheapest of all of them.

Exercise 27, p. 468.
1. I work faster than Alec does.
2. Toshi finished his work the fastest of all.
3. Mimi studies harder than Fred.
4. Jean studies the hardest of all.
5. Is a motorcycle more dangerous than a bike?
6. Kalil speaks more loudly than Haruko does.
7. A turtle moves more slowly than a cat does.
8. This suitcase is heavier than that one.
9. My glasses are clearer than my contact lenses.
10. I can see more clearly with my glasses.

Exercise 31, p. 471.

1. B and D are the same.
2. E is different from A.
3. G and B are similar.
4. A is similar to G.
5. F is the same as A.
6. C and G are different.
7. A and C are similar.

Exercise 40, p. 476.

1. Lucy is tall, but her sister is . . .
2. My old apartment was small, but my new apartment is . . .
3. First Street is noisy, but Second Street is . . .
4. This picture is ugly, but that picture is . . .
5. A car is fast, but a bike is . . .
6. A kitten is weak, but a horse is . . .
7. This watch is expensive, but that watch is . . .
8. Oscar is hard-working, but his brother is . . .

Exercise 43, p. 478.

1. I like strong coffee, but my friend . . .
2. Ellen can speak Spanish, but her husband . . .
3. The children didn't want to go to bed early, but their parents . . .
4. The children weren't tired, but their parents . . .
5. Mark doesn't want to go out to eat, but his friends . . .
6. The doctor isn't friendly, but the nurse . . .
7. I was at home yesterday, but my roommate . . .
8. Scott went to the party, but Jerry . . .
9. The grocery store will be open tomorrow, but the bank . . .
10. I won't be home tonight, but my husband . . .

Chapter 3, Exercise 33, p. 75.

1. No.   [They like to look for food at night.]
2. Yes.
3. Yes.
4. Yes.
5. Yes.
6. No.   [Only female mosquitoes bite.]
7. Yes.

Chapter 3, Exercise 53, p. 88.

Name	Where does she/he live?	What does he/she do?	Where does she/he work?	What pets does he/she have?
ANTONIO	(on a boat)	catches fish	on his boat	a turtle
LENA	in a cabin in the mountains	(teaches skiing)	at a ski school	ten fish
KANE	in an apartment in the city	makes jewelry	(at a jewelry store)	three cats
LISA	in a beach cabin on an island	surfs and swims	has no job	(a snake)
JACK	in a house in the country	designs web pages	at home	a horse

Chapter 4, Exercise 18, p. 106.

PARTNER B

501

Chapter 5, Exercise 20, p. 136.

	a swimming pool	a beach	hiking trails	horses	ocean-view rooms
HOTEL 1	(yes)	yes	yes	no	yes
HOTEL 2	yes	(yes)	yes	yes	no
HOTEL 3	yes	yes	(yes)	yes	yes
HOTEL 4	yes	yes	no	(yes)	yes
HOTEL 5	no	yes	yes	yes	(yes)

Chapter 7, Exercise 17, p. 201.

Partner B

1. an apple
2. some apples
3. some childen
4. an old man
5. some men
6. a word
7. some music
8. some rice
9. an hour
10. an island

Partner A

11. an animal
12. some animals
13. some people
14. some fruit
15. an egg
16. a university
17. an uncle
18. some bananas
19. some bread
20. some vocabulary

Chapter 7, Exercise 26, p. 207.

Partner B's answers:

1. a. some food.
   b. an apple.
   c. a sandwich.
   d. a bowl of soup.
2. a. a glass of milk.
   b. some water.
   c. a cup of tea.
3. a. some medicine.
   b. an ambulance.
4. a. a coat.
   b. a hat.
   c. some warm clothes.
   d. some heat.
5. a. some sleep.
   b. a break.
   c. a relaxing vacation.

Partner A's answers:

6. a. a snack.
   b. some fruit.
   c. an orange.
   d. a piece of chicken.
7. a. some juice.
   b. a bottle of water.
   c. a glass of iced tea.
8. a. a doctor.
   b. some help.
9. a. some boots.
   b. a blanket.
   c. a hot bath.
   d. some gloves.
10. a. some strong coffee.
    b. a break.
    c. a vacation.
    d. a nap.

Chapter 9, Exercise 12, p. 271.

	wake up	eat for breakfast	spend the day	go to bed	absent
JENNY	(7:00 A.M.)	candy bar	in the library	10 P.M.	Because she had a big project to finish.
JIN	8 A.M.	(rice)	at home	midnight	Because her kids were sick.
JADA	7:00 A.M.	raw fish	(at the beach)	11 P.M.	Because she didn't do her homework.
JANICE	9:00 A.M.	eggs	at the hospital	(10 P.M.)	Because she was in a car accident.
JULIANNA	5:00 A.M.	cold cereal	At her restaurant job	9 P.M.	(Because she needed to earn extra money for school tuition.)

Chapter 12, Exercise 4, p. 363.

1. Yes.   [Ostriches and penguins can't fly.]
2. No.   [Elephants can't jump.]
3. Yes.   [Tigers are very good swimmers.]
4. Yes.   [Octopuses change colors when they are excited.]
5. Yes.   [The Australian walking fish can climb trees.]
6. No.   [Sometimes horses stand up for weeks at a time.]
7. No.   [Some turtles can live for 200 or more years.]
8. No.   [Some animals see colors, for example, monkeys, birds, and insects.]
9. Yes.   [Whales can hold their breath for a long time.]

Index

A/an, 6, 8, 196 (*Look on pages 6, 8, and 196.*)	The numbers following the words listed in the index refer to page numbers in the text.
Capital letters, 159*fn.* (*Look at the footnote on page 159.*)	The letters *fn.* mean "footnote." Footnotes are at the bottom of a chart or the bottom of a page.

NOTES

NOTES

NOTES

NOTES